NAOKI URASAWA'S

20th CENTURY BOYS

Naoki Urasawa's
20th Century Boys
Volume 12

VIZ Signature Edition

STORY AND ART BY NAOKI URASAWA

20 SEIKI SHONEN 12 by Naoki URASAWA/Studio Nuts
© 2003 Naoki URASAWA/Studio Nuts
With the cooperation of Takashi NAGASAKI
All rights reserved. Original Japanese
edition published in 2003 by Shogakukan Inc., Tokyo.

English Adaptation/Akemi Wegmüller
Touch-up Art & Lettering/Freeman Wong
Cover & Interior Design/Sam Elzway
Editor/Kit Fox

Printed in Canada

Published by VIZ Media, LLC
P.O. Box 77010
San Francisco, CA 94107

10 9 8 7 6 5 4 3 2 1
First printing, December 2010

NAOKI URASAWA'S 20th CENTURY BOYS

VOL 12

FRIEND'S FACE

Story & Art by

NAOKI URASAWA

With the cooperation of

Takashi NAGASAKI

PROFILES

NAOKI URASAWA'S **20th CENTURY BOYS**

The whereabouts of Kiriko, who turns out to have been a developer of biological weapons... the search for Dr. Yamane...and the true identity of the Friend—as the mysteries become more intertwined, so does the horror!!

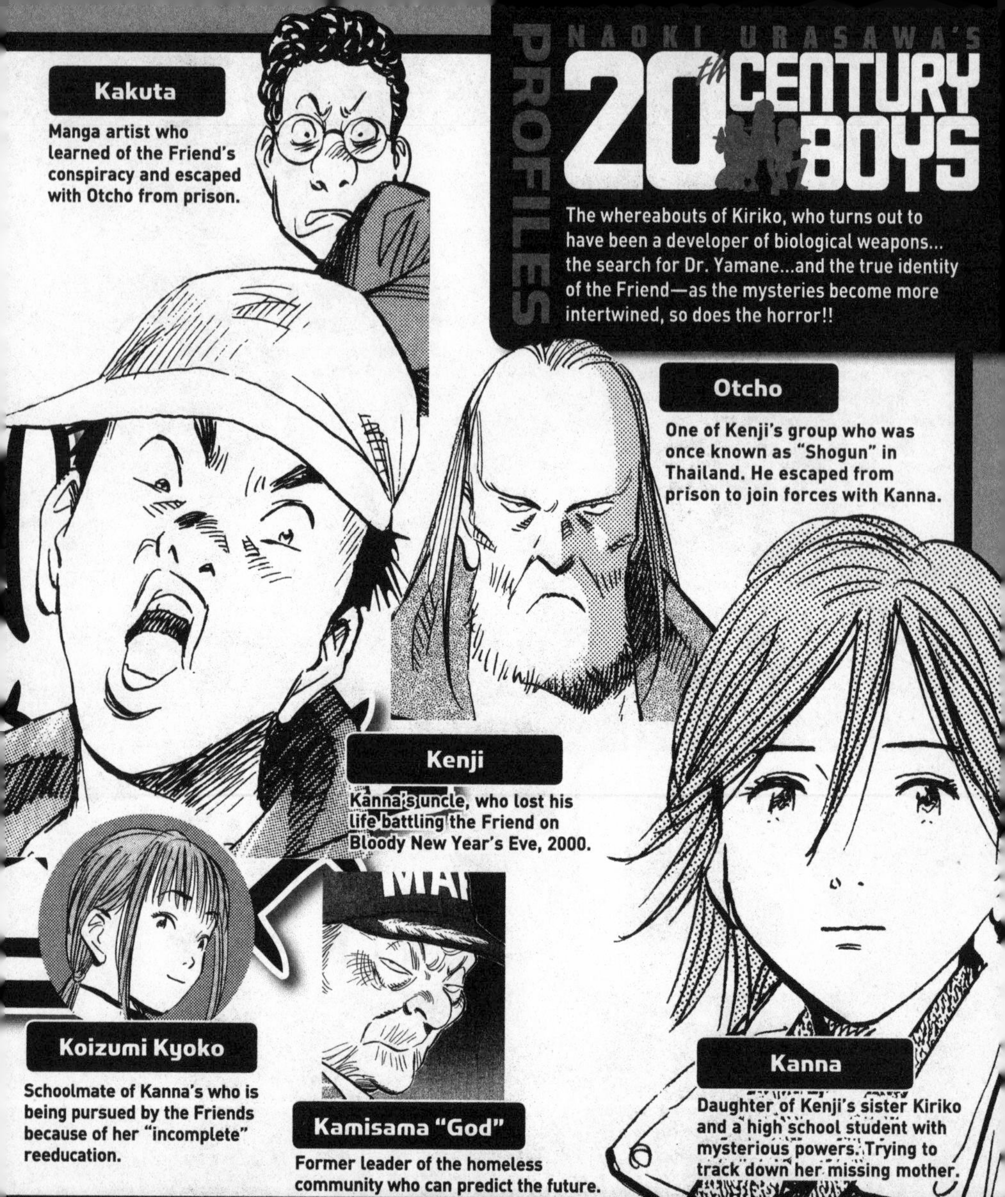

Kakuta

Manga artist who learned of the Friend's conspiracy and escaped with Otcho from prison.

Otcho

One of Kenji's group who was once known as "Shogun" in Thailand. He escaped from prison to join forces with Kanna.

Kenji

Kanna's uncle, who lost his life battling the Friend on Bloody New Year's Eve, 2000.

Koizumi Kyoko

Schoolmate of Kanna's who is being pursued by the Friends because of her "incomplete" reeducation.

Kamisama "God"

Former leader of the homeless community who can predict the future.

Kanna

Daughter of Kenji's sister Kiriko and a high school student with mysterious powers. Trying to track down her missing mother.

airport bombing, the rise of a mystery guru calling himself people's "Friend"...By the time Kenji realized these incidents were following the scenario he'd written in the "Book of Prophecy," he was being hunted down as a terrorist who planned to destroy the planet Earth. What did this "Friend" want, and who was he?!

On December 31, 2000, on what came to be known as Bloody New Year's Eve, biological weapons were scattered worldwide and a giant robot appeared on the streets of Tokyo. Confronting it, Kenji came face to face with the "Friend"—who had orchestrated the entire thing in order to be seen as the world's savior. Kenji was killed in front of his group and Kanna...while the "Friend" rose from the ashes a hero feted around the world.

And now, in 2014, Kanna is seventeen and determined to avenge her beloved uncle's death. She teams up with those of Kenji's friends who are still alive and gets ready to take on the Friends!!

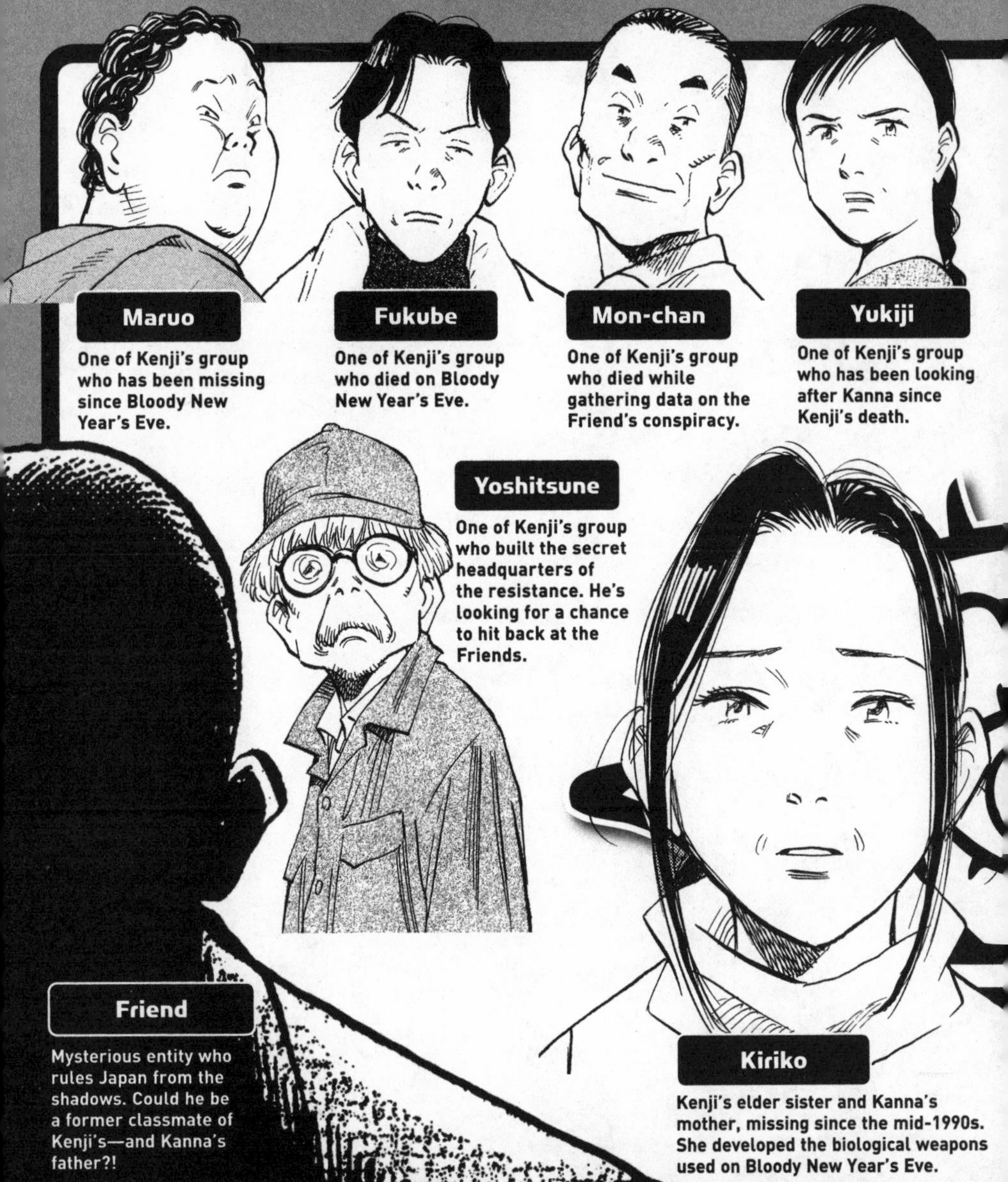

Maruo

One of Kenji's group who has been missing since Bloody New Year's Eve.

Fukube

One of Kenji's group who died on Bloody New Year's Eve.

Mon-chan

One of Kenji's group who died while gathering data on the Friend's conspiracy.

Yukiji

One of Kenji's group who has been looking after Kanna since Kenji's death.

Yoshitsune

One of Kenji's group who built the secret headquarters of the resistance. He's looking for a chance to hit back at the Friends.

Kiriko

Kenji's elder sister and Kanna's mother, missing since the mid-1990s. She developed the biological weapons used on Bloody New Year's Eve.

Friend

Mysterious entity who rules Japan from the shadows. Could he be a former classmate of Kenji's—and Kanna's father?!

The story so far...

Kenji and his friends were born in **1960**, when Japan was powering itself out of post-WWII devastation through rapid economic development.

In 1969, when *Apollo 11* put mankind on the moon for the very first time, and in 1970, when the World Exposition was held in Osaka, Kenji and his friends were elementary schoolers who, like people throughout Japan, dreamed of the exciting future that awaited them in the 21st century. In their secret headquarters, built in an empty lot, they wrote a "Book of Prophecy" filled with the sinister machinations of a League of Evil, whose plan to destroy mankind would be thwarted by a group of heroes. Of course, none of the boys ever imagined their childish fantasies would one day become reality...

But in 1997, when the adult Kenji was raising his missing sister's baby, a series of ominous incidents started taking place around him: viral attacks, an

CONTENTS

VOL 12
FRIEND'S FACE

NAOKI
URASAWA'S

20 CENTURY BOYS

Chapter 1 New Year's Eve

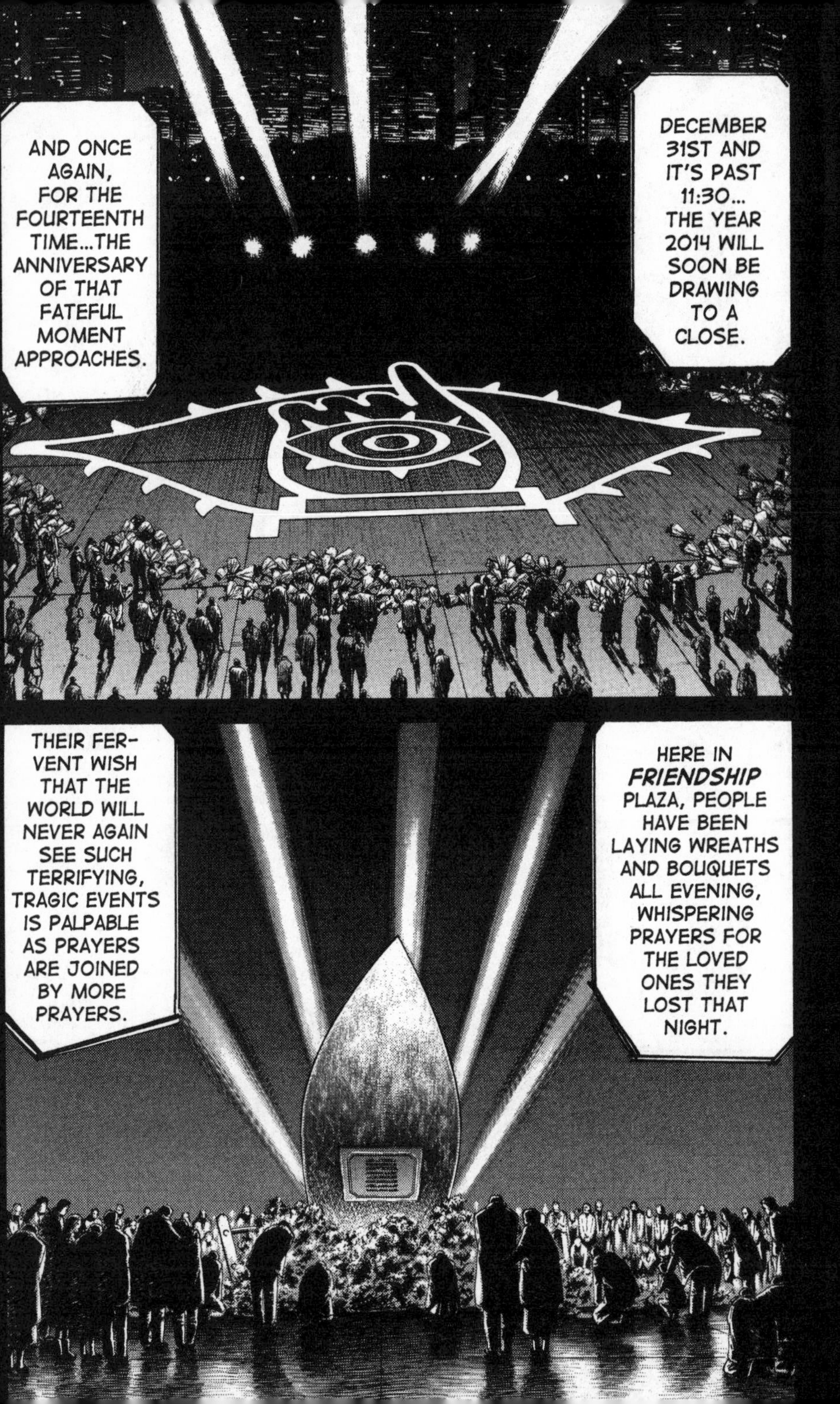

DECEMBER 31ST AND IT'S PAST 11:30... THE YEAR 2014 WILL SOON BE DRAWING TO A CLOSE.
AND ONCE AGAIN, FOR THE FOURTEENTH TIME...THE ANNIVERSARY OF THAT FATEFUL MOMENT APPROACHES.
HERE IN *FRIENDSHIP* PLAZA, PEOPLE HAVE BEEN LAYING WREATHS AND BOUQUETS ALL EVENING, WHISPERING PRAYERS FOR THE LOVED ONES THEY LOST THAT NIGHT.
THEIR FERVENT WISH THAT THE WORLD WILL NEVER AGAIN SEE SUCH TERRIFYING, TRAGIC EVENTS IS PALPABLE AS PRAYERS ARE JOINED BY MORE PRAYERS.

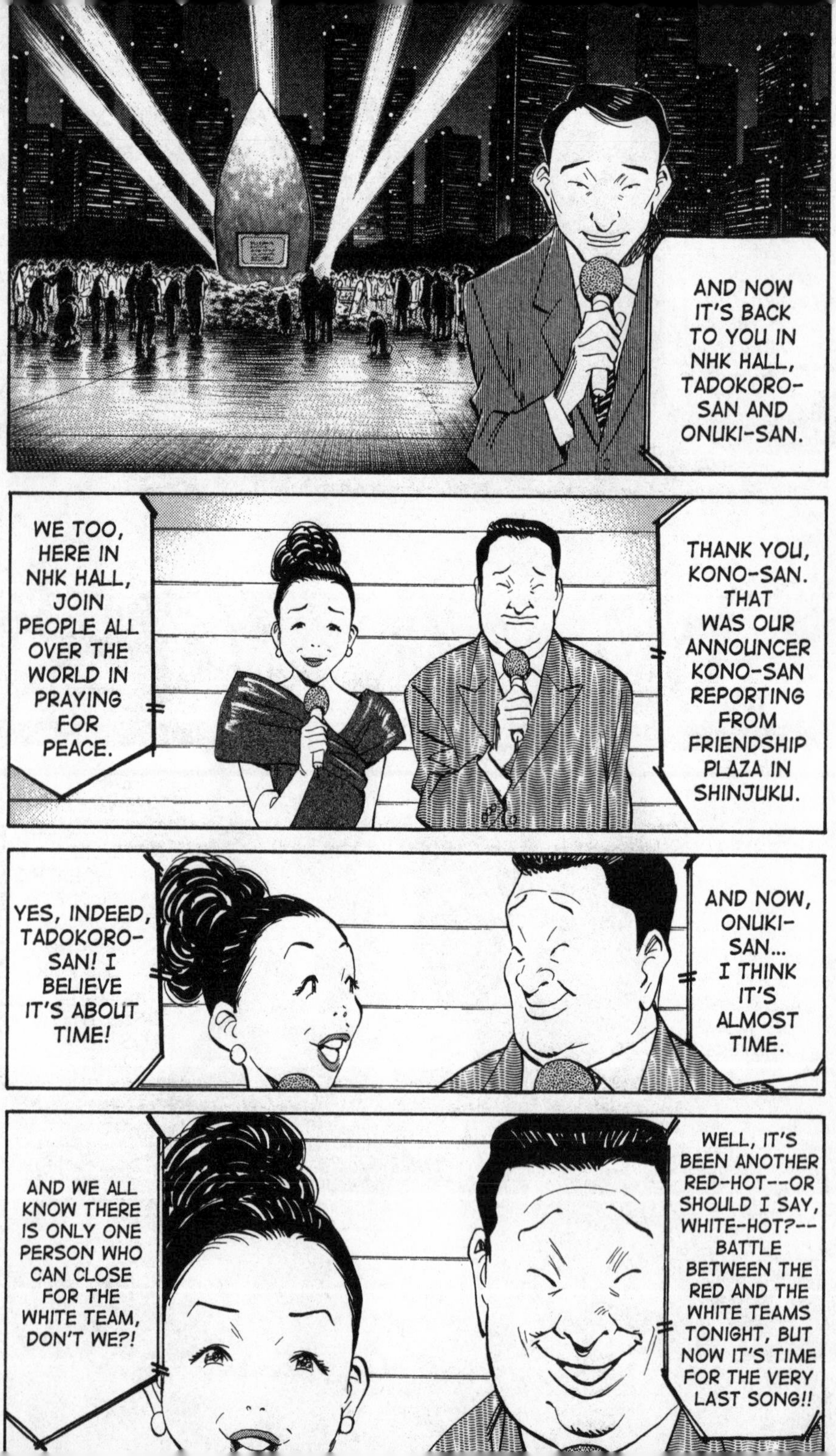
AND NOW IT'S BACK TO YOU IN NHK HALL, TADOKORO-SAN AND ONUKI-SAN.
THANK YOU, KONO-SAN. THAT WAS OUR ANNOUNCER KONO-SAN REPORTING FROM FRIENDSHIP PLAZA IN SHINJUKU.
WE TOO, HERE IN NHK HALL, JOIN PEOPLE ALL OVER THE WORLD IN PRAYING FOR PEACE.
AND NOW, ONUKI-SAN... I THINK IT'S ALMOST TIME.
YES, INDEED, TADOKORO-SAN! I BELIEVE IT'S ABOUT TIME!
WELL, IT'S BEEN ANOTHER RED-HOT--OR SHOULD I SAY, WHITE-HOT?--BATTLE BETWEEN THE RED AND THE WHITE TEAMS TONIGHT, BUT NOW IT'S TIME FOR THE VERY LAST SONG!!
AND WE ALL KNOW THERE IS ONLY ONE PERSON WHO CAN CLOSE FOR THE WHITE TEAM, DON'T WE?!

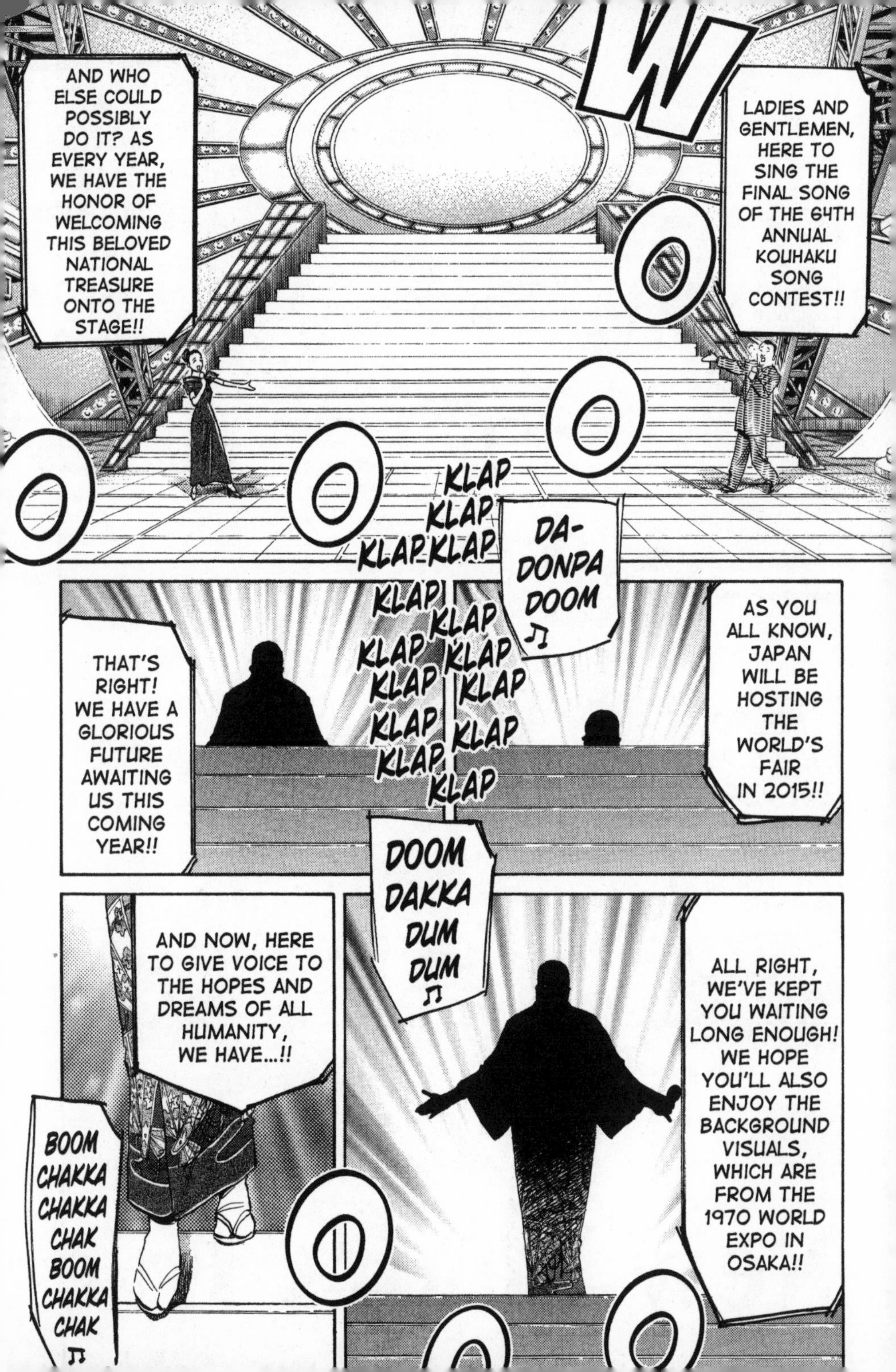
W
LADIES AND GENTLEMEN, HERE TO SING THE FINAL SONG OF THE 64TH ANNUAL KOUHAKU SONG CONTEST!!
AND WHO ELSE COULD POSSIBLY DO IT? AS EVERY YEAR, WE HAVE THE HONOR OF WELCOMING THIS BELOVED NATIONAL TREASURE ONTO THE STAGE!!
DA-DONPA DOOM ♫
KLAP KLAP KLAP KLAP
KLAP KLAP KLAP KLAP KLAP KLAP KLAP KLAP KLAP KLAP
AS YOU ALL KNOW, JAPAN WILL BE HOSTING THE WORLD'S FAIR IN 2015!!
THAT'S RIGHT! WE HAVE A GLORIOUS FUTURE AWAITING US THIS COMING YEAR!!
DOOM DAKKA DUM DUM ♫
ALL RIGHT, WE'VE KEPT YOU WAITING LONG ENOUGH! WE HOPE YOU'LL ALSO ENJOY THE BACKGROUND VISUALS, WHICH ARE FROM THE 1970 WORLD EXPO IN OSAKA!!
AND NOW, HERE TO GIVE VOICE TO THE HOPES AND DREAMS OF ALL HUMANITY, WE HAVE...!!
BOOM CHAKKA CHAKKA CHAK BOOM CHAKKA CHAK ♫

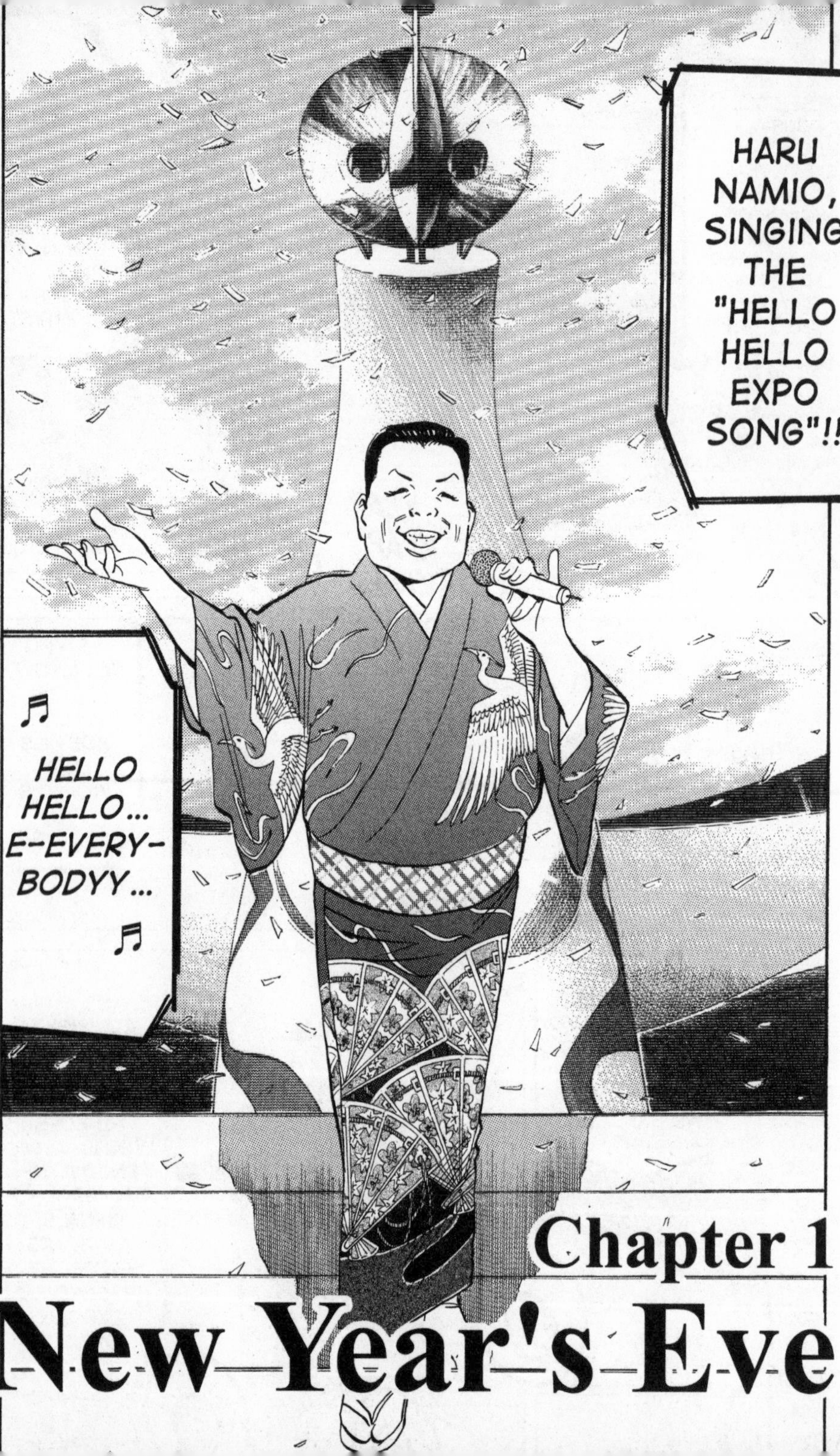
HARU NAMIO, SINGING THE "HELLO HELLO EXPO SONG"!!
♬ HELLO HELLO... E-EVERY-BODYY... ♬

Chapter 1
New Year's Eve

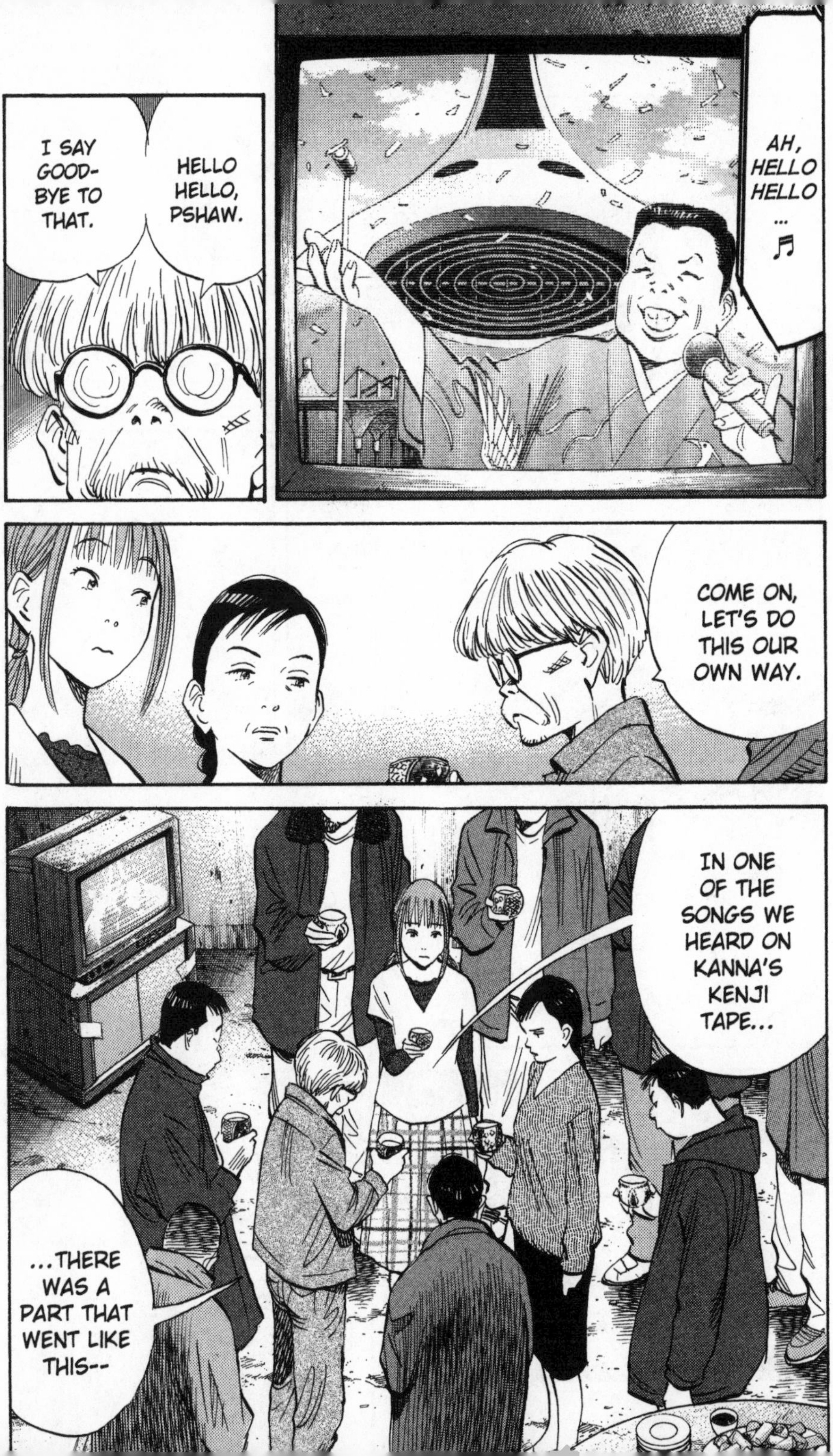
AH, HELLO HELLO ... ♫
HELLO HELLO, PSHAW.
I SAY GOOD-BYE TO THAT.
COME ON, LET'S DO THIS OUR OWN WAY.
IN ONE OF THE SONGS WE HEARD ON KANNA'S KENJI TAPE...
...THERE WAS A PART THAT WENT LIKE THIS--

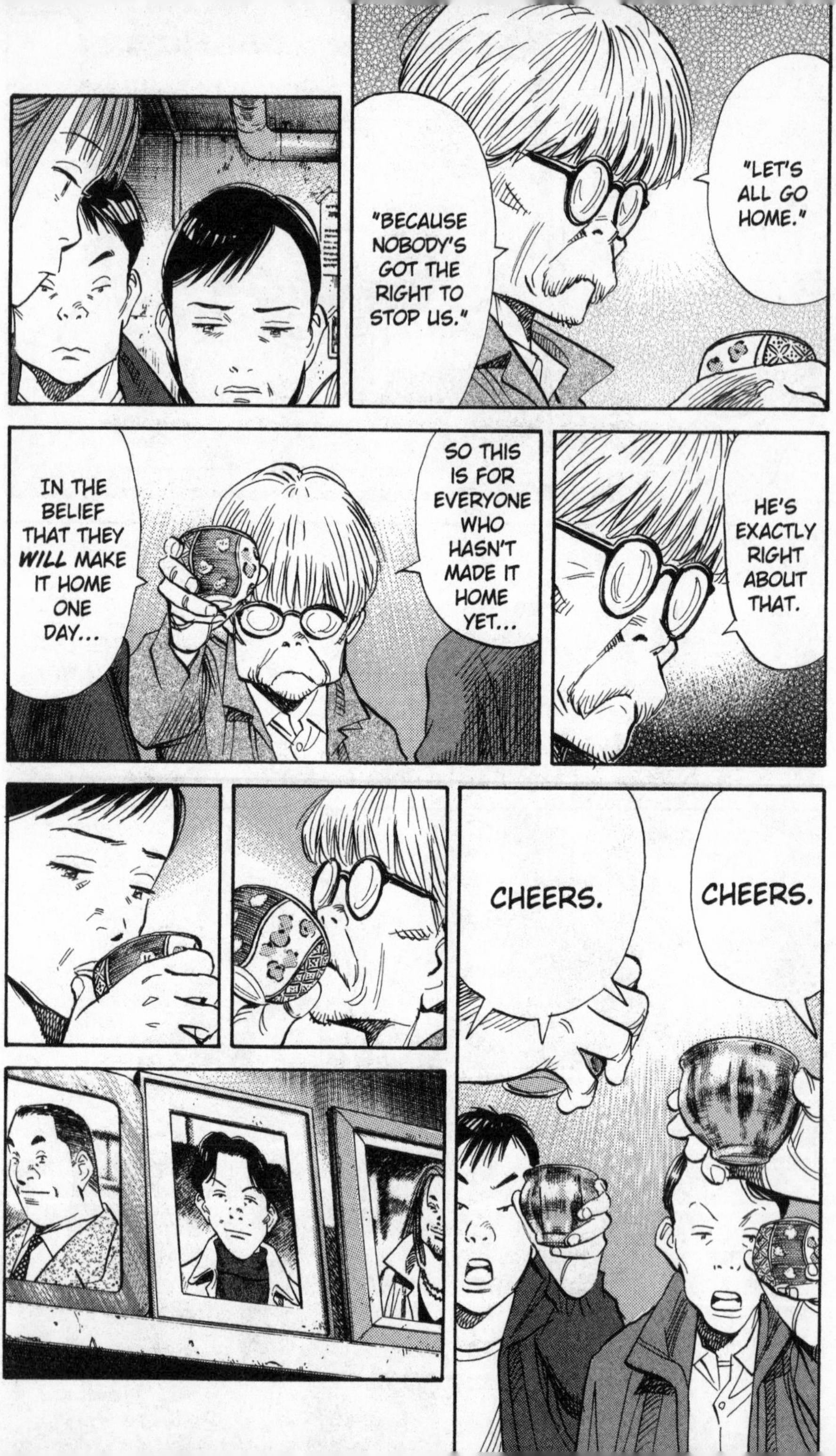
"LET'S ALL GO HOME."
"BECAUSE NOBODY'S GOT THE RIGHT TO STOP US."
HE'S EXACTLY RIGHT ABOUT THAT.
SO THIS IS FOR EVERYONE WHO HASN'T MADE IT HOME YET...
IN THE BELIEF THAT THEY *WILL* MAKE IT HOME ONE DAY...
CHEERS.
CHEERS.

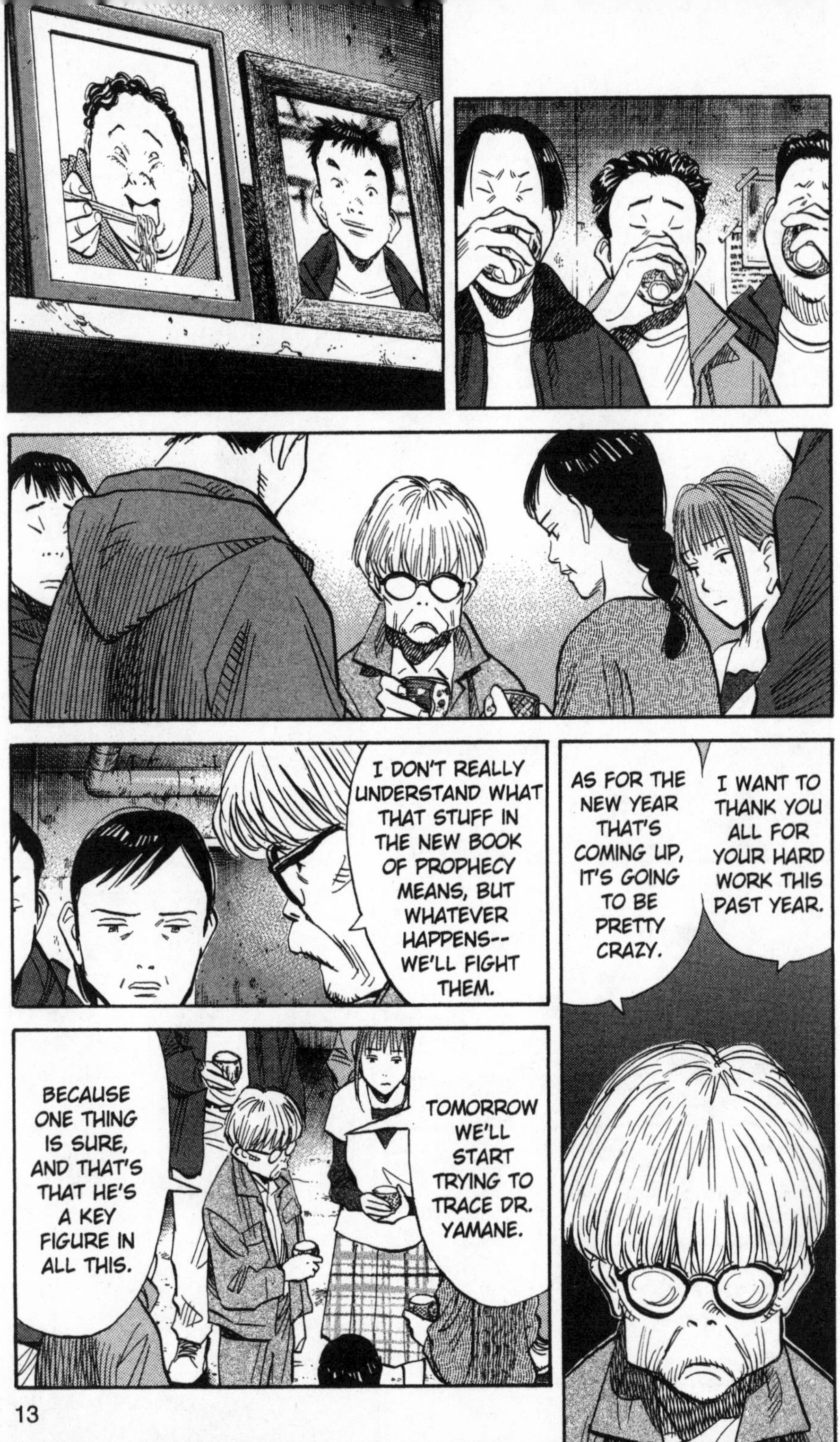
I WANT TO THANK YOU ALL FOR YOUR HARD WORK THIS PAST YEAR.
AS FOR THE NEW YEAR THAT'S COMING UP, IT'S GOING TO BE PRETTY CRAZY.
I DON'T REALLY UNDERSTAND WHAT THAT STUFF IN THE NEW BOOK OF PROPHECY MEANS, BUT WHATEVER HAPPENS-- WE'LL FIGHT THEM.
TOMORROW WE'LL START TRYING TO TRACE DR. YAMANE.
BECAUSE ONE THING IS SURE, AND THAT'S THAT HE'S A KEY FIGURE IN ALL THIS.

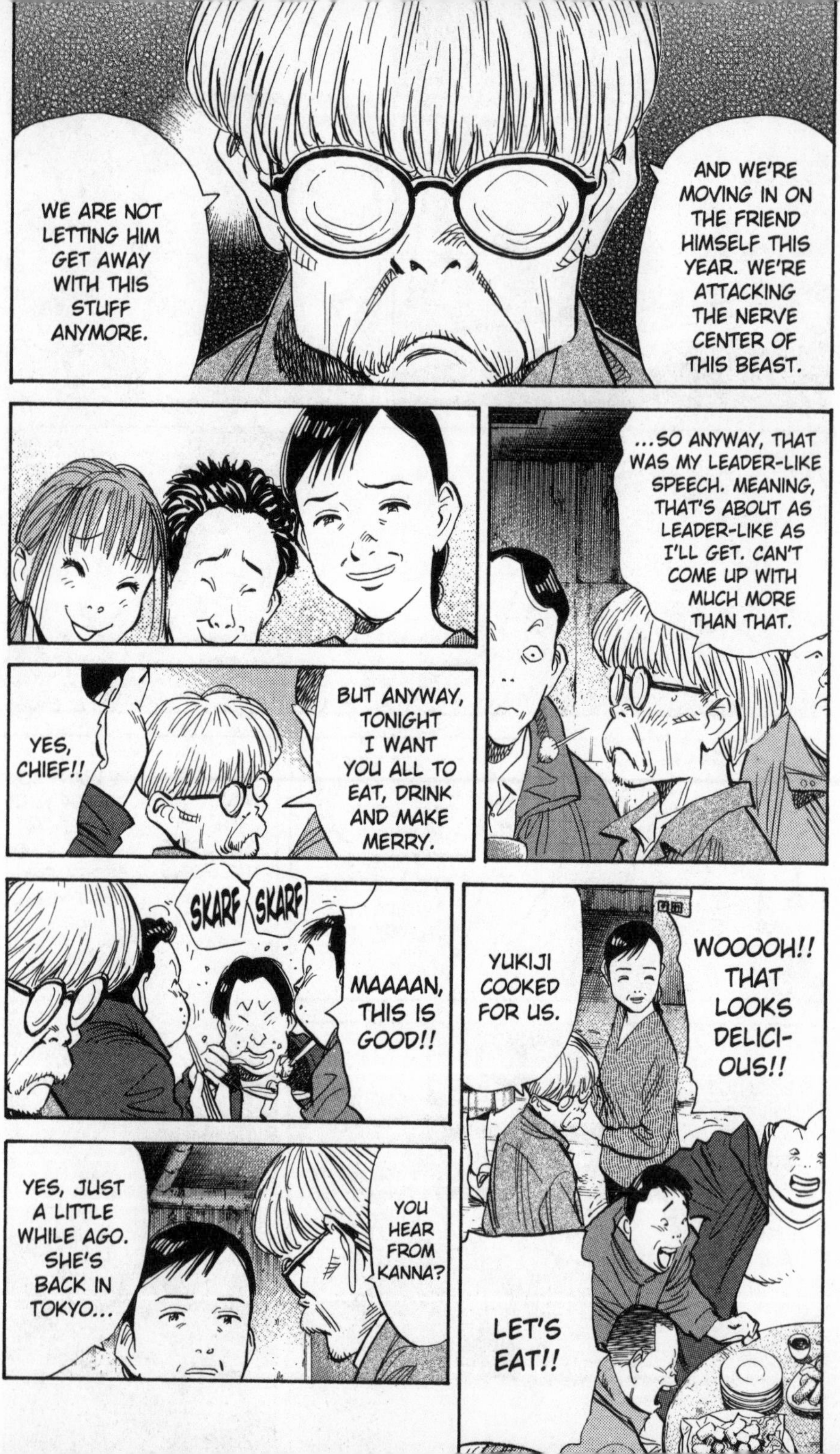
AND WE'RE MOVING IN ON THE FRIEND HIMSELF THIS YEAR. WE'RE ATTACKING THE NERVE CENTER OF THIS BEAST.
WE ARE NOT LETTING HIM GET AWAY WITH THIS STUFF ANYMORE.
...SO ANYWAY, THAT WAS MY LEADER-LIKE SPEECH. MEANING, THAT'S ABOUT AS LEADER-LIKE AS I'LL GET. CAN'T COME UP WITH MUCH MORE THAN THAT.
BUT ANYWAY, TONIGHT I WANT YOU ALL TO EAT, DRINK AND MAKE MERRY.
YES, CHIEF!!
WOOOOH!! THAT LOOKS DELICI-OUS!!
YUKIJI COOKED FOR US.
LET'S EAT!!
MAAAAN, THIS IS GOOD!!
SKARF
SKARF
YOU HEAR FROM KANNA?
YES, JUST A LITTLE WHILE AGO. SHE'S BACK IN TOKYO...

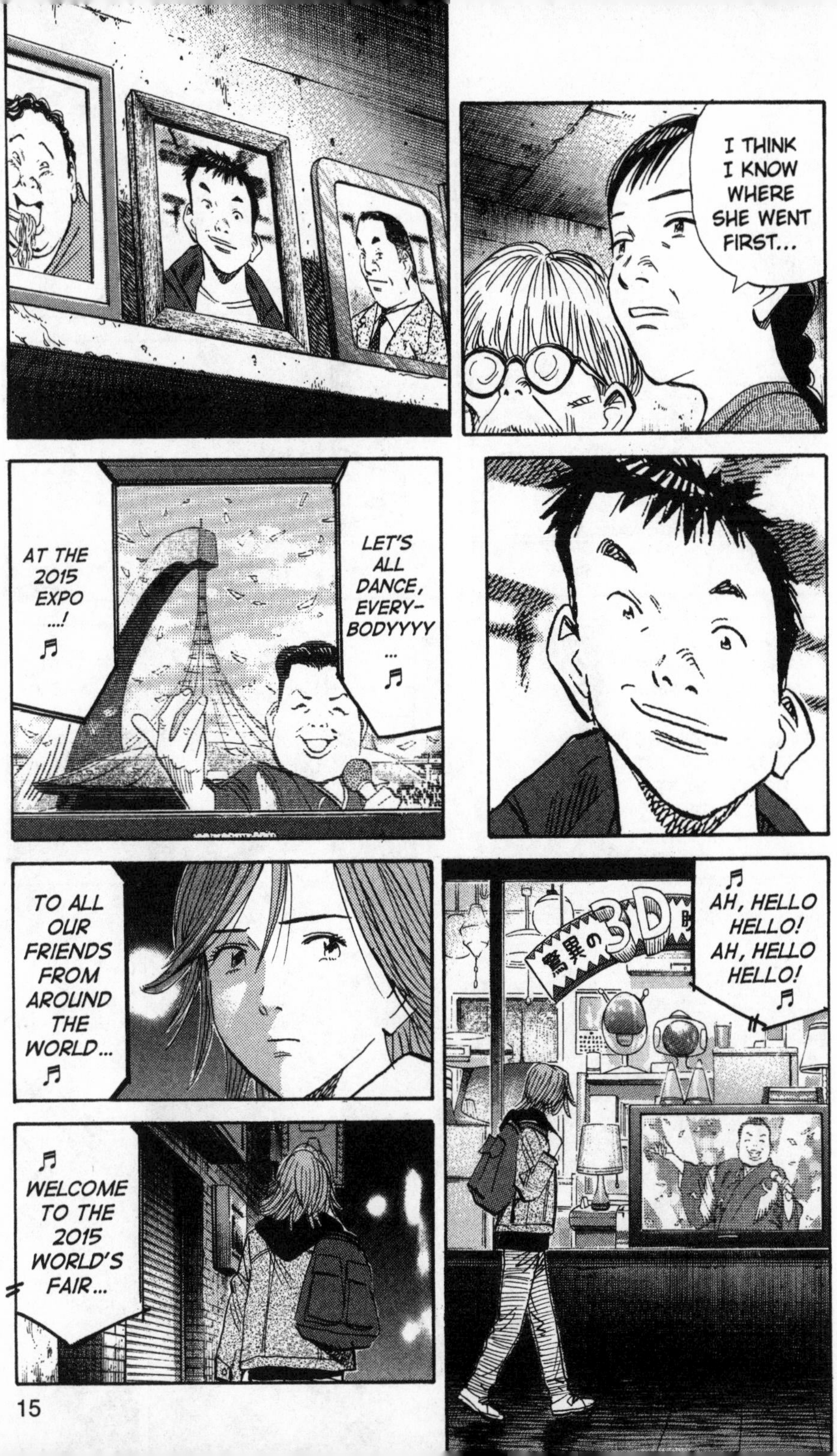
I THINK I KNOW WHERE SHE WENT FIRST...
LET'S ALL DANCE, EVERYBODYYYY ... ♬
AT THE 2015 EXPO ...! ♬
♬ AH, HELLO HELLO! AH, HELLO HELLO! ♬
驚異の3D
TO ALL OUR FRIENDS FROM AROUND THE WORLD... ♬
♬ WELCOME TO THE 2015 WORLD'S FAIR...

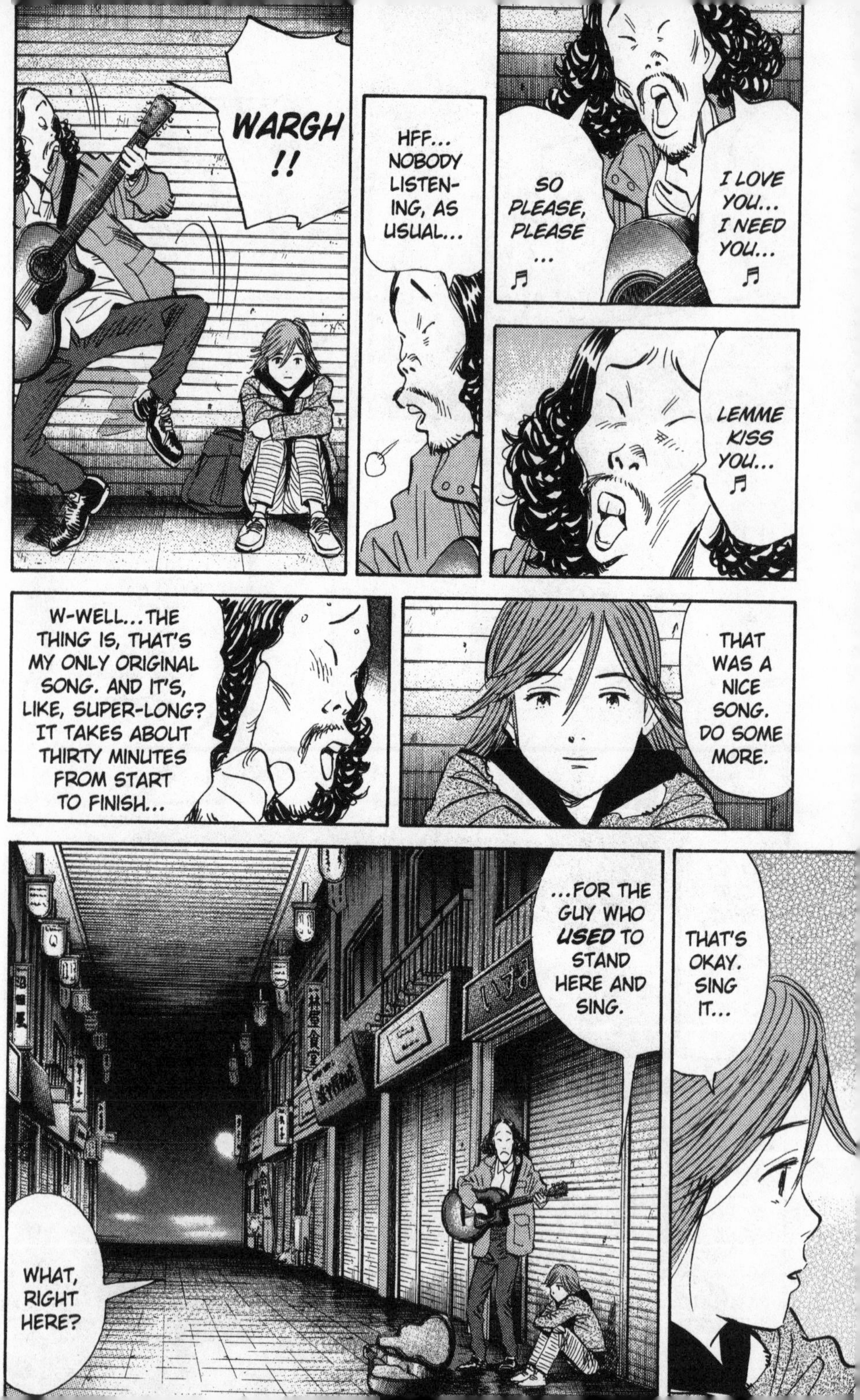
I LOVE YOU... I NEED YOU... ♬
SO PLEASE, PLEASE ... ♬
LEMME KISS YOU... ♬
HFF... NOBODY LISTEN-ING, AS USUAL...
WARGH !!
THAT WAS A NICE SONG. DO SOME MORE.
W-WELL...THE THING IS, THAT'S MY ONLY ORIGINAL SONG. AND IT'S, LIKE, SUPER-LONG? IT TAKES ABOUT THIRTY MINUTES FROM START TO FINISH...
THAT'S OKAY. SING IT...
...FOR THE GUY WHO *USED* TO STAND HERE AND SING.
WHAT, RIGHT HERE?

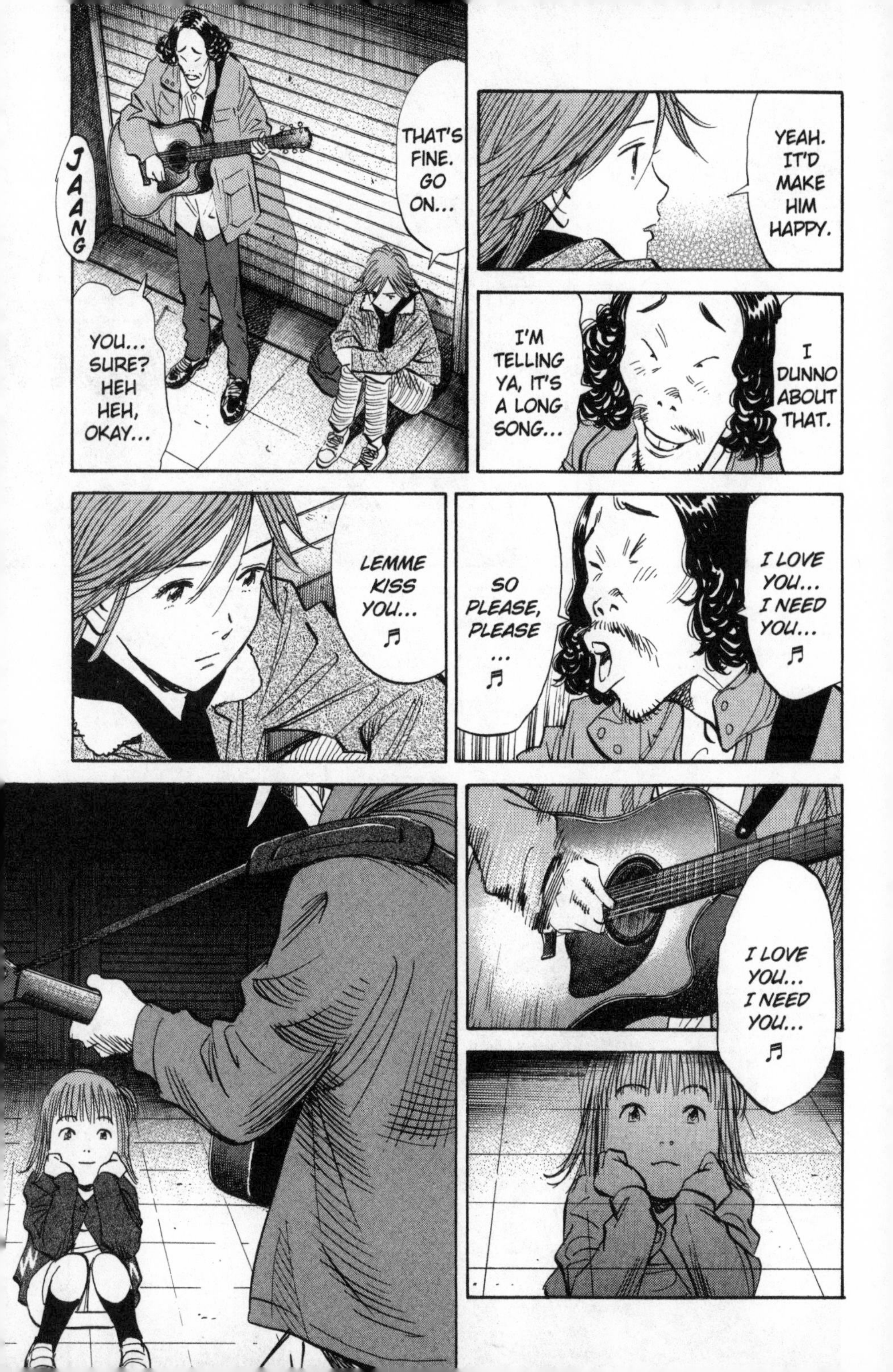
YEAH. IT'D MAKE HIM HAPPY.
I DUNNO ABOUT THAT.
I'M TELLING YA, IT'S A LONG SONG...
THAT'S FINE. GO ON...
JAAANG
YOU... SURE? HEH HEH, OKAY...
I LOVE YOU... I NEED YOU... ♬
SO PLEASE, PLEASE ... ♬
LEMME KISS YOU... ♬
I LOVE YOU... I NEED YOU... ♬

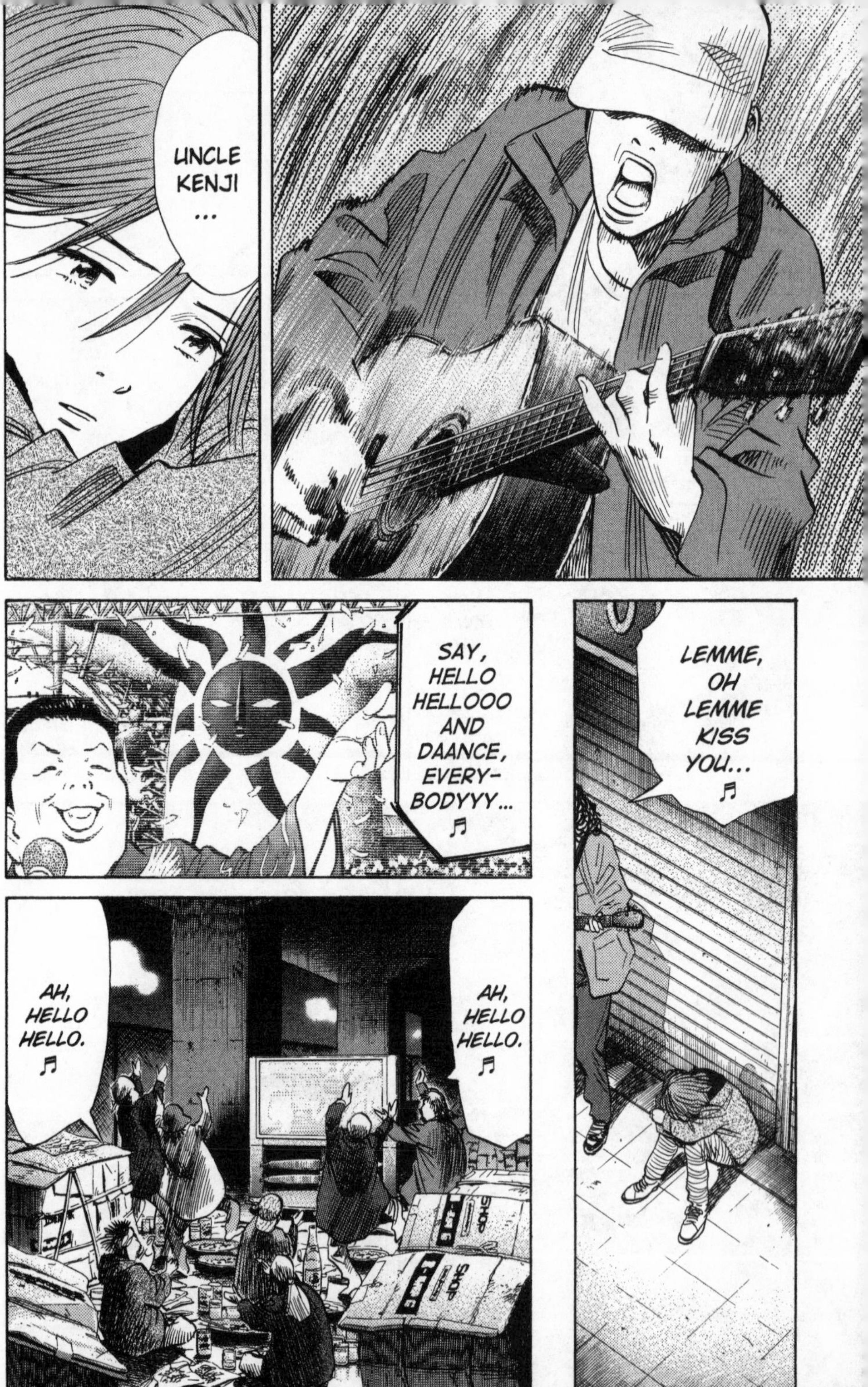
UNCLE KENJI ...
LEMME, OH LEMME KISS YOU... ♬
SAY, HELLO HELLOOO AND DAANCE, EVERY-BODYYY... ♬
AH, HELLO HELLO. ♬
AH, HELLO HELLO. ♬

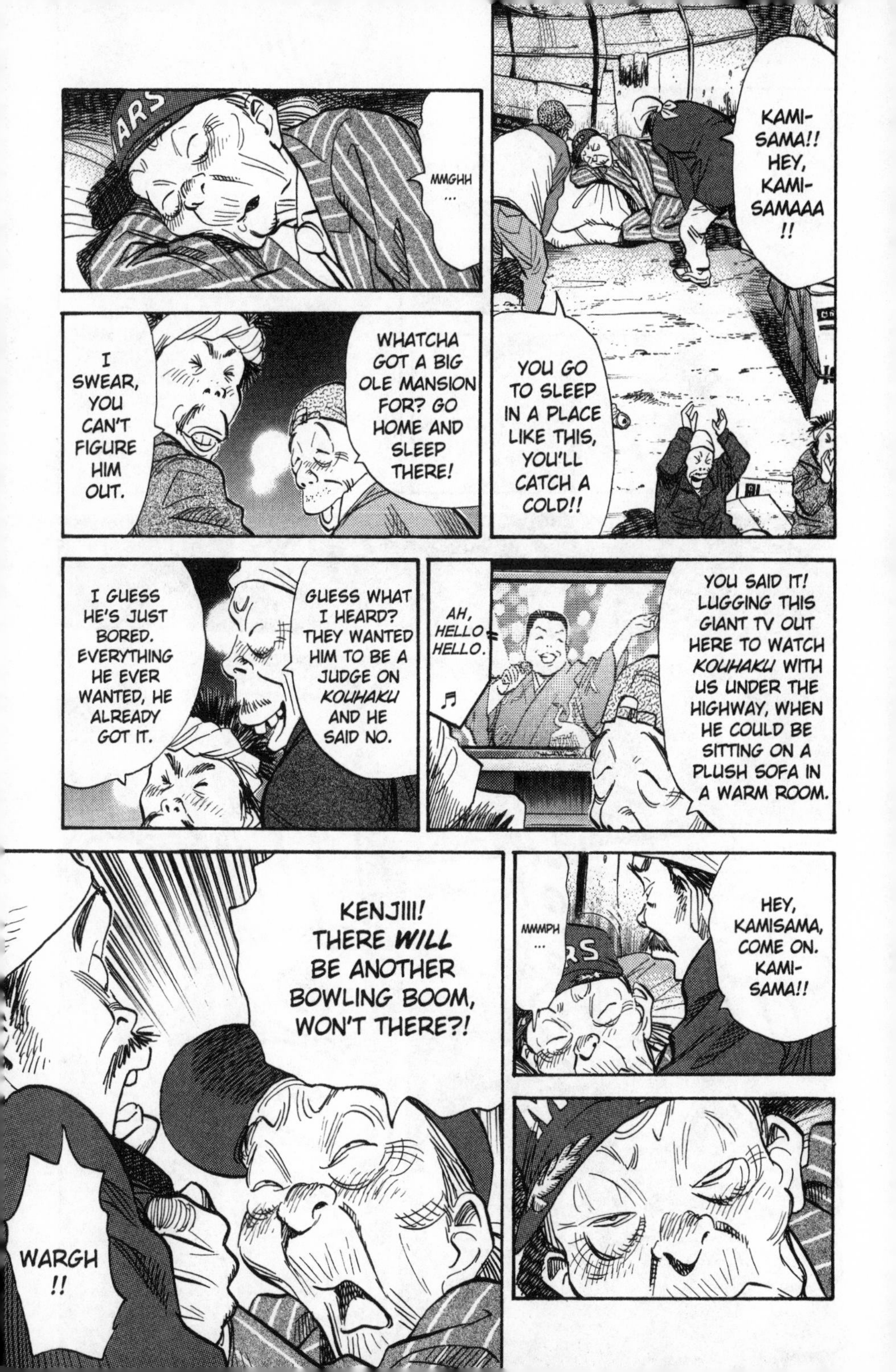
KAMI-SAMA!! HEY, KAMI-SAMAAAA!!
YOU GO TO SLEEP IN A PLACE LIKE THIS, YOU'LL CATCH A COLD!!
MMGHH...
WHATCHA GOT A BIG OLE MANSION FOR? GO HOME AND SLEEP THERE!
I SWEAR, YOU CAN'T FIGURE HIM OUT.
YOU SAID IT! LUGGING THIS GIANT TV OUT HERE TO WATCH *KOUHAKU* WITH US UNDER THE HIGHWAY, WHEN HE COULD BE SITTING ON A PLUSH SOFA IN A WARM ROOM.
AH, HELLO HELLO.
GUESS WHAT I HEARD? THEY WANTED HIM TO BE A JUDGE ON *KOUHAKU* AND HE SAID NO.
I GUESS HE'S JUST BORED. EVERYTHING HE EVER WANTED, HE ALREADY GOT IT.
HEY, KAMISAMA, COME ON. KAMI-SAMA!!
MMMPH...
KENJIII! THERE ***WILL*** BE ANOTHER BOWLING BOOM, WON'T THERE?!
WARGH!!

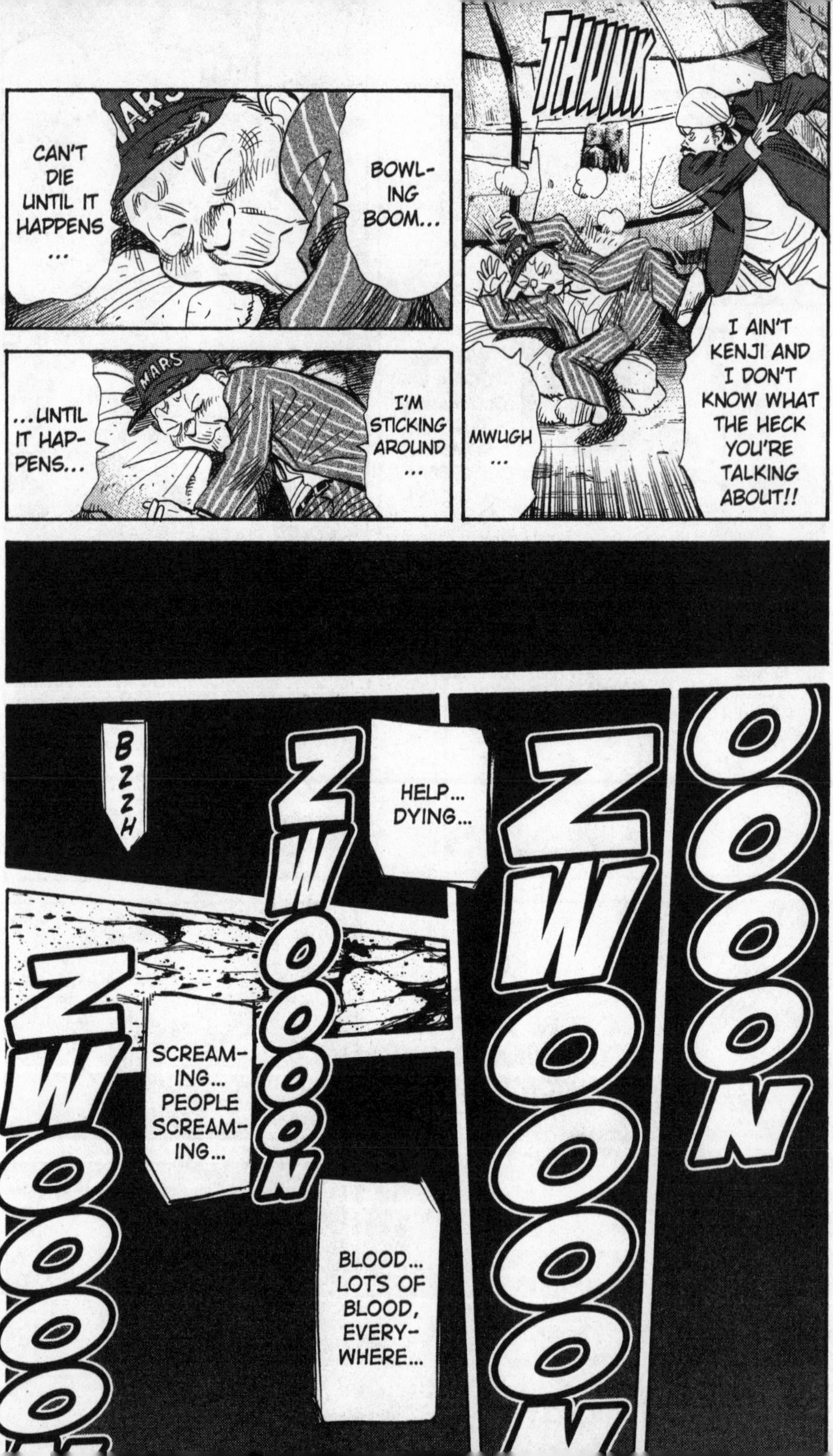
THUNK
I AIN'T KENJI AND I DON'T KNOW WHAT THE HECK YOU'RE TALKING ABOUT!!
MWUGH...
BOWL-ING BOOM...
CAN'T DIE UNTIL IT HAPPENS...
I'M STICKING AROUND...
...UNTIL IT HAP-PENS...
OOOOOON
ZWOOOOOO
HELP... DYING...
ZWOOOOON
BZZH
SCREAM-ING... PEOPLE SCREAM-ING...
BLOOD... LOTS OF BLOOD, EVERY-WHERE...
ZWOOOOO

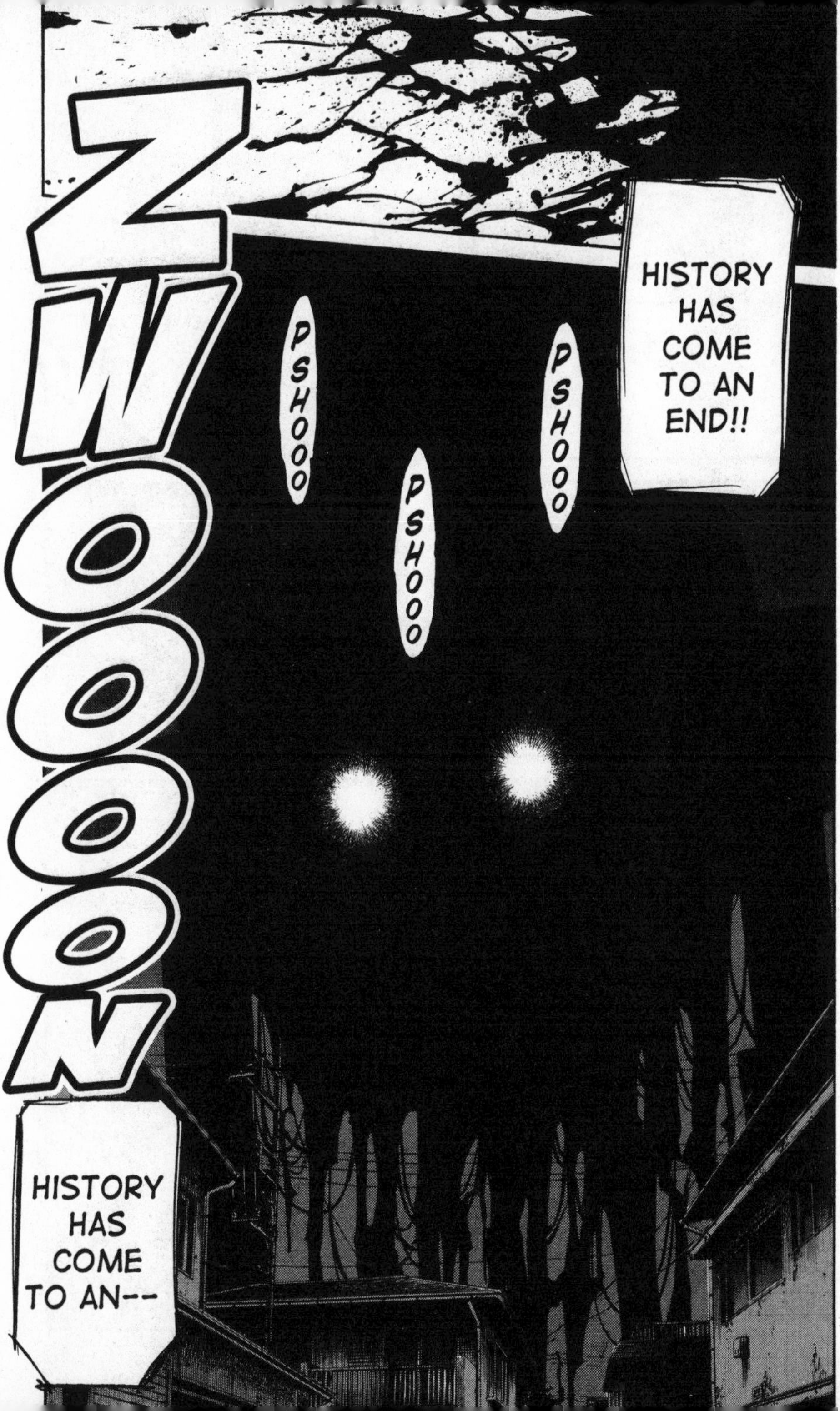
HISTORY HAS COME TO AN END!!
PSHOOOO
PSHOOOO
PSHOOOO
ZWOOOOON
HISTORY HAS COME TO AN--

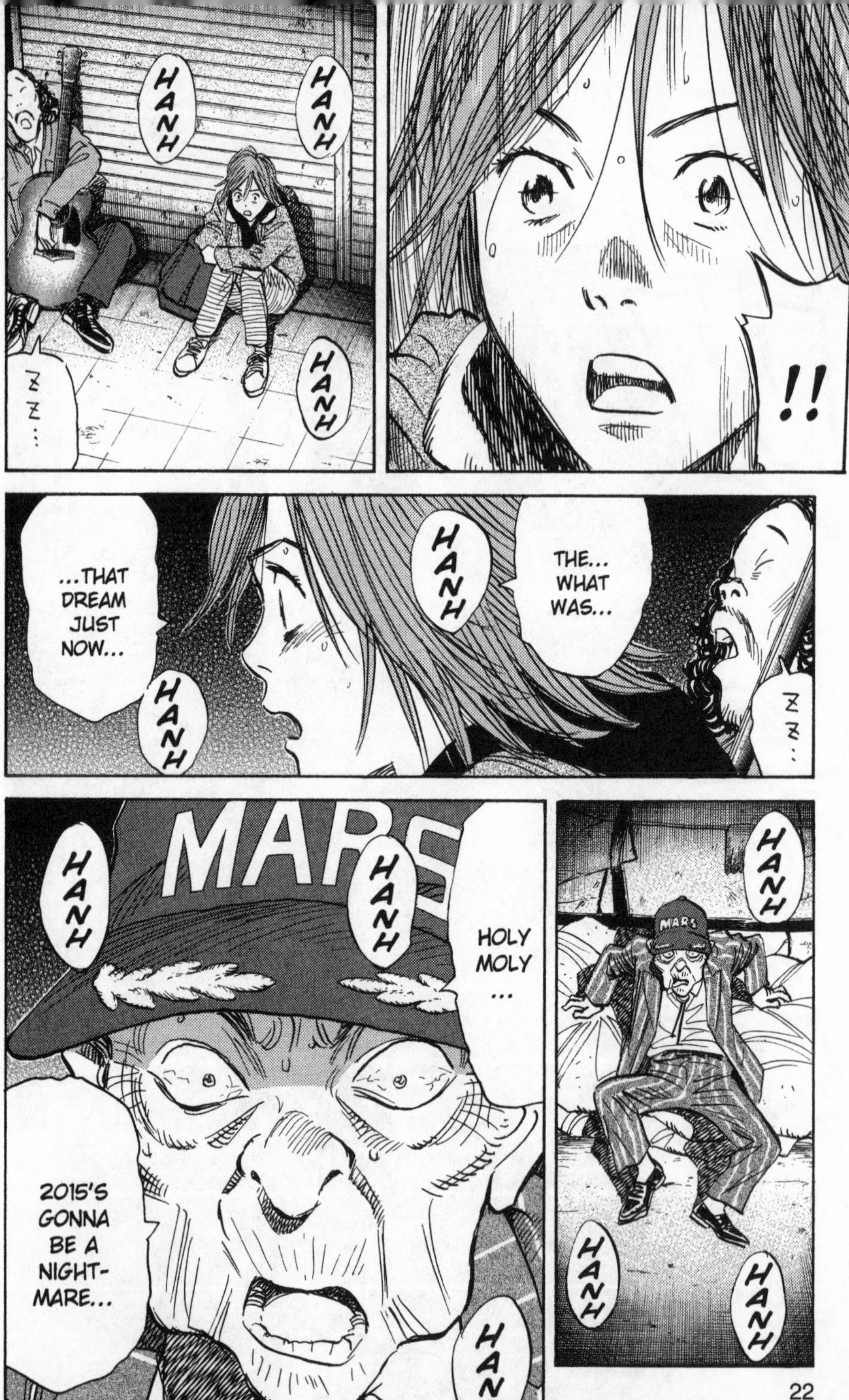
!!
HANH
HANH
HANH
Z Z...
Z Z...
THE... WHAT WAS...
HANH
...THAT DREAM JUST NOW...
HANH
HANH
HANH
HANH
HOLY MOLY ...
HANH
HANH
2015'S GONNA BE A NIGHT-MARE...
HANH

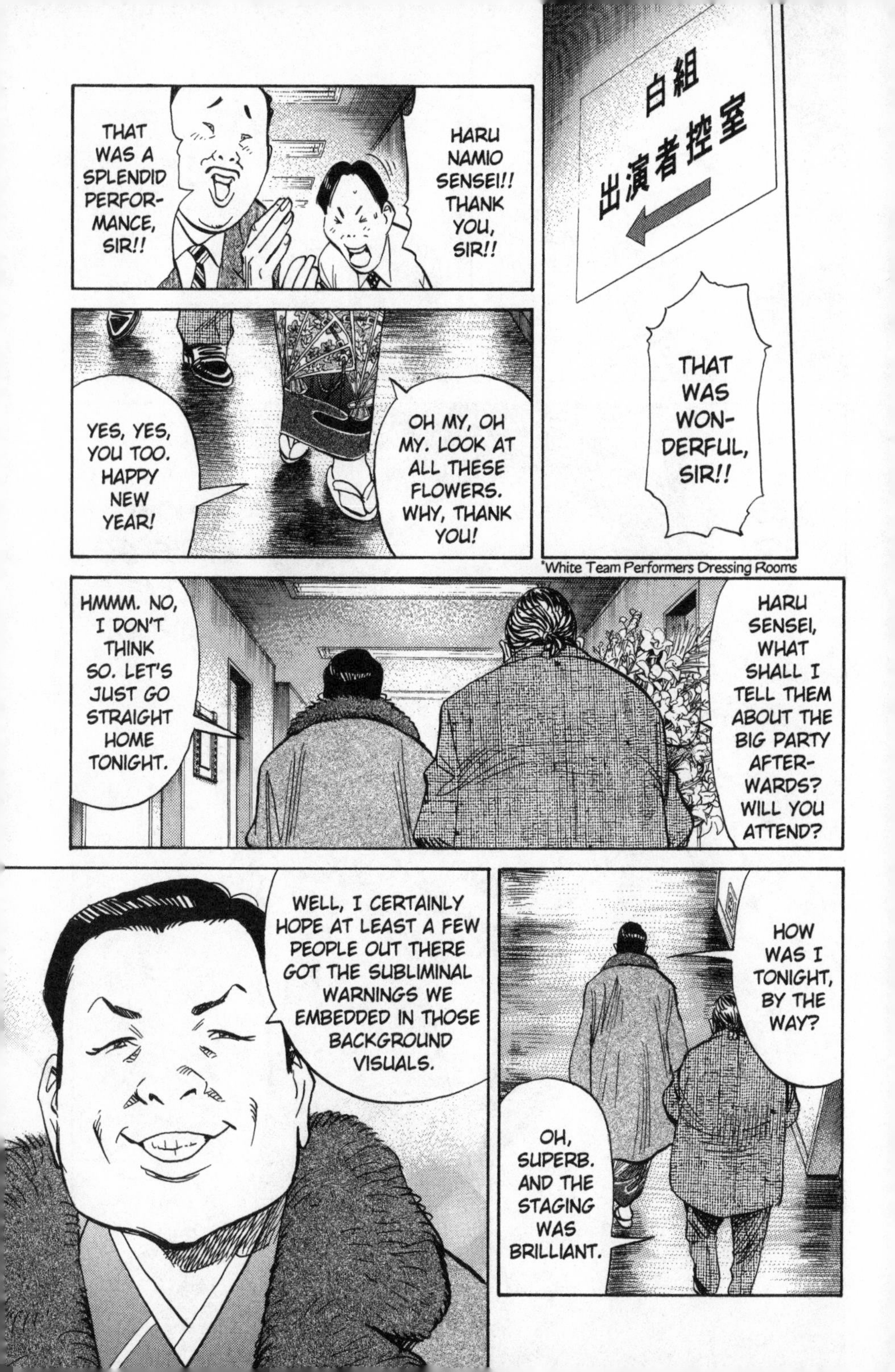
白組
出演者控室
THAT WAS WONDERFUL, SIR!!
HARU NAMIO SENSEI!! THANK YOU, SIR!!
THAT WAS A SPLENDID PERFORMANCE, SIR!!
OH MY, OH MY. LOOK AT ALL THESE FLOWERS. WHY, THANK YOU!
YES, YES, YOU TOO. HAPPY NEW YEAR!
HARU SENSEI, WHAT SHALL I TELL THEM ABOUT THE BIG PARTY AFTERWARDS? WILL YOU ATTEND?
HMMM. NO, I DON'T THINK SO. LET'S JUST GO STRAIGHT HOME TONIGHT.
HOW WAS I TONIGHT, BY THE WAY?
OH, SUPERB. AND THE STAGING WAS BRILLIANT.
WELL, I CERTAINLY HOPE AT LEAST A FEW PEOPLE OUT THERE GOT THE SUBLIMINAL WARNINGS WE EMBEDDED IN THOSE BACKGROUND VISUALS.
*White Team Performers Dressing Rooms

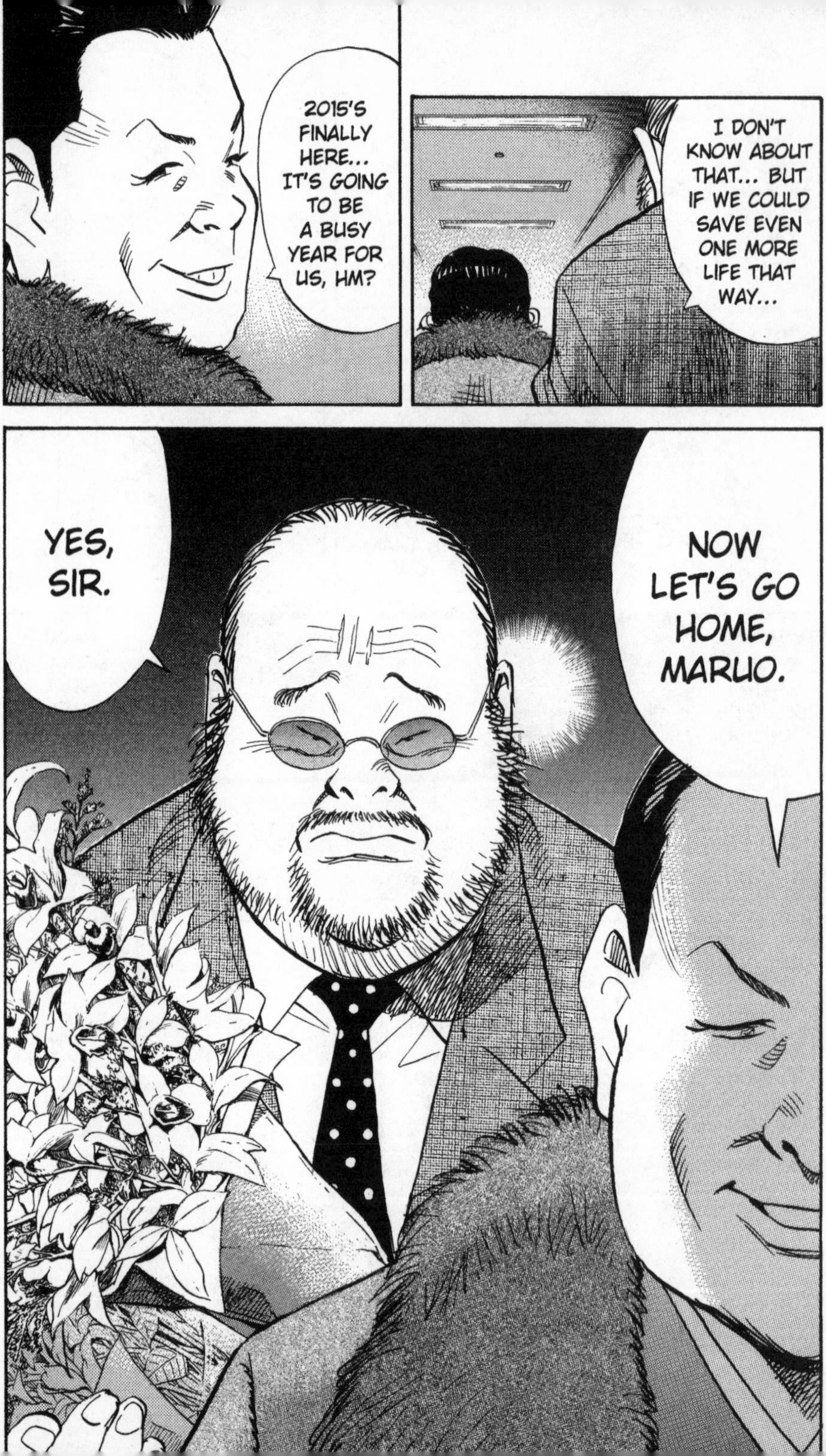
I DON'T KNOW ABOUT THAT... BUT IF WE COULD SAVE EVEN ONE MORE LIFE THAT WAY...
2015'S FINALLY HERE... IT'S GOING TO BE A BUSY YEAR FOR US, HM?
NOW LET'S GO HOME, MARUO.
YES, SIR.

Chapter 2 Shrine Visit

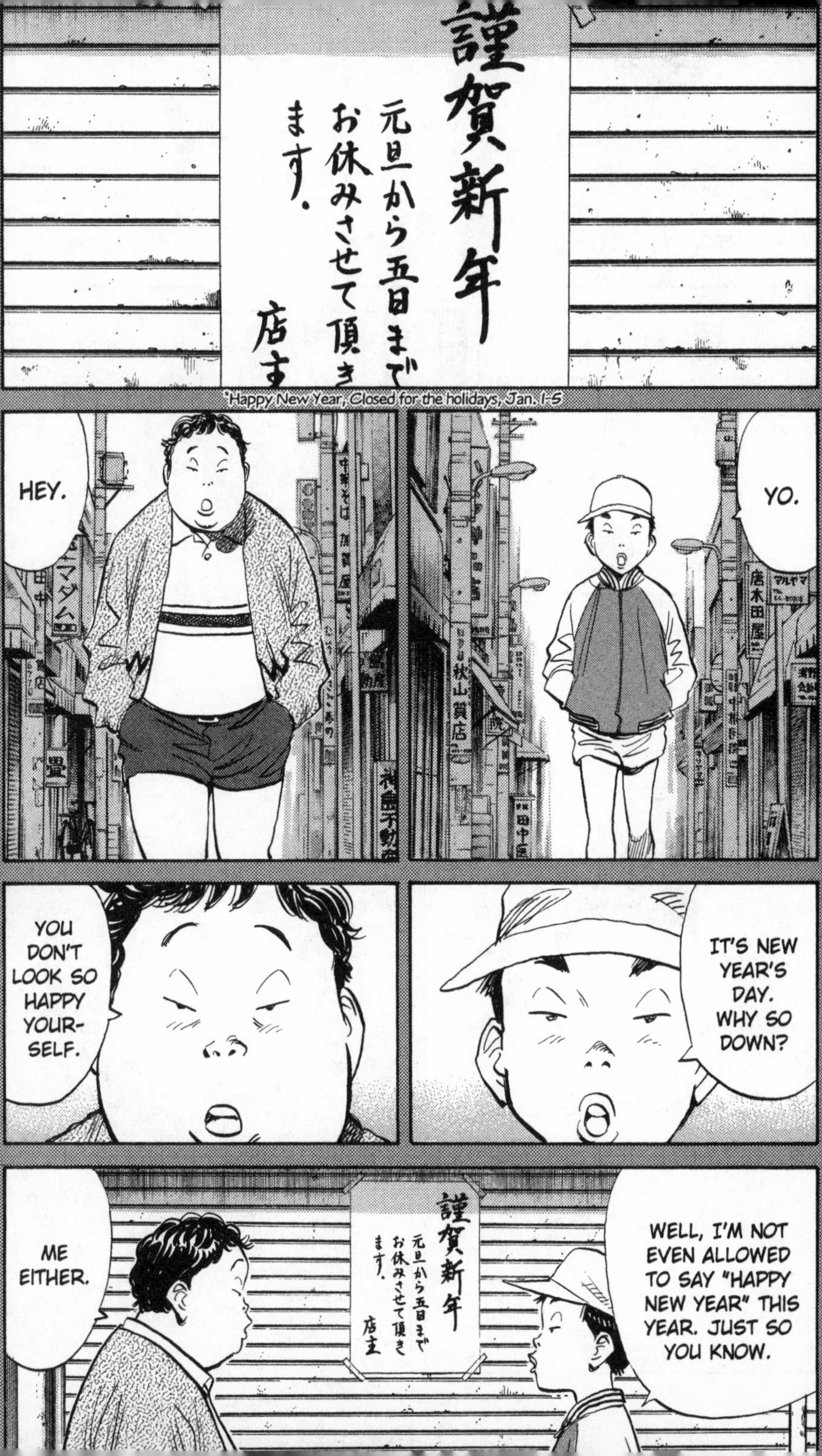
謹賀新年
元旦から五日まで
お休みさせて頂き
ます。
店主
*Happy New Year, Closed for the holidays, Jan. 1-5
YO.
HEY.
IT'S NEW YEAR'S DAY. WHY SO DOWN?
YOU DON'T LOOK SO HAPPY YOURSELF.
WELL, I'M NOT EVEN ALLOWED TO SAY "HAPPY NEW YEAR" THIS YEAR. JUST SO YOU KNOW.
ME EITHER.

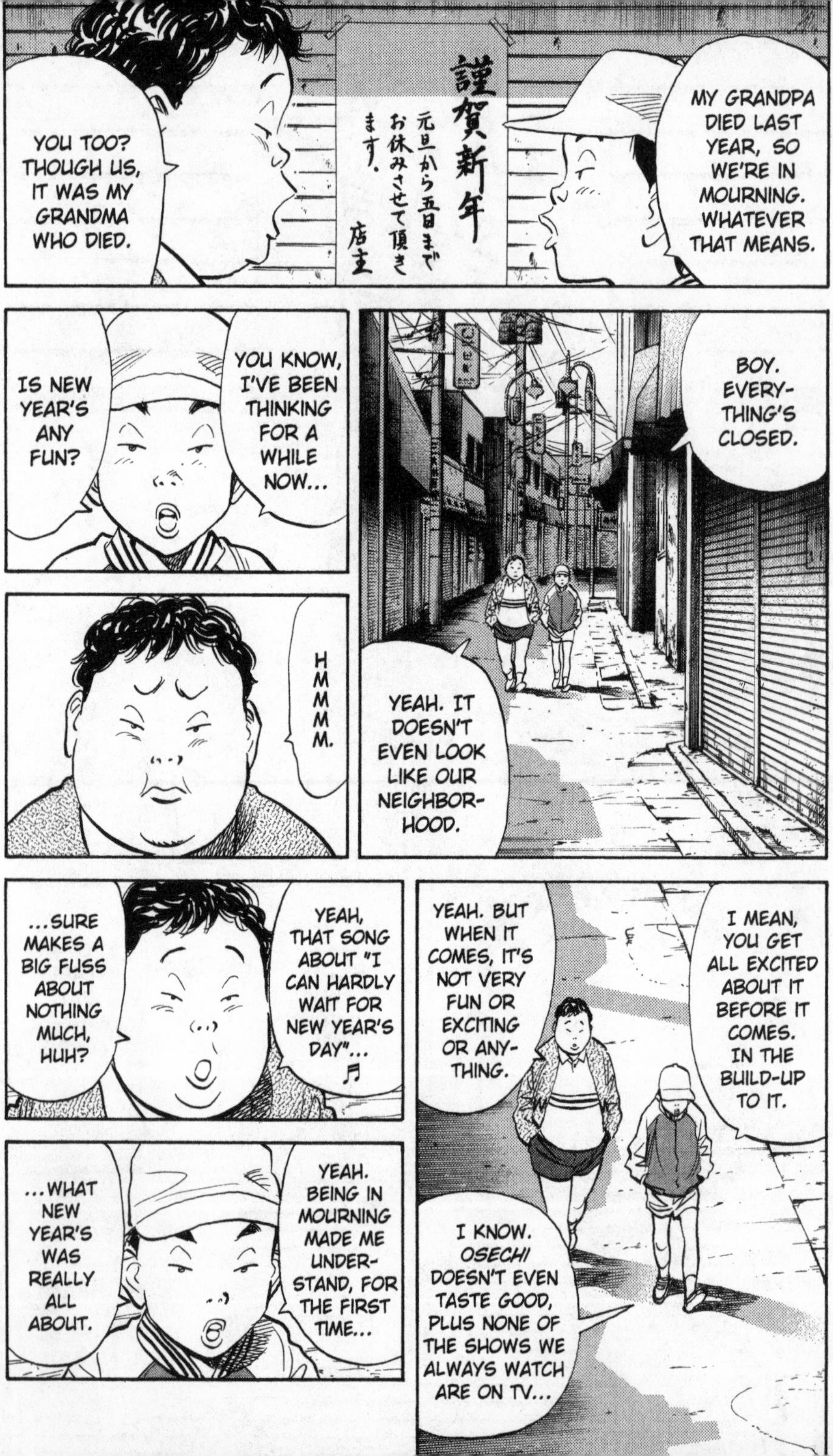
MY GRANDPA DIED LAST YEAR, SO WE'RE IN MOURNING. WHATEVER THAT MEANS.
謹賀新年
元旦から五日までお休みさせて頂きます。
店主
YOU TOO? THOUGH US, IT WAS MY GRANDMA WHO DIED.
BOY. EVERY-THING'S CLOSED.
YEAH. IT DOESN'T EVEN LOOK LIKE OUR NEIGHBOR-HOOD.
YOU KNOW, I'VE BEEN THINKING FOR A WHILE NOW...
IS NEW YEAR'S ANY FUN?
HMMMMM.
I MEAN, YOU GET ALL EXCITED ABOUT IT BEFORE IT COMES. IN THE BUILD-UP TO IT.
YEAH. BUT WHEN IT COMES, IT'S NOT VERY FUN OR EXCITING OR ANY-THING.
I KNOW. *OSECHI* DOESN'T EVEN TASTE GOOD, PLUS NONE OF THE SHOWS WE ALWAYS WATCH ARE ON TV...
YEAH, THAT SONG ABOUT "I CAN HARDLY WAIT FOR NEW YEAR'S DAY"... ♬
...SURE MAKES A BIG FUSS ABOUT NOTHING MUCH, HUH?
YEAH. BEING IN MOURNING MADE ME UNDER-STAND, FOR THE FIRST TIME...
...WHAT NEW YEAR'S WAS REALLY ALL ABOUT.

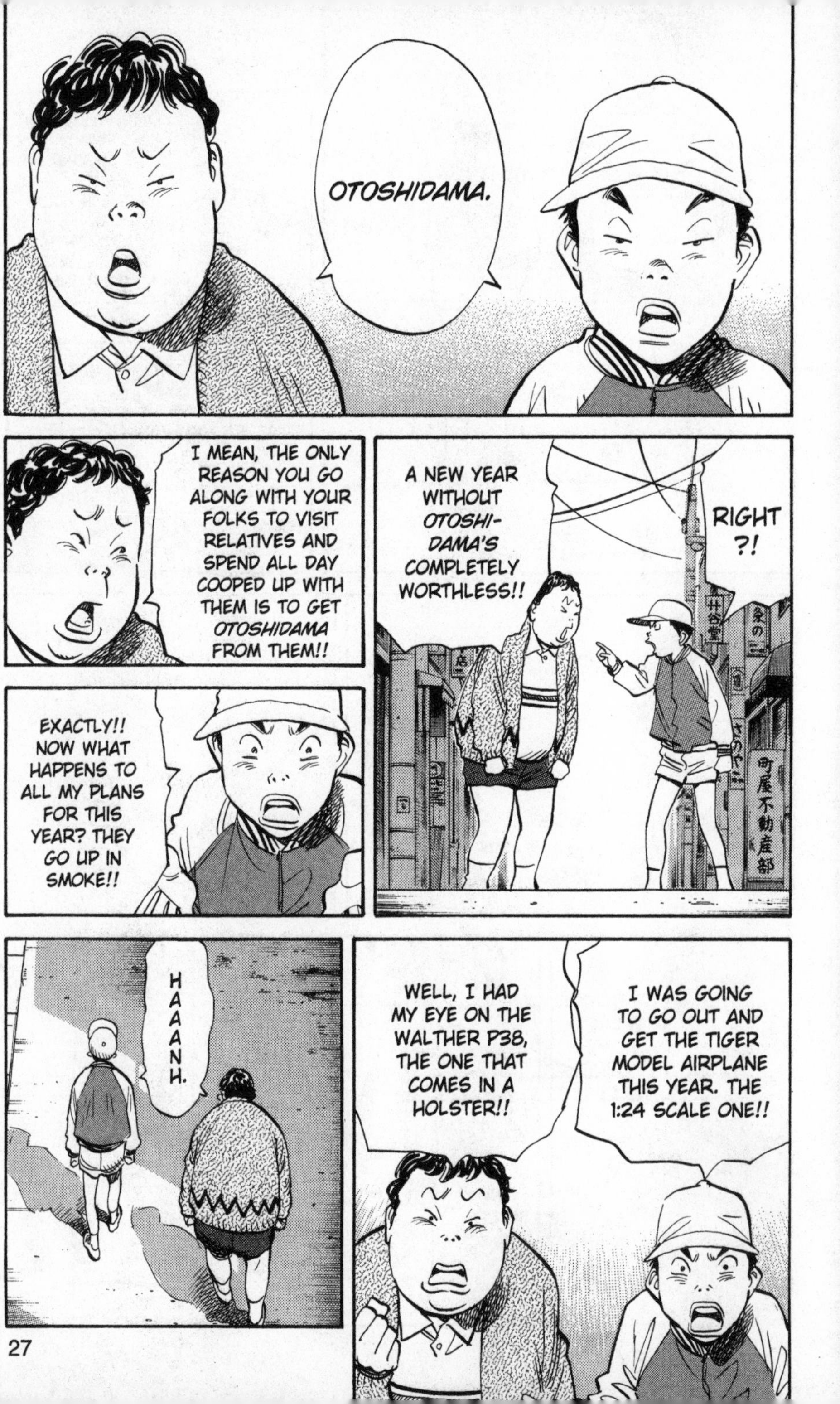
OTOSHIDAMA.
A NEW YEAR WITHOUT OTOSHI-DAMA'S COMPLETELY WORTHLESS!!
RIGHT ?!
I MEAN, THE ONLY REASON YOU GO ALONG WITH YOUR FOLKS TO VISIT RELATIVES AND SPEND ALL DAY COOPED UP WITH THEM IS TO GET OTOSHIDAMA FROM THEM!!
EXACTLY!! NOW WHAT HAPPENS TO ALL MY PLANS FOR THIS YEAR? THEY GO UP IN SMOKE!!
I WAS GOING TO GO OUT AND GET THE TIGER MODEL AIRPLANE THIS YEAR. THE 1:24 SCALE ONE!!
WELL, I HAD MY EYE ON THE WALTHER P38, THE ONE THAT COMES IN A HOLSTER!!
HAAAANH.

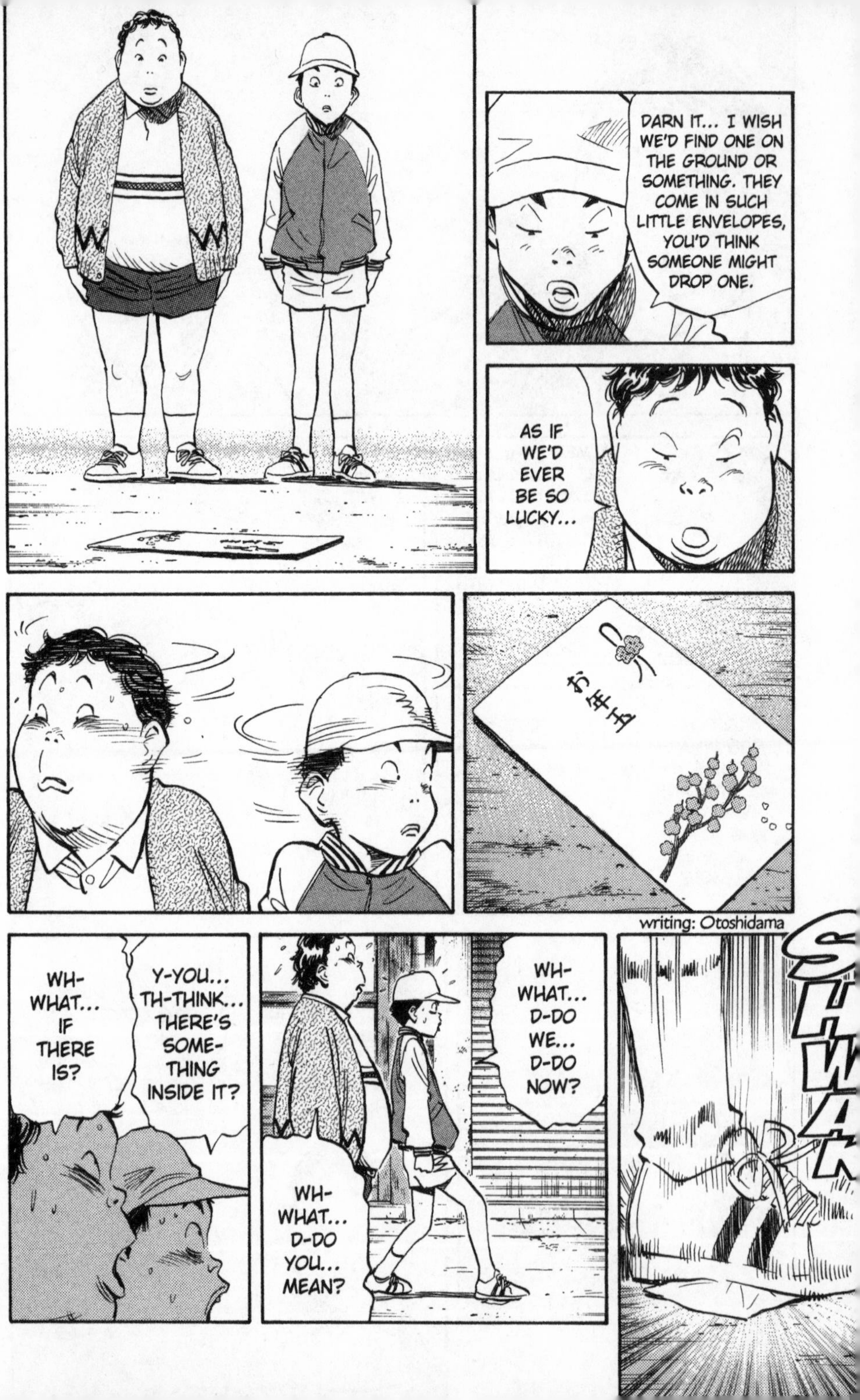
DARN IT... I WISH WE'D FIND ONE ON THE GROUND OR SOMETHING. THEY COME IN SUCH LITTLE ENVELOPES, YOU'D THINK SOMEONE MIGHT DROP ONE.
AS IF WE'D EVER BE SO LUCKY...
お年玉
writing: Otoshidama
SHWAK
WH-WHAT... D-DO WE... D-DO NOW?
WH-WHAT... D-DO YOU... MEAN?
Y-YOU... TH-THINK... THERE'S SOME-THING INSIDE IT?
WH-WHAT... IF THERE IS?

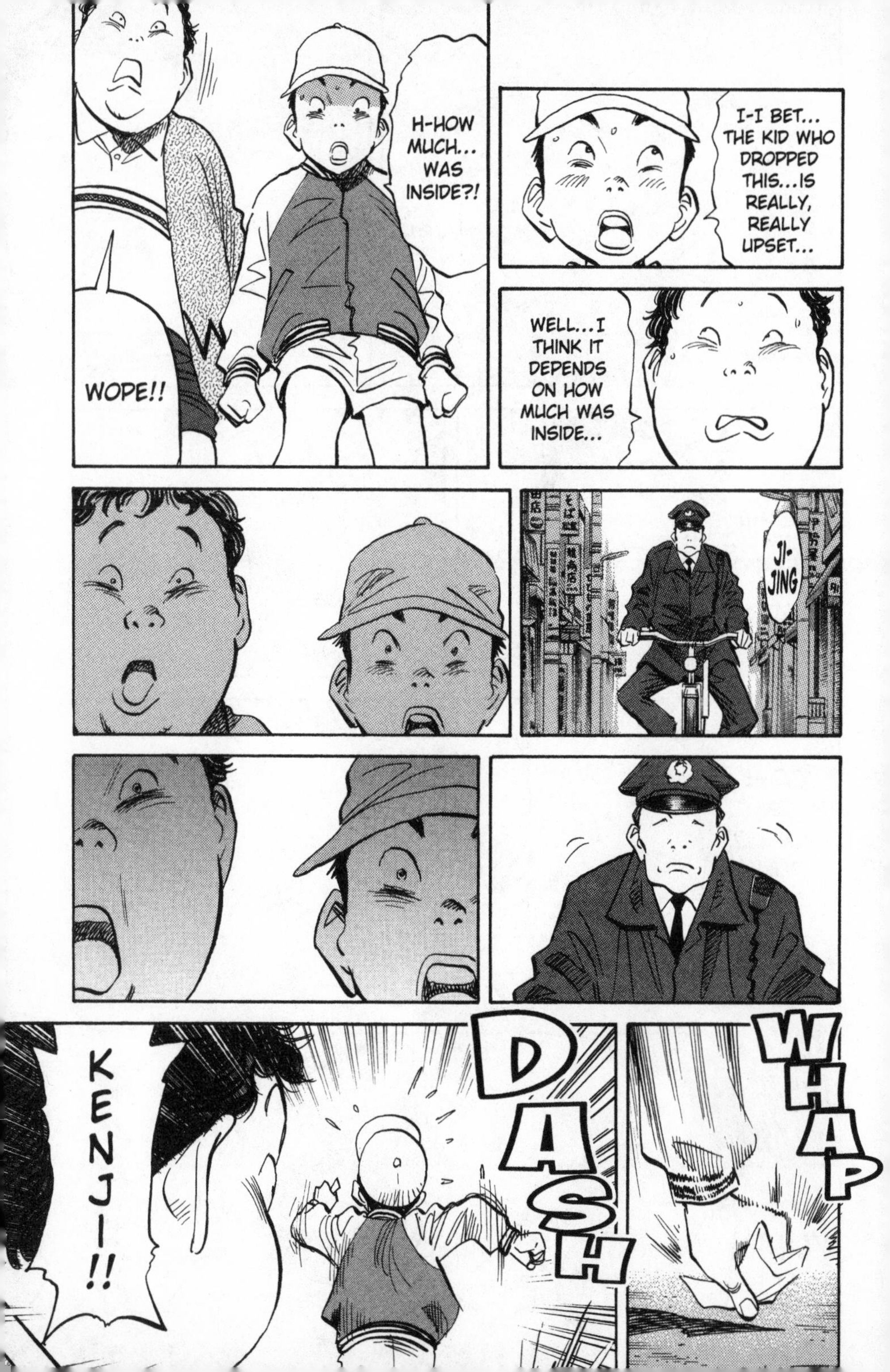
I-I BET... THE KID WHO DROPPED THIS...IS REALLY, REALLY UPSET...
WELL...I THINK IT DEPENDS ON HOW MUCH WAS INSIDE...
H-HOW MUCH... WAS INSIDE?!
WOPE!!
JI-JING
WHAP
DASH
KENJI!!

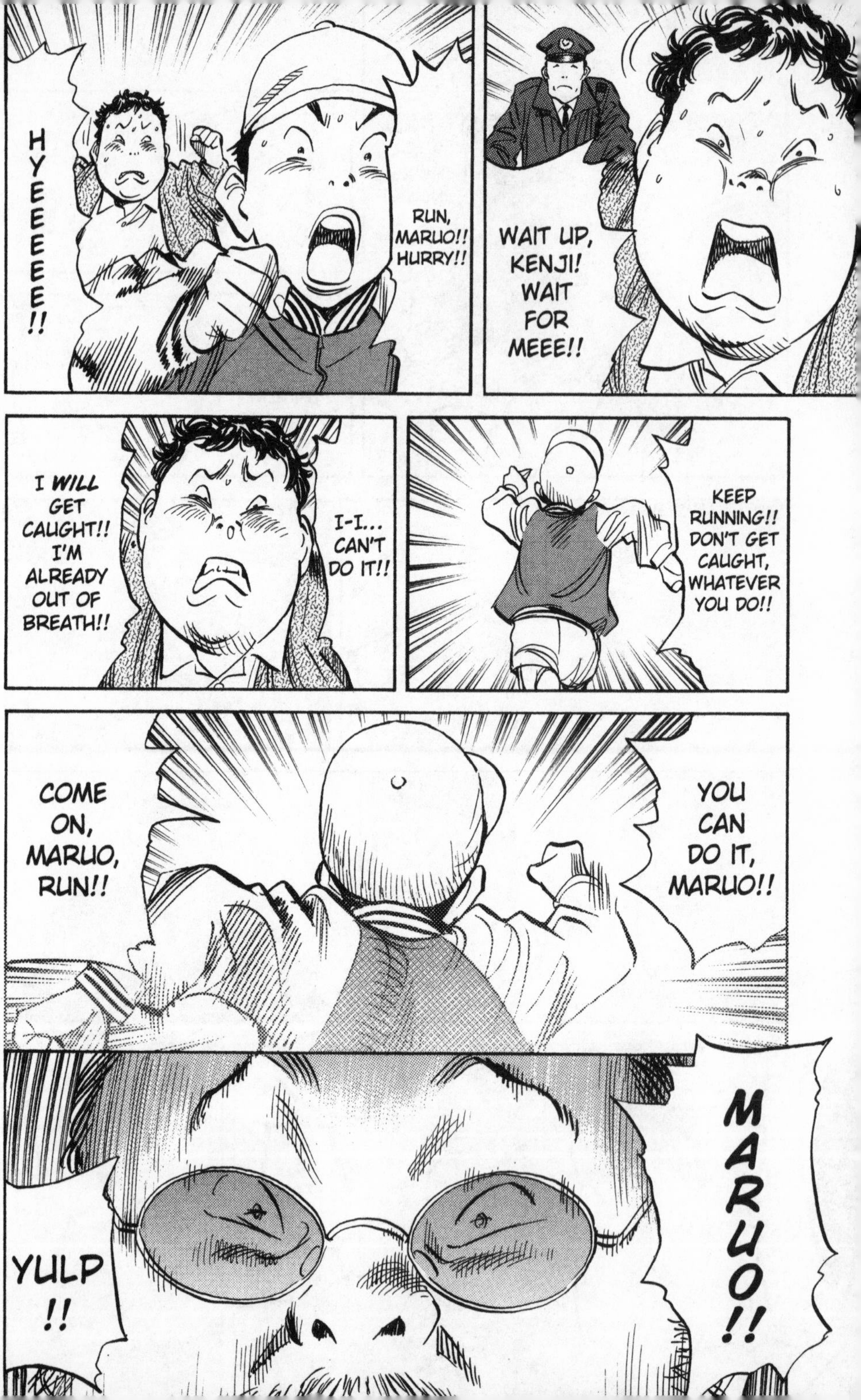
WAIT UP, KENJI! WAIT FOR MEEE!!
RUN, MARUO!! HURRY!!
HYEEEEEE!!
KEEP RUNNING!! DON'T GET CAUGHT, WHATEVER YOU DO!!
I-I... CAN'T DO IT!!
I *WILL* GET CAUGHT!! I'M ALREADY OUT OF BREATH!!
YOU CAN DO IT, MARUO!!
COME ON, MARUO, RUN!!
MARUO!!
YULP!!

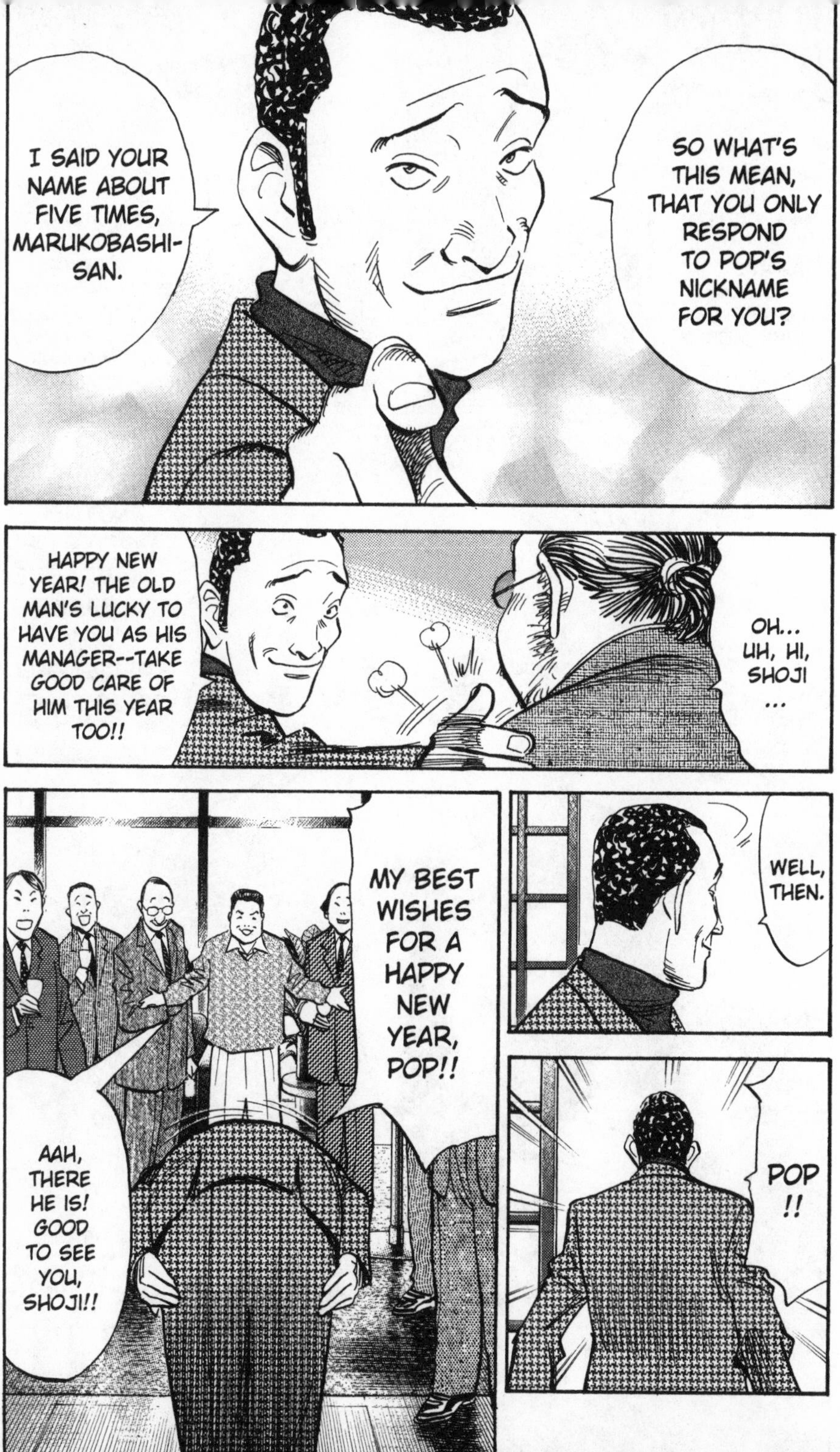
SO WHAT'S THIS MEAN, THAT YOU ONLY RESPOND TO POP'S NICKNAME FOR YOU?
I SAID YOUR NAME ABOUT FIVE TIMES, MARUKOBASHI-SAN.
OH... UH, HI, SHOJI ...
HAPPY NEW YEAR! THE OLD MAN'S LUCKY TO HAVE YOU AS HIS MANAGER--TAKE GOOD CARE OF HIM THIS YEAR TOO!!
WELL, THEN.
POP !!
MY BEST WISHES FOR A HAPPY NEW YEAR, POP!!
AAH, THERE HE IS! GOOD TO SEE YOU, SHOJI!!

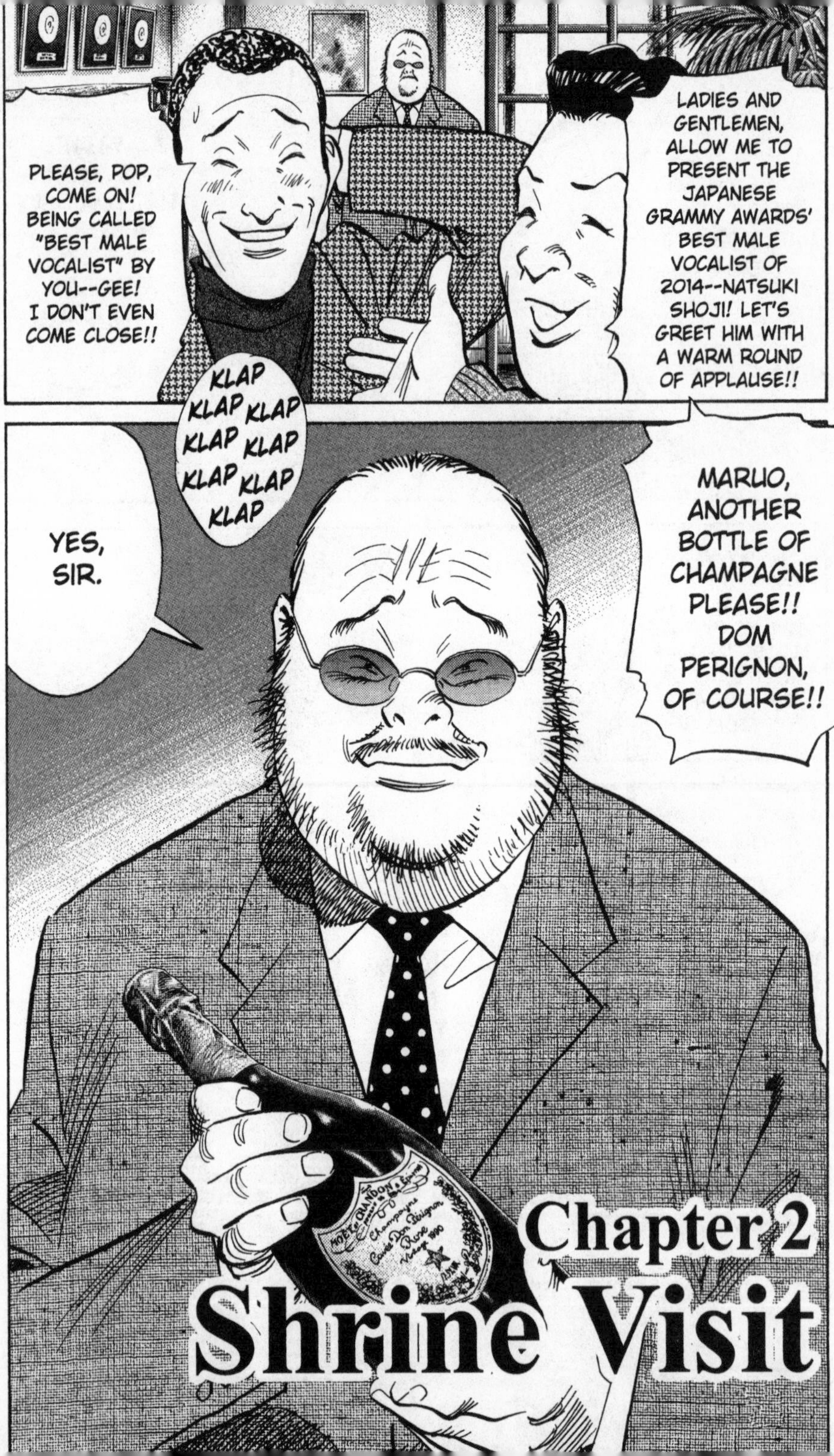
LADIES AND GENTLEMEN, ALLOW ME TO PRESENT THE JAPANESE GRAMMY AWARDS' BEST MALE VOCALIST OF 2014--NATSUKI SHOJI! LET'S GREET HIM WITH A WARM ROUND OF APPLAUSE!!
PLEASE, POP, COME ON! BEING CALLED "BEST MALE VOCALIST" BY YOU--GEE! I DON'T EVEN COME CLOSE!!
KLAP KLAP KLAP KLAP KLAP KLAP KLAP KLAP
MARUO, ANOTHER BOTTLE OF CHAMPAGNE PLEASE!! DOM PERIGNON, OF COURSE!!
YES, SIR.
Chapter 2
Shrine Visit

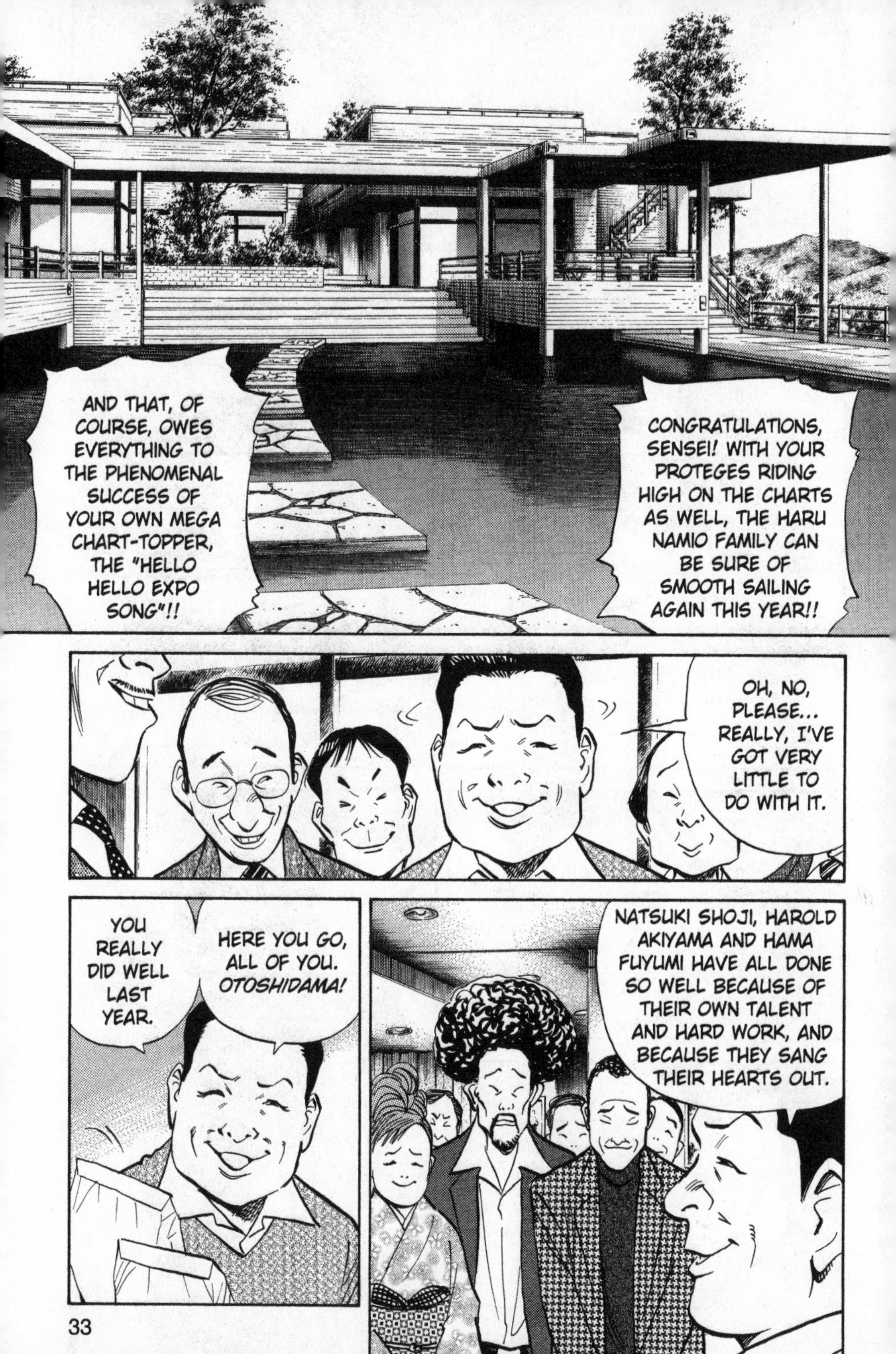
CONGRATULATIONS, SENSEI! WITH YOUR PROTEGES RIDING HIGH ON THE CHARTS AS WELL, THE HARU NAMIO FAMILY CAN BE SURE OF SMOOTH SAILING AGAIN THIS YEAR!!
AND THAT, OF COURSE, OWES EVERYTHING TO THE PHENOMENAL SUCCESS OF YOUR OWN MEGA CHART-TOPPER, THE "HELLO HELLO EXPO SONG"!!
OH, NO, PLEASE... REALLY, I'VE GOT VERY LITTLE TO DO WITH IT.
NATSUKI SHOJI, HAROLD AKIYAMA AND HAMA FUYUMI HAVE ALL DONE SO WELL BECAUSE OF THEIR OWN TALENT AND HARD WORK, AND BECAUSE THEY SANG THEIR HEARTS OUT.
HERE YOU GO, ALL OF YOU. *OTOSHIDAMA!*
YOU REALLY DID WELL LAST YEAR.

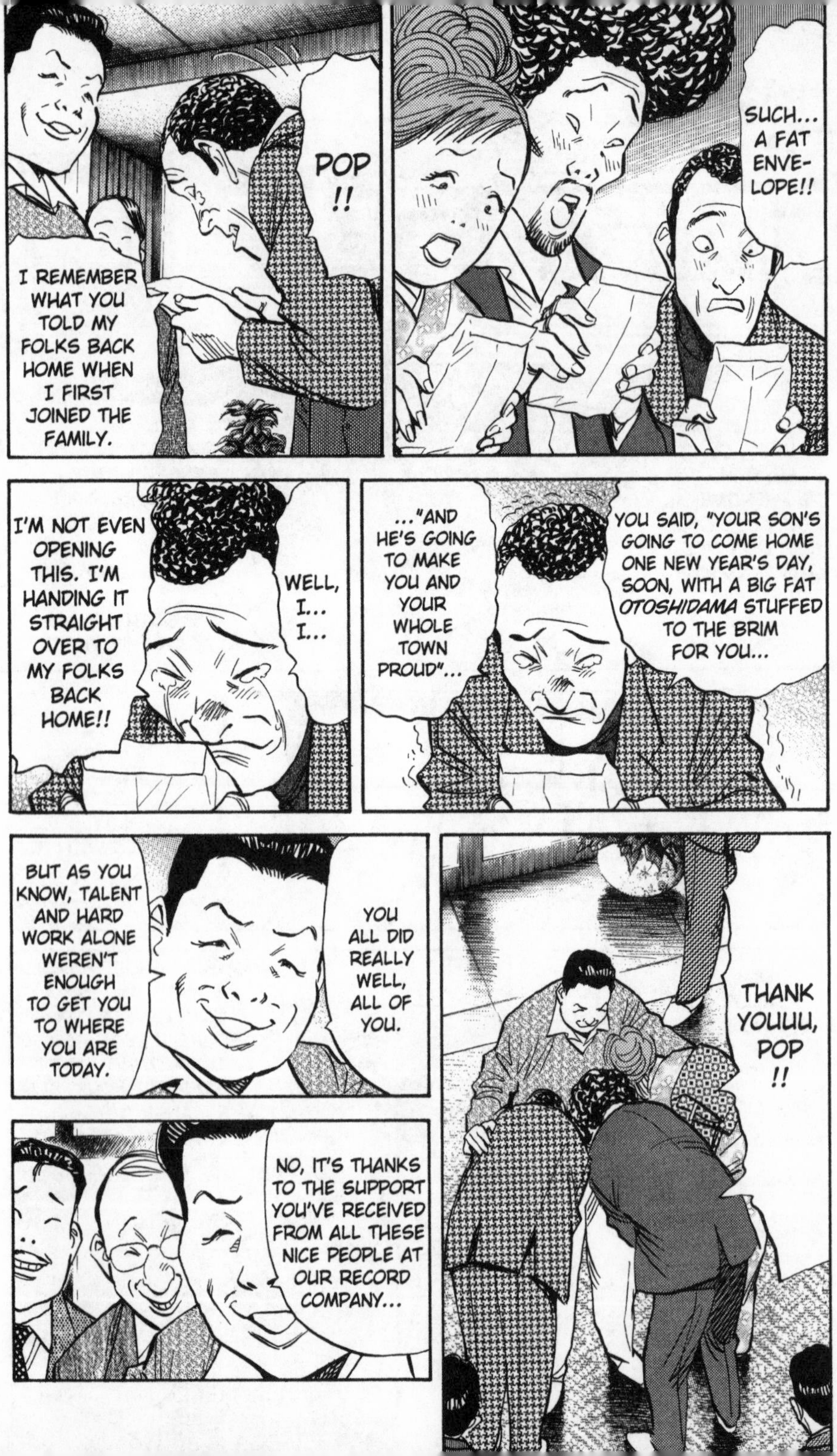
SUCH... A FAT ENVE-LOPE!!
POP !!
I REMEMBER WHAT YOU TOLD MY FOLKS BACK HOME WHEN I FIRST JOINED THE FAMILY.
YOU SAID, "YOUR SON'S GOING TO COME HOME ONE NEW YEAR'S DAY, SOON, WITH A BIG FAT *OTOSHIDAMA* STUFFED TO THE BRIM FOR YOU...
..."AND HE'S GOING TO MAKE YOU AND YOUR WHOLE TOWN PROUD"...
WELL, I... I...
I'M NOT EVEN OPENING THIS. I'M HANDING IT STRAIGHT OVER TO MY FOLKS BACK HOME!!
THANK YOUUU, POP !!
YOU ALL DID REALLY WELL, ALL OF YOU.
BUT AS YOU KNOW, TALENT AND HARD WORK ALONE WEREN'T ENOUGH TO GET YOU TO WHERE YOU ARE TODAY.
NO, IT'S THANKS TO THE SUPPORT YOU'VE RECEIVED FROM ALL THESE NICE PEOPLE AT OUR RECORD COMPANY...

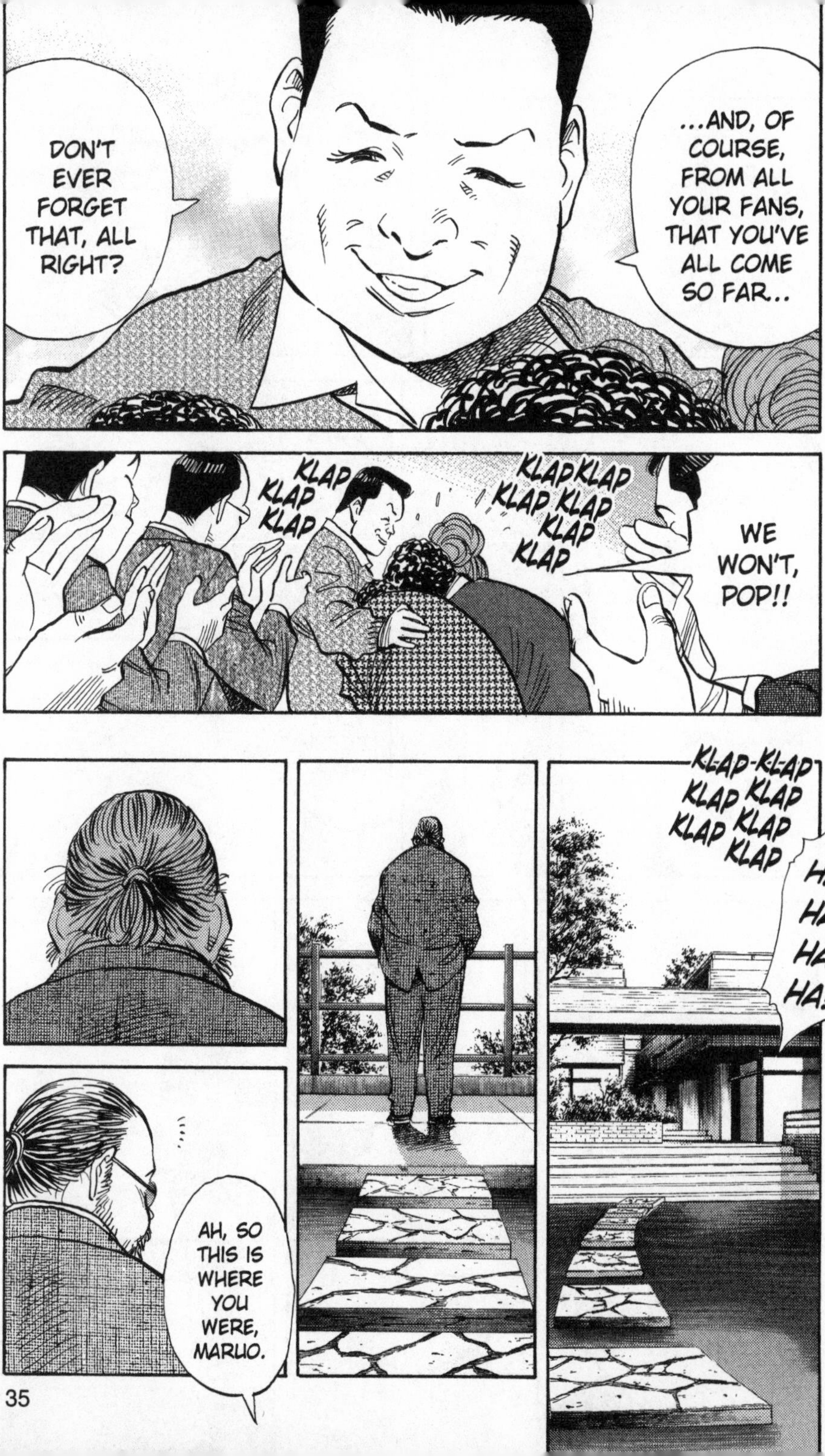
...AND, OF COURSE, FROM ALL YOUR FANS, THAT YOU'VE ALL COME SO FAR...
DON'T EVER FORGET THAT, ALL RIGHT?
WE WON'T, POP!!
KLAP KLAP KLAP KLAP KLAP KLAP
KLAP KLAP KLAP
KLAP-KLAP KLAP KLAP KLAP KLAP KLAP
HA HA HA HA!
...
AH, SO THIS IS WHERE YOU WERE, MARUO.

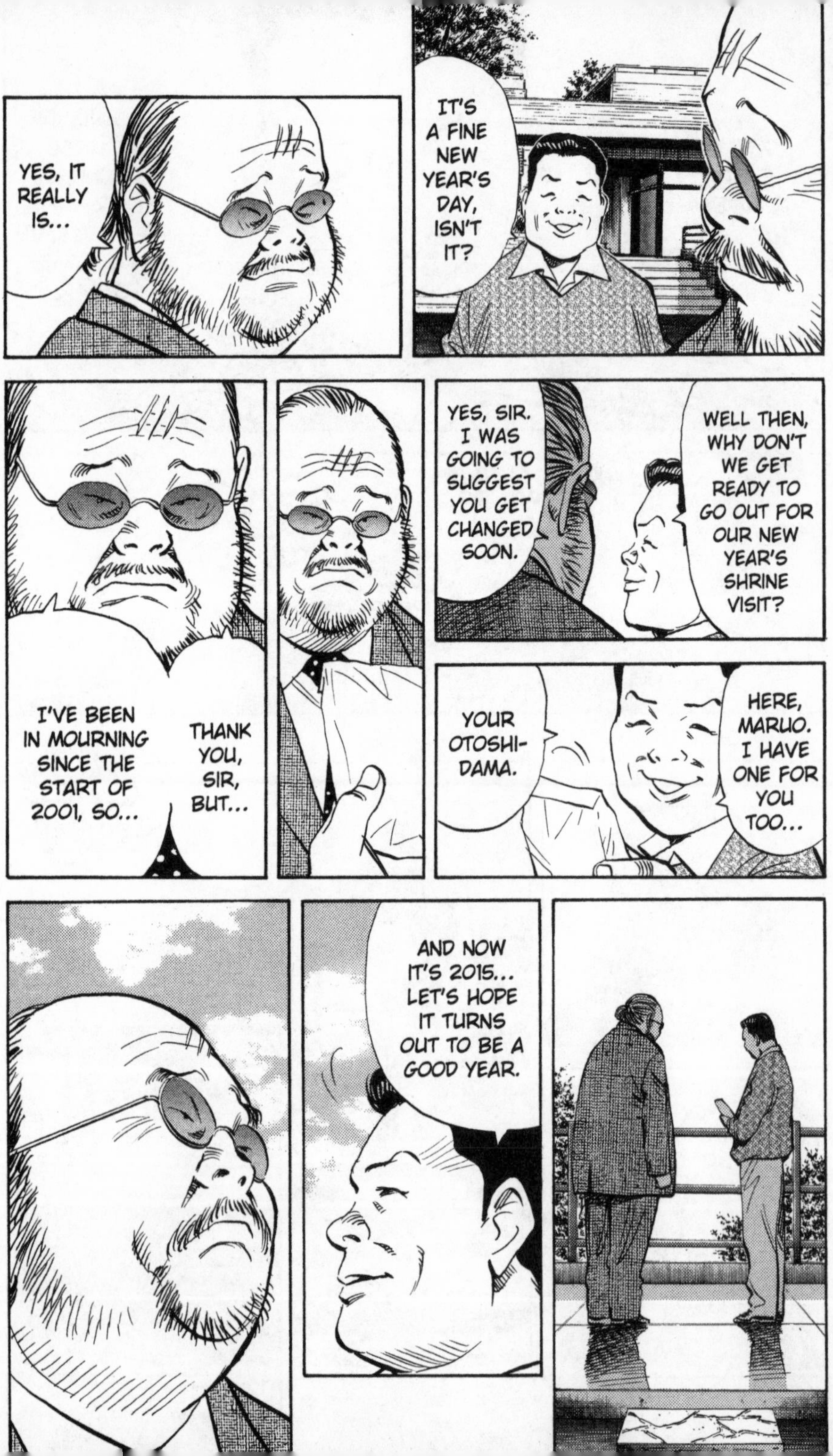
IT'S A FINE NEW YEAR'S DAY, ISN'T IT?
YES, IT REALLY IS...
WELL THEN, WHY DON'T WE GET READY TO GO OUT FOR OUR NEW YEAR'S SHRINE VISIT?
YES, SIR. I WAS GOING TO SUGGEST YOU GET CHANGED SOON.
HERE, MARUO. I HAVE ONE FOR YOU TOO...
YOUR OTOSHI-DAMA.
THANK YOU, SIR, BUT...
I'VE BEEN IN MOURNING SINCE THE START OF 2001, SO...
AND NOW IT'S 2015... LET'S HOPE IT TURNS OUT TO BE A GOOD YEAR.

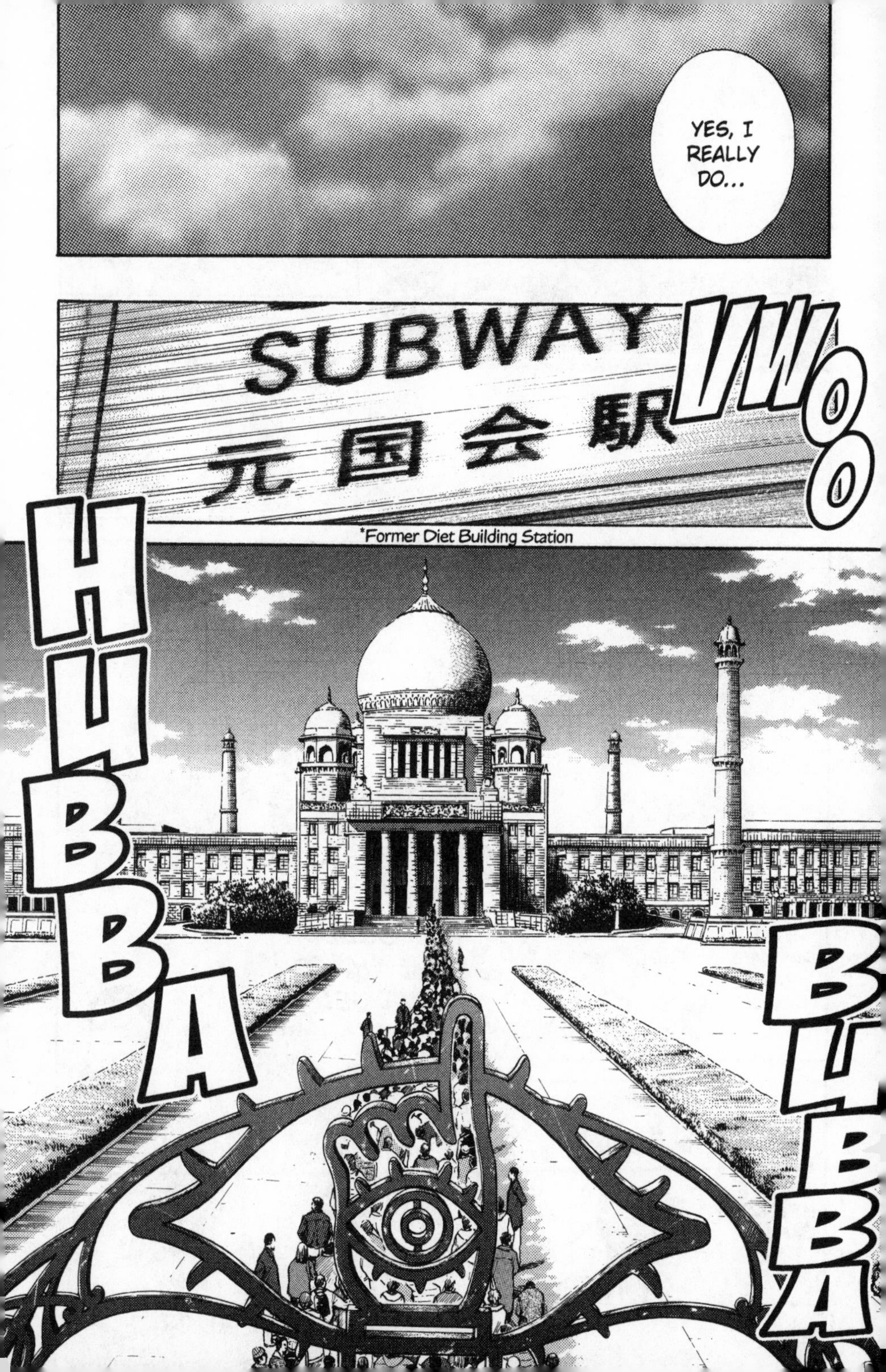
YES, I REALLY DO...
SUBWAY
元国会駅
VWOOO
*Former Diet Building Station
HUBBA
BUBBA

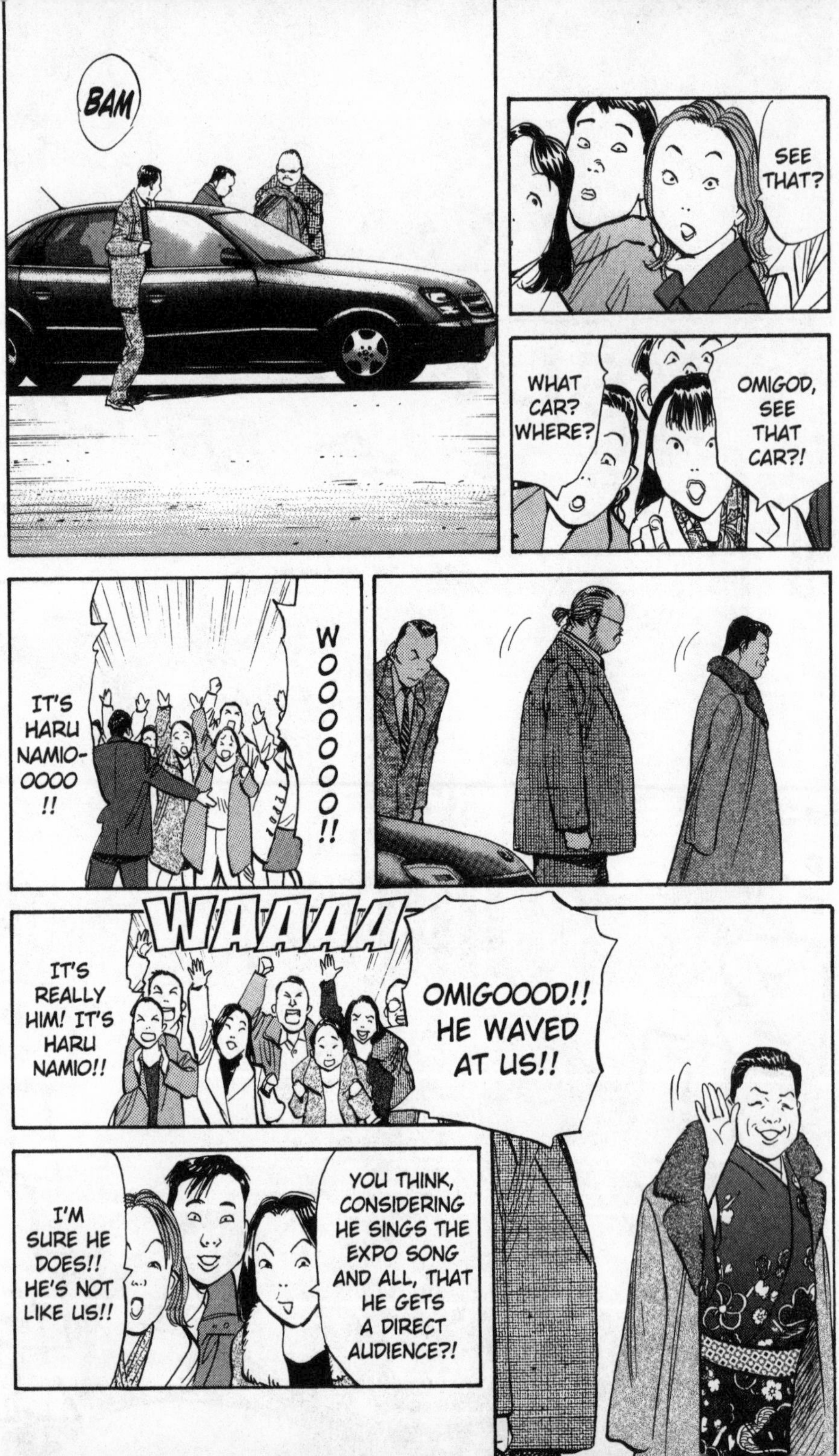
SEE THAT?
OMIGOD, SEE THAT CAR?!
WHAT CAR? WHERE?
BAM
WOOOOOOOO!!
IT'S HARU NAMIO-OOOO!!
OMIGOOOD!! HE WAVED AT US!!
WAAAA
IT'S REALLY HIM! IT'S HARU NAMIO!!
YOU THINK, CONSIDERING HE SINGS THE EXPO SONG AND ALL, THAT HE GETS A DIRECT AUDIENCE?!
I'M SURE HE DOES!! HE'S NOT LIKE US!!

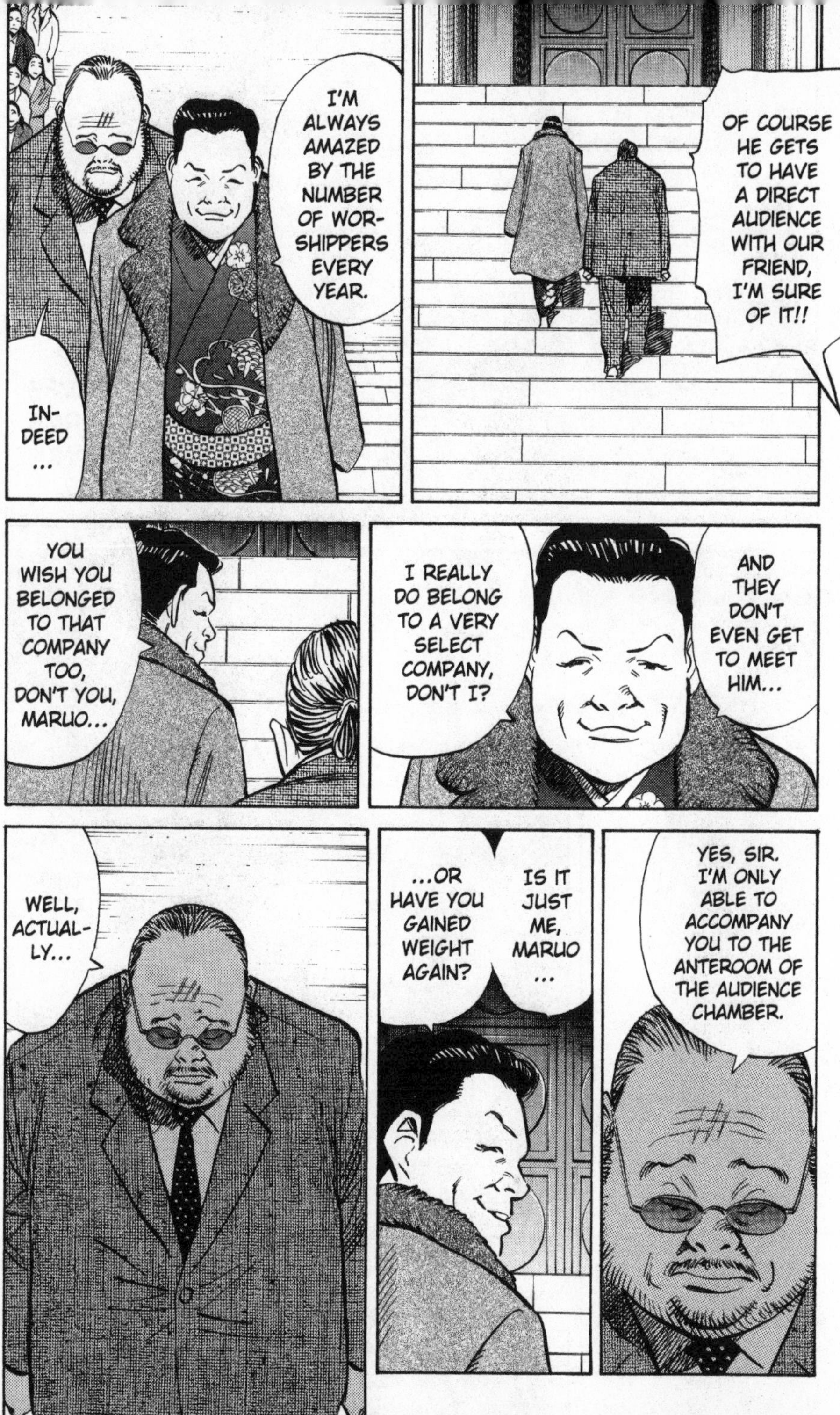
OF COURSE HE GETS TO HAVE A DIRECT AUDIENCE WITH OUR FRIEND, I'M SURE OF IT!!
I'M ALWAYS AMAZED BY THE NUMBER OF WORSHIPPERS EVERY YEAR.
INDEED...
AND THEY DON'T EVEN GET TO MEET HIM...
I REALLY DO BELONG TO A VERY SELECT COMPANY, DON'T I?
YOU WISH YOU BELONGED TO THAT COMPANY TOO, DON'T YOU, MARUO...
YES, SIR. I'M ONLY ABLE TO ACCOMPANY YOU TO THE ANTEROOM OF THE AUDIENCE CHAMBER.
IS IT JUST ME, MARUO...
...OR HAVE YOU GAINED WEIGHT AGAIN?
WELL, ACTUALLY...

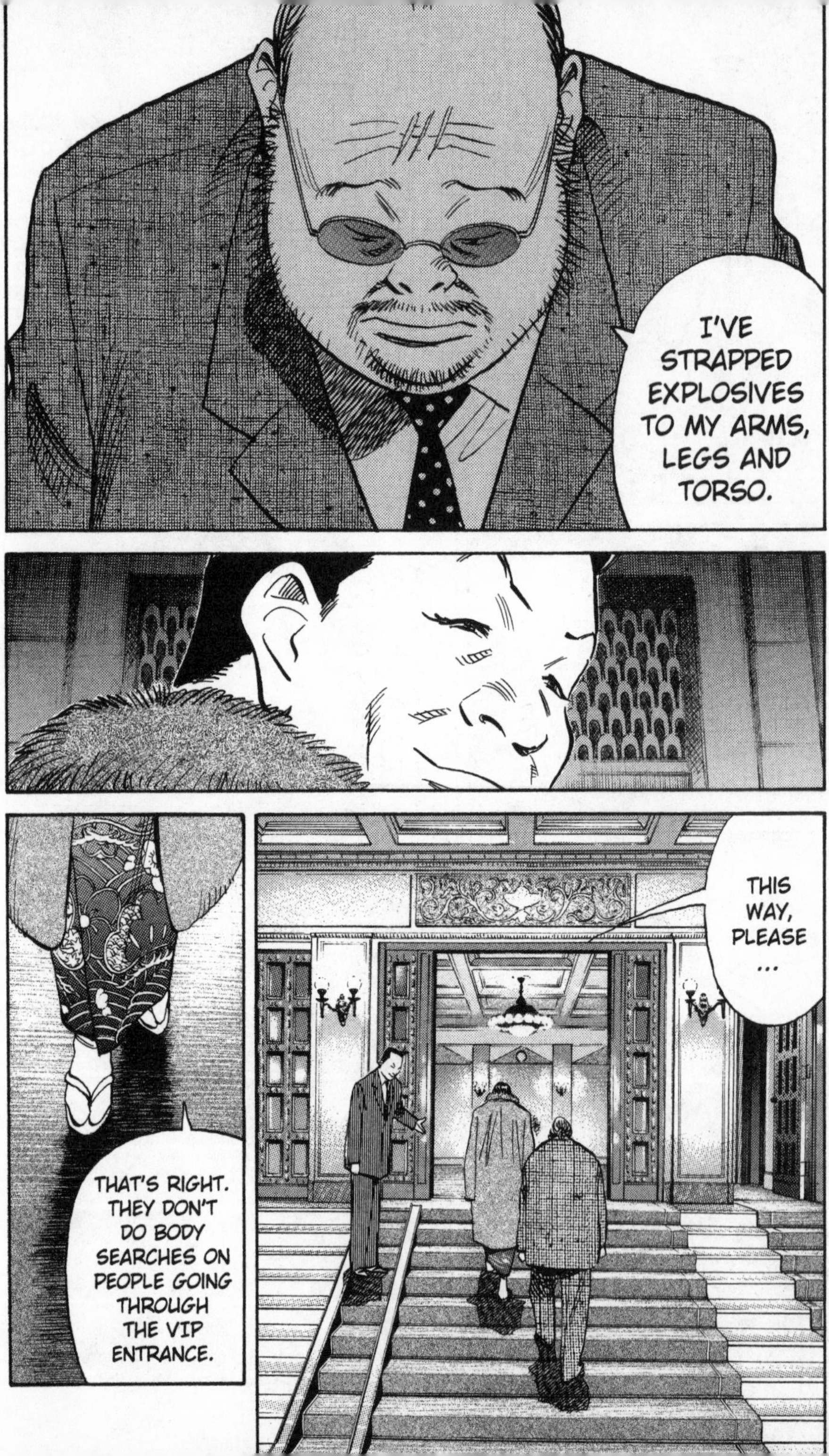
I'VE STRAPPED EXPLOSIVES TO MY ARMS, LEGS AND TORSO.
THIS WAY, PLEASE ...
THAT'S RIGHT. THEY DON'T DO BODY SEARCHES ON PEOPLE GOING THROUGH THE VIP ENTRANCE.

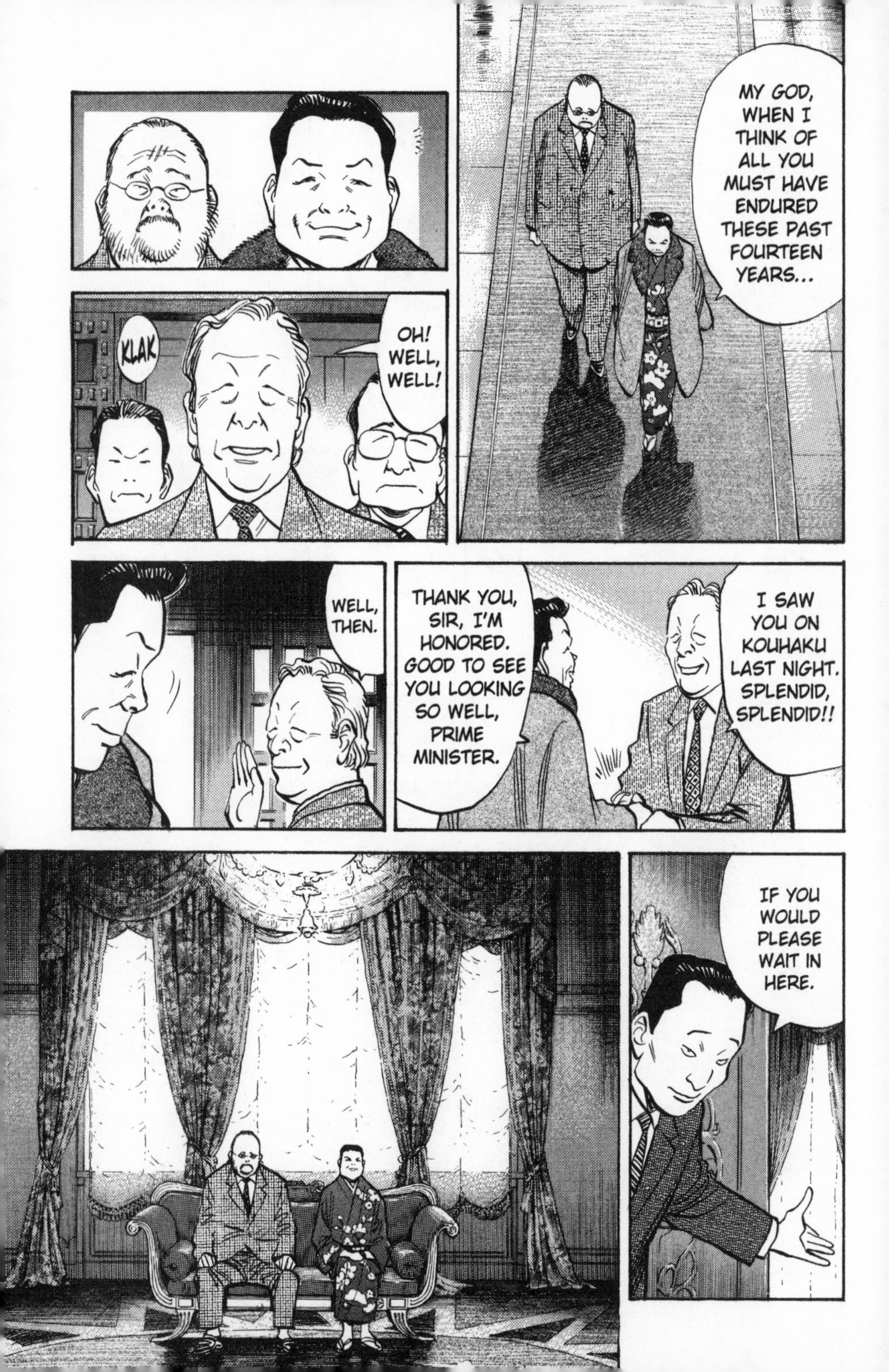
MY GOD, WHEN I THINK OF ALL YOU MUST HAVE ENDURED THESE PAST FOURTEEN YEARS...
OH! WELL, WELL!
KLAK
I SAW YOU ON KOUHAKU LAST NIGHT. SPLENDID, SPLENDID!!
THANK YOU, SIR, I'M HONORED. GOOD TO SEE YOU LOOKING SO WELL, PRIME MINISTER.
WELL, THEN.
IF YOU WOULD PLEASE WAIT IN HERE.

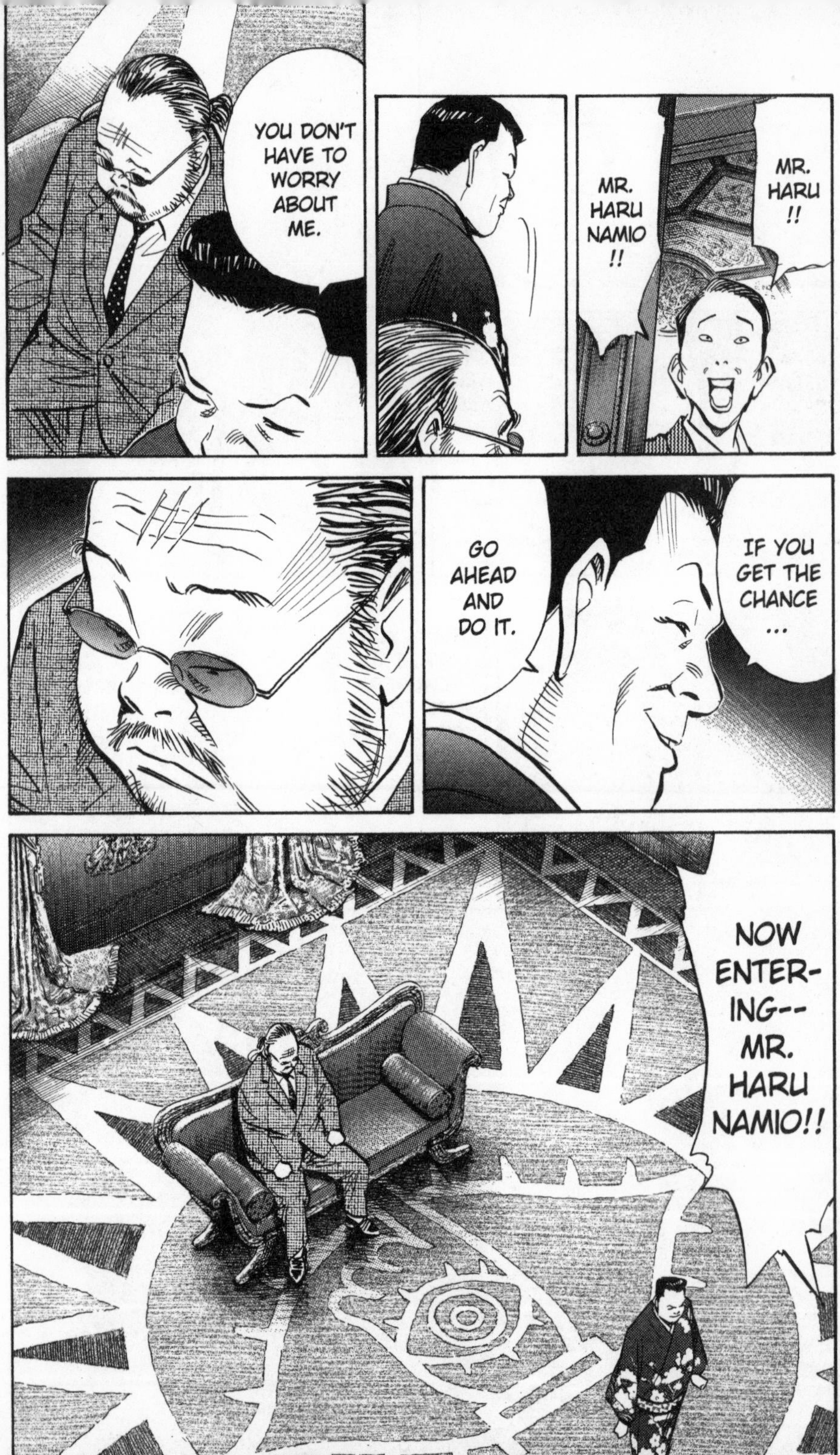
MR. HARU!!
MR. HARU NAMIO!!
YOU DON'T HAVE TO WORRY ABOUT ME.
IF YOU GET THE CHANCE...
GO AHEAD AND DO IT.
NOW ENTERING-- MR. HARU NAMIO!!

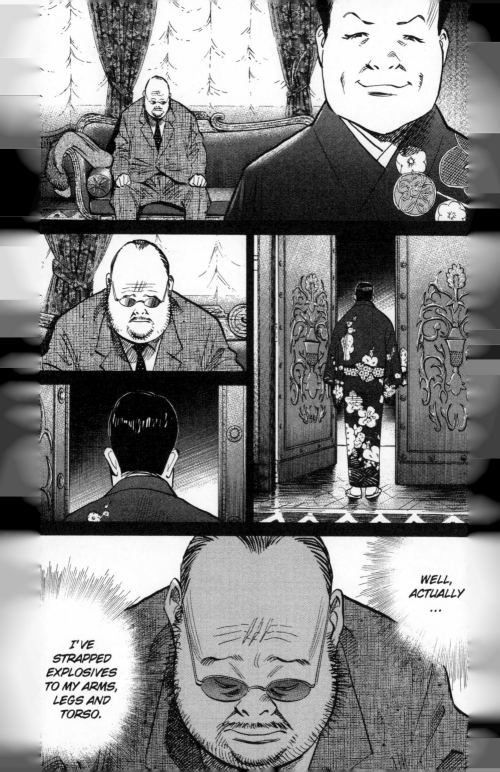

WELL, ACTUALLY ...

I'VE STRAPPED EXPLOSIVES TO MY ARMS, LEGS AND TORSO.

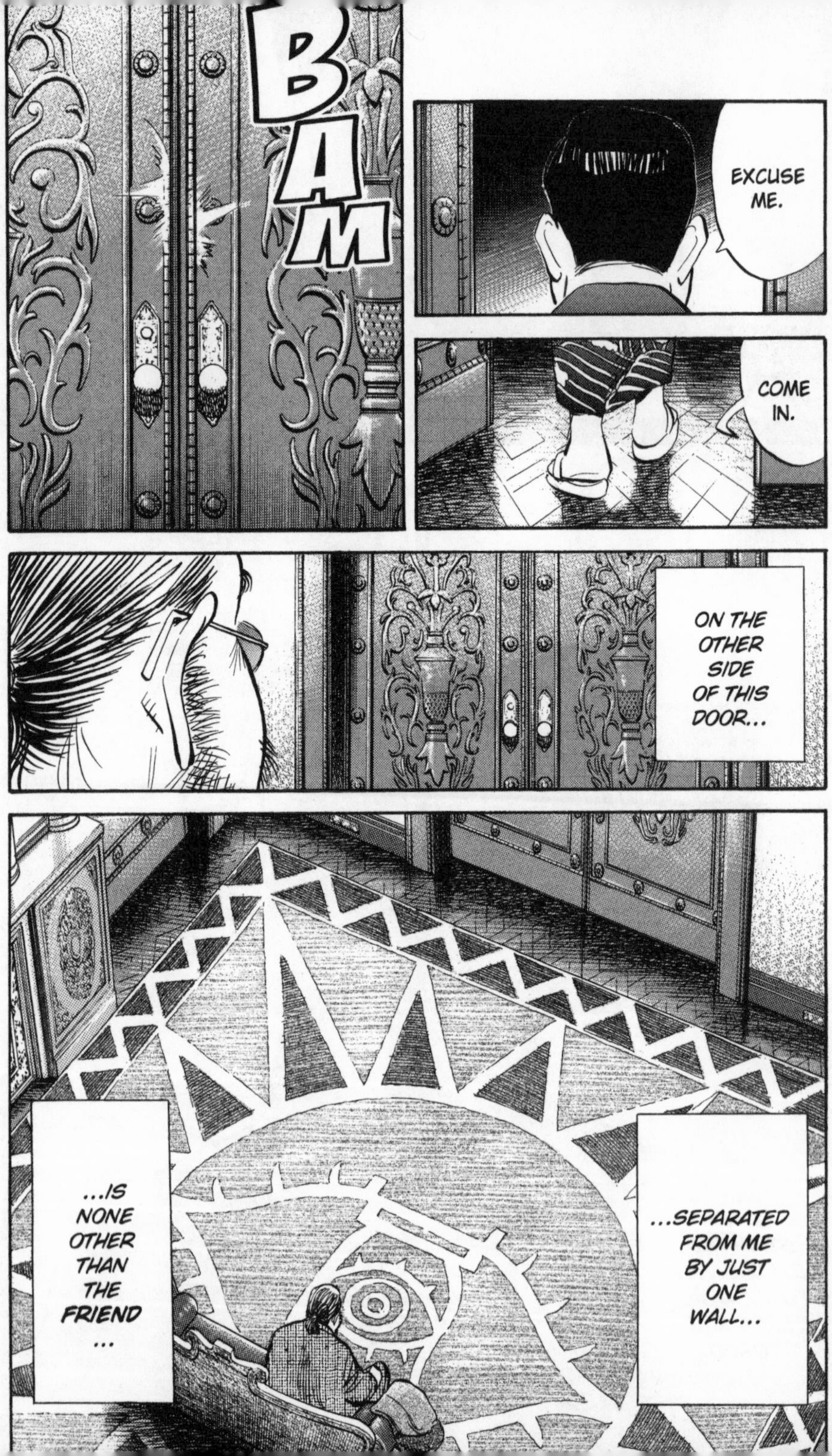
EXCUSE ME.
COME IN.
BAM
ON THE OTHER SIDE OF THIS DOOR...
...SEPARATED FROM ME BY JUST ONE WALL...
...IS NONE OTHER THAN THE FRIEND ...

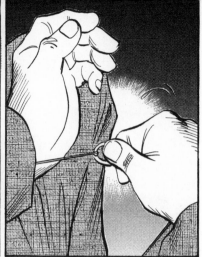

ALL I HAVE TO DO IS YANK ON THIS CORD...

KENJI...

...AND THAT SETTLES EVERYTHING...

Chapter 3
Suicide Bomber

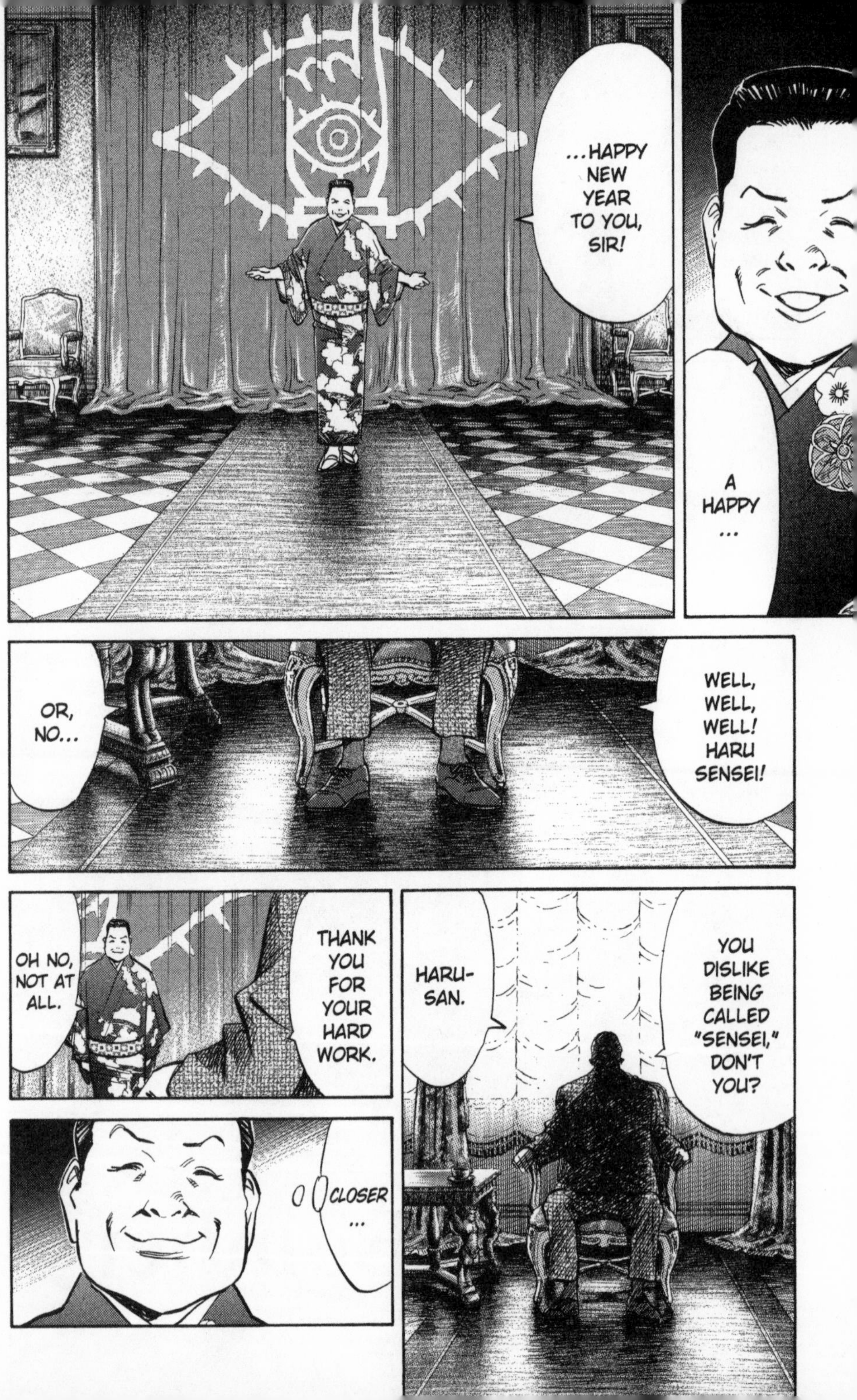
A HAPPY ...
...HAPPY NEW YEAR TO YOU, SIR!
WELL, WELL, WELL! HARU SENSEI!
OR, NO...
YOU DISLIKE BEING CALLED "SENSEI," DON'T YOU?
HARU-SAN.
THANK YOU FOR YOUR HARD WORK.
OH NO, NOT AT ALL.
CLOSER ...

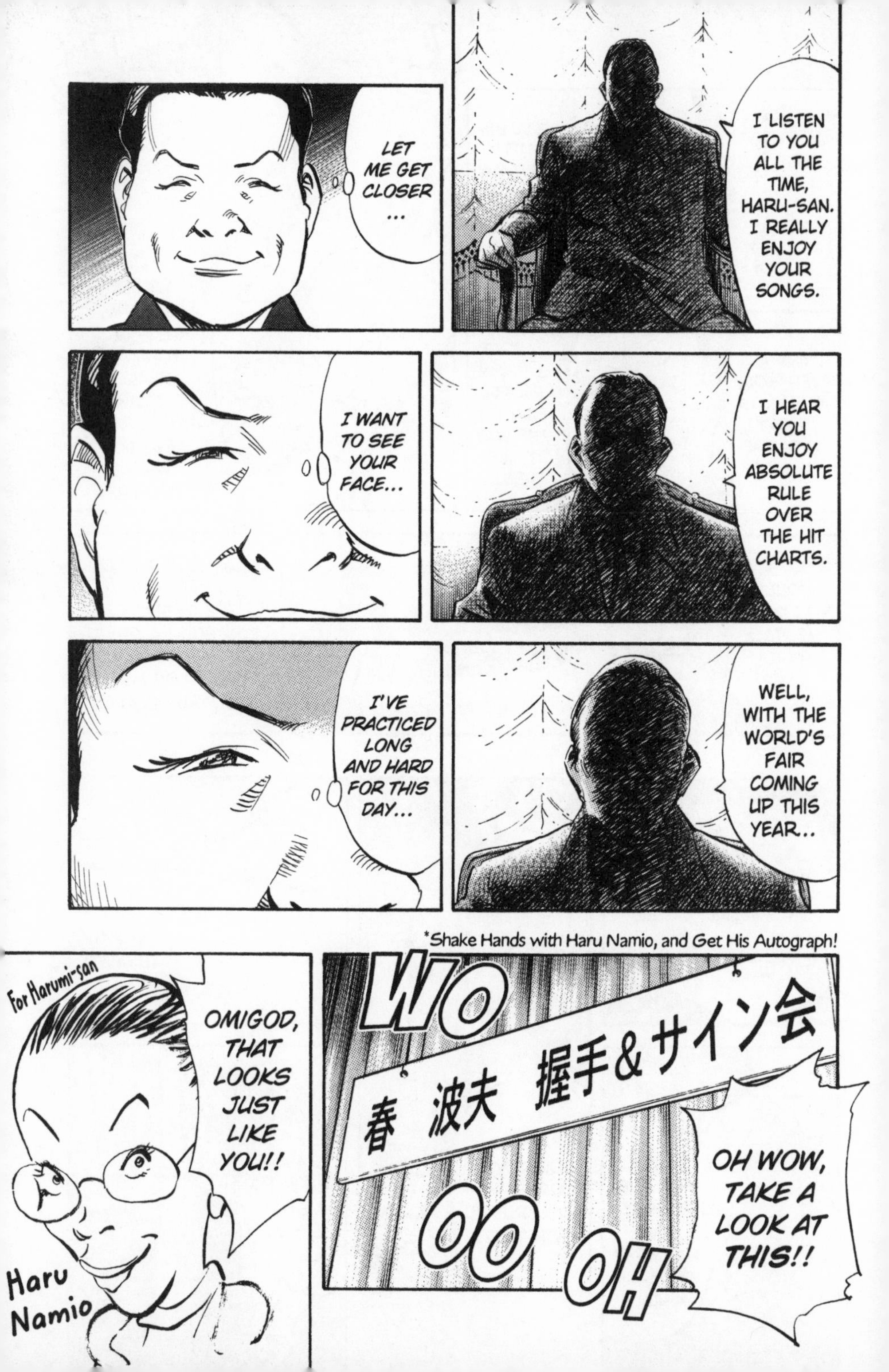
I LISTEN TO YOU ALL THE TIME, HARU-SAN. I REALLY ENJOY YOUR SONGS.
LET ME GET CLOSER ...
I HEAR YOU ENJOY ABSOLUTE RULE OVER THE HIT CHARTS.
I WANT TO SEE YOUR FACE...
WELL, WITH THE WORLD'S FAIR COMING UP THIS YEAR..
I'VE PRACTICED LONG AND HARD FOR THIS DAY...
WO
春波夫 握手&サイン会
OO
OH
OH WOW, TAKE A LOOK AT THIS!!
*Shake Hands with Haru Namio, and Get His Autograph!
OMIGOD, THAT LOOKS JUST LIKE YOU!!
For Harumi-san
Haru Namio

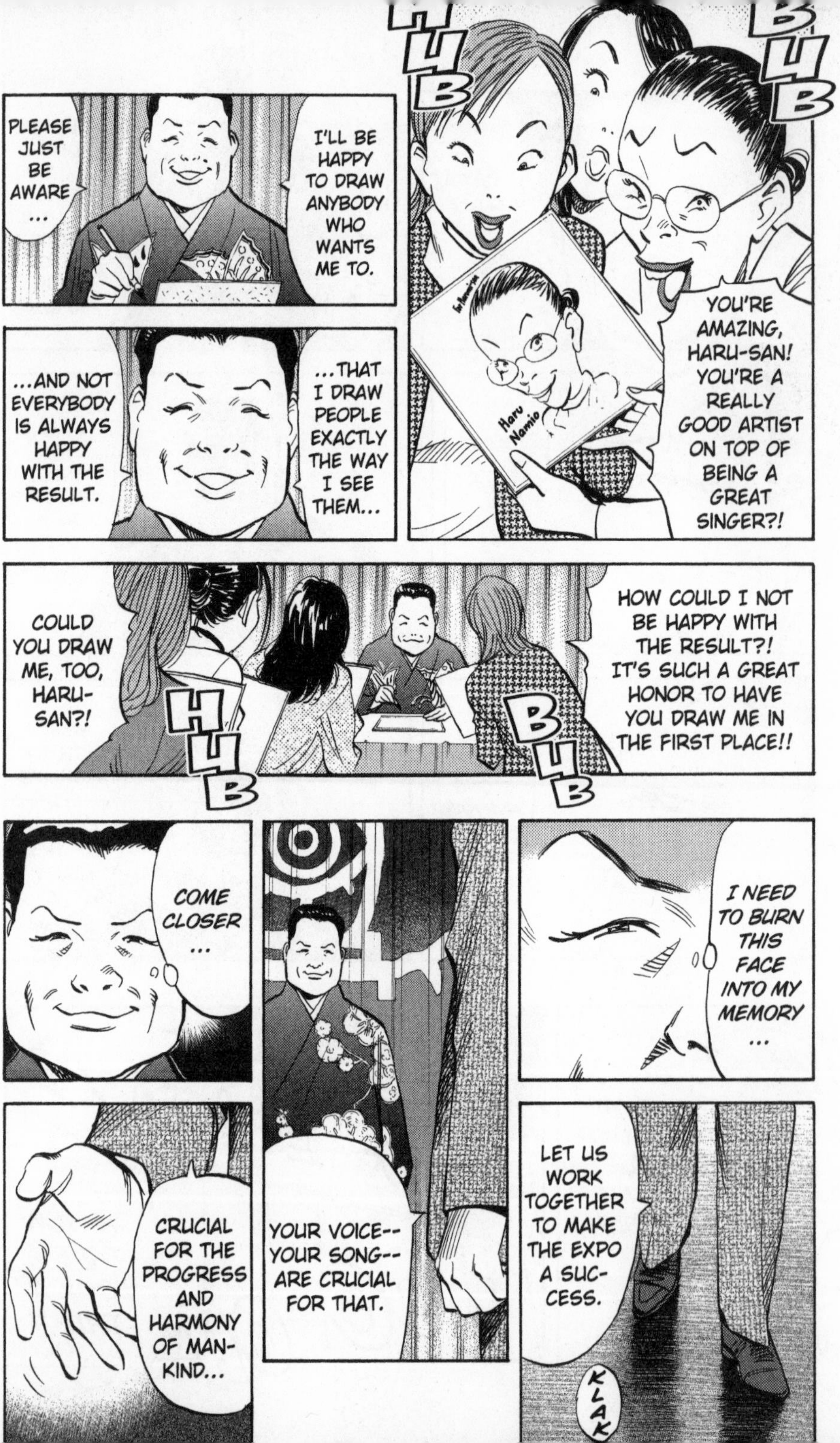
HUB BUB
YOU'RE AMAZING, HARU-SAN! YOU'RE A REALLY GOOD ARTIST ON TOP OF BEING A GREAT SINGER?!
Haru Namio
I'LL BE HAPPY TO DRAW ANYBODY WHO WANTS ME TO.
PLEASE JUST BE AWARE...
...THAT I DRAW PEOPLE EXACTLY THE WAY I SEE THEM...
...AND NOT EVERYBODY IS ALWAYS HAPPY WITH THE RESULT.
HOW COULD I NOT BE HAPPY WITH THE RESULT?! IT'S SUCH A GREAT HONOR TO HAVE YOU DRAW ME IN THE FIRST PLACE!!
HUB BUB
COULD YOU DRAW ME, TOO, HARU-SAN?!
I NEED TO BURN THIS FACE INTO MY MEMORY...
LET US WORK TOGETHER TO MAKE THE EXPO A SUC-CESS.
KLAK
YOUR VOICE-- YOUR SONG-- ARE CRUCIAL FOR THAT.
COME CLOSER...
CRUCIAL FOR THE PROGRESS AND HARMONY OF MAN-KIND...

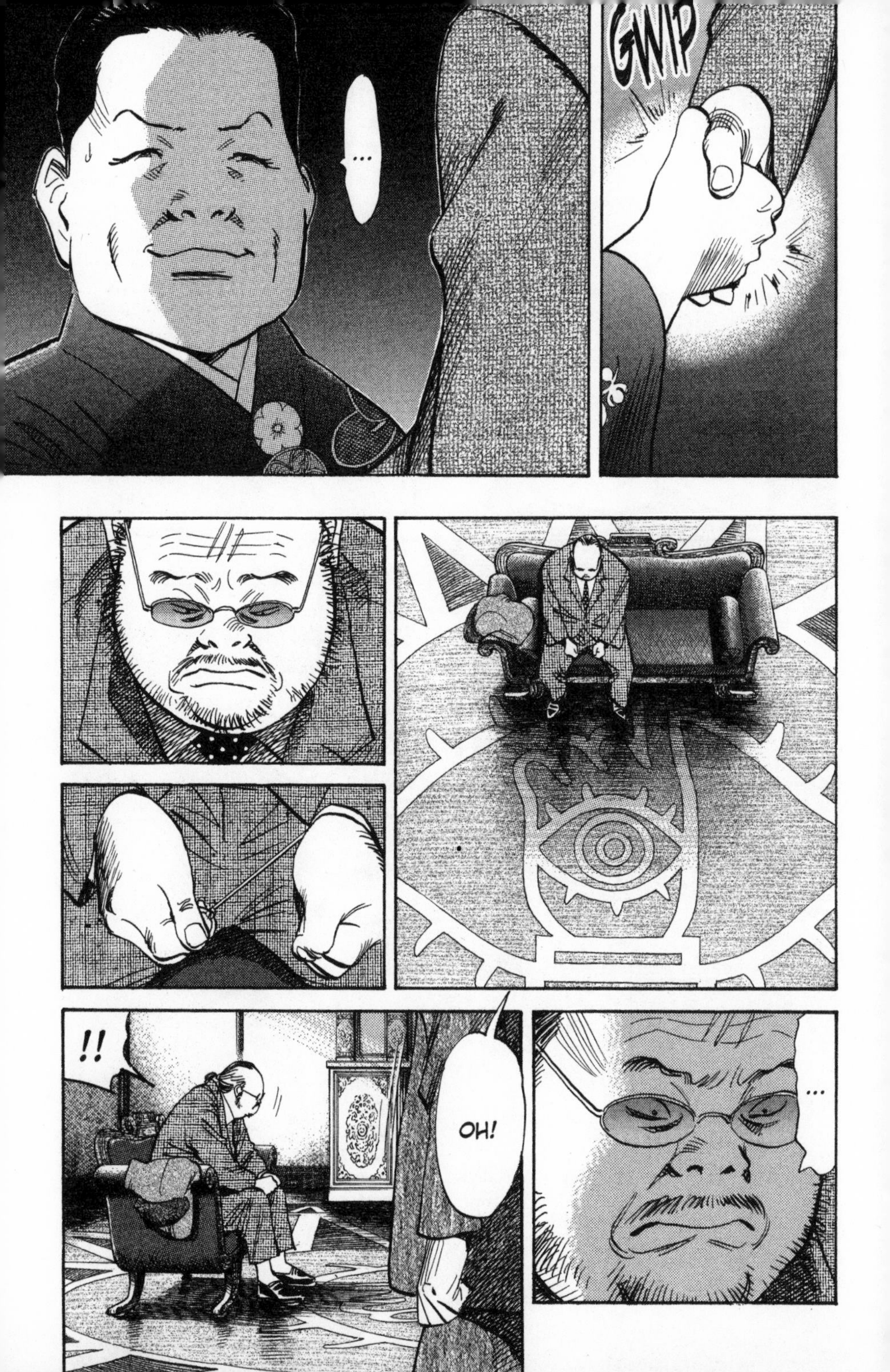
GWIP
...
...
OH!
!!

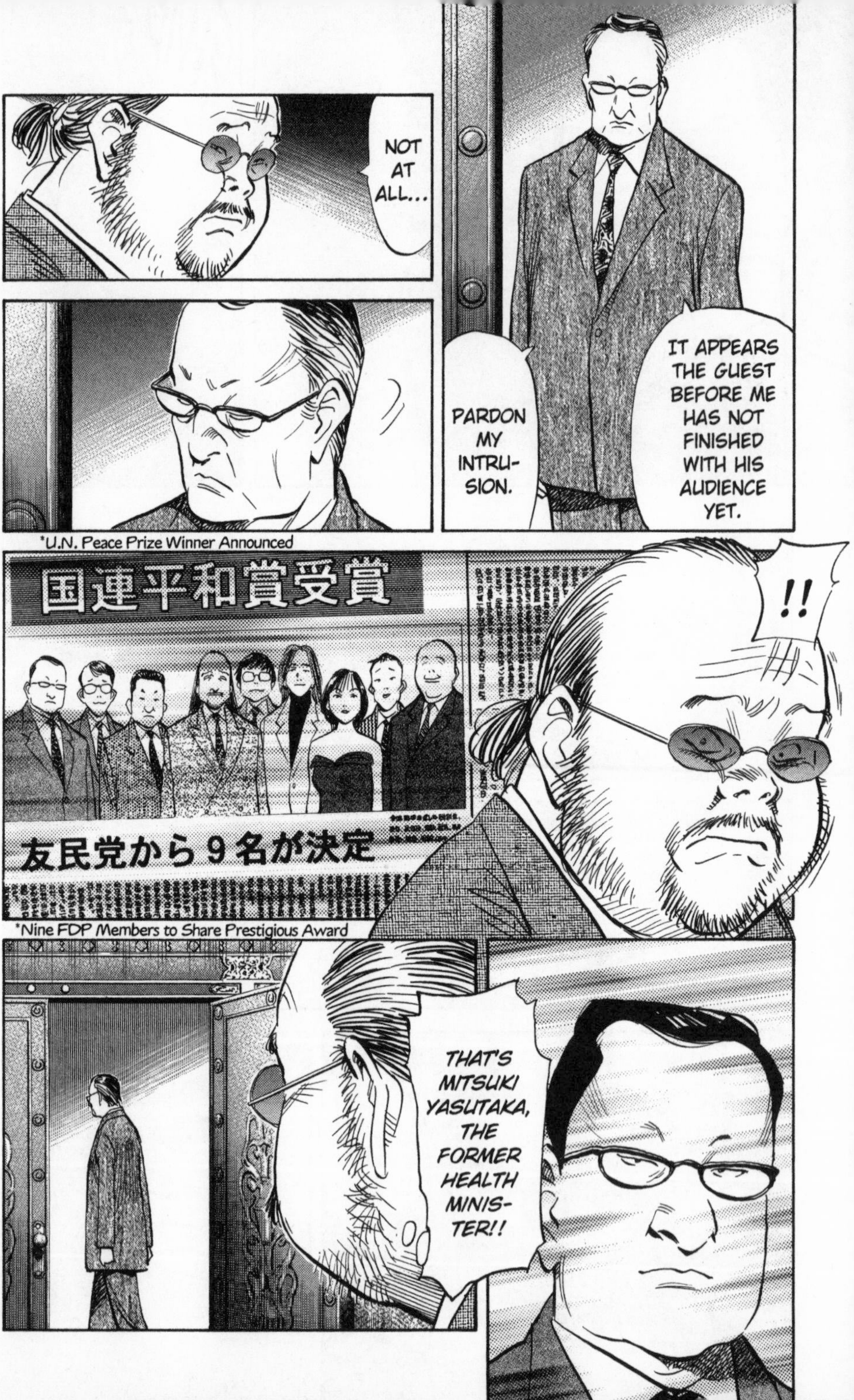
IT APPEARS THE GUEST BEFORE ME HAS NOT FINISHED WITH HIS AUDIENCE YET.
PARDON MY INTRUSION.
NOT AT ALL...
!!
*U.N. Peace Prize Winner Announced
国連平和賞受賞
友民党から９名が決定
*Nine FDP Members to Share Prestigious Award
THAT'S MITSUKI YASUTAKA, THE FORMER HEALTH MINISTER!!

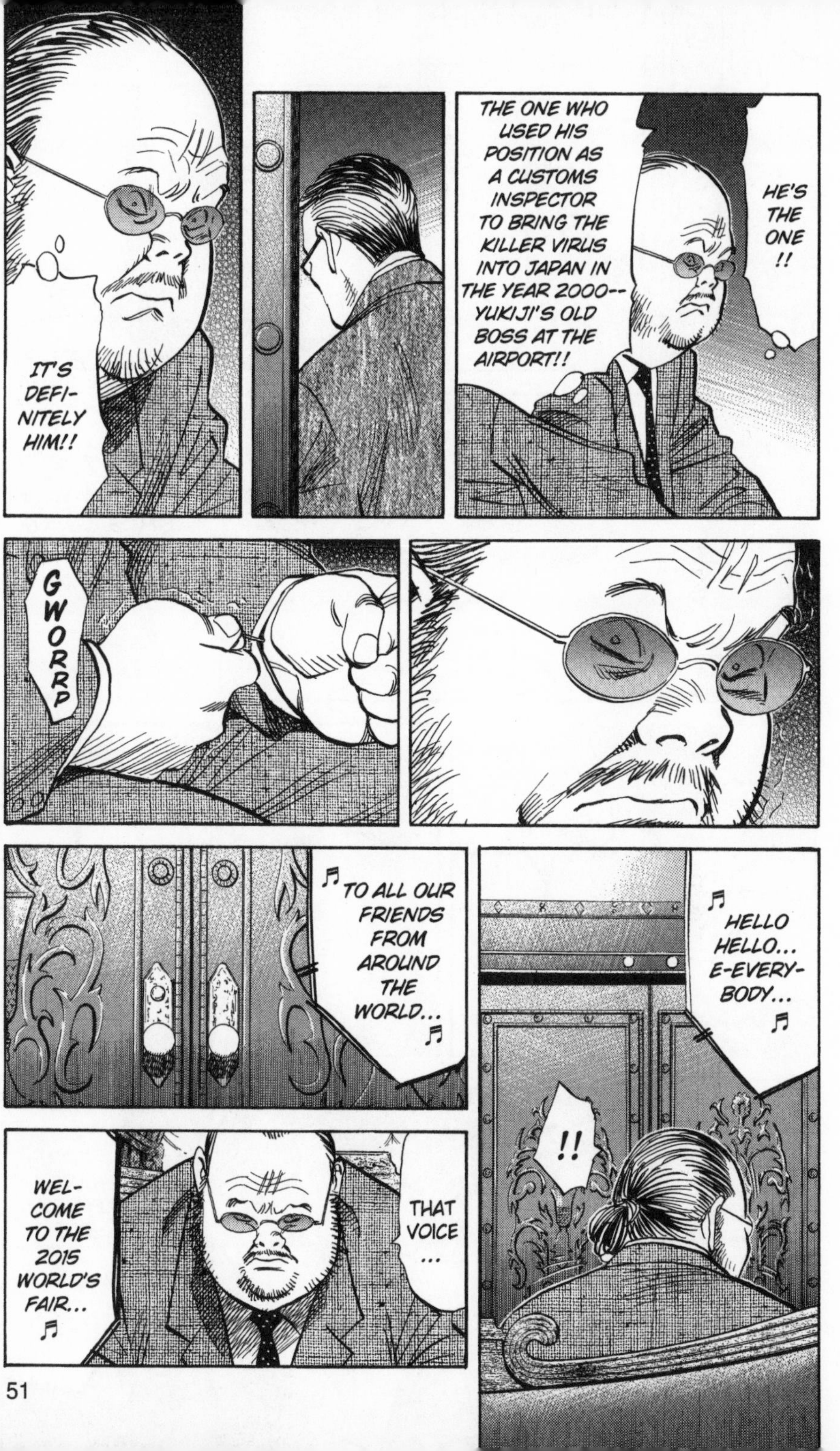
HE'S THE ONE!!
THE ONE WHO USED HIS POSITION AS A CUSTOMS INSPECTOR TO BRING THE KILLER VIRUS INTO JAPAN IN THE YEAR 2000-- YUKIJI'S OLD BOSS AT THE AIRPORT!!
IT'S DEFI-NITELY HIM!!
GWORRP
♬ HELLO HELLO... E-EVERY-BODY... ♬
!!
♬ TO ALL OUR FRIENDS FROM AROUND THE WORLD... ♬
THAT VOICE ...
WEL-COME TO THE 2015 WORLD'S FAIR... ♬

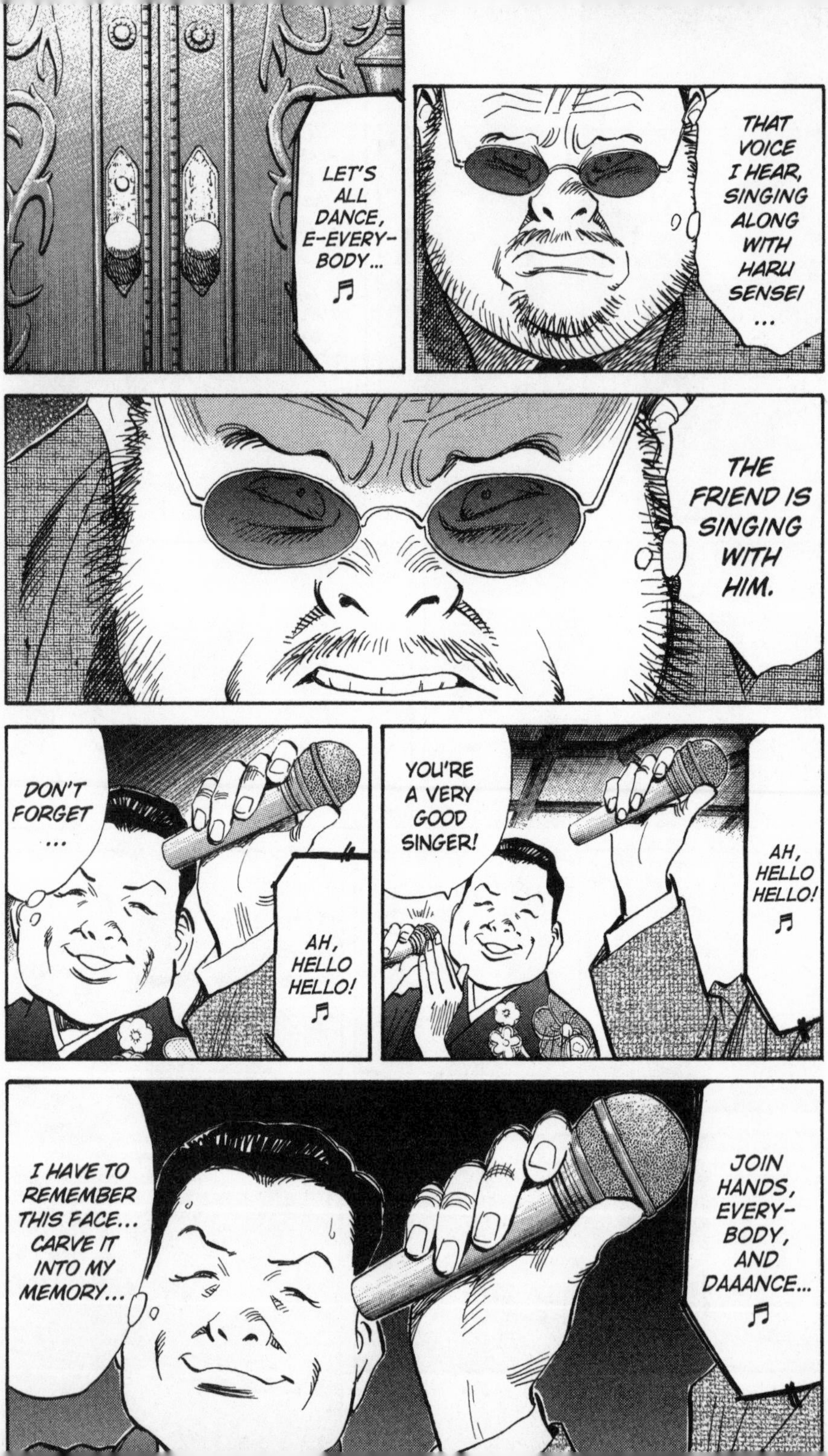
THAT VOICE I HEAR, SINGING ALONG WITH HARU SENSEI ...
LET'S ALL DANCE, E-EVERY-BODY... ♬
THE FRIEND IS SINGING WITH HIM.
AH, HELLO HELLO! ♬
YOU'RE A VERY GOOD SINGER!
AH, HELLO HELLO! ♬
DON'T FORGET ...
JOIN HANDS, EVERY-BODY, AND DAAANCE... ♬
I HAVE TO REMEMBER THIS FACE... CARVE IT INTO MY MEMORY...

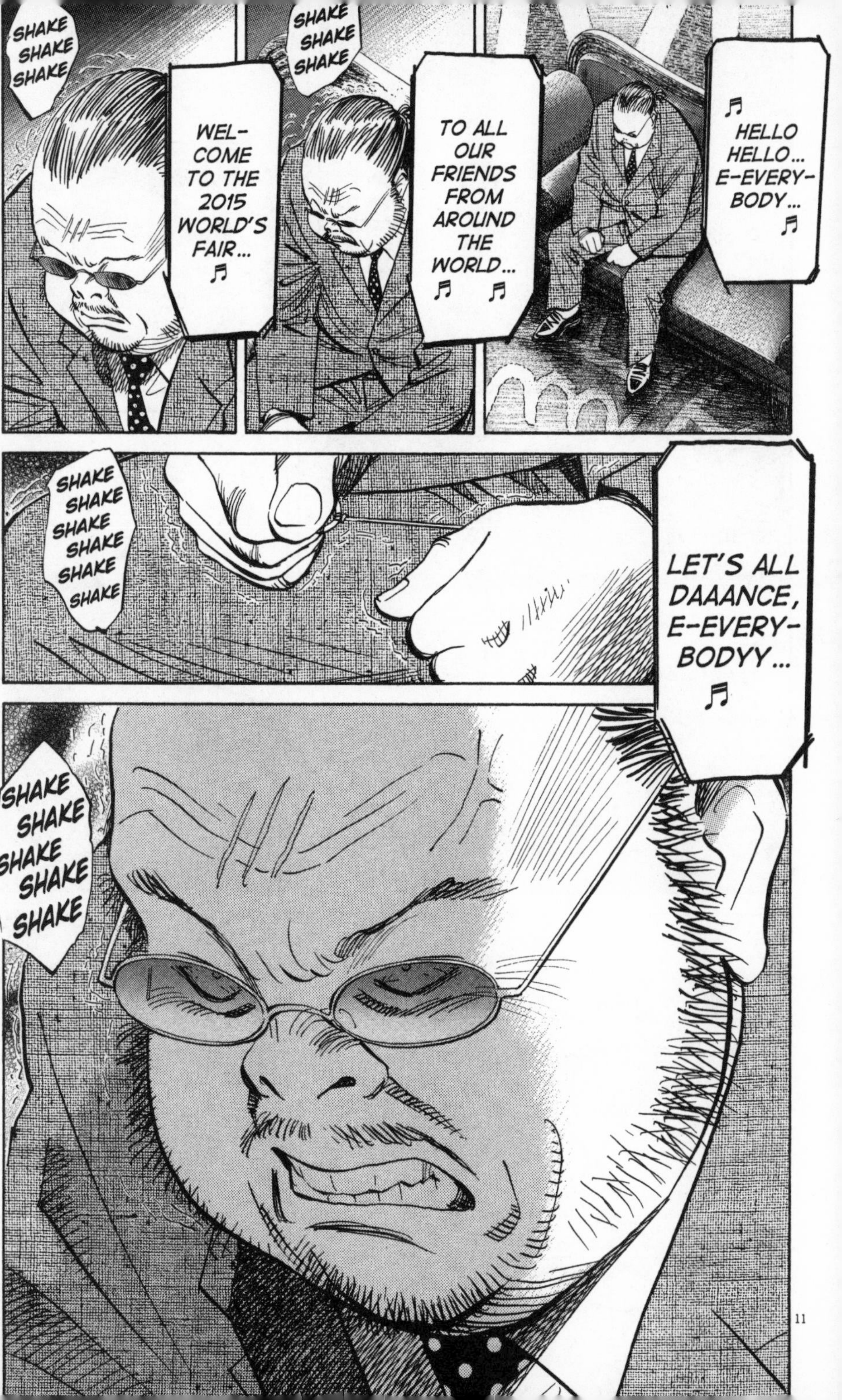
♬ HELLO HELLO... E-EVERY-BODY... ♬
SHAKE SHAKE SHAKE
TO ALL OUR FRIENDS FROM AROUND THE WORLD... ♬ ♬
WEL-COME TO THE 2015 WORLD'S FAIR... ♬
SHAKE SHAKE SHAKE
LET'S ALL DAAANCE, E-EVERY-BODYY... ♬
SHAKE SHAKE SHAKE SHAKE SHAKE SHAKE
SHAKE SHAKE SHAKE SHAKE SHAKE

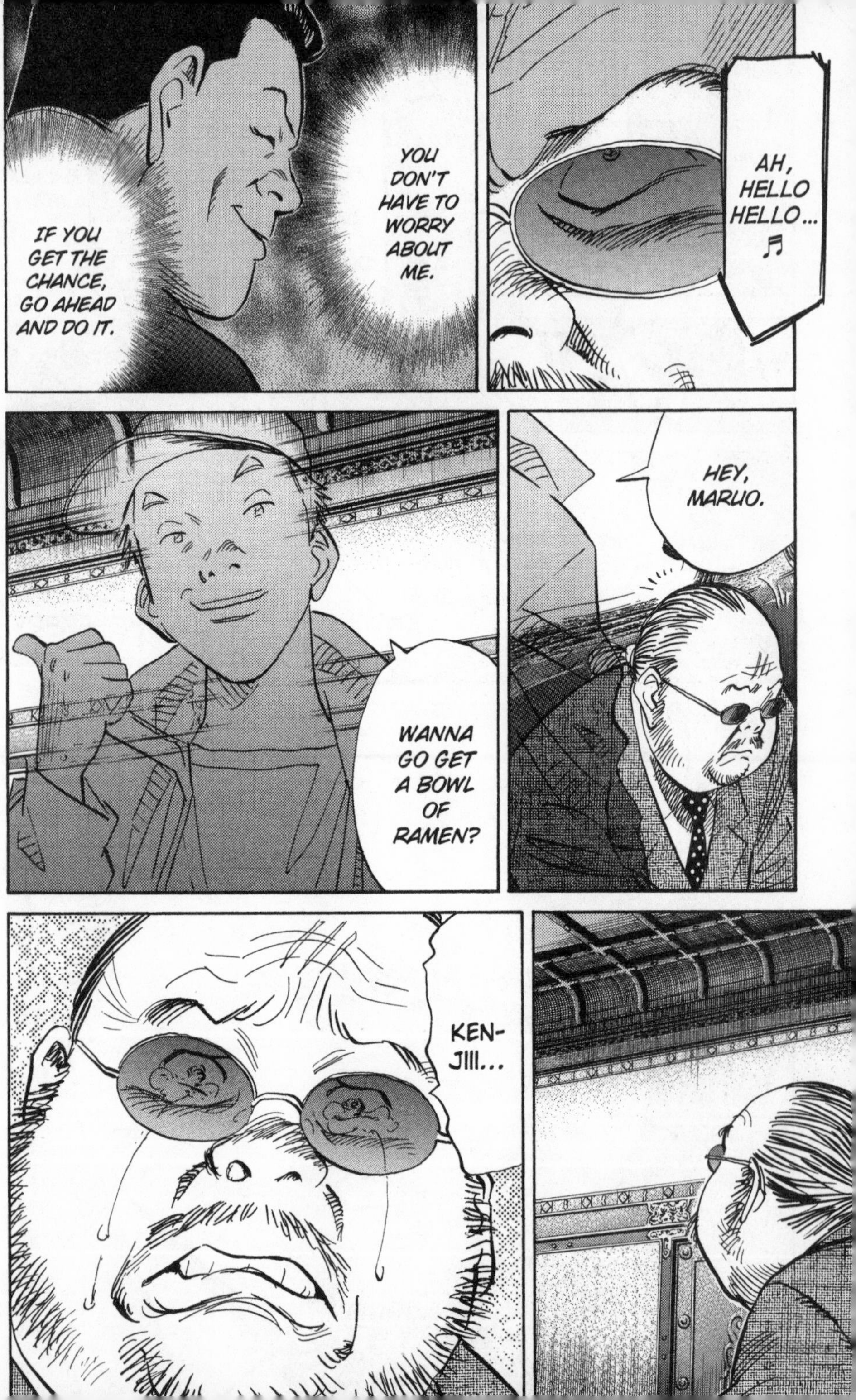
AH, HELLO HELLO... ♪
YOU DON'T HAVE TO WORRY ABOUT ME.
IF YOU GET THE CHANCE, GO AHEAD AND DO IT.
HEY, MARUO.
WANNA GO GET A BOWL OF RAMEN?
KEN-JIII...

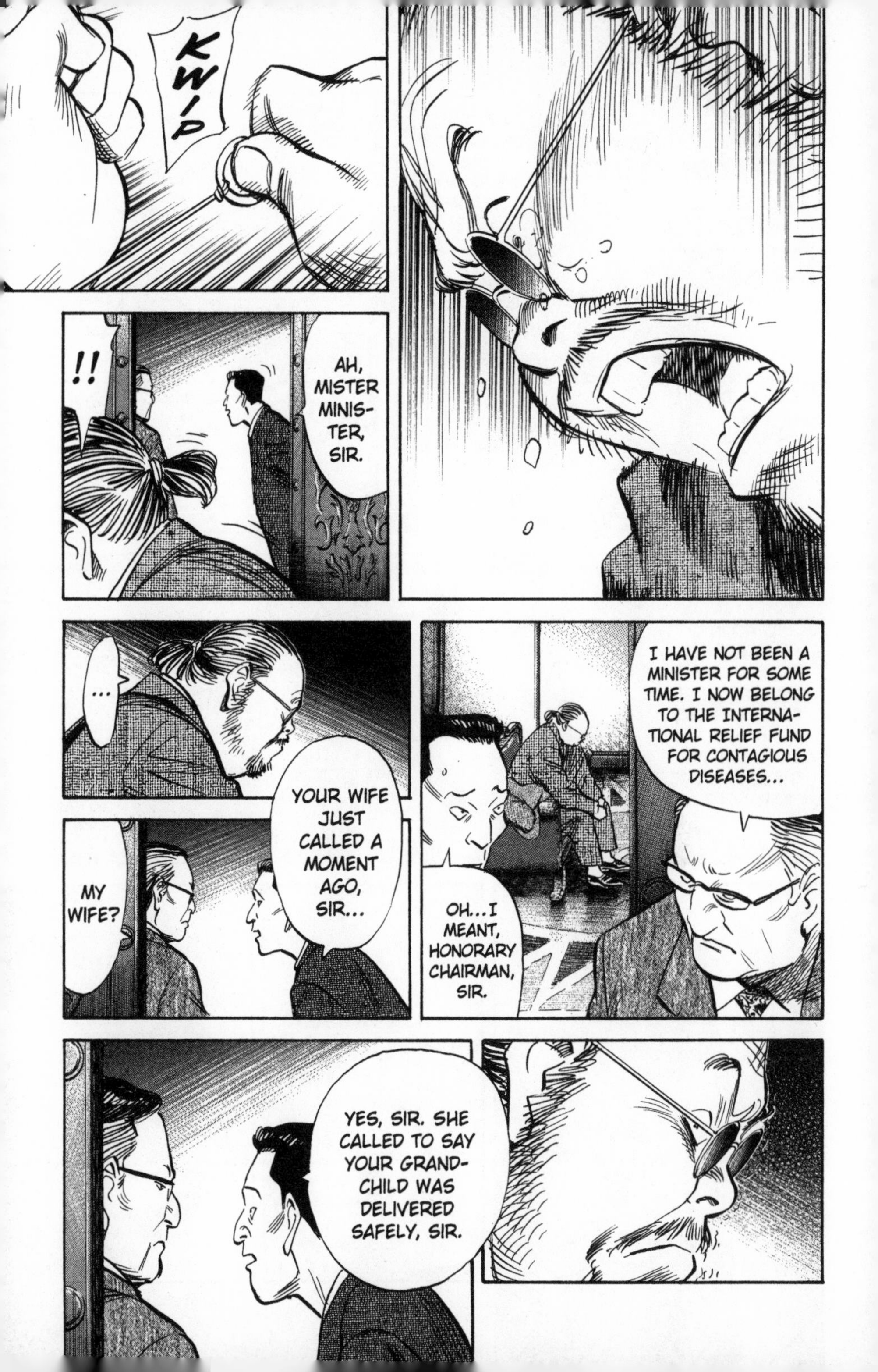
KWIP
AH, MISTER MINISTER, SIR.
!!
I HAVE NOT BEEN A MINISTER FOR SOME TIME. I NOW BELONG TO THE INTERNATIONAL RELIEF FUND FOR CONTAGIOUS DISEASES...
OH...I MEANT, HONORARY CHAIRMAN, SIR.
...
YOUR WIFE JUST CALLED A MOMENT AGO, SIR...
MY WIFE?
YES, SIR. SHE CALLED TO SAY YOUR GRANDCHILD WAS DELIVERED SAFELY, SIR.

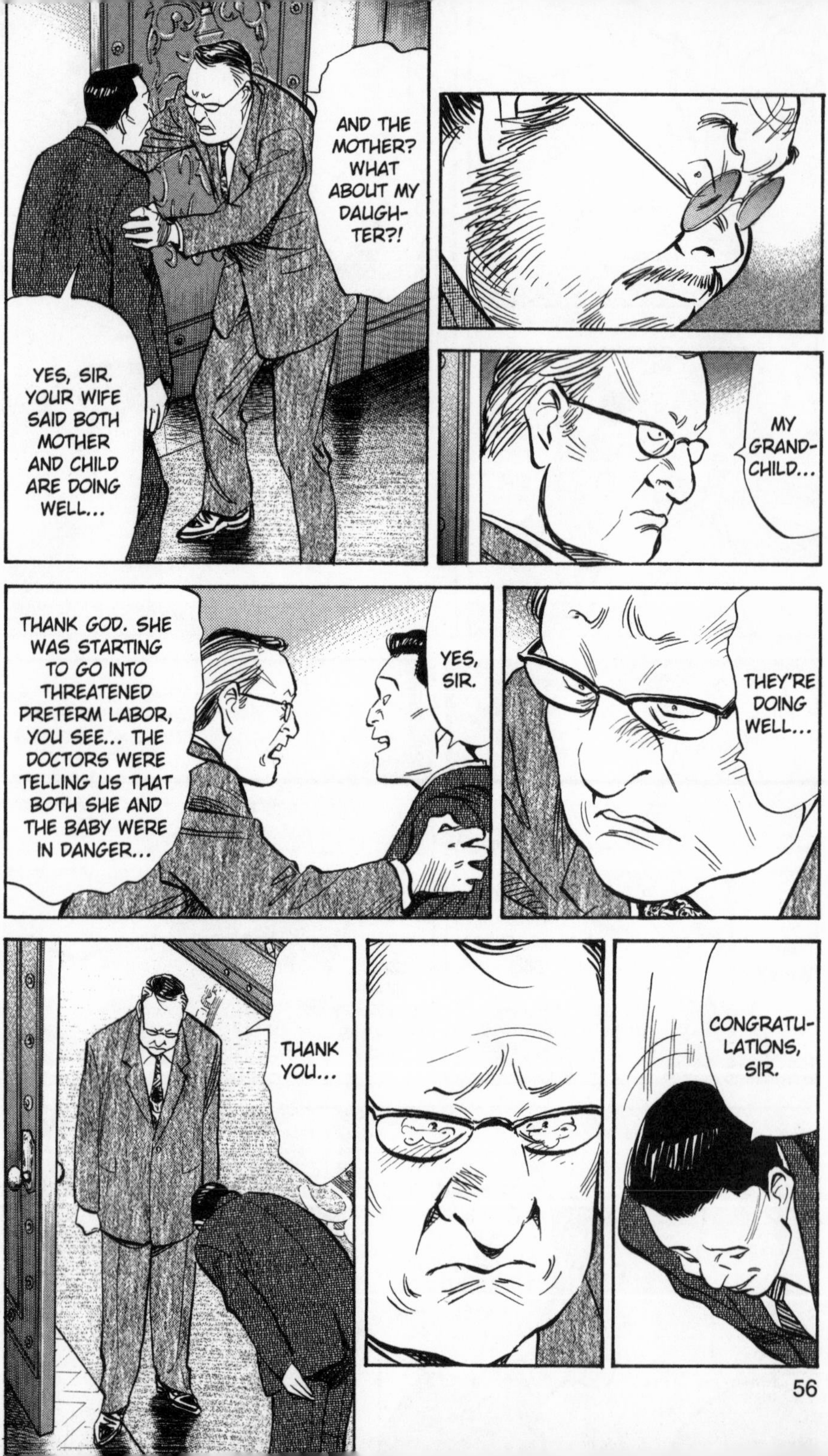
MY GRAND-CHILD...
AND THE MOTHER? WHAT ABOUT MY DAUGH-TER?!
YES, SIR. YOUR WIFE SAID BOTH MOTHER AND CHILD ARE DOING WELL...
THEY'RE DOING WELL...
THANK GOD. SHE WAS STARTING TO GO INTO THREATENED PRETERM LABOR, YOU SEE... THE DOCTORS WERE TELLING US THAT BOTH SHE AND THE BABY WERE IN DANGER...
YES, SIR.
CONGRATU-LATIONS, SIR.
THANK YOU...

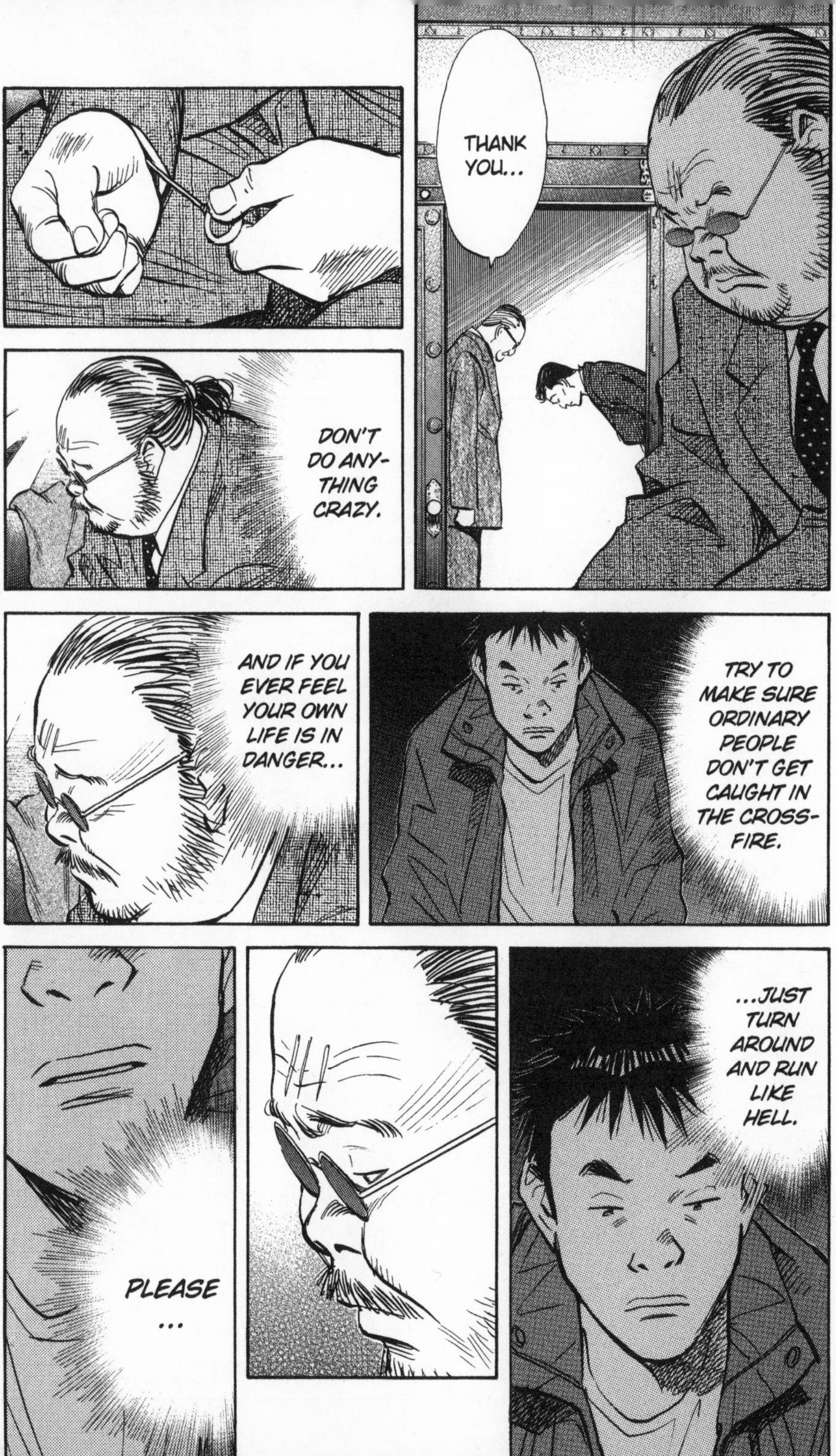
THANK YOU...
DON'T DO ANYTHING CRAZY.
TRY TO MAKE SURE ORDINARY PEOPLE DON'T GET CAUGHT IN THE CROSSFIRE.
AND IF YOU EVER FEEL YOUR OWN LIFE IS IN DANGER...
...JUST TURN AROUND AND RUN LIKE HELL.
PLEASE ...

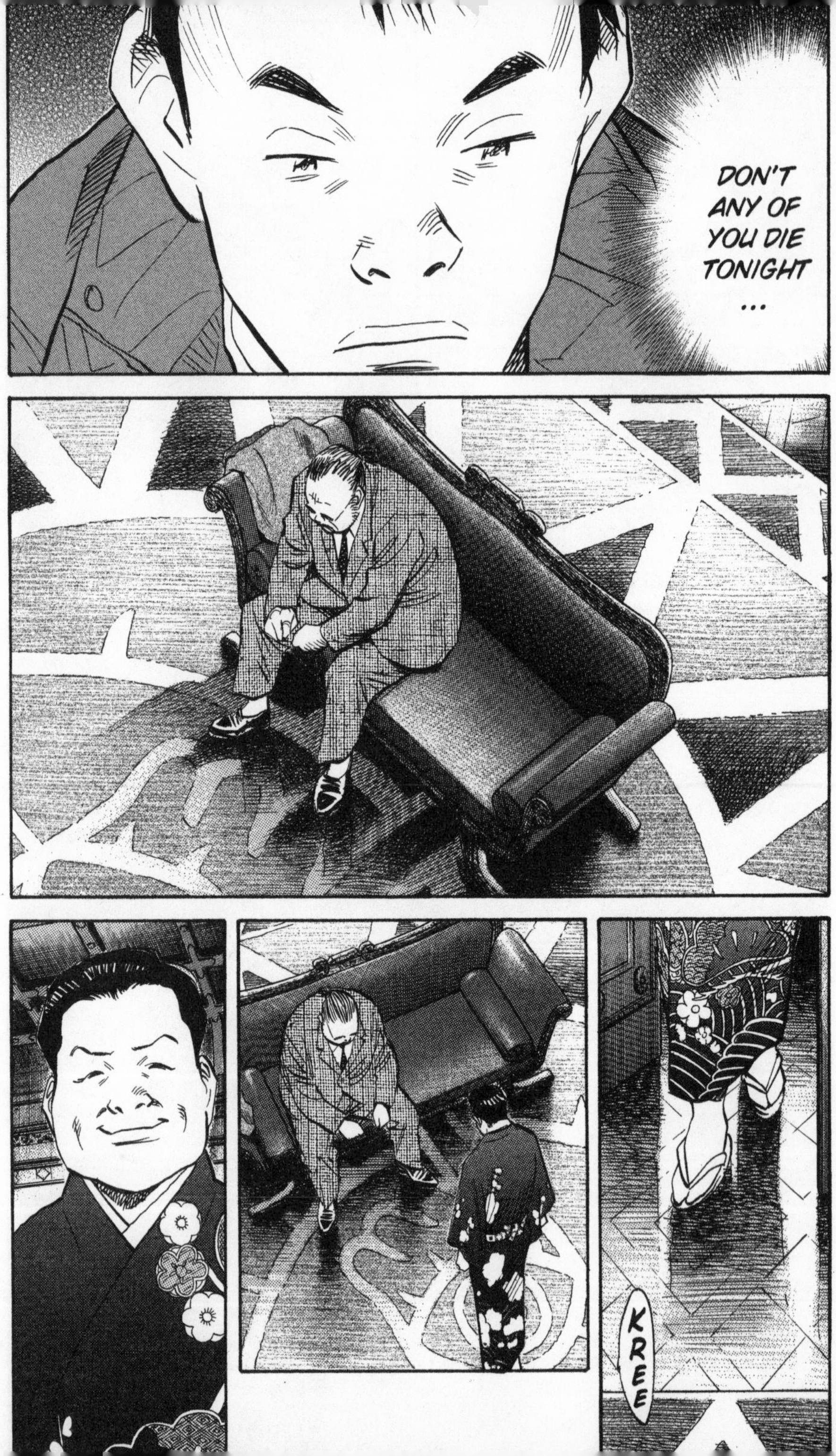
DON'T ANY OF YOU DIE TONIGHT ...
KREE

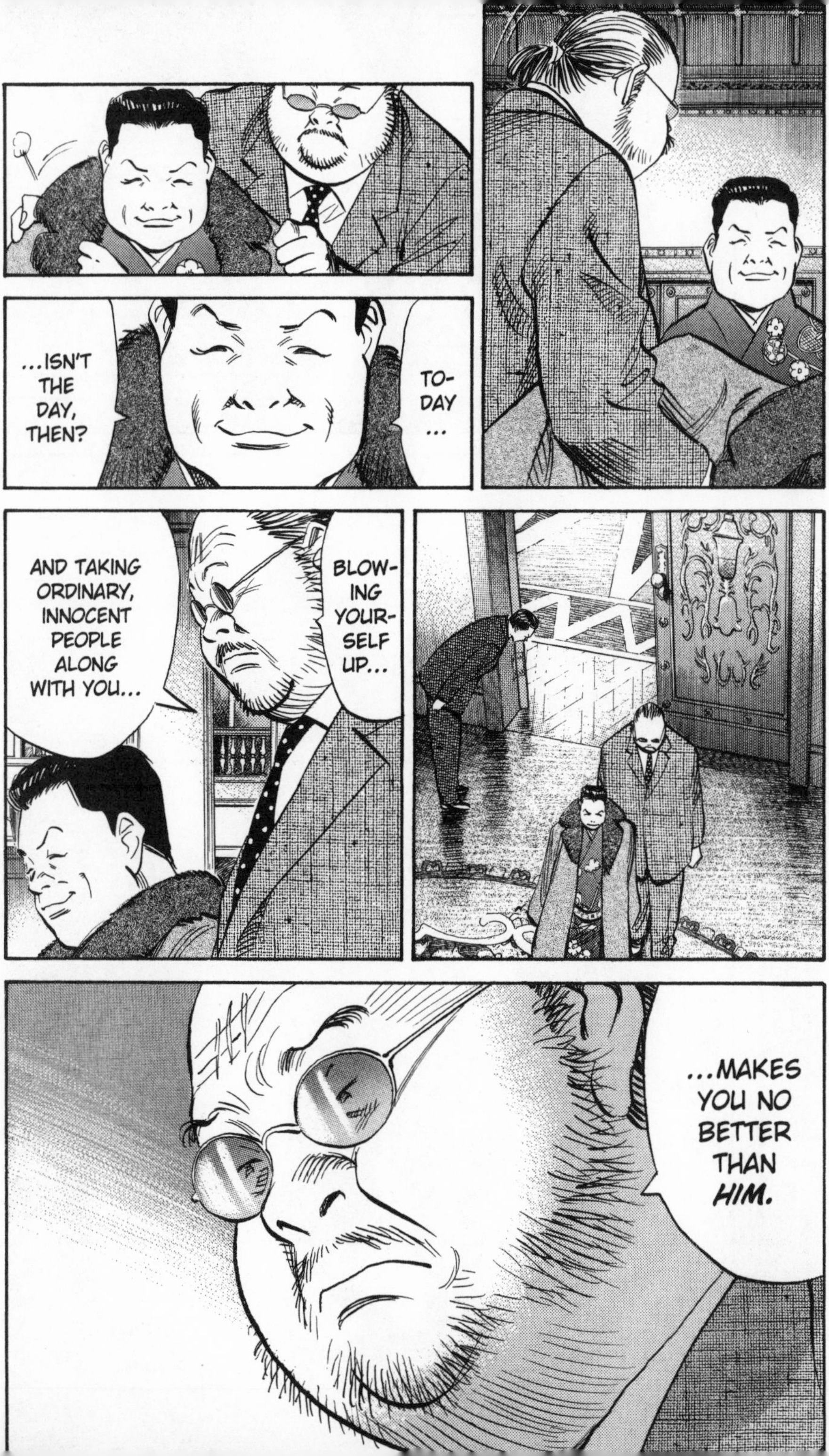
TO-DAY...
...ISN'T THE DAY, THEN?
BLOWING-ING YOUR-SELF UP...
AND TAKING ORDINARY, INNOCENT PEOPLE ALONG WITH YOU...
...MAKES YOU NO BETTER THAN *HIM.*

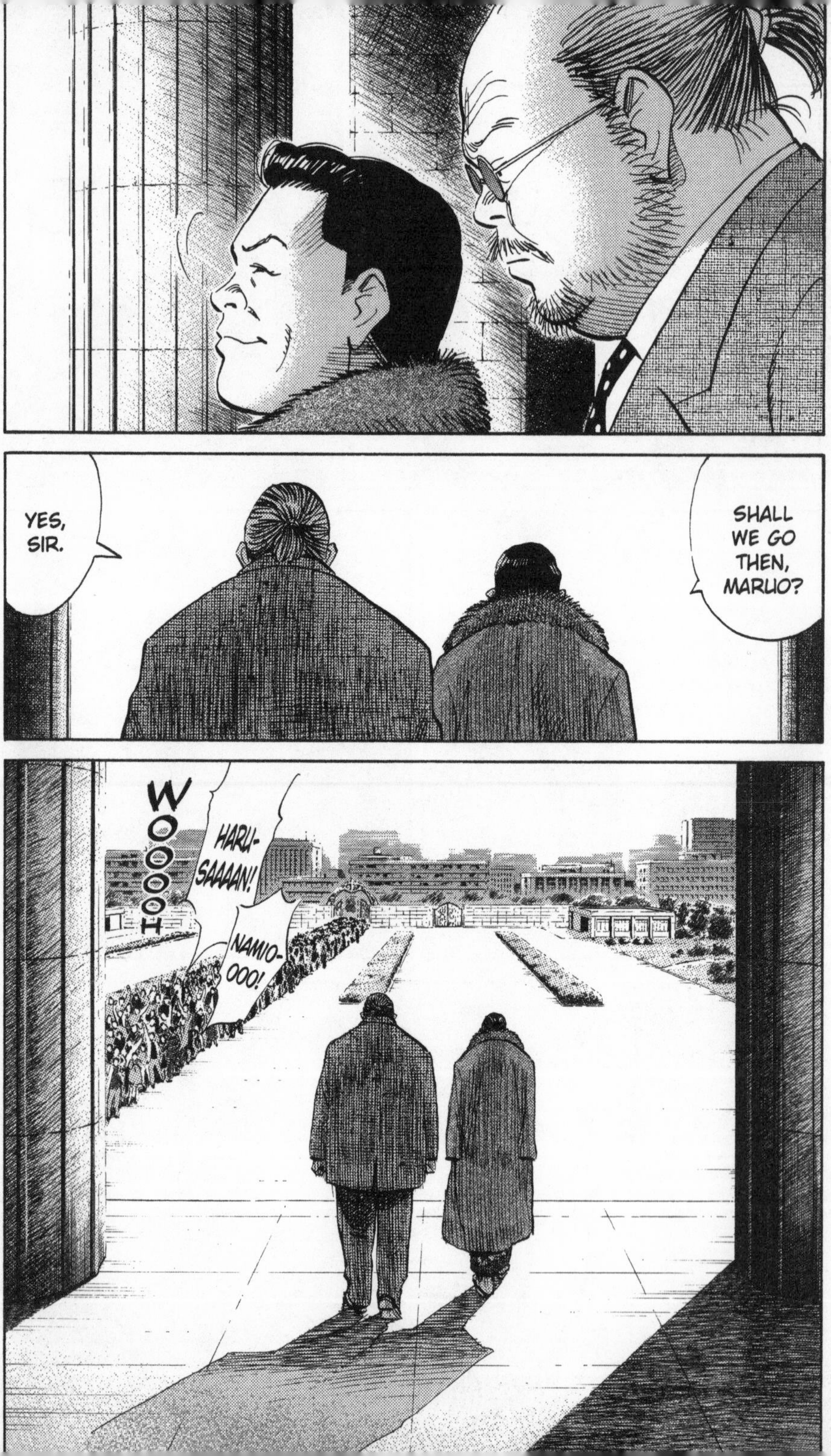
SHALL WE GO THEN, MARUO?
YES, SIR.
HARU-SAAAAN!
WOOOOOH
NAMIO-OOO!

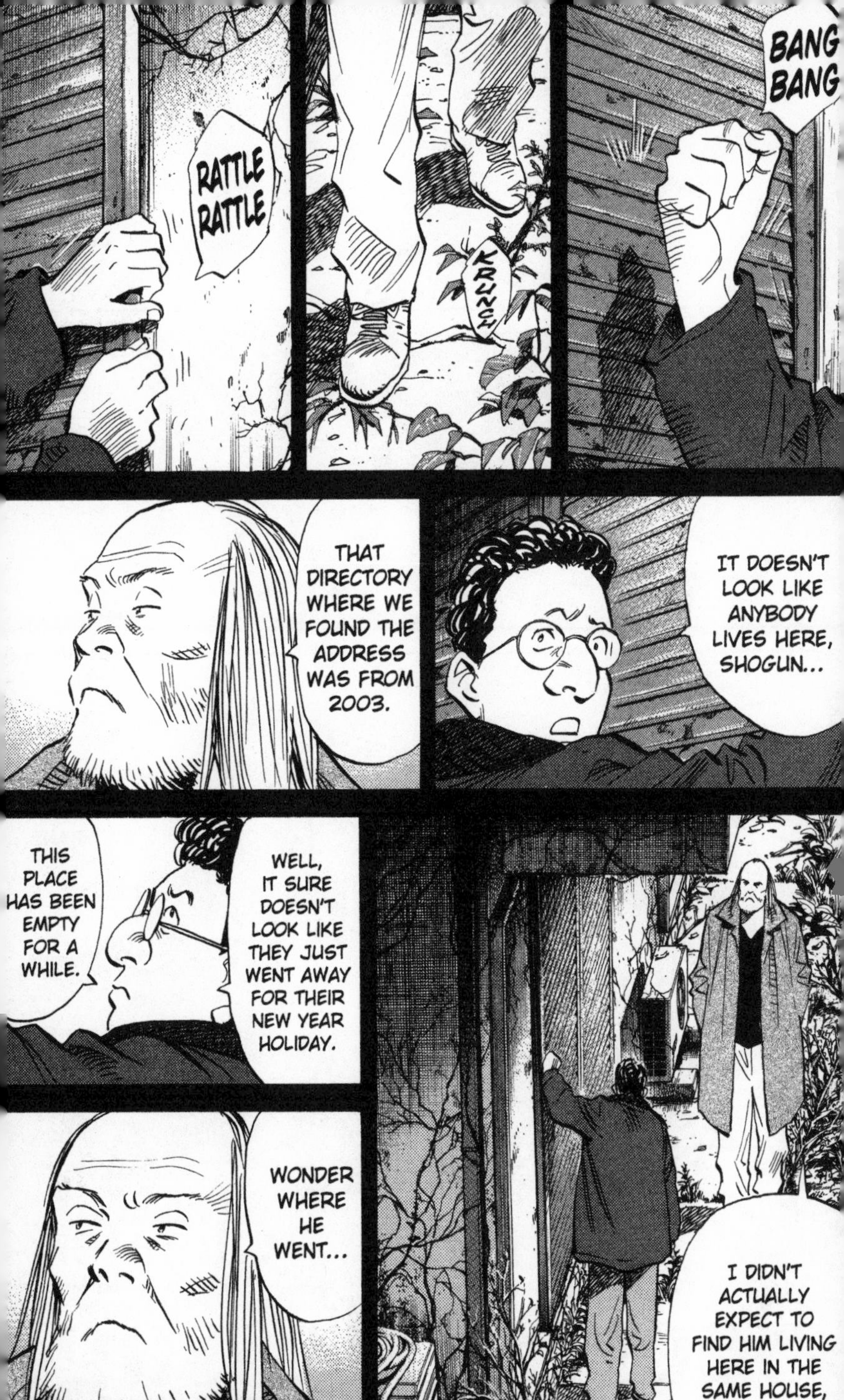
BANG BANG
KRUNCH
RATTLE RATTLE
IT DOESN'T LOOK LIKE ANYBODY LIVES HERE, SHOGUN...
THAT DIRECTORY WHERE WE FOUND THE ADDRESS WAS FROM 2003.
I DIDN'T ACTUALLY EXPECT TO FIND HIM LIVING HERE IN THE SAME HOUSE, TWELVE YEARS LATER.
WELL, IT SURE DOESN'T LOOK LIKE THEY JUST WENT AWAY FOR THEIR NEW YEAR HOLIDAY.
THIS PLACE HAS BEEN EMPTY FOR A WHILE.
WONDER WHERE HE WENT...

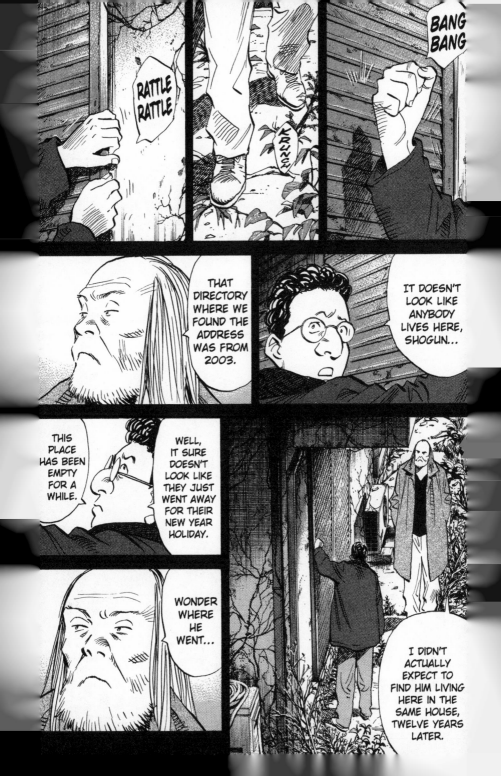

IT WAS THE PLACE BOTH HE AND I LOVED BEST...

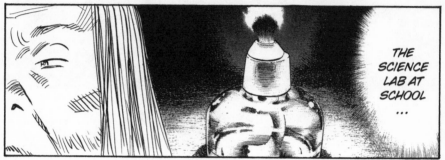

THE SCIENCE LAB AT SCHOOL ...

DOCTOR YAMANE...

Chapter 4
Secret Message

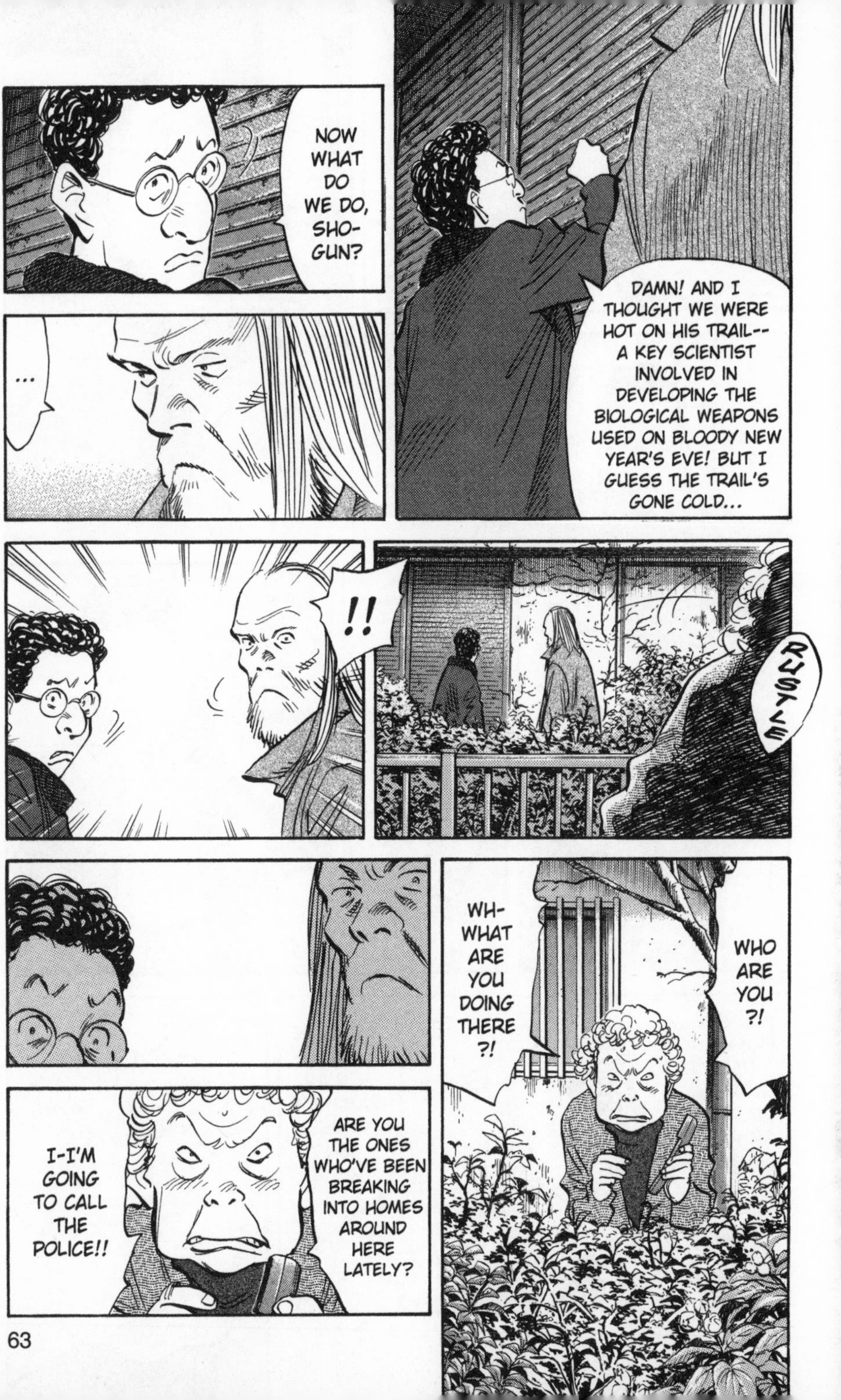
DAMN! AND I THOUGHT WE WERE HOT ON HIS TRAIL-- A KEY SCIENTIST INVOLVED IN DEVELOPING THE BIOLOGICAL WEAPONS USED ON BLOODY NEW YEAR'S EVE! BUT I GUESS THE TRAIL'S GONE COLD...
NOW WHAT DO WE DO, SHO-GUN?
...
RUSTLE
!!
WHO ARE YOU ?!
WH- WHAT ARE YOU DOING THERE ?!
ARE YOU THE ONES WHO'VE BEEN BREAKING INTO HOMES AROUND HERE LATELY?
I-I'M GOING TO CALL THE POLICE!!

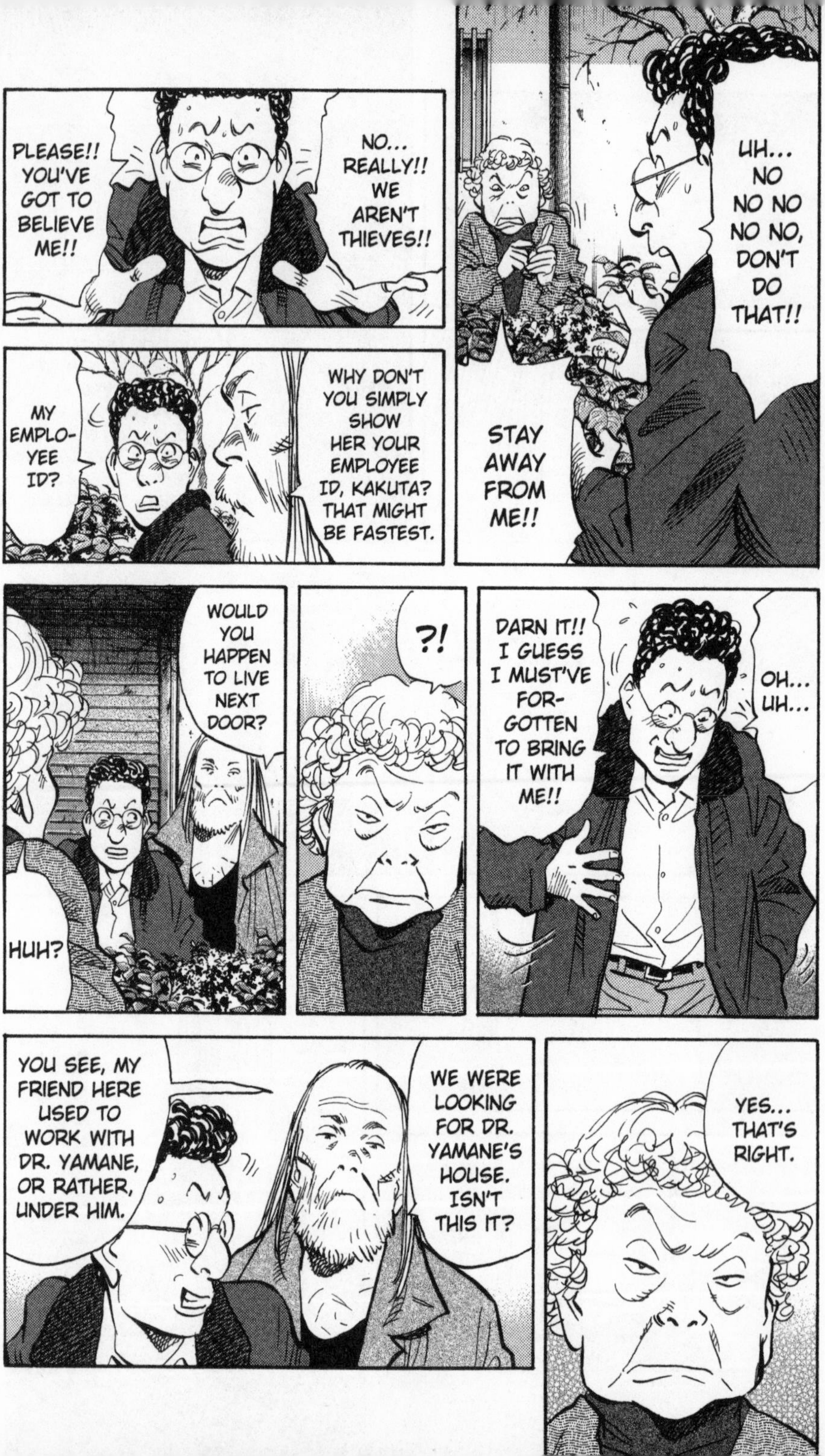
UH... NO NO NO NO NO, DON'T DO THAT!!
STAY AWAY FROM ME!!
NO... REALLY!! WE AREN'T THIEVES!!
PLEASE!! YOU'VE GOT TO BELIEVE ME!!
WHY DON'T YOU SIMPLY SHOW HER YOUR EMPLOYEE ID, KAKUTA? THAT MIGHT BE FASTEST.
MY EMPLOYEE ID?
OH... UH...
DARN IT!! I GUESS I MUST'VE FORGOTTEN TO BRING IT WITH ME!!
?!
WOULD YOU HAPPEN TO LIVE NEXT DOOR?
HUH?
YES... THAT'S RIGHT.
WE WERE LOOKING FOR DR. YAMANE'S HOUSE. ISN'T THIS IT?
YOU SEE, MY FRIEND HERE USED TO WORK WITH DR. YAMANE, OR RATHER, UNDER HIM.

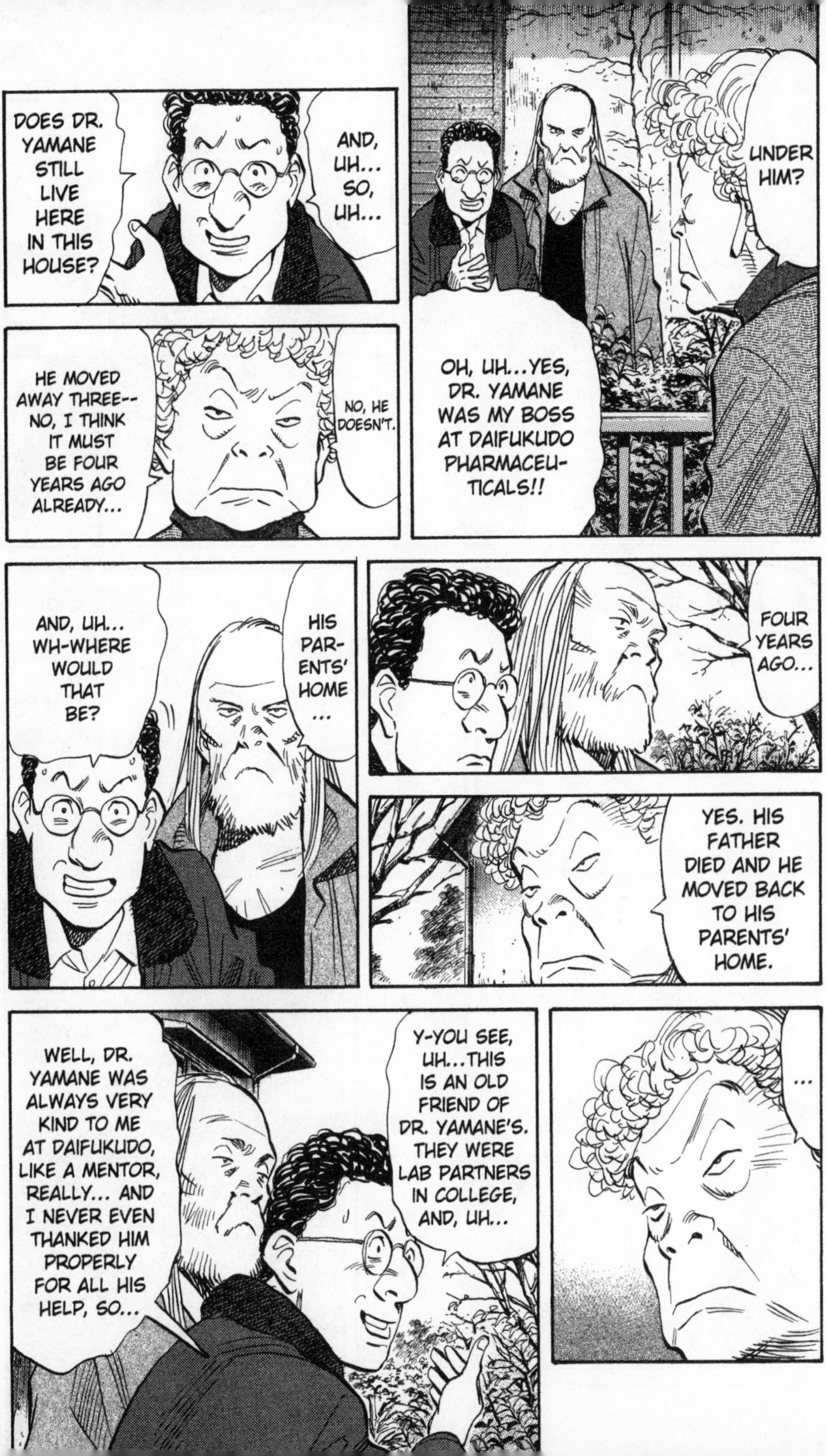
UNDER HIM?
OH, UH...YES, DR. YAMANE WAS MY BOSS AT DAIFUKUDO PHARMACEUTICALS!!
AND, UH... SO, UH...
DOES DR. YAMANE STILL LIVE HERE IN THIS HOUSE?
NO, HE DOESN'T.
HE MOVED AWAY THREE--NO, I THINK IT MUST BE FOUR YEARS AGO ALREADY...
FOUR YEARS AGO...
YES. HIS FATHER DIED AND HE MOVED BACK TO HIS PARENTS' HOME.
HIS PARENTS' HOME...
AND, UH... WH-WHERE WOULD THAT BE?
...
Y-YOU SEE, UH...THIS IS AN OLD FRIEND OF DR. YAMANE'S. THEY WERE LAB PARTNERS IN COLLEGE, AND, UH...
WELL, DR. YAMANE WAS ALWAYS VERY KIND TO ME AT DAIFUKUDO, LIKE A MENTOR, REALLY... AND I NEVER EVEN THANKED HIM PROPERLY FOR ALL HIS HELP, SO...

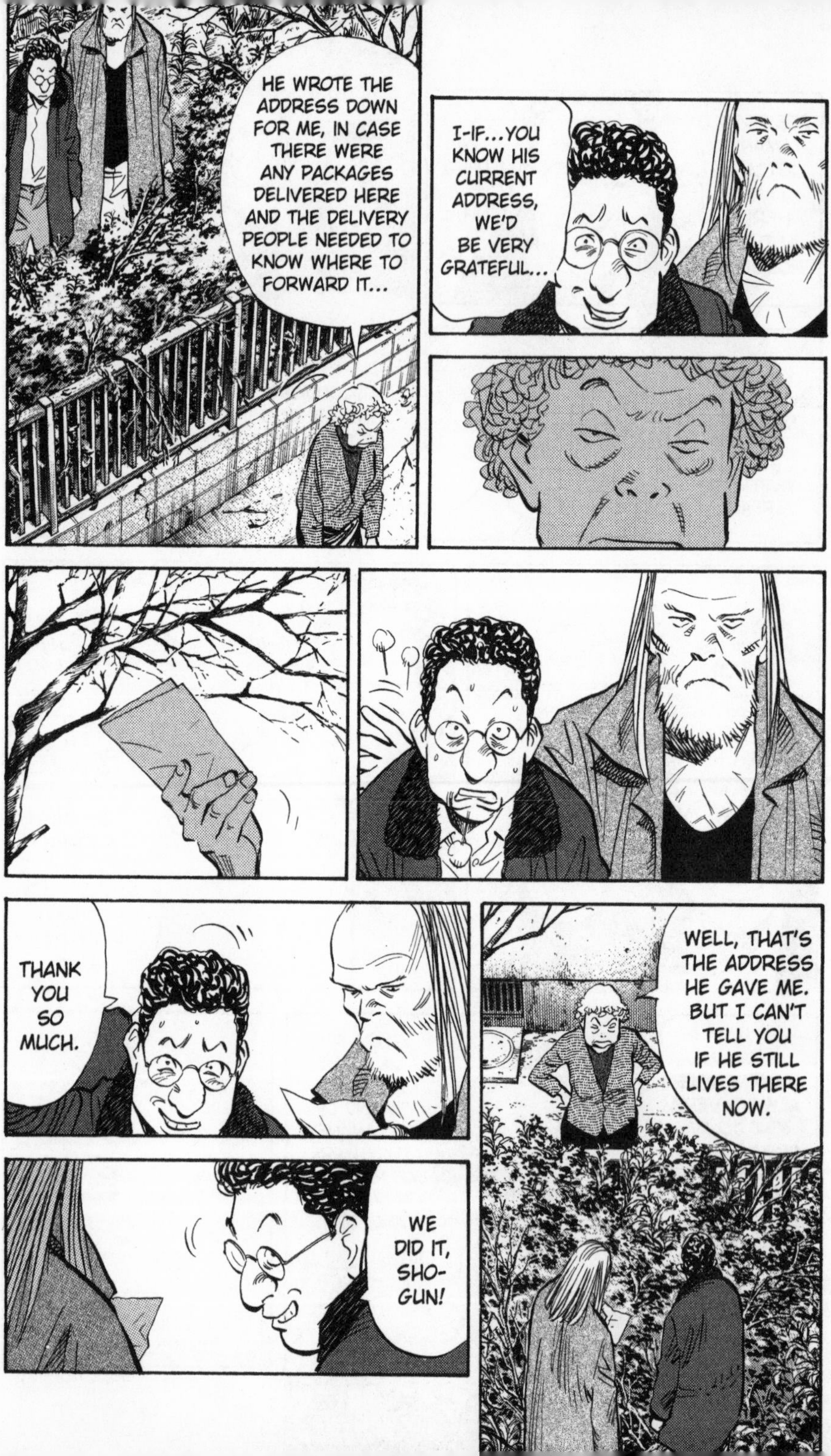
I-IF...YOU KNOW HIS CURRENT ADDRESS, WE'D BE VERY GRATEFUL...
HE WROTE THE ADDRESS DOWN FOR ME, IN CASE THERE WERE ANY PACKAGES DELIVERED HERE AND THE DELIVERY PEOPLE NEEDED TO KNOW WHERE TO FORWARD IT...
WELL, THAT'S THE ADDRESS HE GAVE ME. BUT I CAN'T TELL YOU IF HE STILL LIVES THERE NOW.
THANK YOU SO MUCH.
WE DID IT, SHO-GUN!

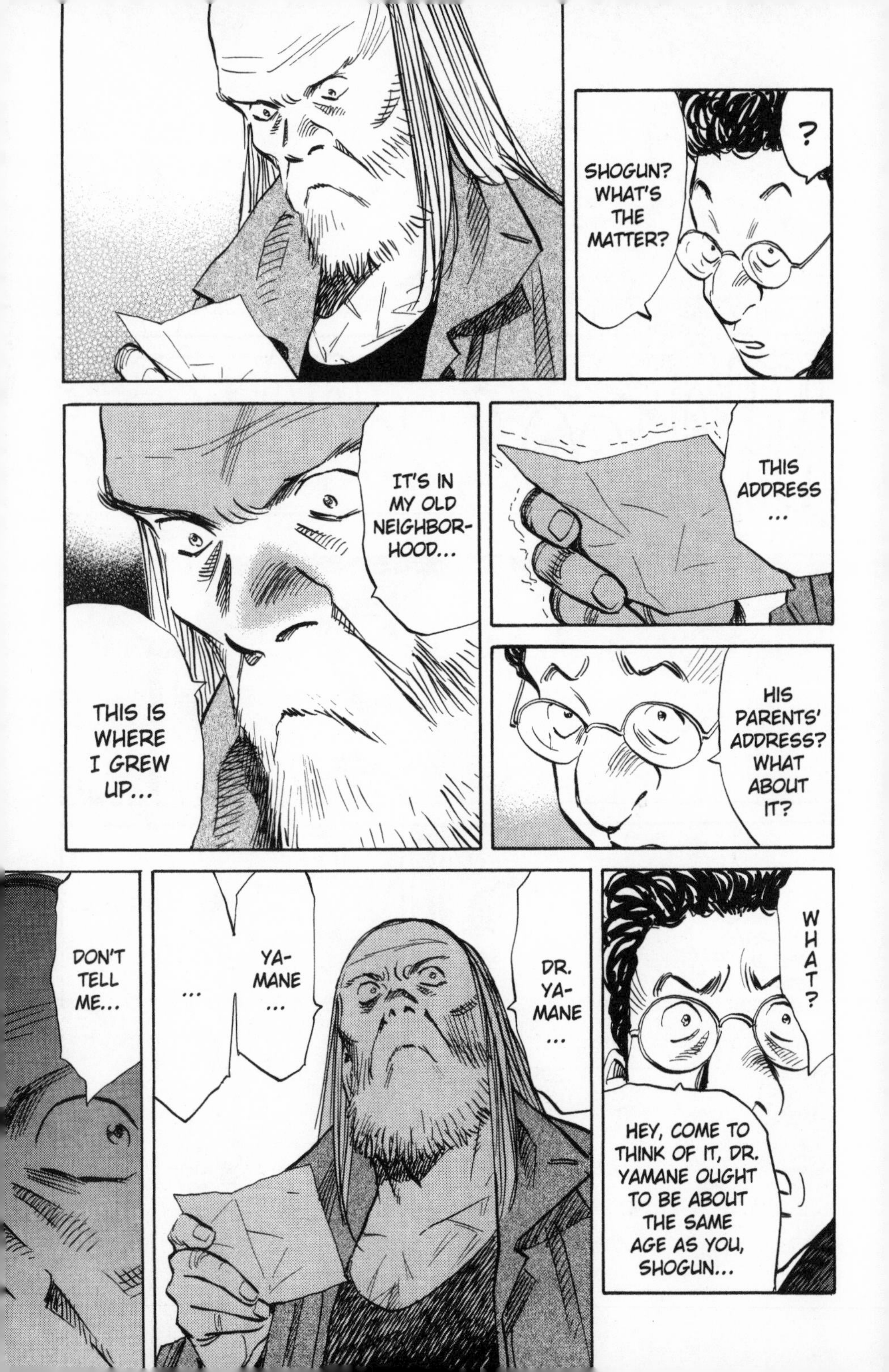
?
SHOGUN? WHAT'S THE MATTER?
THIS ADDRESS ...
HIS PARENTS' ADDRESS? WHAT ABOUT IT?
IT'S IN MY OLD NEIGHBOR-HOOD...
THIS IS WHERE I GREW UP...
WHAT?
HEY, COME TO THINK OF IT, DR. YAMANE OUGHT TO BE ABOUT THE SAME AGE AS YOU, SHOGUN...
DR. YA-MANE ...
YA-MANE ...
...
DON'T TELL ME...

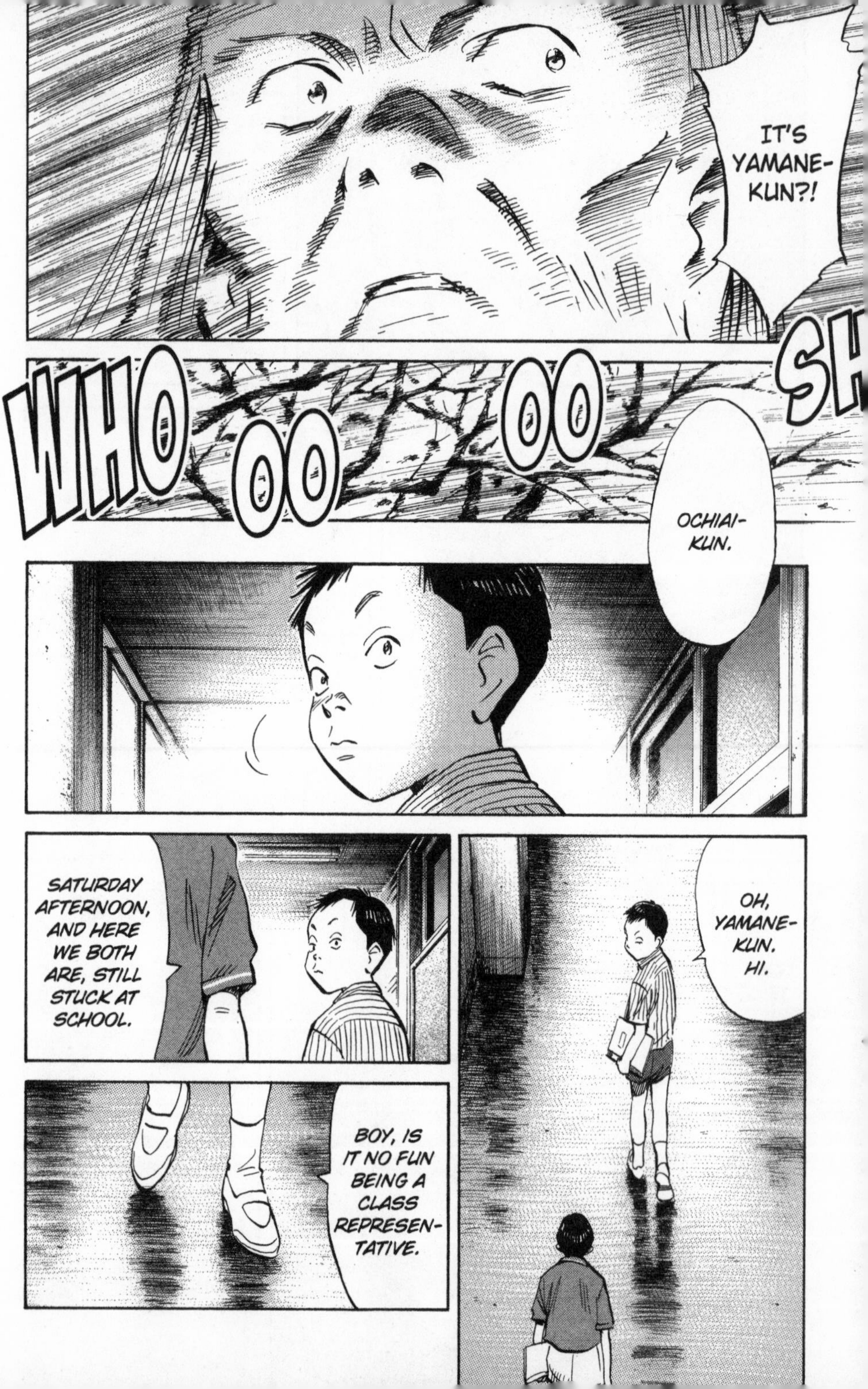
IT'S YAMANE-KUN?!
WHOOOOOOSH
OCHIAI-KUN.
OH, YAMANE-KUN. HI.
SATURDAY AFTERNOON, AND HERE WE BOTH ARE, STILL STUCK AT SCHOOL.
BOY, IS IT NO FUN BEING A CLASS REPRESENTATIVE.

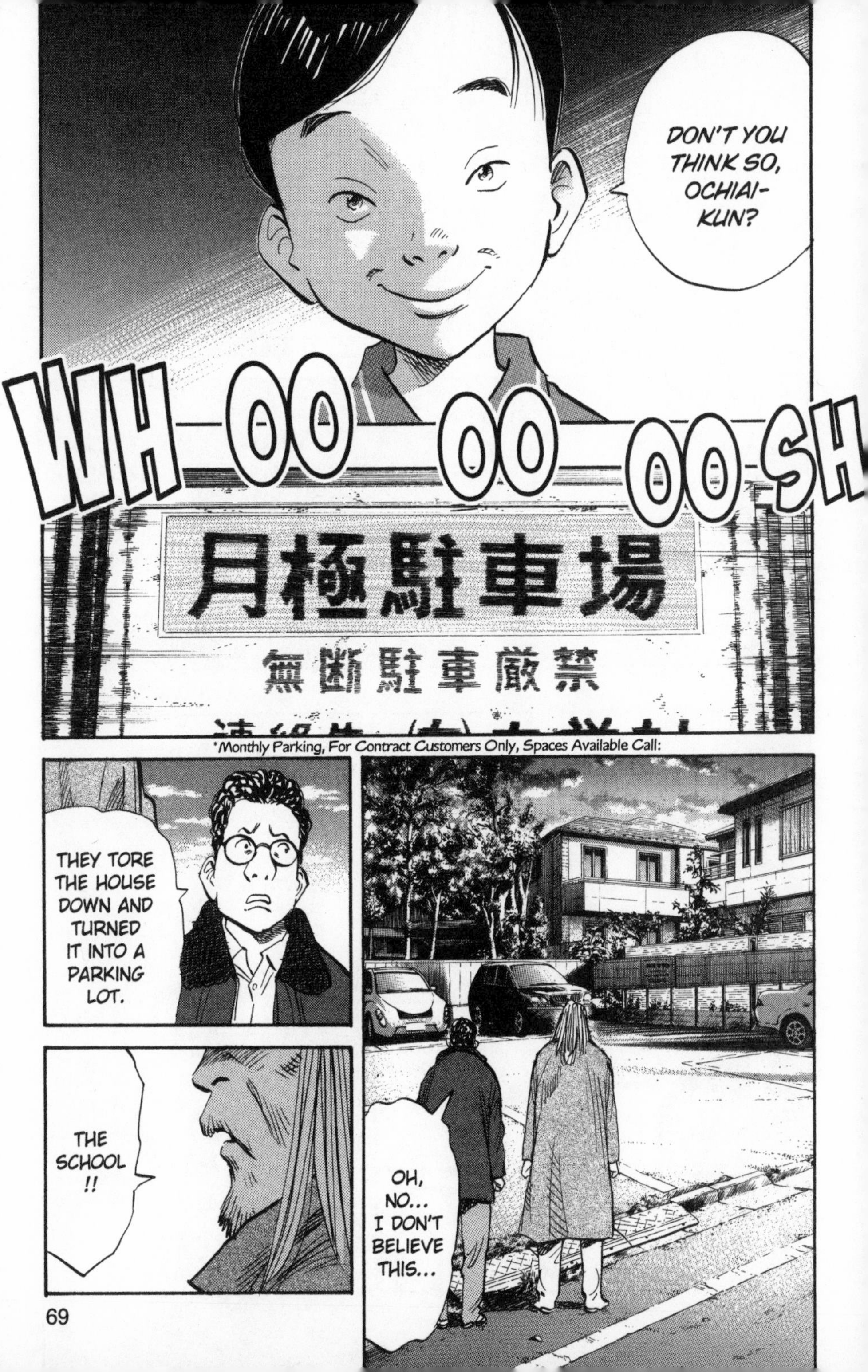
DON'T YOU THINK SO, OCHIAI-KUN?
WHOOOOOOSH
月極駐車場
無断駐車厳禁
OH, NO... I DON'T BELIEVE THIS...
THEY TORE THE HOUSE DOWN AND TURNED IT INTO A PARKING LOT.
THE SCHOOL !!
*Monthly Parking, For Contract Customers Only, Spaces Available Call:

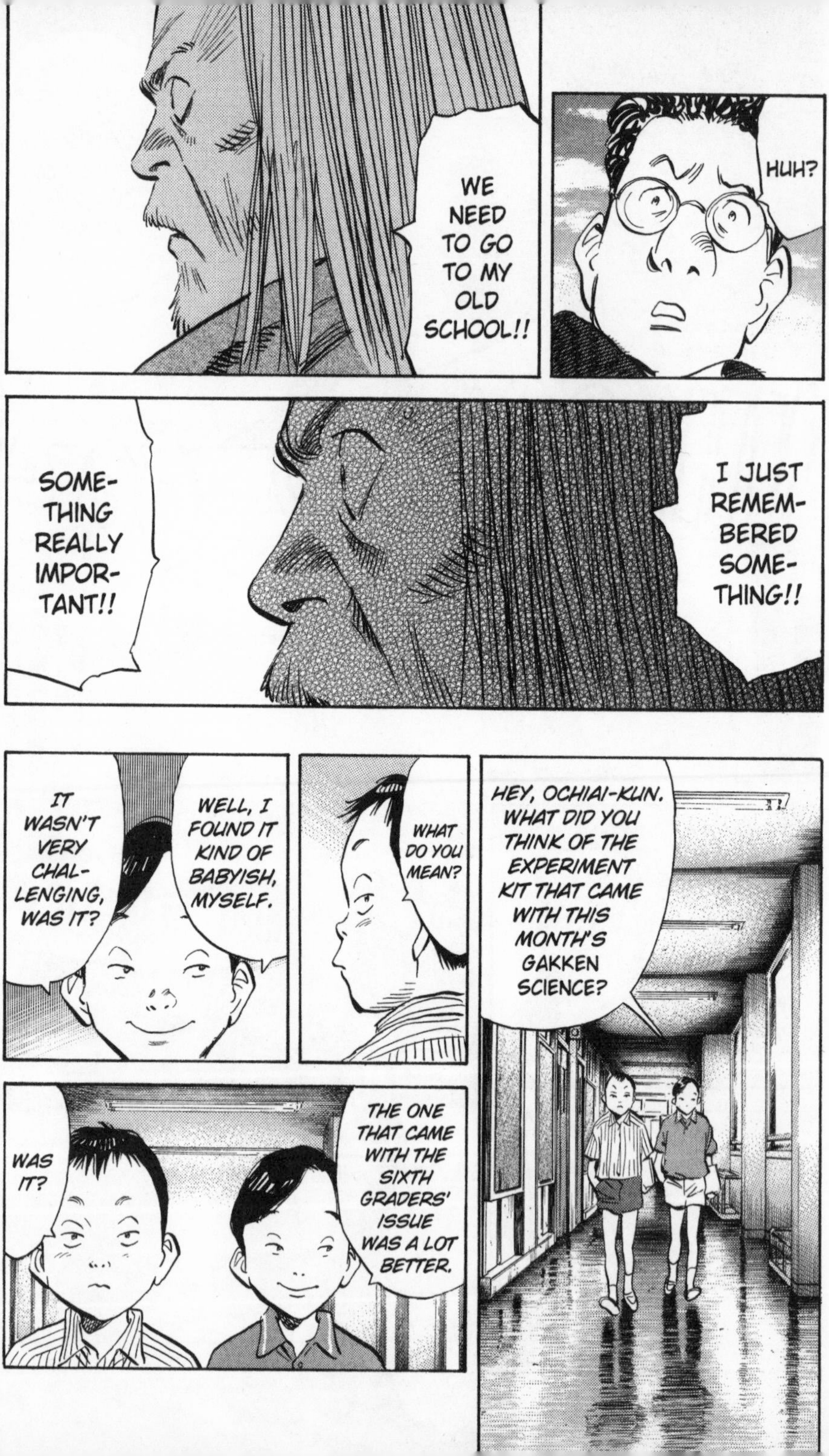
HUH?
WE NEED TO GO TO MY OLD SCHOOL!!
I JUST REMEMBERED SOMETHING!!
SOMETHING REALLY IMPORTANT!!
HEY, OCHIAI-KUN. WHAT DID YOU THINK OF THE EXPERIMENT KIT THAT CAME WITH THIS MONTH'S GAKKEN SCIENCE?
WHAT DO YOU MEAN?
WELL, I FOUND IT KIND OF BABYISH, MYSELF.
IT WASN'T VERY CHALLENGING, WAS IT?
THE ONE THAT CAME WITH THE SIXTH GRADERS' ISSUE WAS A LOT BETTER.
WAS IT?

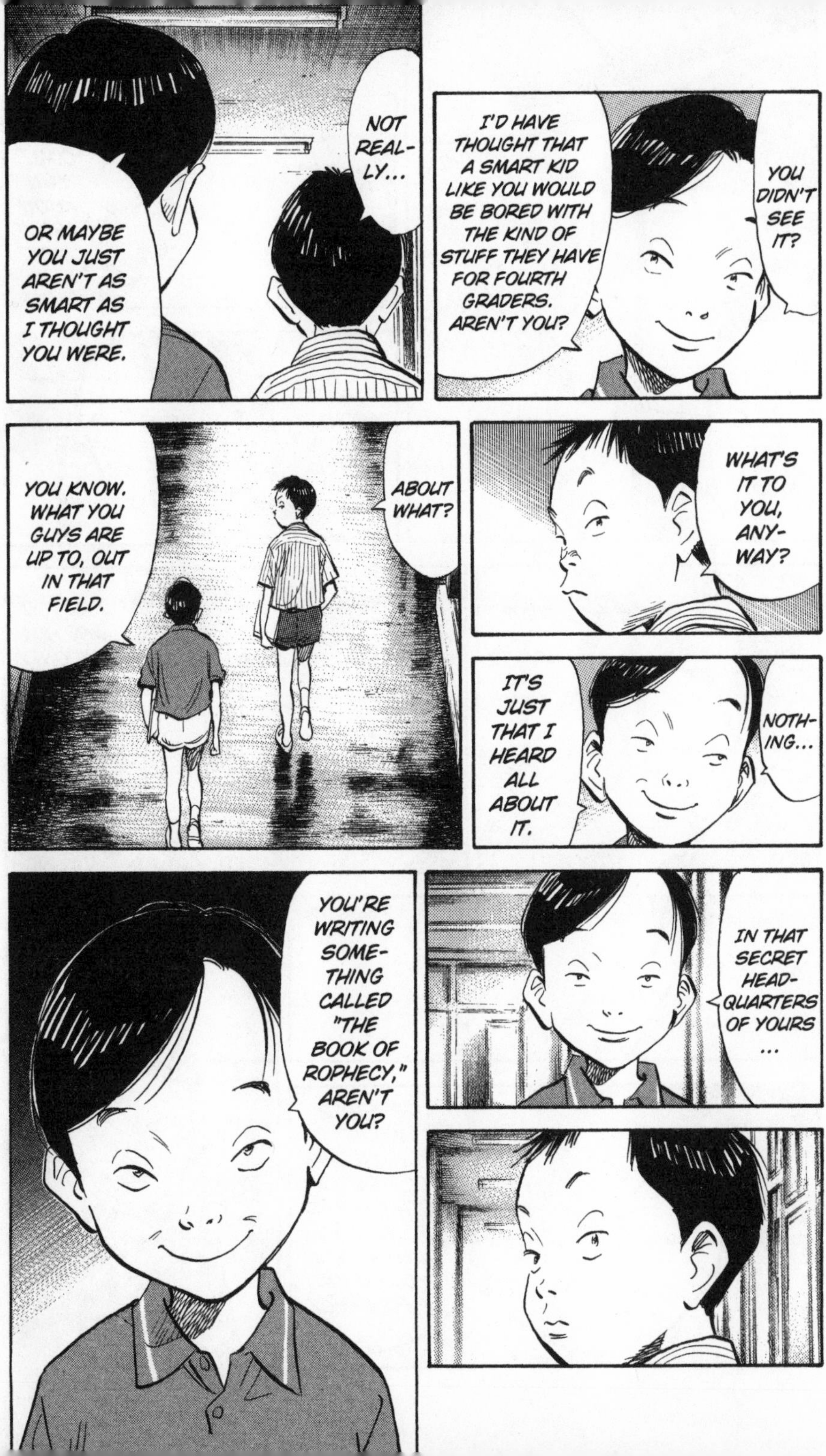
YOU DIDN'T SEE IT?
I'D HAVE THOUGHT THAT A SMART KID LIKE YOU WOULD BE BORED WITH THE KIND OF STUFF THEY HAVE FOR FOURTH GRADERS. AREN'T YOU?
NOT REAL-LY...
OR MAYBE YOU JUST AREN'T AS SMART AS I THOUGHT YOU WERE.
WHAT'S IT TO YOU, ANY-WAY?
NOTH-ING...
IT'S JUST THAT I HEARD ALL ABOUT IT.
ABOUT WHAT?
YOU KNOW. WHAT YOU GUYS ARE UP TO, OUT IN THAT FIELD.
IN THAT SECRET HEAD-QUARTERS OF YOURS ...
YOU'RE WRITING SOME-THING CALLED "THE BOOK OF ROPHECY," AREN'T YOU?

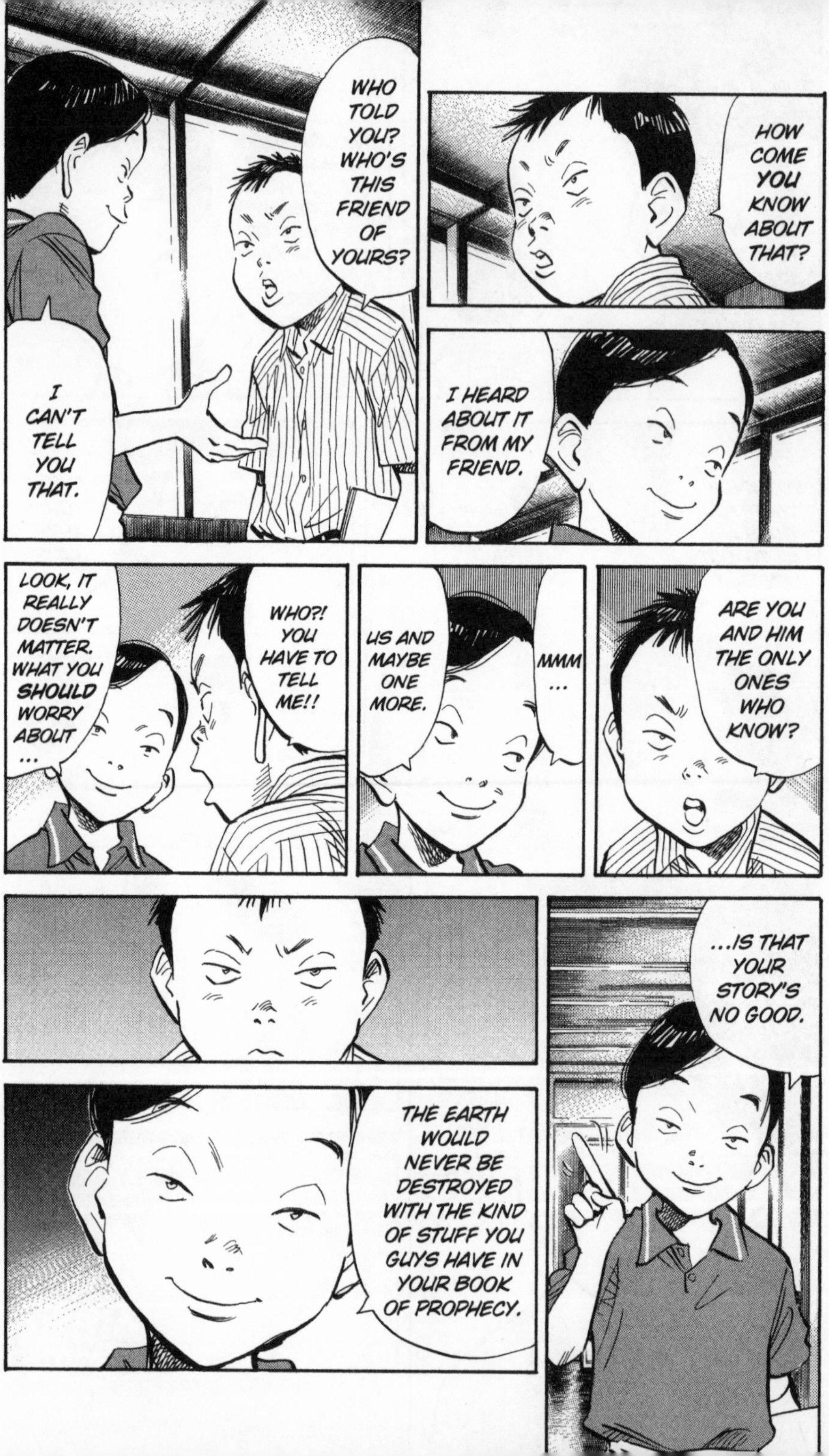
HOW COME YOU KNOW ABOUT THAT?
I HEARD ABOUT IT FROM MY FRIEND.
WHO TOLD YOU? WHO'S THIS FRIEND OF YOURS?
I CAN'T TELL YOU THAT.
ARE YOU AND HIM THE ONLY ONES WHO KNOW?
MMM...
US AND MAYBE ONE MORE.
WHO?! YOU HAVE TO TELL ME!!
LOOK, IT REALLY DOESN'T MATTER. WHAT YOU SHOULD WORRY ABOUT...
...IS THAT YOUR STORY'S NO GOOD.
THE EARTH WOULD NEVER BE DESTROYED WITH THE KIND OF STUFF YOU GUYS HAVE IN YOUR BOOK OF PROPHECY.

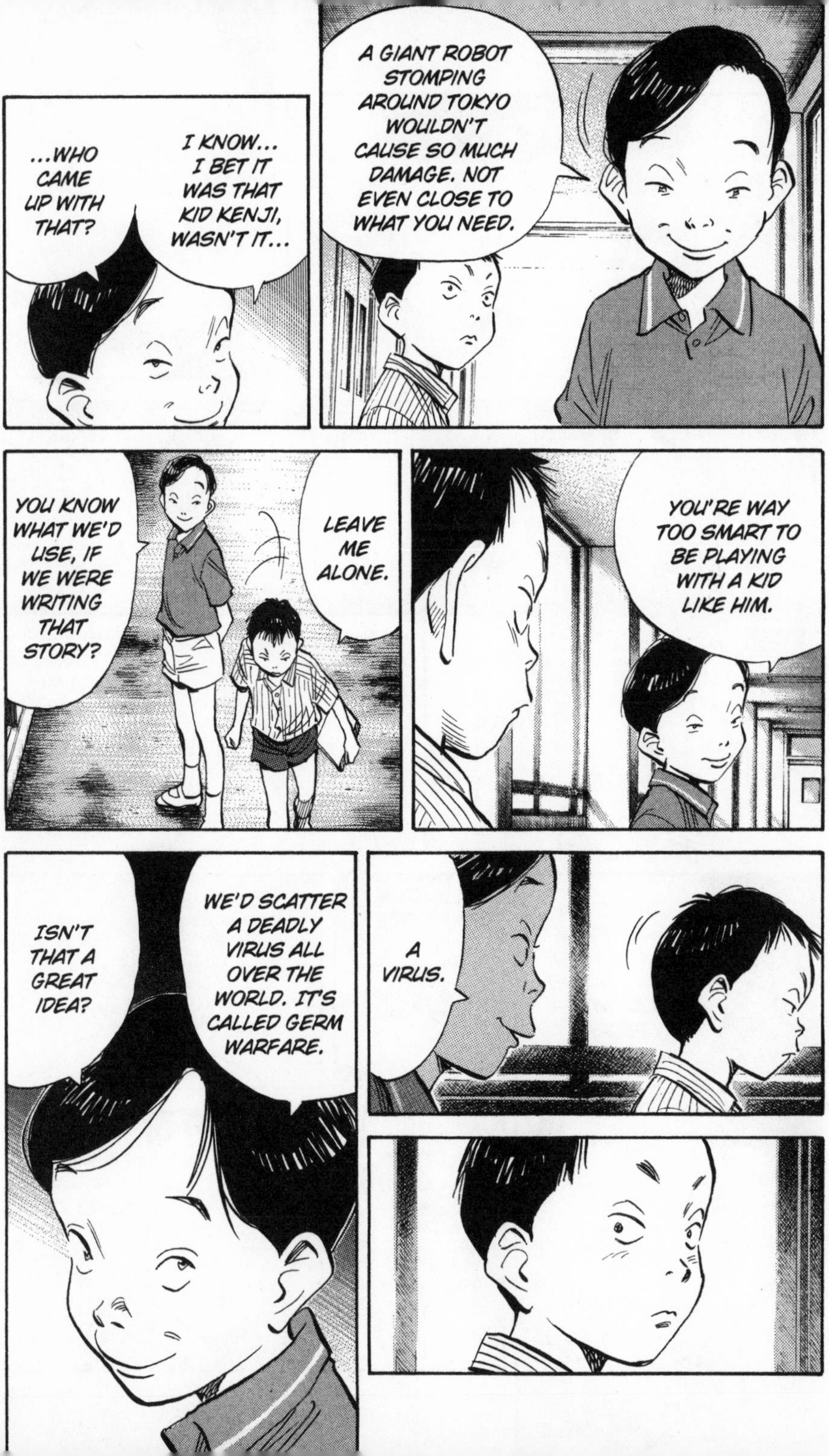
A GIANT ROBOT STOMPING AROUND TOKYO WOULDN'T CAUSE SO MUCH DAMAGE. NOT EVEN CLOSE TO WHAT YOU NEED.
I KNOW... I BET IT WAS THAT KID KENJI, WASN'T IT...
...WHO CAME UP WITH THAT?
YOU'RE WAY TOO SMART TO BE PLAYING WITH A KID LIKE HIM.
LEAVE ME ALONE.
YOU KNOW WHAT WE'D USE, IF WE WERE WRITING THAT STORY?
A VIRUS.
WE'D SCATTER A DEADLY VIRUS ALL OVER THE WORLD. IT'S CALLED GERM WARFARE.
ISN'T THAT A GREAT IDEA?

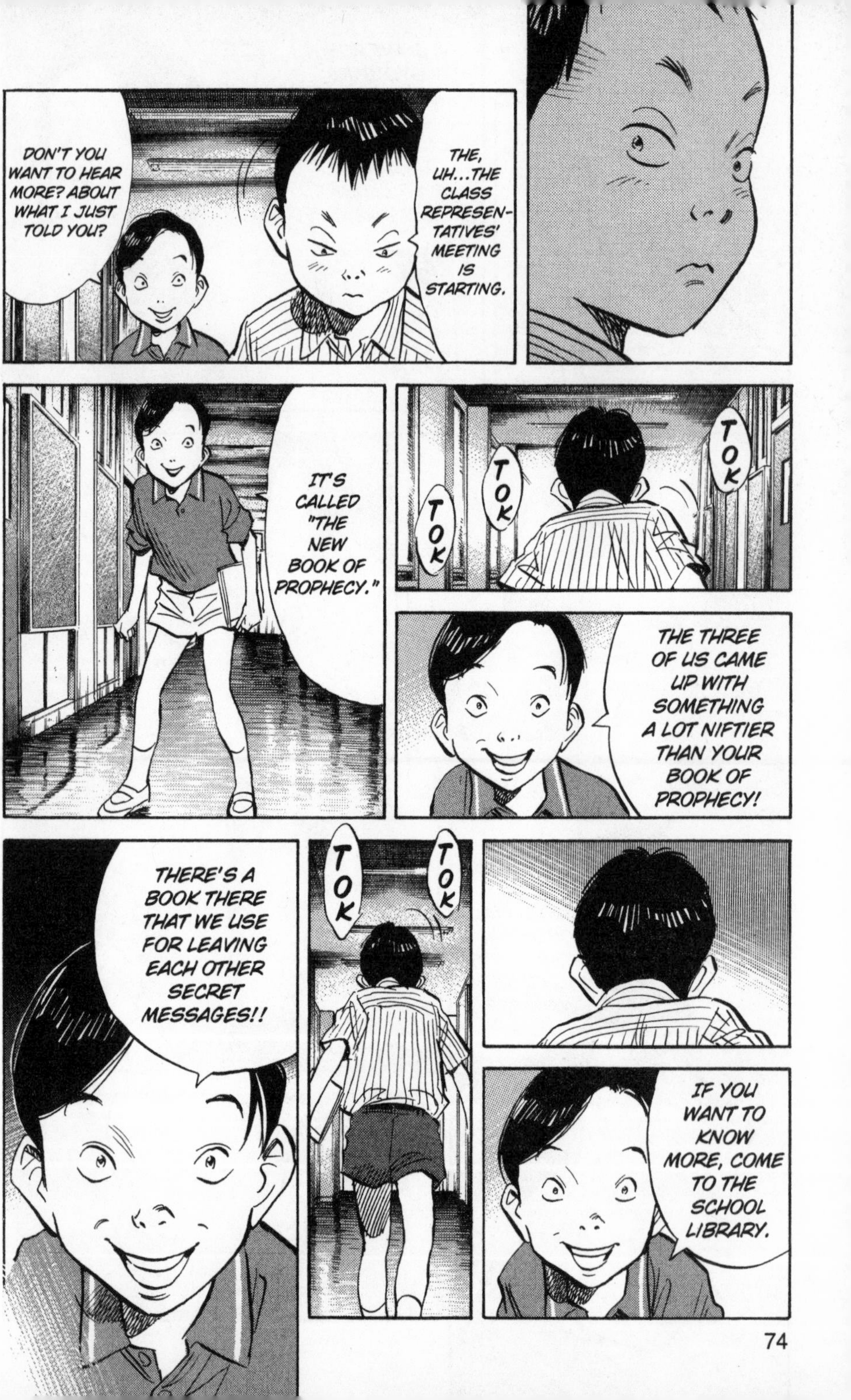
THE, UH...THE CLASS REPRESEN-TATIVES' MEETING IS STARTING.
DON'T YOU WANT TO HEAR MORE? ABOUT WHAT I JUST TOLD YOU?
TOK
TOK
TOK
THE THREE OF US CAME UP WITH SOMETHING A LOT NIFTIER THAN YOUR BOOK OF PROPHECY!
IT'S CALLED "THE NEW BOOK OF PROPHECY."
IF YOU WANT TO KNOW MORE, COME TO THE SCHOOL LIBRARY.
TOK
TOK
THERE'S A BOOK THERE THAT WE USE FOR LEAVING EACH OTHER SECRET MESSAGES!!

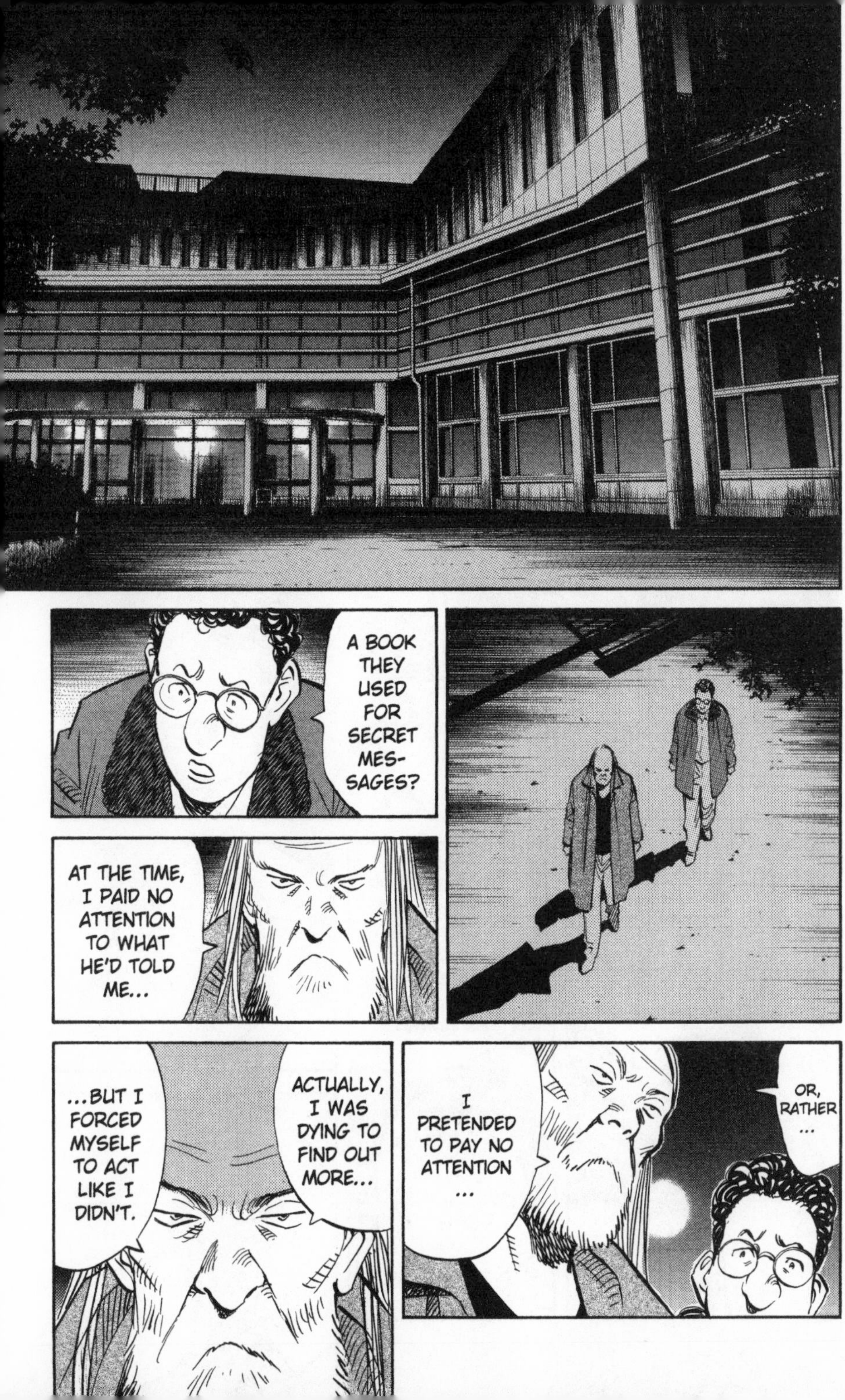
A BOOK THEY USED FOR SECRET MES-SAGES?
AT THE TIME, I PAID NO ATTENTION TO WHAT HE'D TOLD ME...
OR, RATHER...
I PRETENDED TO PAY NO ATTENTION...
ACTUALLY, I WAS DYING TO FIND OUT MORE...
...BUT I FORCED MYSELF TO ACT LIKE I DIDN'T.

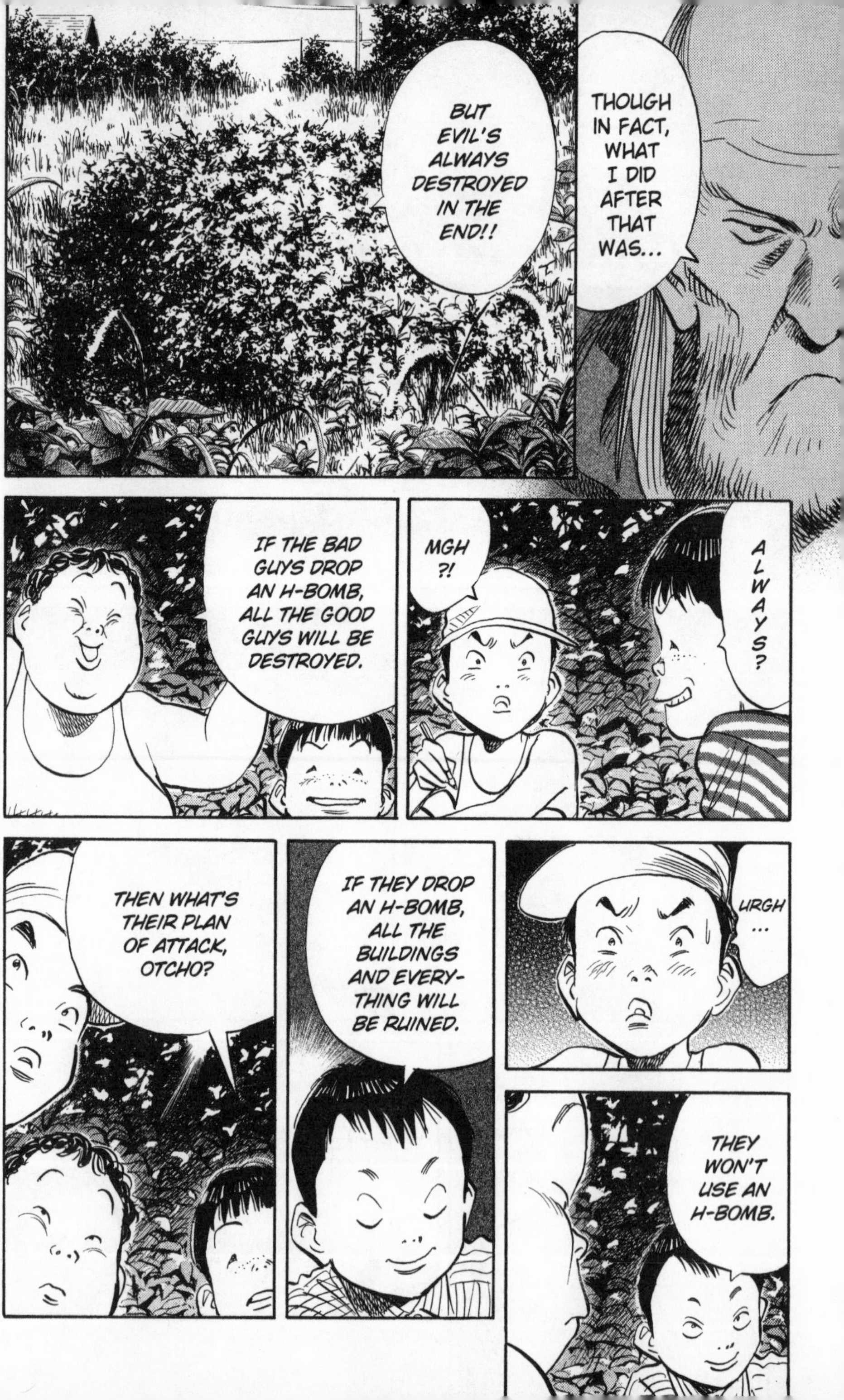
THOUGH IN FACT, WHAT I DID AFTER THAT WAS...
BUT EVIL'S ALWAYS DESTROYED IN THE END!!
ALWAYS?
MGH ?!
IF THE BAD GUYS DROP AN H-BOMB, ALL THE GOOD GUYS WILL BE DESTROYED.
URGH ...
THEY WON'T USE AN H-BOMB.
IF THEY DROP AN H-BOMB, ALL THE BUILDINGS AND EVERY-THING WILL BE RUINED.
THEN WHAT'S THEIR PLAN OF ATTACK, OTCHO?

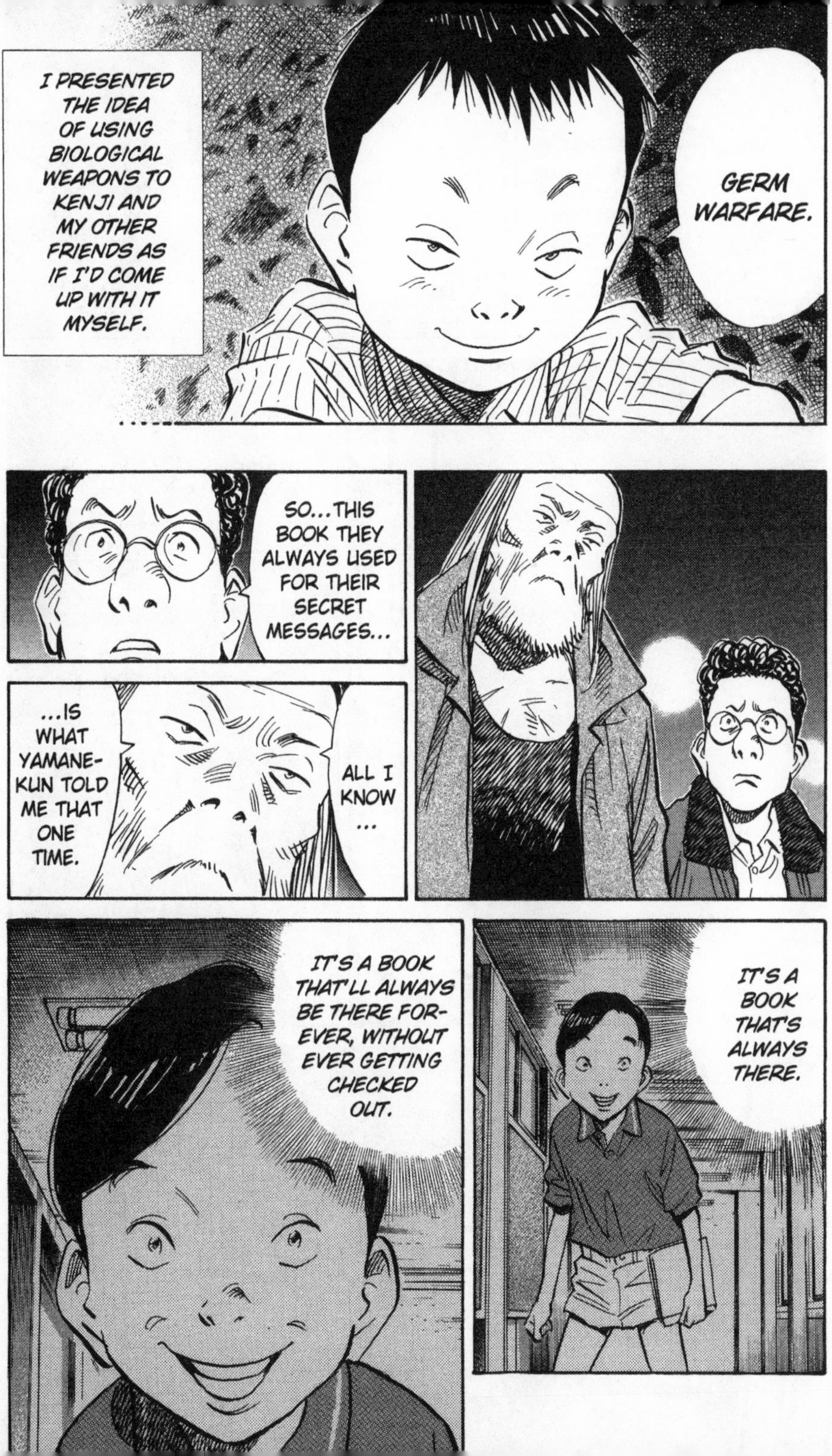
GERM WARFARE.
I PRESENTED THE IDEA OF USING BIOLOGICAL WEAPONS TO KENJI AND MY OTHER FRIENDS AS IF I'D COME UP WITH IT MYSELF.
SO... THIS BOOK THEY ALWAYS USED FOR THEIR SECRET MESSAGES...
ALL I KNOW ...
...IS WHAT YAMANE-KUN TOLD ME THAT ONE TIME.
IT'S A BOOK THAT'S ALWAYS THERE.
IT'S A BOOK THAT'LL ALWAYS BE THERE FOR-EVER, WITHOUT EVER GETTING CHECKED OUT.

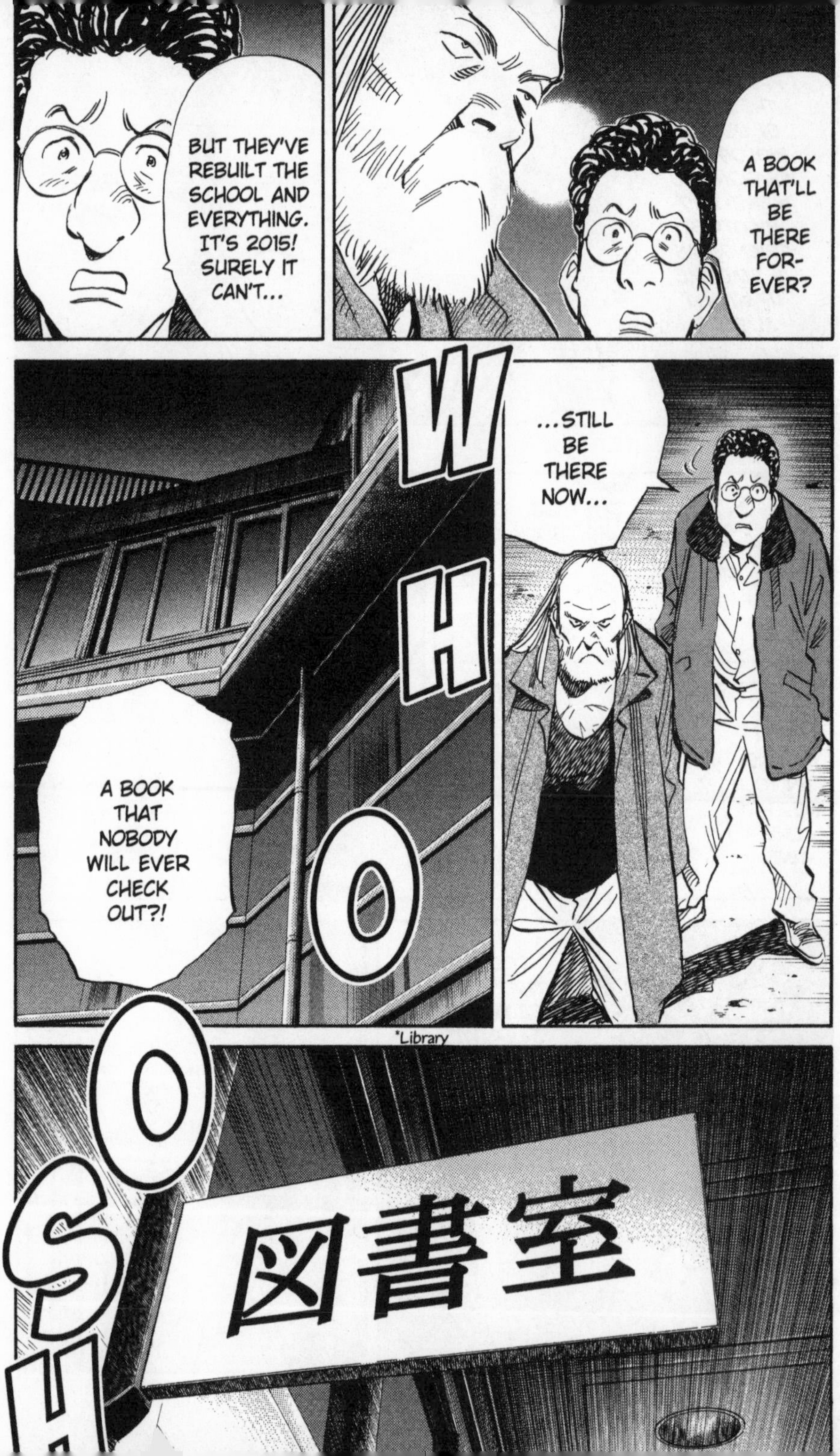
A BOOK THAT'LL BE THERE FOR-EVER?
BUT THEY'VE REBUILT THE SCHOOL AND EVERYTHING. IT'S 2015! SURELY IT CAN'T...
...STILL BE THERE NOW...
A BOOK THAT NOBODY WILL EVER CHECK OUT?!
WHOOSH
*Library
図書室

Chapter 5

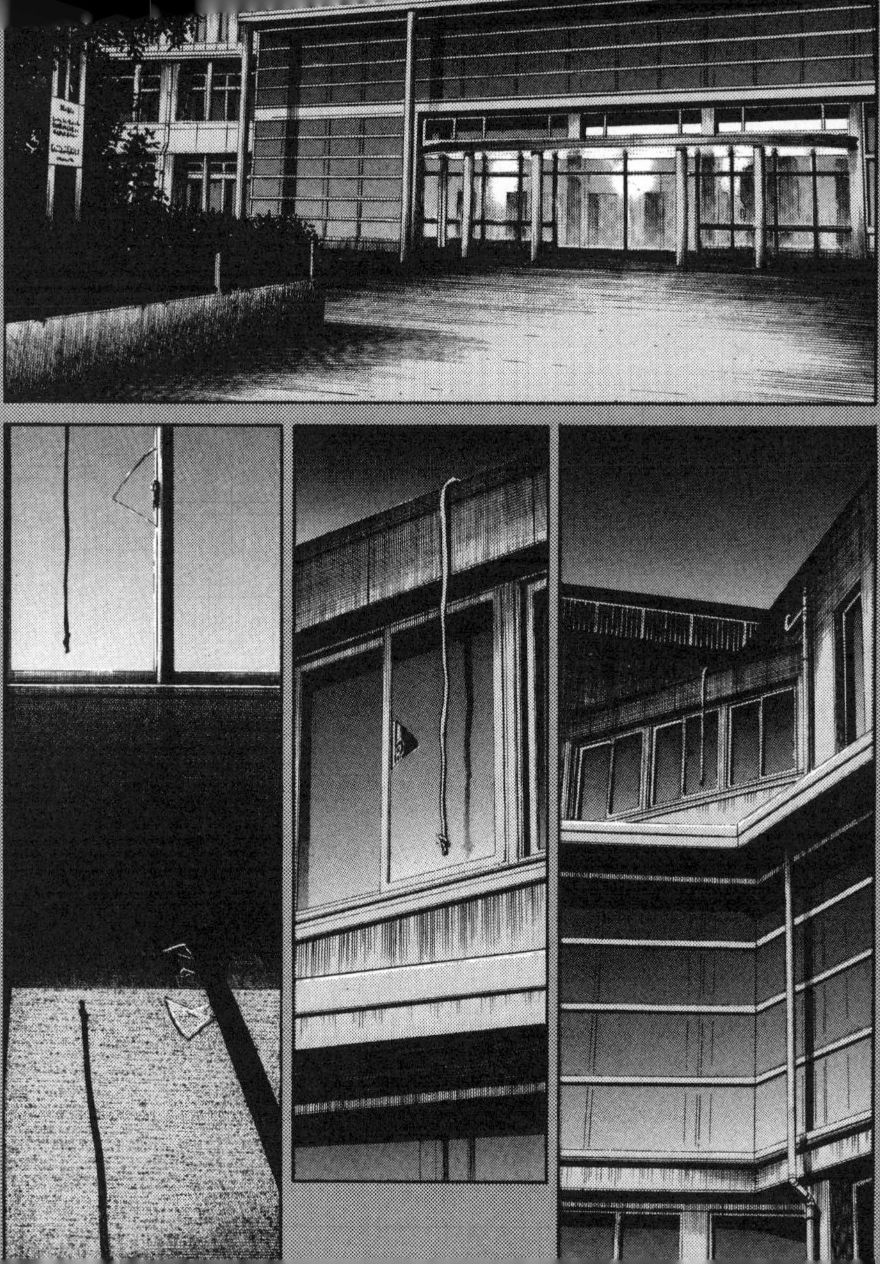

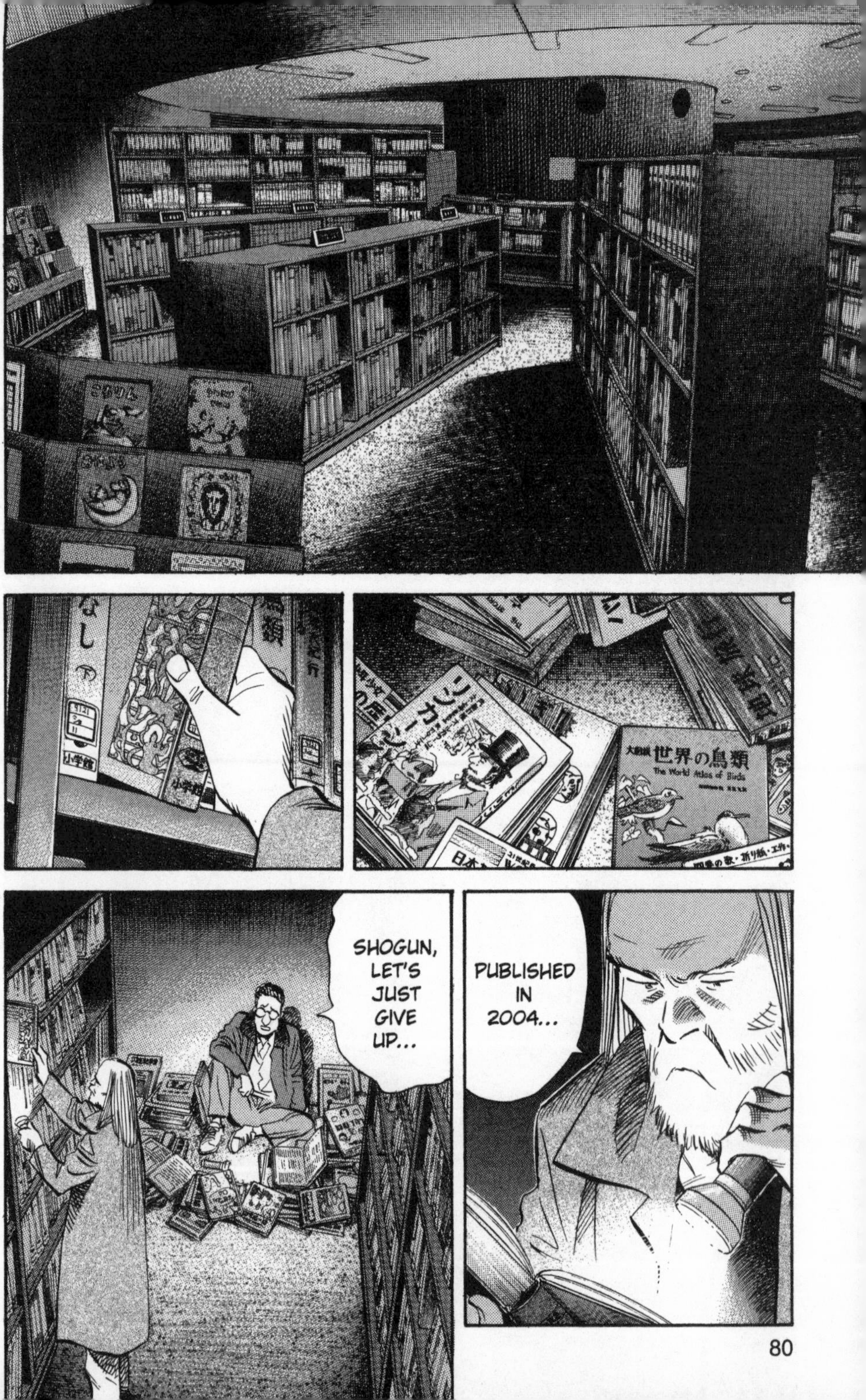
世界の鳥類
The World Atlas of Birds
小学館
PUBLISHED IN 2004...
SHOGUN, LET'S JUST GIVE UP...

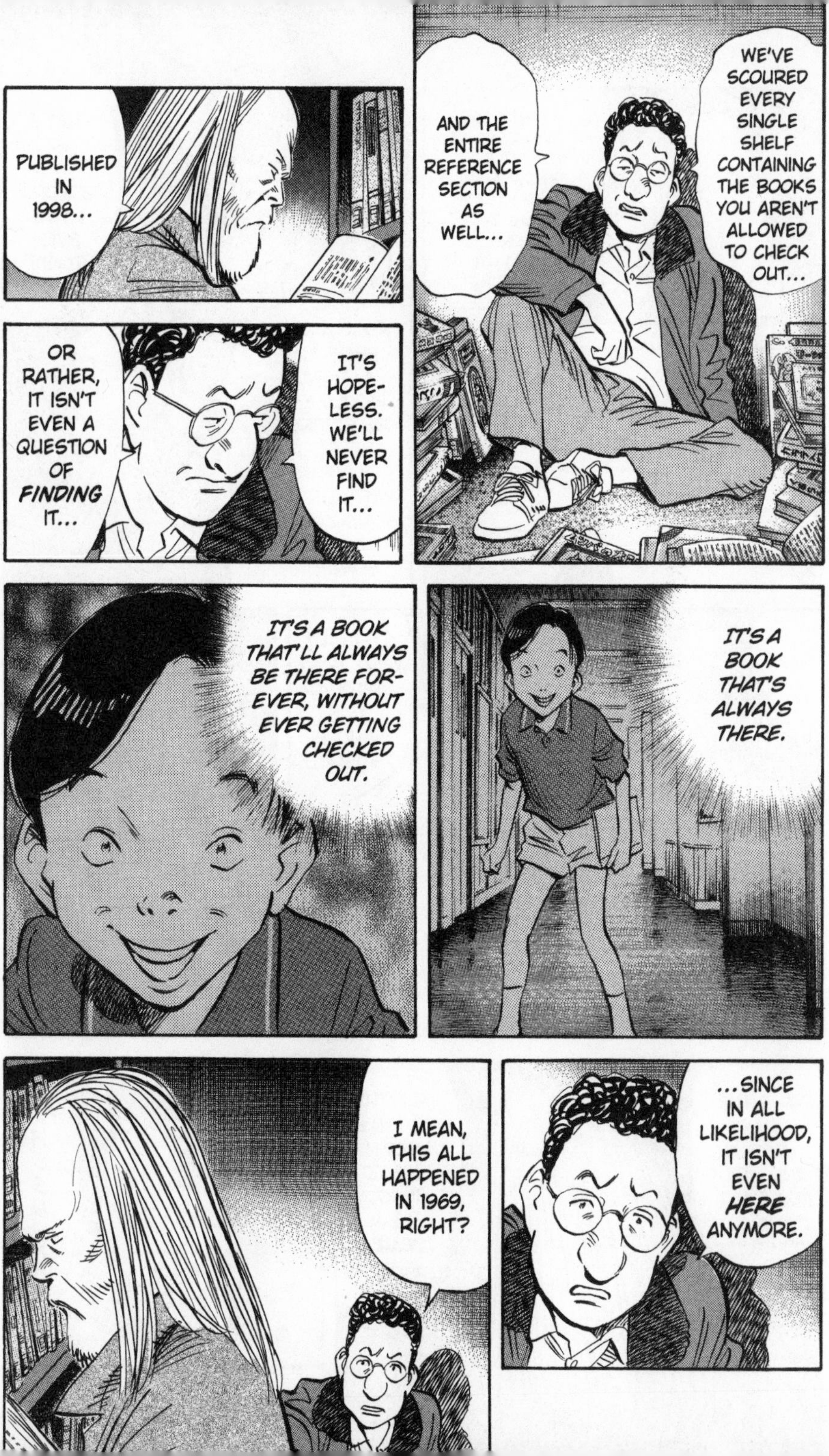
WE'VE SCOURED EVERY SINGLE SHELF CONTAINING THE BOOKS YOU AREN'T ALLOWED TO CHECK OUT...
AND THE ENTIRE REFERENCE SECTION AS WELL...
PUBLISHED IN 1998...
IT'S HOPE-LESS. WE'LL NEVER FIND IT...
OR RATHER, IT ISN'T EVEN A QUESTION OF *FINDING* IT...
IT'S A BOOK THAT'S ALWAYS THERE.
IT'S A BOOK THAT'LL ALWAYS BE THERE FOR-EVER, WITHOUT EVER GETTING CHECKED OUT.
...SINCE IN ALL LIKELIHOOD, IT ISN'T EVEN *HERE* ANYMORE.
I MEAN, THIS ALL HAPPENED IN 1969, RIGHT?

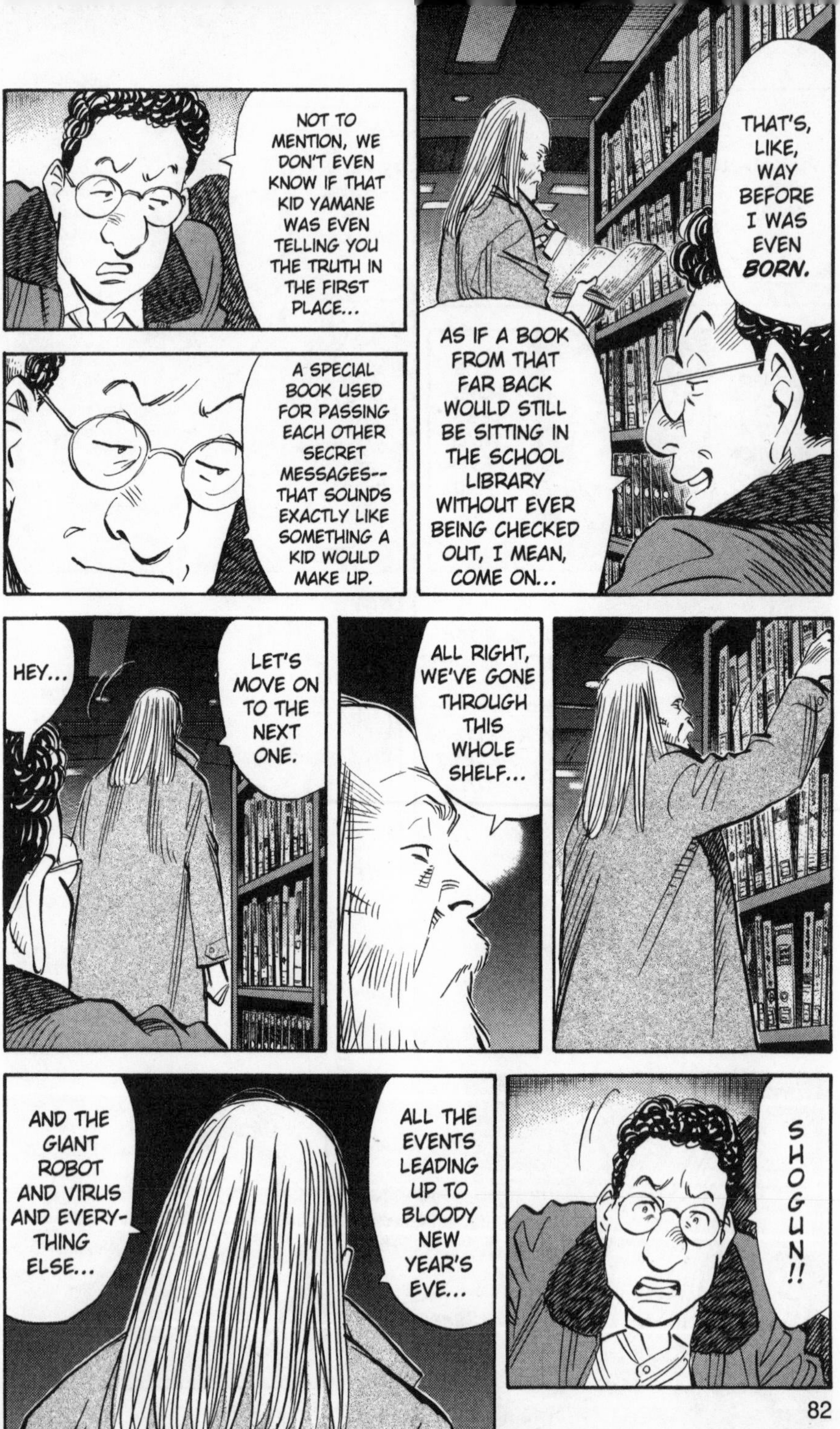

THAT'S, LIKE, WAY BEFORE I WAS EVEN ***BORN.***
AS IF A BOOK FROM THAT FAR BACK WOULD STILL BE SITTING IN THE SCHOOL LIBRARY WITHOUT EVER BEING CHECKED OUT, I MEAN, COME ON...
NOT TO MENTION, WE DON'T EVEN KNOW IF THAT KID YAMANE WAS EVEN TELLING YOU THE TRUTH IN THE FIRST PLACE...
A SPECIAL BOOK USED FOR PASSING EACH OTHER SECRET MESSAGES-- THAT SOUNDS EXACTLY LIKE SOMETHING A KID WOULD MAKE UP.
ALL RIGHT, WE'VE GONE THROUGH THIS WHOLE SHELF...
LET'S MOVE ON TO THE NEXT ONE.
HEY...
SHOGUN!!
ALL THE EVENTS LEADING UP TO BLOODY NEW YEAR'S EVE...
AND THE GIANT ROBOT AND VIRUS AND EVERYTHING ELSE...

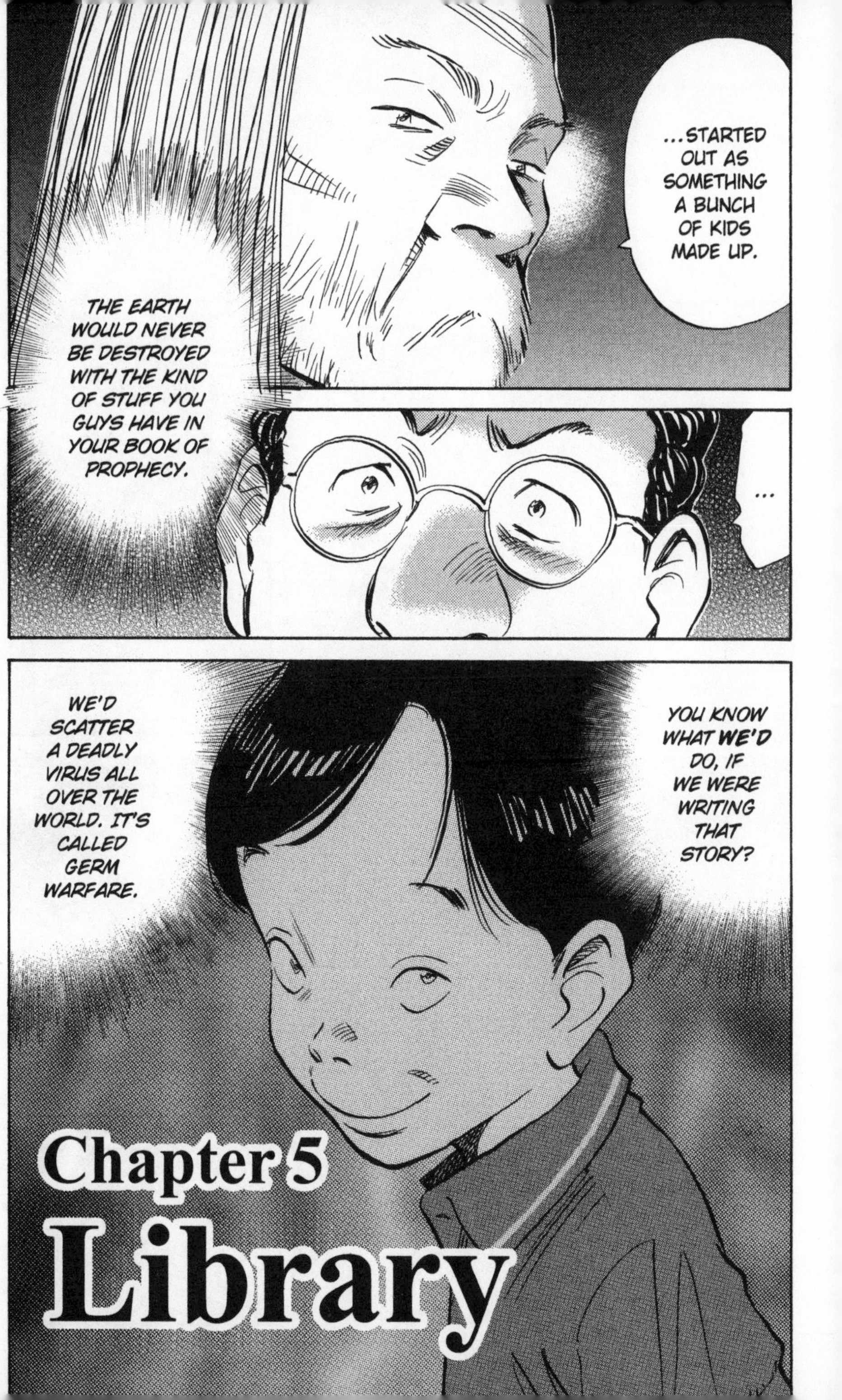
...STARTED OUT AS SOMETHING A BUNCH OF KIDS MADE UP.
THE EARTH WOULD NEVER BE DESTROYED WITH THE KIND OF STUFF YOU GUYS HAVE IN YOUR BOOK OF PROPHECY.
...
YOU KNOW WHAT **WE'D** DO, IF WE WERE WRITING THAT STORY?
WE'D SCATTER A DEADLY VIRUS ALL OVER THE WORLD. IT'S CALLED GERM WARFARE.
Chapter 5
Library

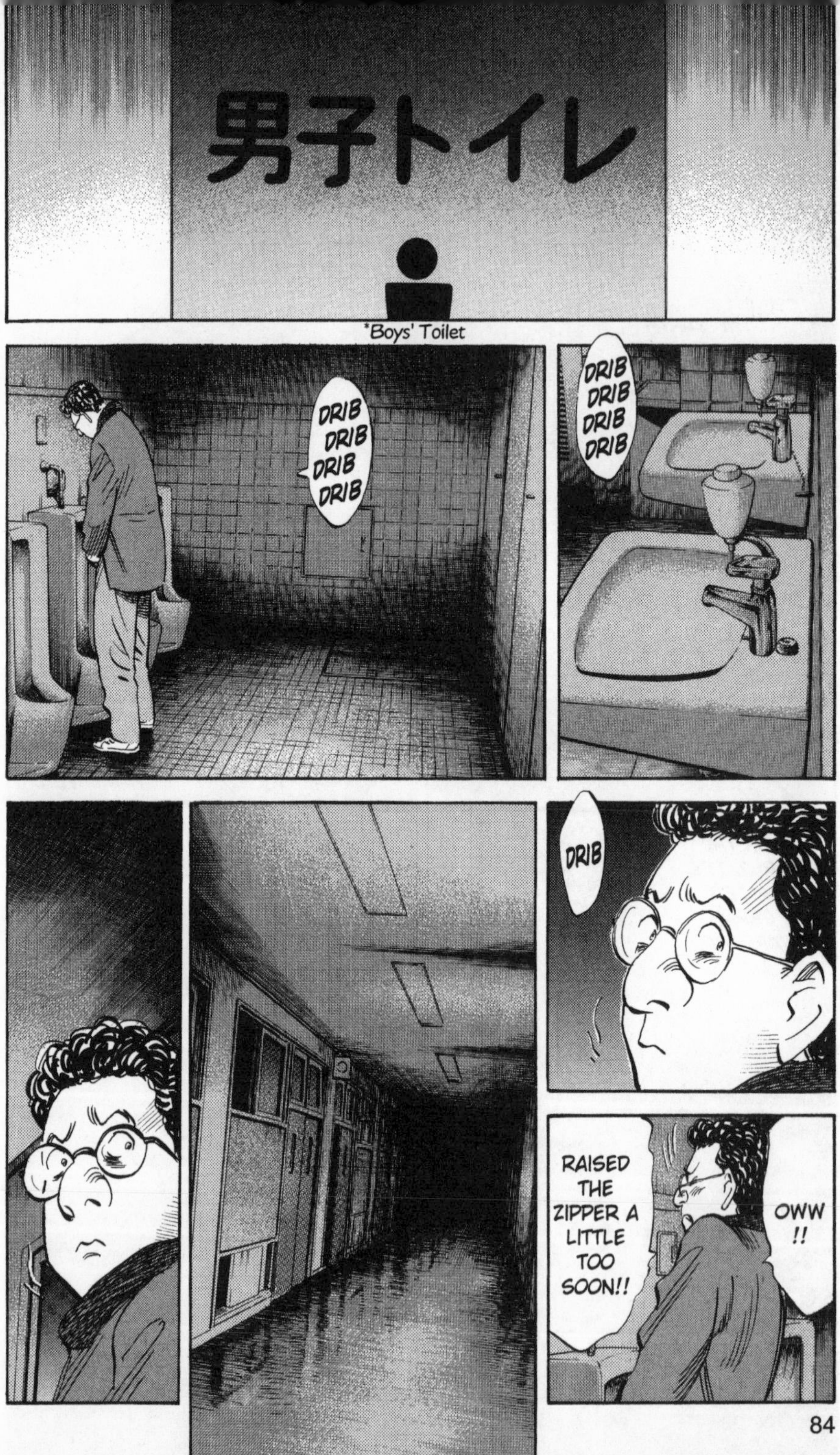
男子トイレ
*Boys' Toilet
DRIB DRIB DRIB DRIB
DRIB DRIB DRIB DRIB
DRIB
OWW!!
RAISED THE ZIPPER A LITTLE TOO SOON!!

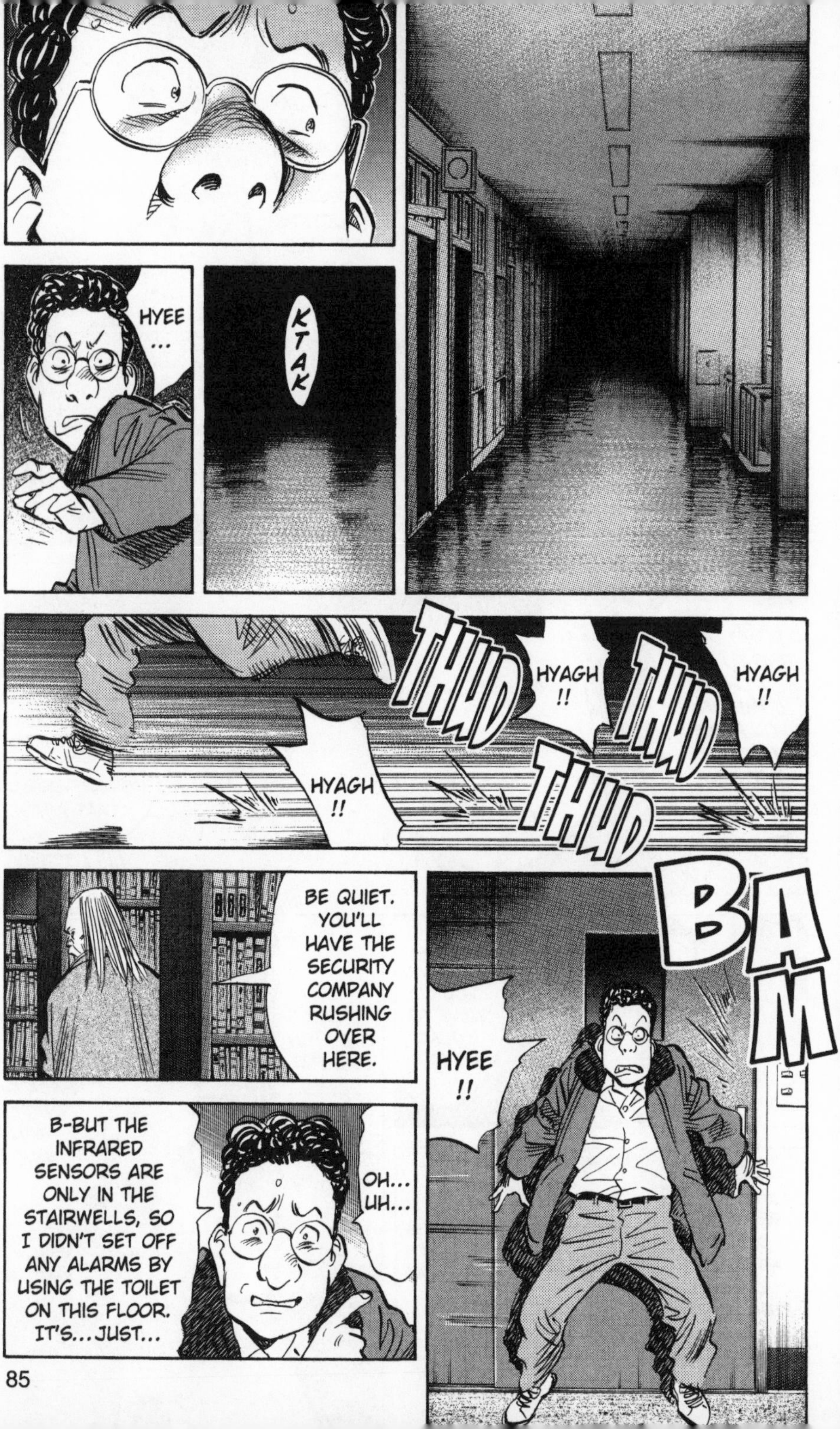
KTAK
HYEE ...
HYAGH !!
THUD
THUD
HYAGH !!
THUD
HYAGH !!
BAM
HYEE !!
BE QUIET. YOU'LL HAVE THE SECURITY COMPANY RUSHING OVER HERE.
OH... UH...
B-BUT THE INFRARED SENSORS ARE ONLY IN THE STAIRWELLS, SO I DIDN'T SET OFF ANY ALARMS BY USING THE TOILET ON THIS FLOOR. IT'S...JUST...

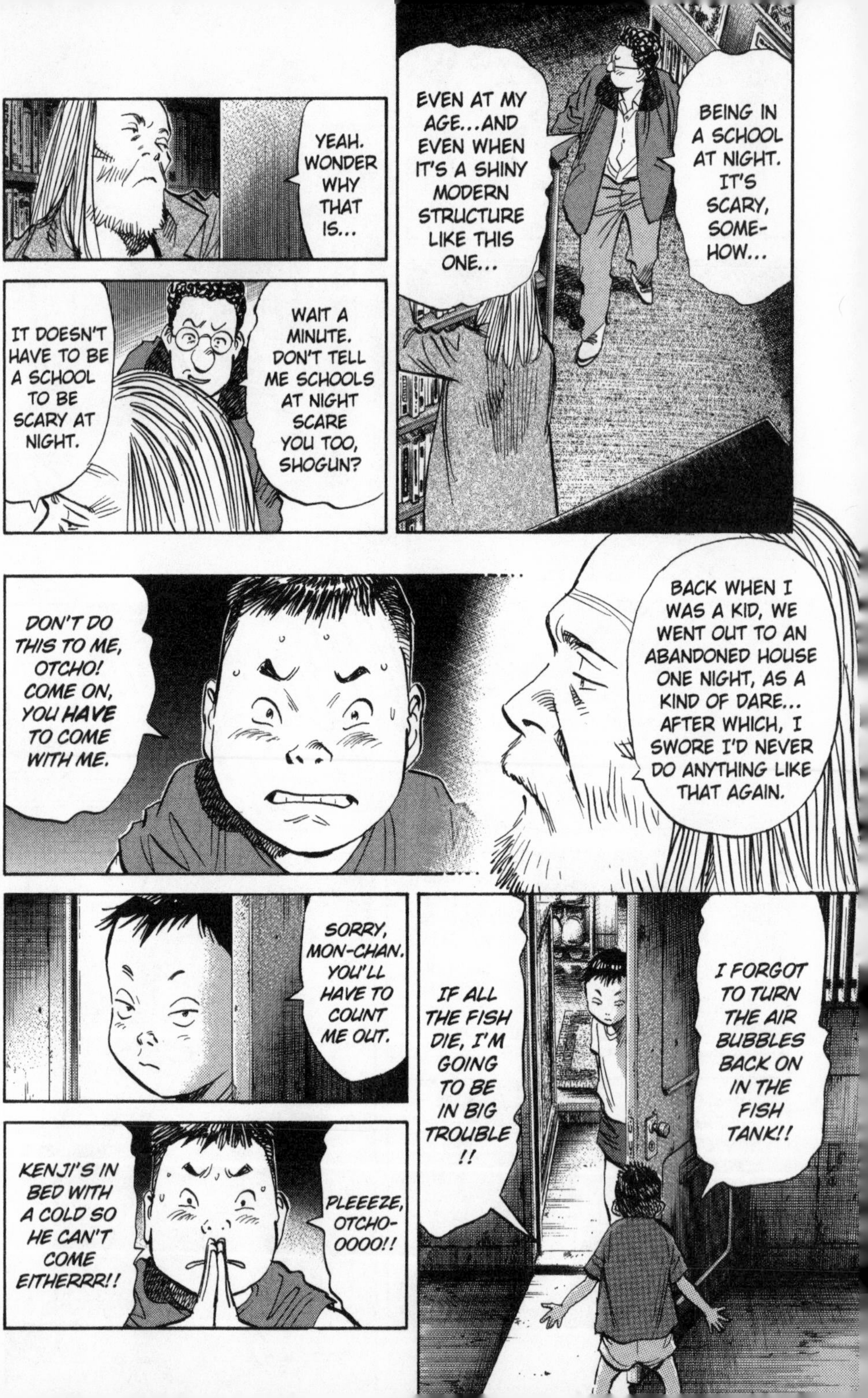
BEING IN A SCHOOL AT NIGHT. IT'S SCARY, SOME-HOW...
EVEN AT MY AGE...AND EVEN WHEN IT'S A SHINY MODERN STRUCTURE LIKE THIS ONE...
YEAH. WONDER WHY THAT IS...
WAIT A MINUTE. DON'T TELL ME SCHOOLS AT NIGHT SCARE YOU TOO, SHOGUN?
IT DOESN'T HAVE TO BE A SCHOOL TO BE SCARY AT NIGHT.
BACK WHEN I WAS A KID, WE WENT OUT TO AN ABANDONED HOUSE ONE NIGHT, AS A KIND OF DARE... AFTER WHICH, I SWORE I'D NEVER DO ANYTHING LIKE THAT AGAIN.
*DON'T DO THIS TO ME, OTCHO! COME ON, YOU **HAVE** TO COME WITH ME.*
I FORGOT TO TURN THE AIR BUBBLES BACK ON IN THE FISH TANK!!
IF ALL THE FISH DIE, I'M GOING TO BE IN BIG TROUBLE!!
SORRY, MON-CHAN. YOU'LL HAVE TO COUNT ME OUT.
PLEEEZE, OTCHO-OOOO!!
KENJI'S IN BED WITH A COLD SO HE CAN'T COME EITHERRR!!

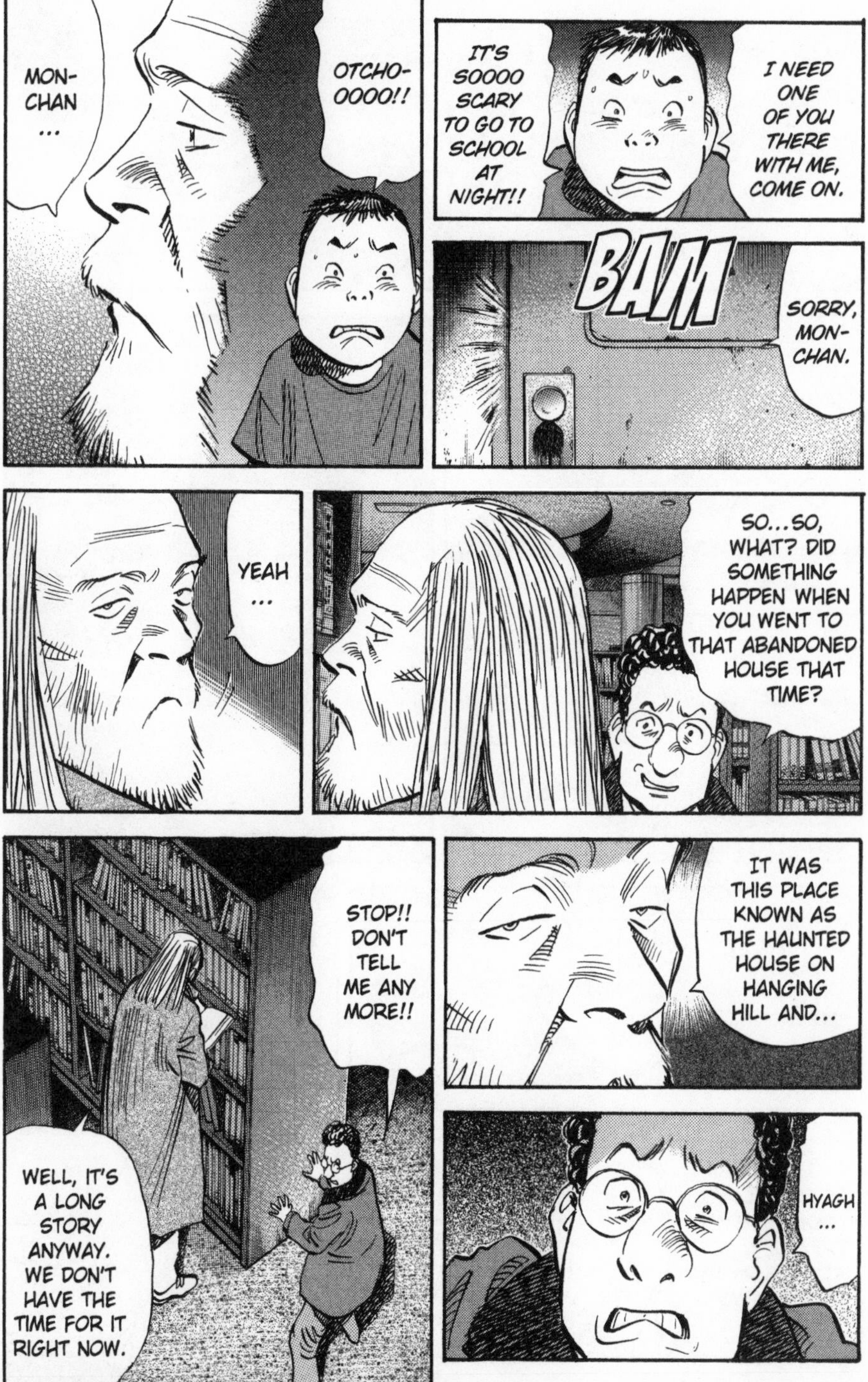
I NEED ONE OF YOU THERE WITH ME, COME ON.
IT'S SOOOO SCARY TO GO TO SCHOOL AT NIGHT!!
BAM
SORRY, MON-CHAN.
OTCHO-OOOO!!
MON-CHAN ...
SO...SO, WHAT? DID SOMETHING HAPPEN WHEN YOU WENT TO THAT ABANDONED HOUSE THAT TIME?
YEAH ...
IT WAS THIS PLACE KNOWN AS THE HAUNTED HOUSE ON HANGING HILL AND...
HYAGH ...
STOP!! DON'T TELL ME ANY MORE!!
WELL, IT'S A LONG STORY ANYWAY. WE DON'T HAVE THE TIME FOR IT RIGHT NOW.

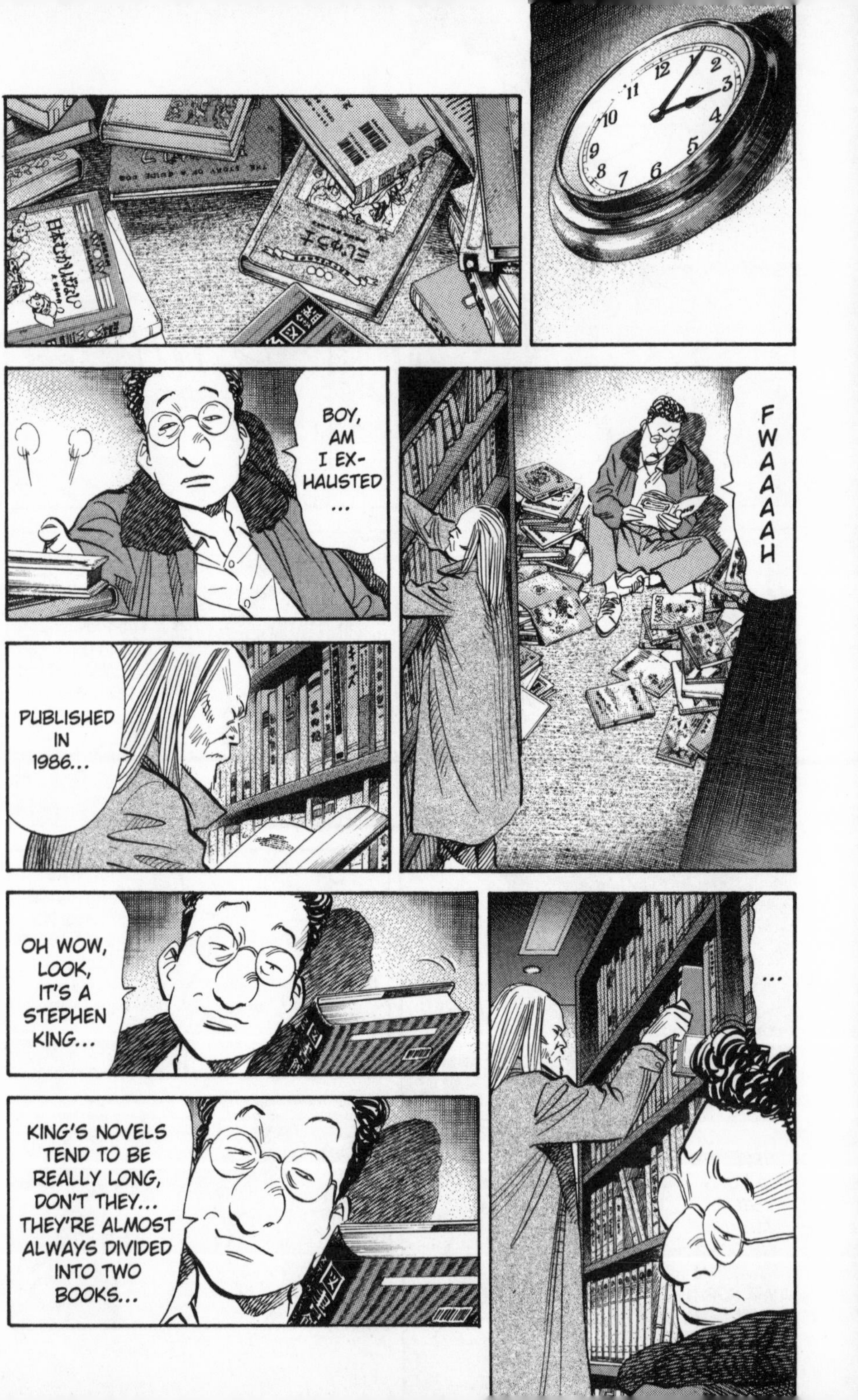
FWAAAAH
BOY, AM I EX-HAUSTED ...
PUBLISHED IN 1986...
...
OH WOW, LOOK, IT'S A STEPHEN KING...
KING'S NOVELS TEND TO BE REALLY LONG, DON'T THEY... THEY'RE ALMOST ALWAYS DIVIDED INTO TWO BOOKS...

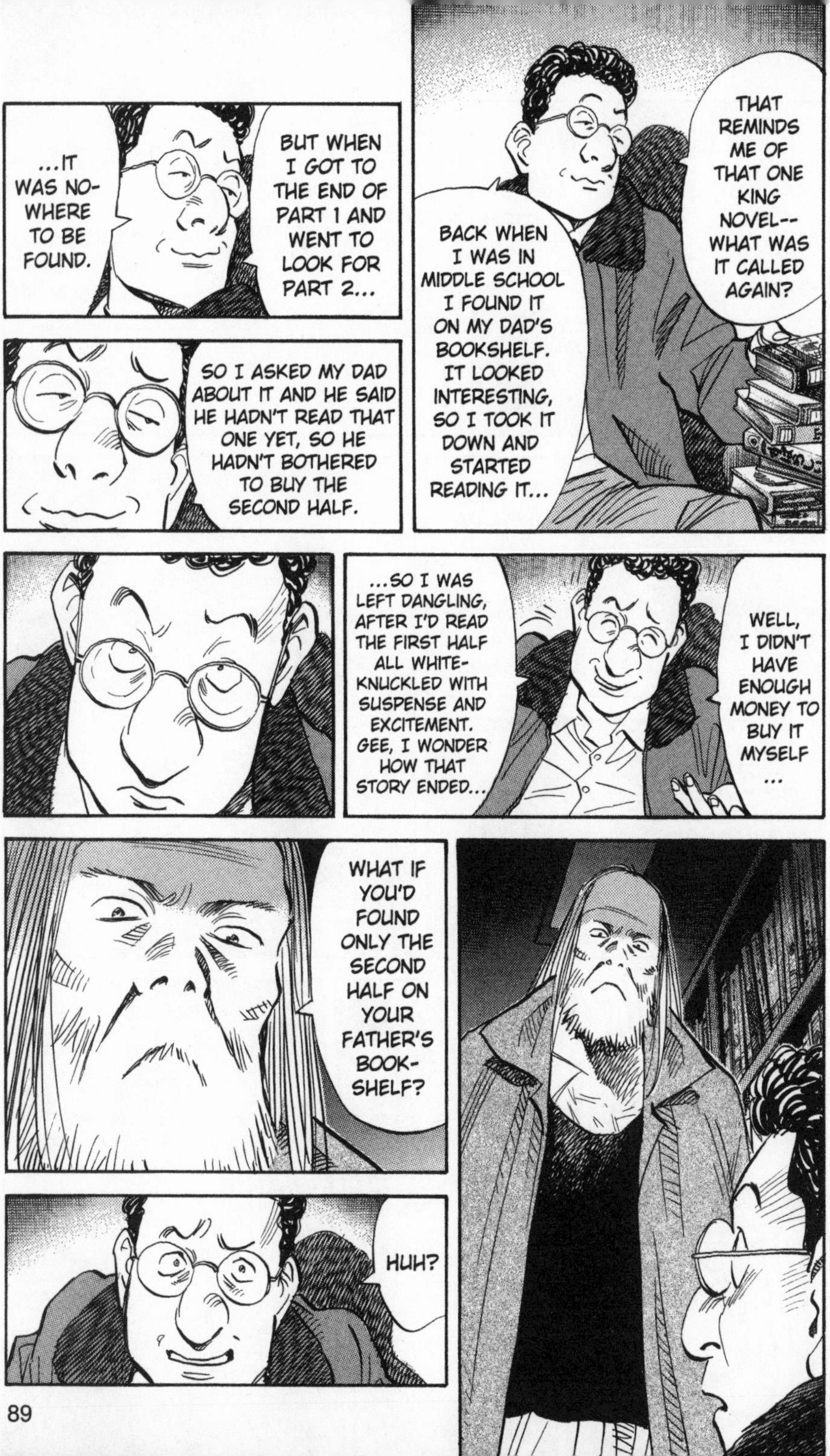
THAT REMINDS ME OF THAT ONE KING NOVEL--WHAT WAS IT CALLED AGAIN?
BACK WHEN I WAS IN MIDDLE SCHOOL I FOUND IT ON MY DAD'S BOOKSHELF. IT LOOKED INTERESTING, SO I TOOK IT DOWN AND STARTED READING IT...
BUT WHEN I GOT TO THE END OF PART 1 AND WENT TO LOOK FOR PART 2...
...IT WAS NOWHERE TO BE FOUND.
SO I ASKED MY DAD ABOUT IT AND HE SAID HE HADN'T READ THAT ONE YET, SO HE HADN'T BOTHERED TO BUY THE SECOND HALF.
WELL, I DIDN'T HAVE ENOUGH MONEY TO BUY IT MYSELF ...
...SO I WAS LEFT DANGLING, AFTER I'D READ THE FIRST HALF ALL WHITE-KNUCKLED WITH SUSPENSE AND EXCITEMENT. GEE, I WONDER HOW THAT STORY ENDED...
WHAT IF YOU'D FOUND ONLY THE SECOND HALF ON YOUR FATHER'S BOOKSHELF?
HUH?

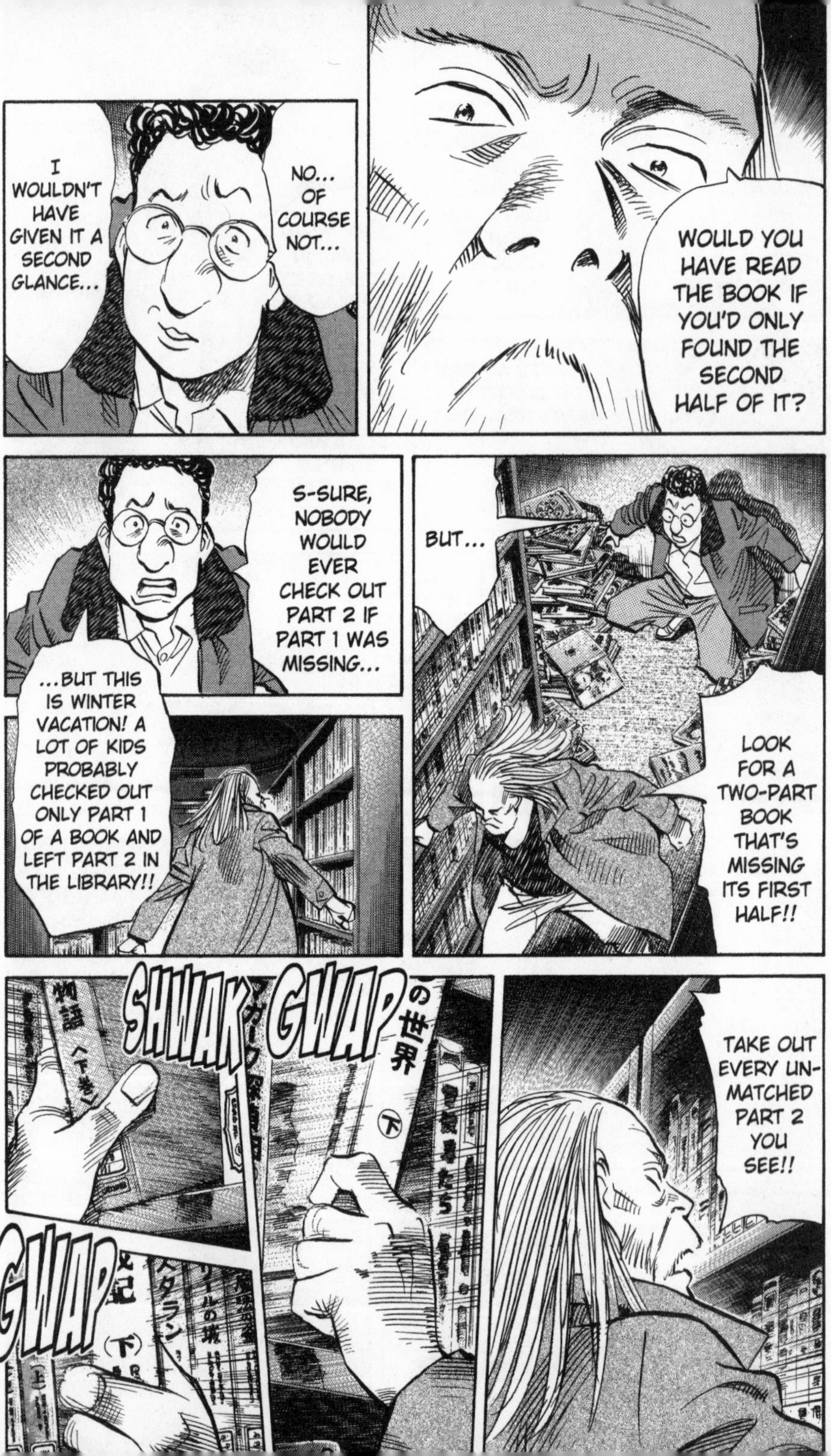
WOULD YOU HAVE READ THE BOOK IF YOU'D ONLY FOUND THE SECOND HALF OF IT?
NO... OF COURSE NOT...
I WOULDN'T HAVE GIVEN IT A SECOND GLANCE...
BUT...
LOOK FOR A TWO-PART BOOK THAT'S MISSING ITS FIRST HALF!!
S-SURE, NOBODY WOULD EVER CHECK OUT PART 2 IF PART 1 WAS MISSING...
...BUT THIS IS WINTER VACATION! A LOT OF KIDS PROBABLY CHECKED OUT ONLY PART 1 OF A BOOK AND LEFT PART 2 IN THE LIBRARY!!
TAKE OUT EVERY UN-MATCHED PART 2 YOU SEE!!
GWAP
SHWAK
GWAP

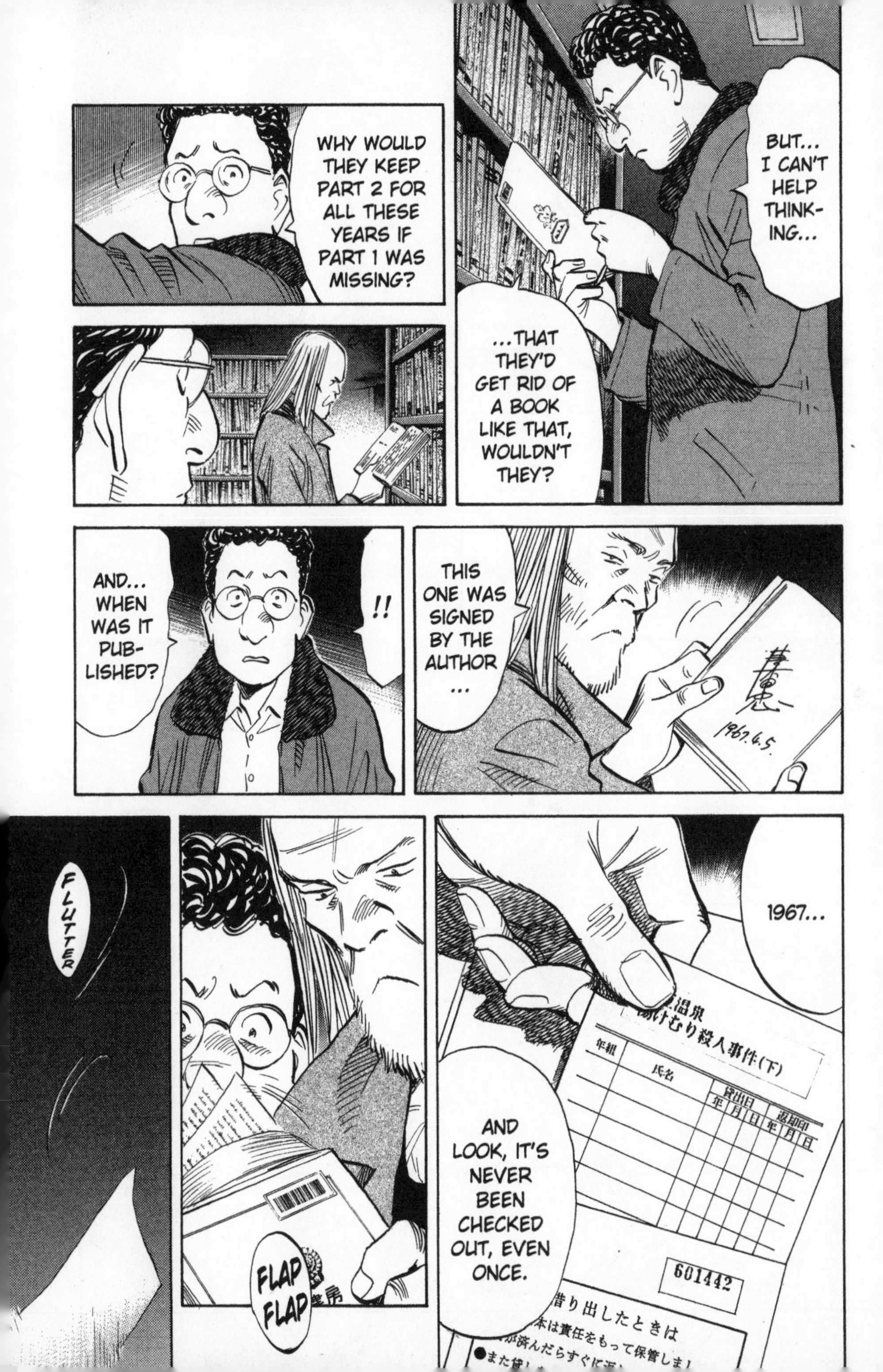
BUT... I CAN'T HELP THINKING...
...THAT THEY'D GET RID OF A BOOK LIKE THAT, WOULDN'T THEY?
WHY WOULD THEY KEEP PART 2 FOR ALL THESE YEARS IF PART 1 WAS MISSING?
THIS ONE WAS SIGNED BY THE AUTHOR ...
1967.4.5.
!!
AND... WHEN WAS IT PUBLISHED?
1967...
けむり殺人事件(下)
年組
氏名
貸出日
返却日
年 月 日
601442
借り出したときは
本は責任をもって保管しま
AND LOOK, IT'S NEVER BEEN CHECKED OUT, EVEN ONCE.
FLAP FLAP
FLUTTER

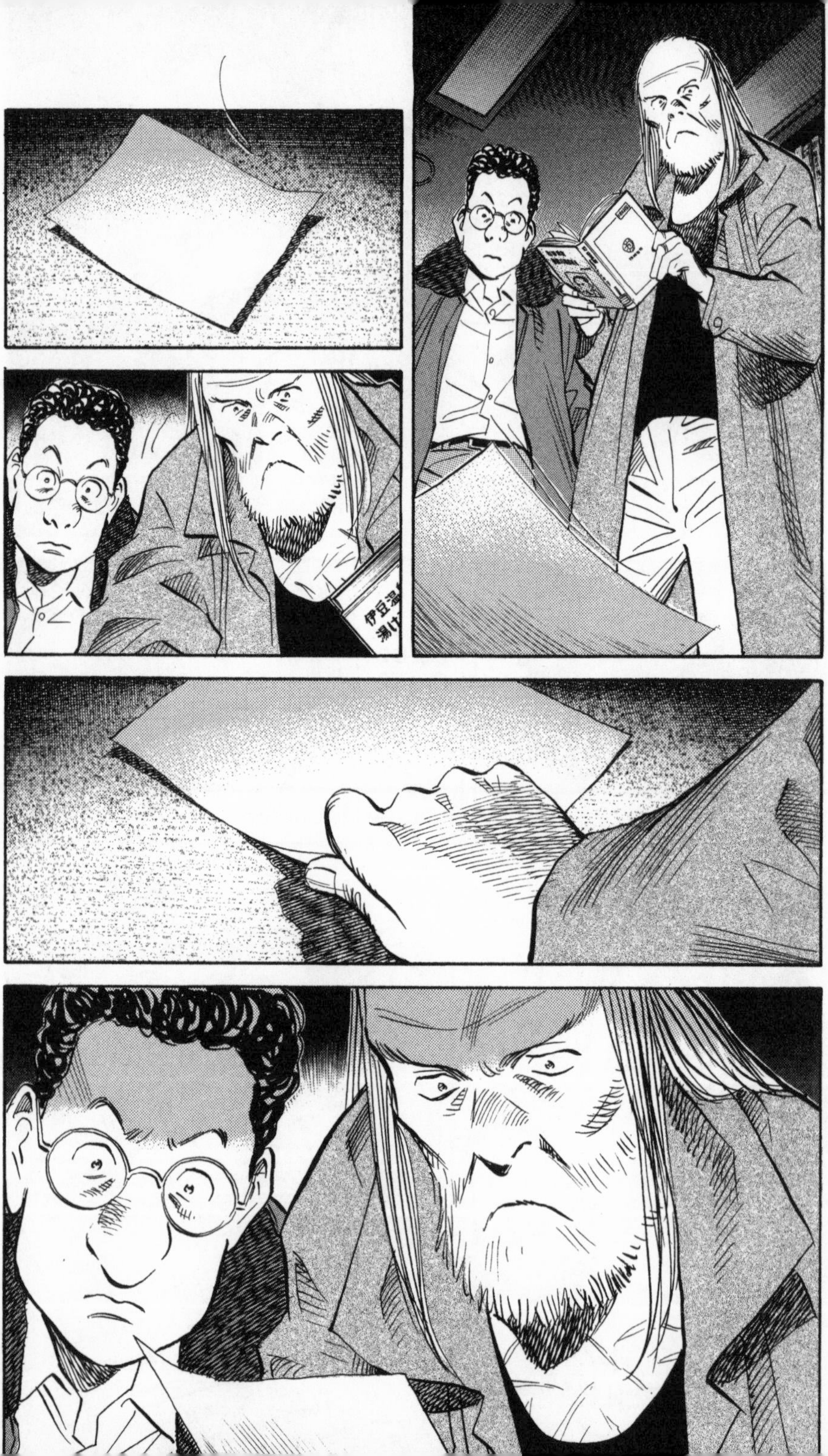
伊豆温
湯け

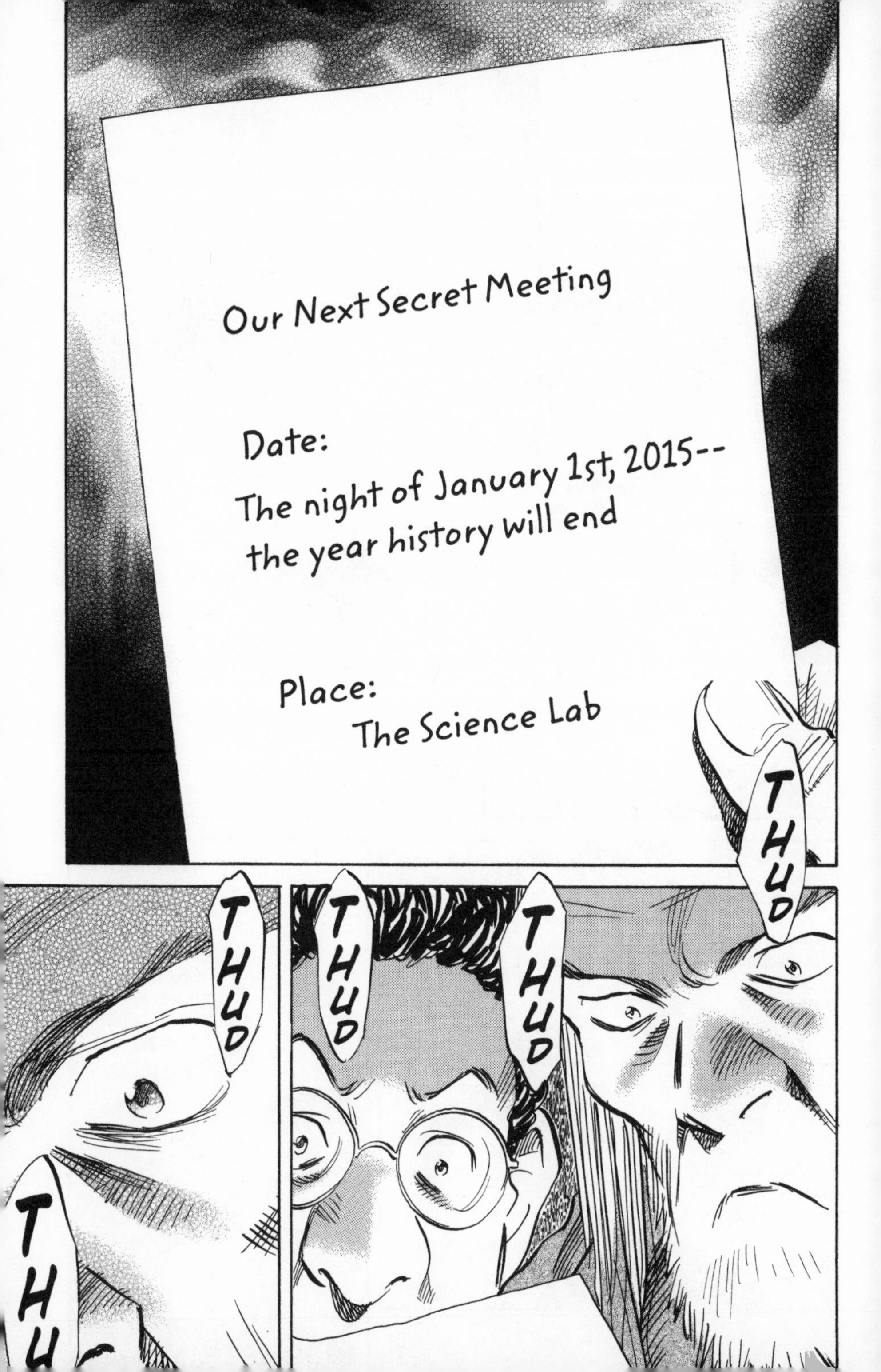
Our Next Secret Meeting
Date:
The night of January 1st, 2015--
the year history will end
Place:
The Science Lab
THUD
THUD
THUD
THUD
THU

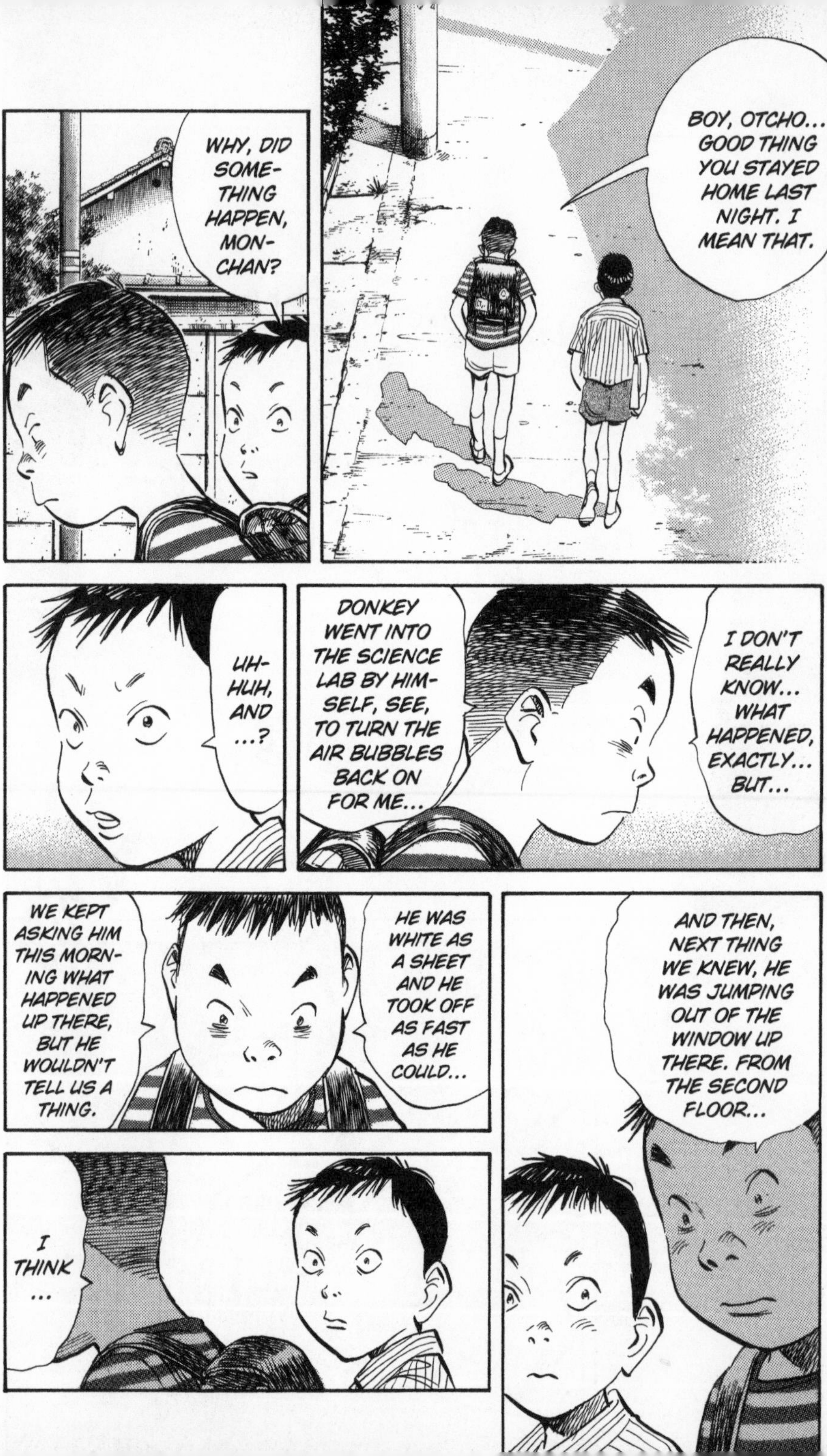
BOY, OTCHO... GOOD THING YOU STAYED HOME LAST NIGHT. I MEAN THAT.
WHY, DID SOME-THING HAPPEN, MON-CHAN?
I DON'T REALLY KNOW... WHAT HAPPENED, EXACTLY... BUT...
DONKEY WENT INTO THE SCIENCE LAB BY HIM-SELF, SEE, TO TURN THE AIR BUBBLES BACK ON FOR ME...
UH-HUH, AND ...?
AND THEN, NEXT THING WE KNEW, HE WAS JUMPING OUT OF THE WINDOW UP THERE. FROM THE SECOND FLOOR...
HE WAS WHITE AS A SHEET AND HE TOOK OFF AS FAST AS HE COULD...
WE KEPT ASKING HIM THIS MORN-ING WHAT HAPPENED UP THERE, BUT HE WOULDN'T TELL US A THING.
I THINK ...

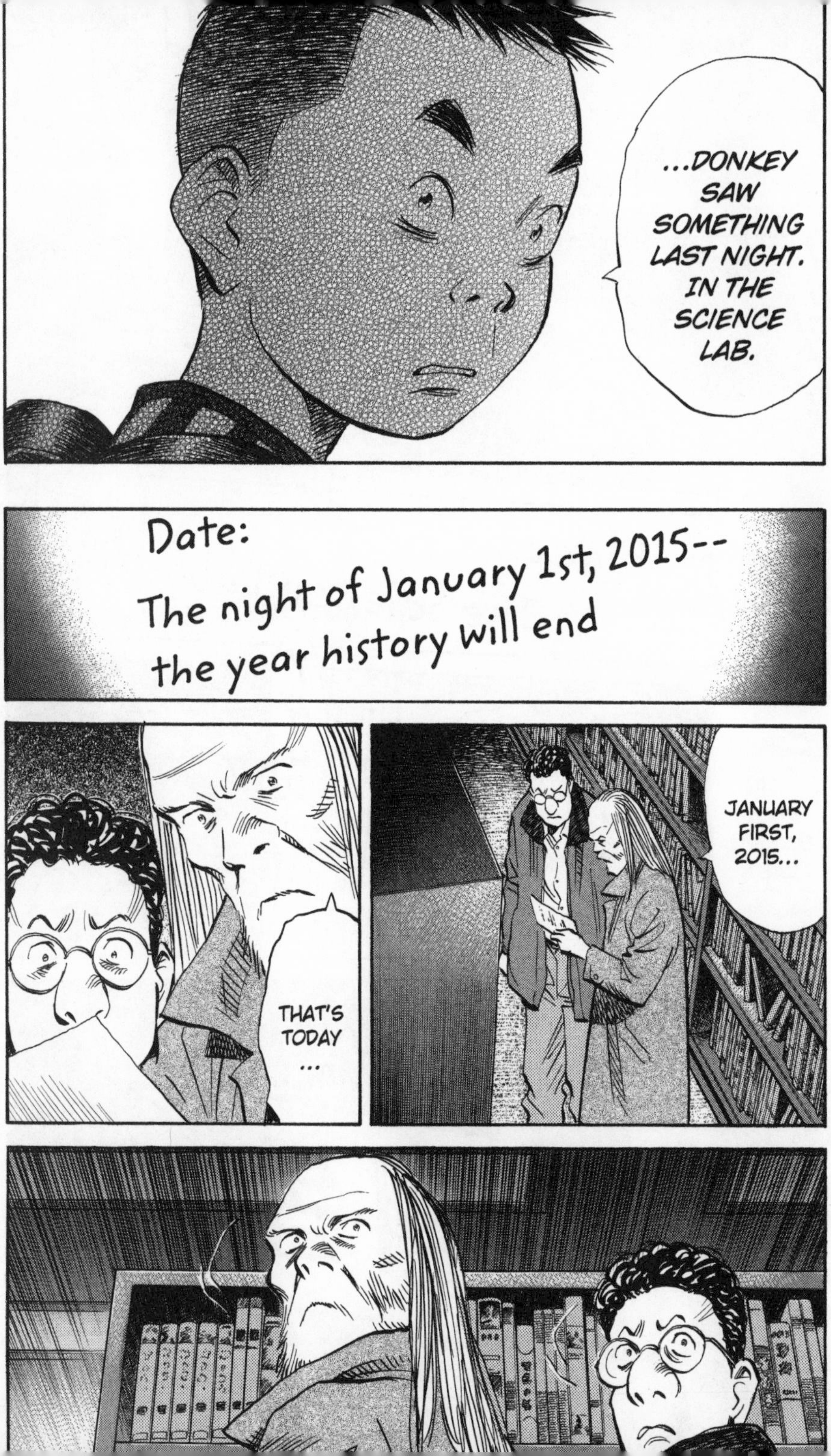
...DONKEY SAW SOMETHING LAST NIGHT. IN THE SCIENCE LAB.
Date:
The night of January 1st, 2015--
the year history will end
JANUARY FIRST, 2015...
THAT'S TODAY ...

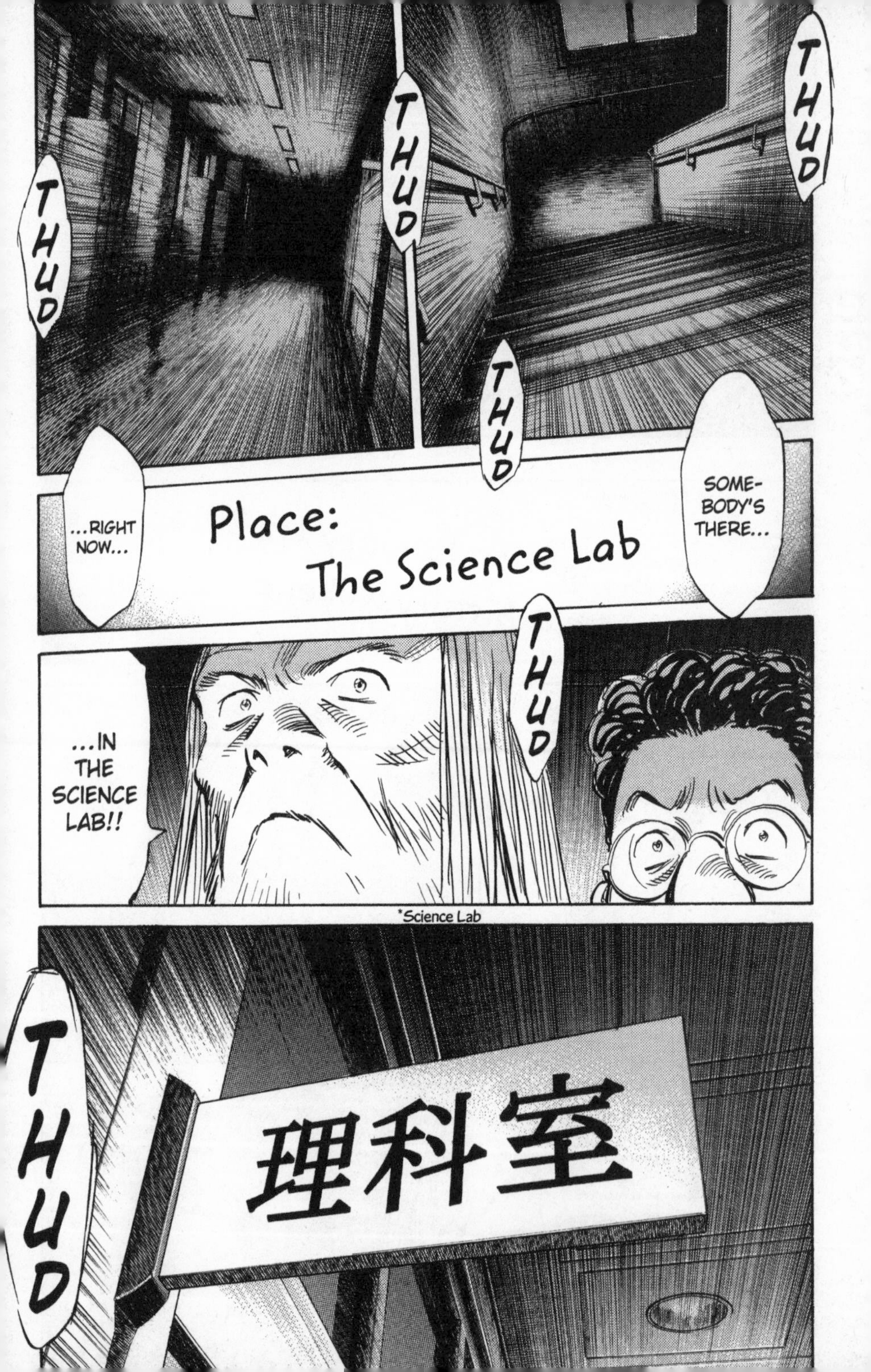
THUD
THUD
THUD
THUD
SOME-BODY'S THERE...
Place: The Science Lab
...RIGHT NOW...
THUD
...IN THE SCIENCE LAB!!
*Science Lab
理科室
THUD

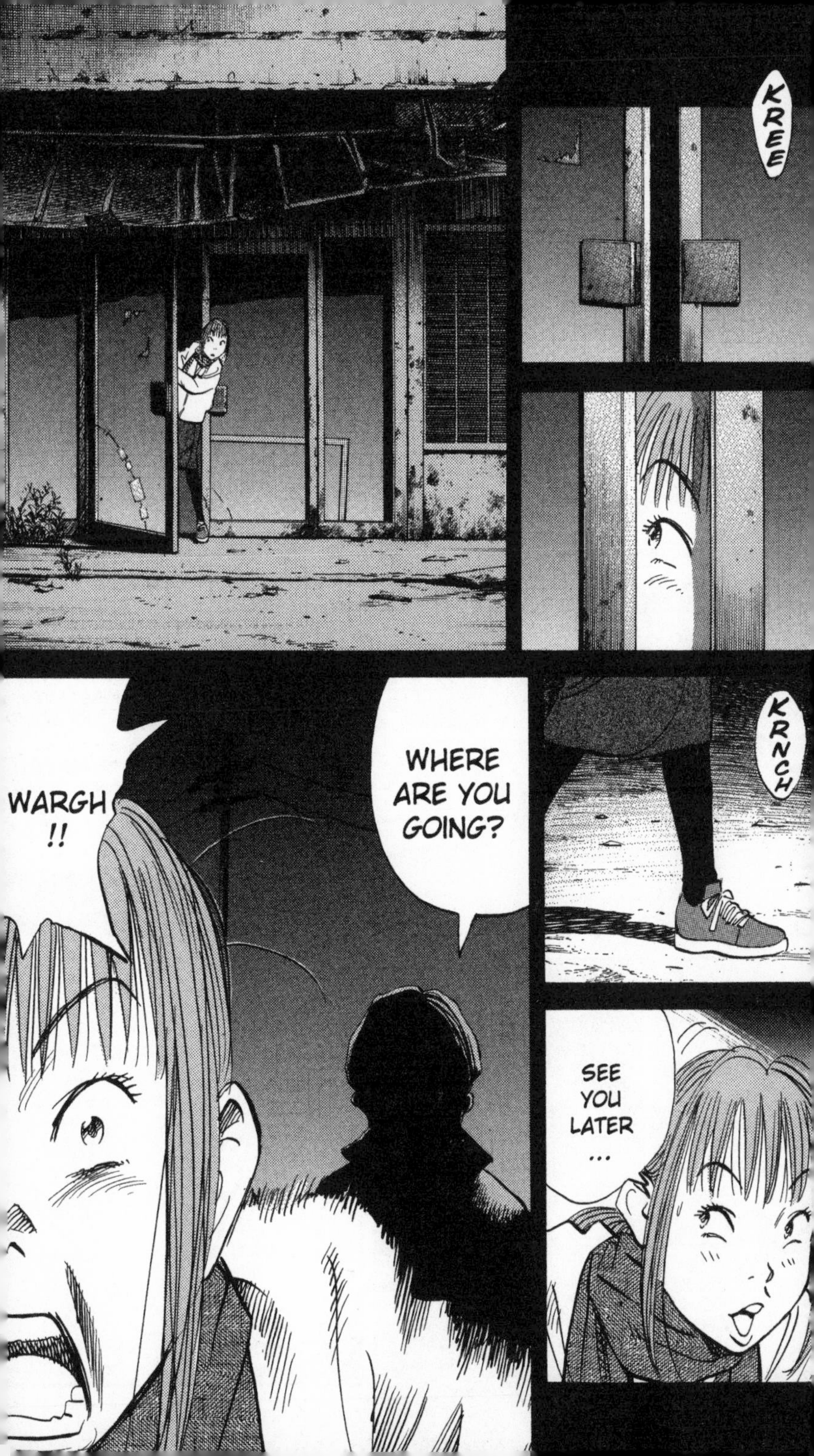
KREE
KRNCH
SEE YOU LATER ...
WHERE ARE YOU GOING?
WARGH !!

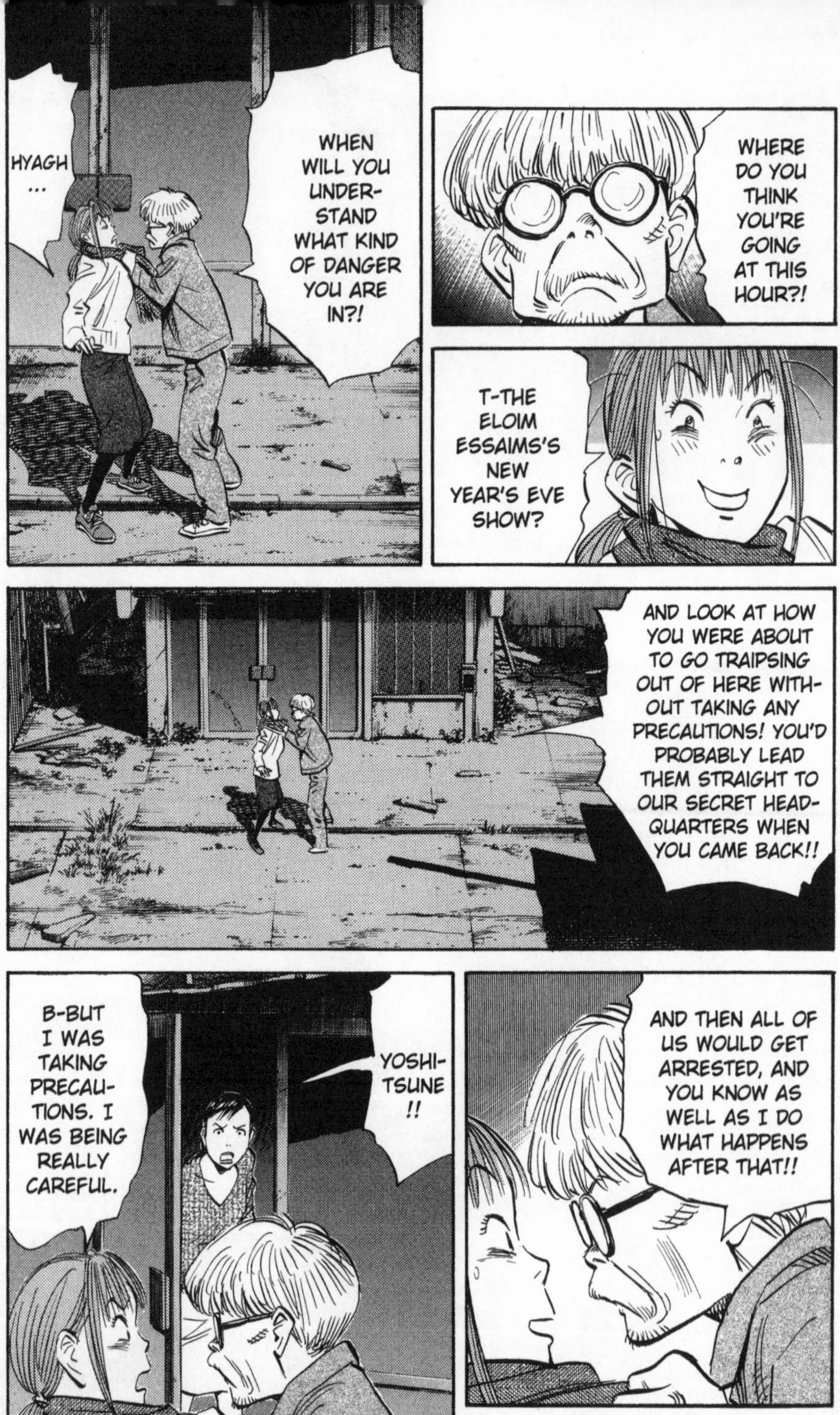
WHERE DO YOU THINK YOU'RE GOING AT THIS HOUR?!
T-THE ELOIM ESSAIMS'S NEW YEAR'S EVE SHOW?
WHEN WILL YOU UNDER-STAND WHAT KIND OF DANGER YOU ARE IN?!
HYAGH ...
AND LOOK AT HOW YOU WERE ABOUT TO GO TRAIPSING OUT OF HERE WITH-OUT TAKING ANY PRECAUTIONS! YOU'D PROBABLY LEAD THEM STRAIGHT TO OUR SECRET HEAD-QUARTERS WHEN YOU CAME BACK!!
AND THEN ALL OF US WOULD GET ARRESTED, AND YOU KNOW AS WELL AS I DO WHAT HAPPENS AFTER THAT!!
B-BUT I WAS TAKING PRECAU-TIONS. I WAS BEING REALLY CAREFUL.
YOSHI-TSUNE !!

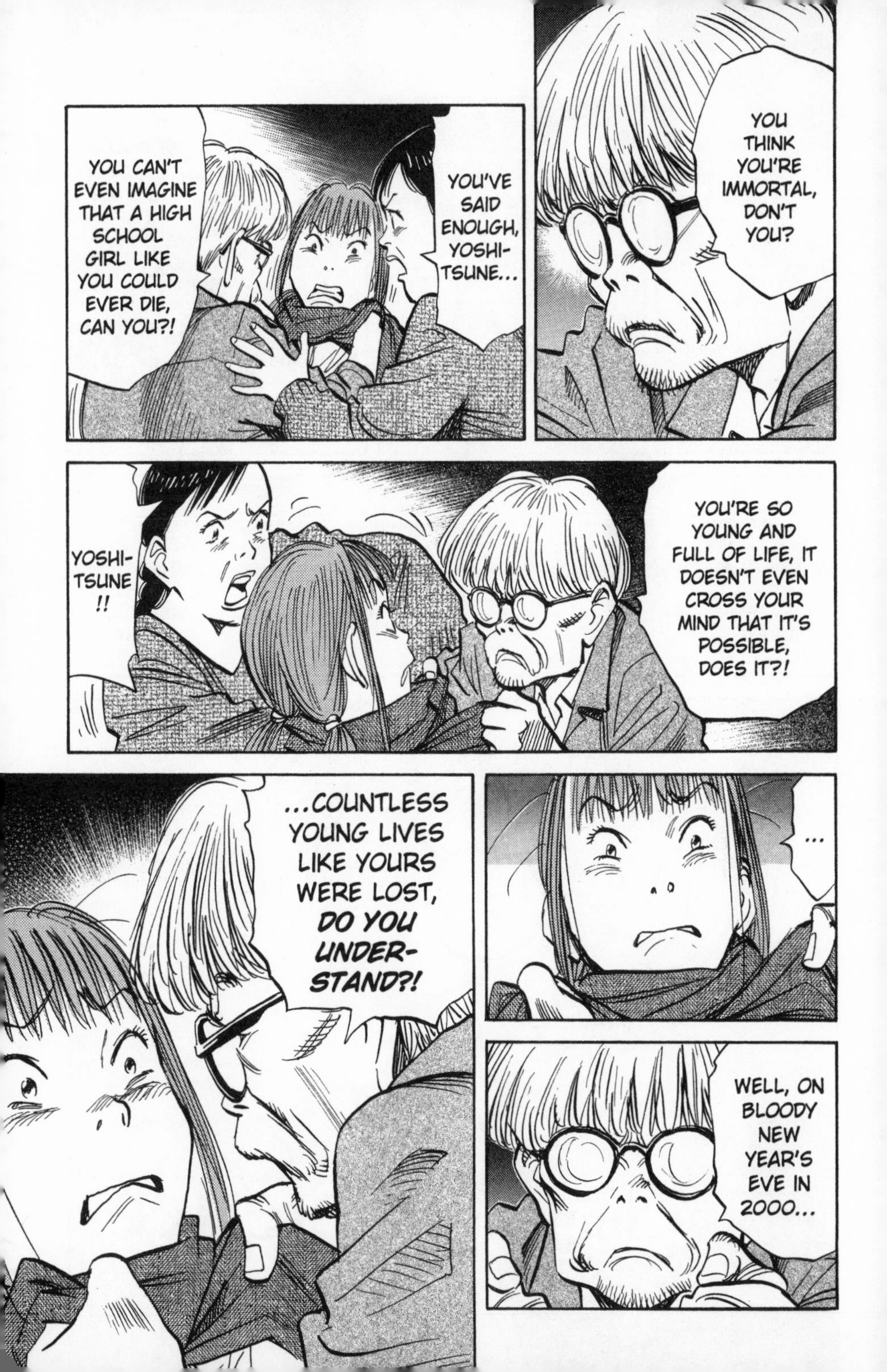
YOU THINK YOU'RE IMMORTAL, DON'T YOU?
YOU'VE SAID ENOUGH, YOSHI-TSUNE...
YOU CAN'T EVEN IMAGINE THAT A HIGH SCHOOL GIRL LIKE YOU COULD EVER DIE, CAN YOU?!
YOU'RE SO YOUNG AND FULL OF LIFE, IT DOESN'T EVEN CROSS YOUR MIND THAT IT'S POSSIBLE, DOES IT?!
YOSHI-TSUNE !!
...
WELL, ON BLOODY NEW YEAR'S EVE IN 2000...
...COUNTLESS YOUNG LIVES LIKE YOURS WERE LOST, ***DO YOU UNDER-STAND?!***

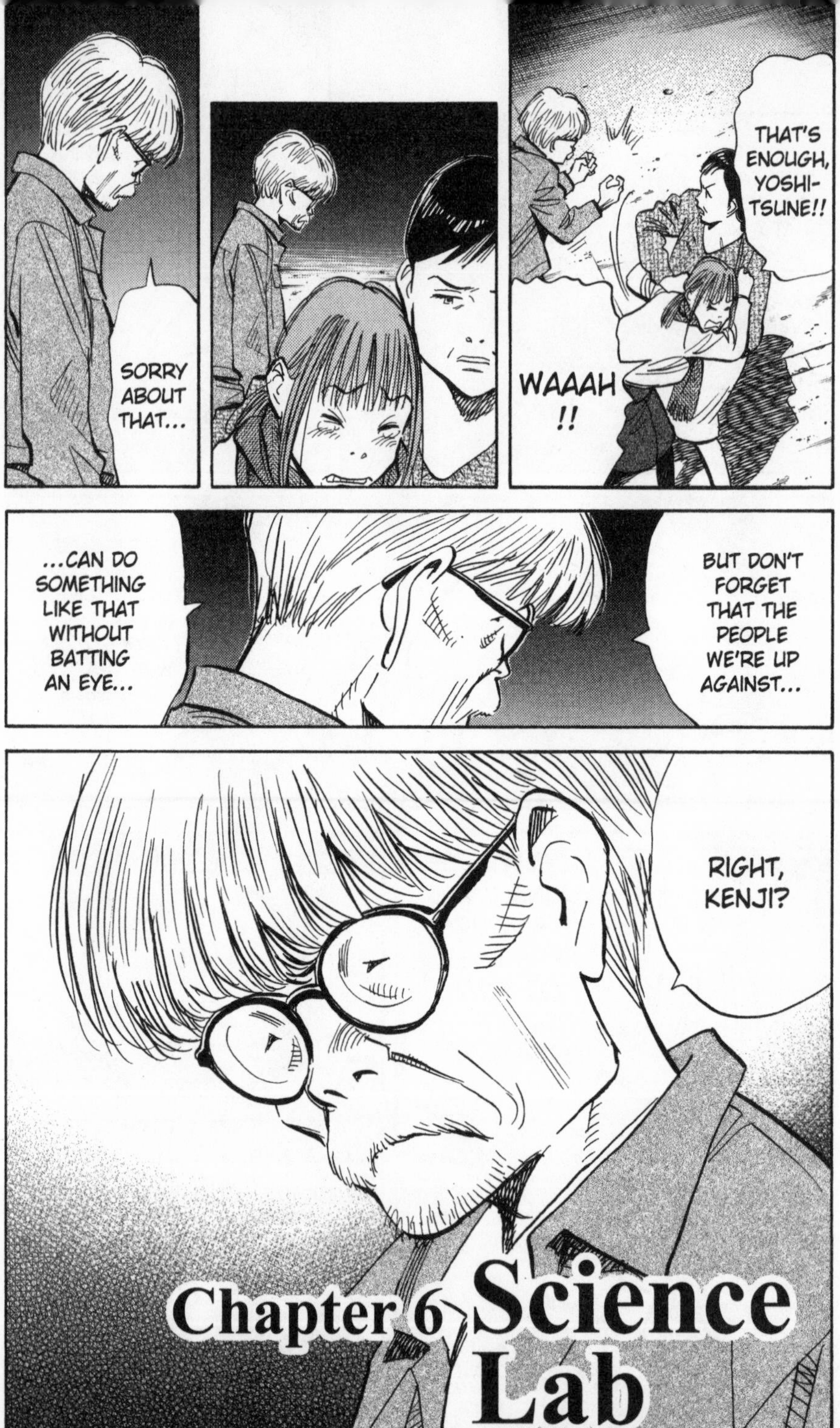
THAT'S ENOUGH, YOSHI-TSUNE!!
WAAAH !!
SORRY ABOUT THAT...
BUT DON'T FORGET THAT THE PEOPLE WE'RE UP AGAINST...
...CAN DO SOMETHING LIKE THAT WITHOUT BATTING AN EYE...
RIGHT, KENJI?

Chapter 6 Science Lab

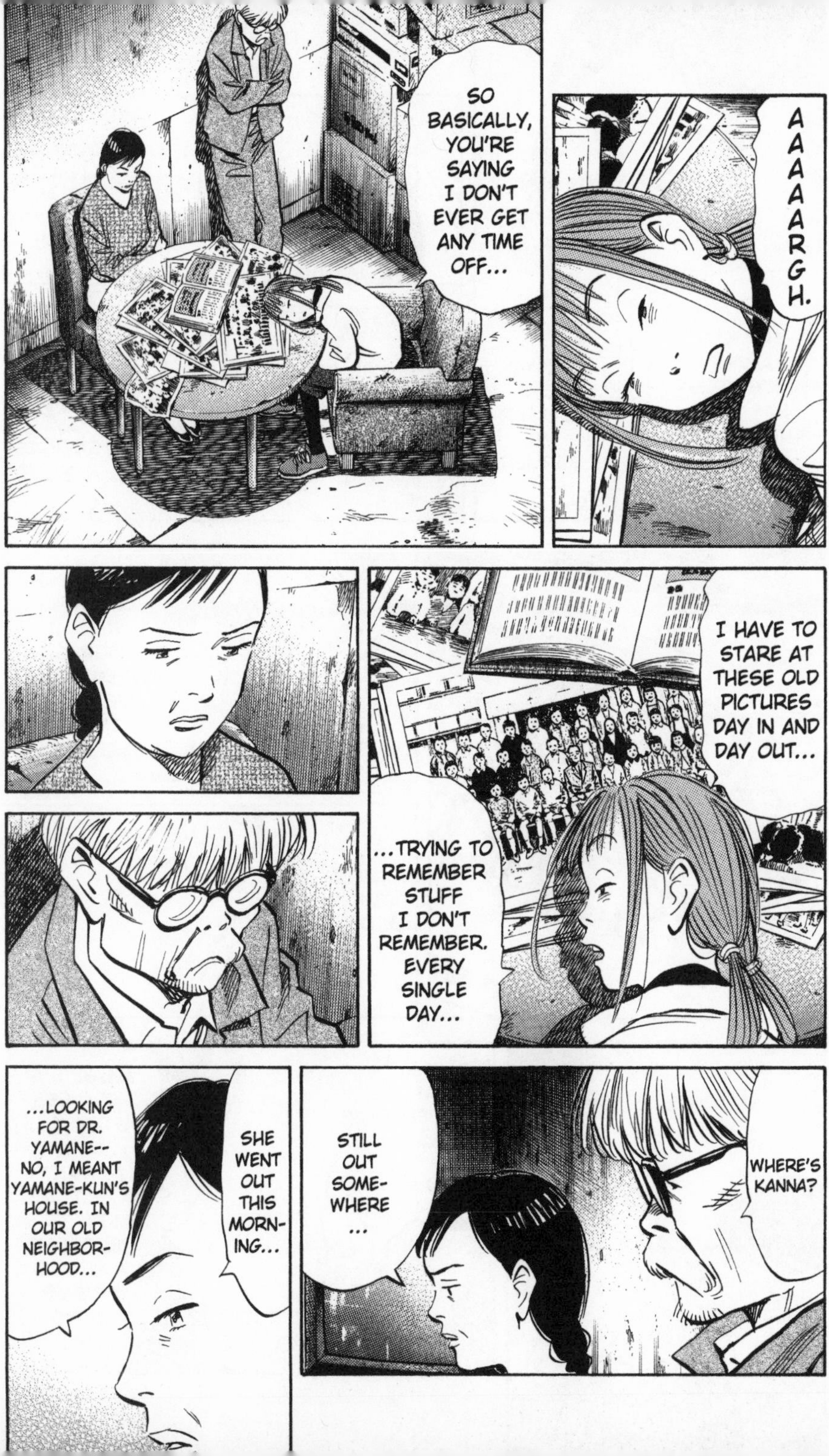
AAAAARGH.
SO BASICALLY, YOU'RE SAYING I DON'T EVER GET ANY TIME OFF...
I HAVE TO STARE AT THESE OLD PICTURES DAY IN AND DAY OUT...
...TRYING TO REMEMBER STUFF I DON'T REMEMBER. EVERY SINGLE DAY...
WHERE'S KANNA?
STILL OUT SOME-WHERE...
SHE WENT OUT THIS MORN-ING...
...LOOKING FOR DR. YAMANE-- NO, I MEANT YAMANE-KUN'S HOUSE. IN OUR OLD NEIGHBOR-HOOD...

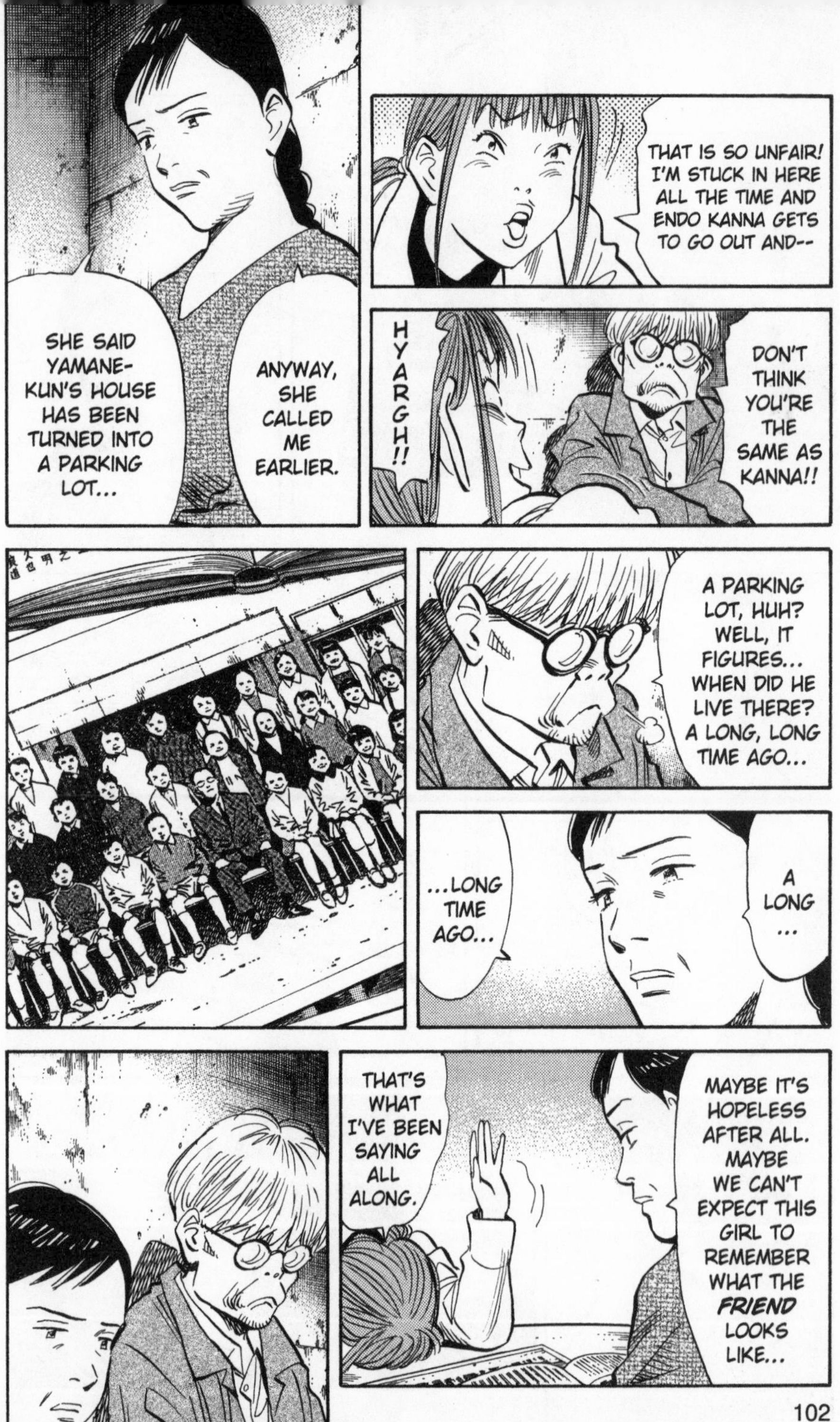
THAT IS SO UNFAIR! I'M STUCK IN HERE ALL THE TIME AND ENDO KANNA GETS TO GO OUT AND--
DON'T THINK YOU'RE THE SAME AS KANNA!!
HYARGH!!
ANYWAY, SHE CALLED ME EARLIER.
SHE SAID YAMANE-KUN'S HOUSE HAS BEEN TURNED INTO A PARKING LOT...
A PARKING LOT, HUH? WELL, IT FIGURES... WHEN DID HE LIVE THERE? A LONG, LONG TIME AGO...
A LONG ...
...LONG TIME AGO...
MAYBE IT'S HOPELESS AFTER ALL. MAYBE WE CAN'T EXPECT THIS GIRL TO REMEMBER WHAT THE FRIEND LOOKS LIKE...
THAT'S WHAT I'VE BEEN SAYING ALL ALONG.

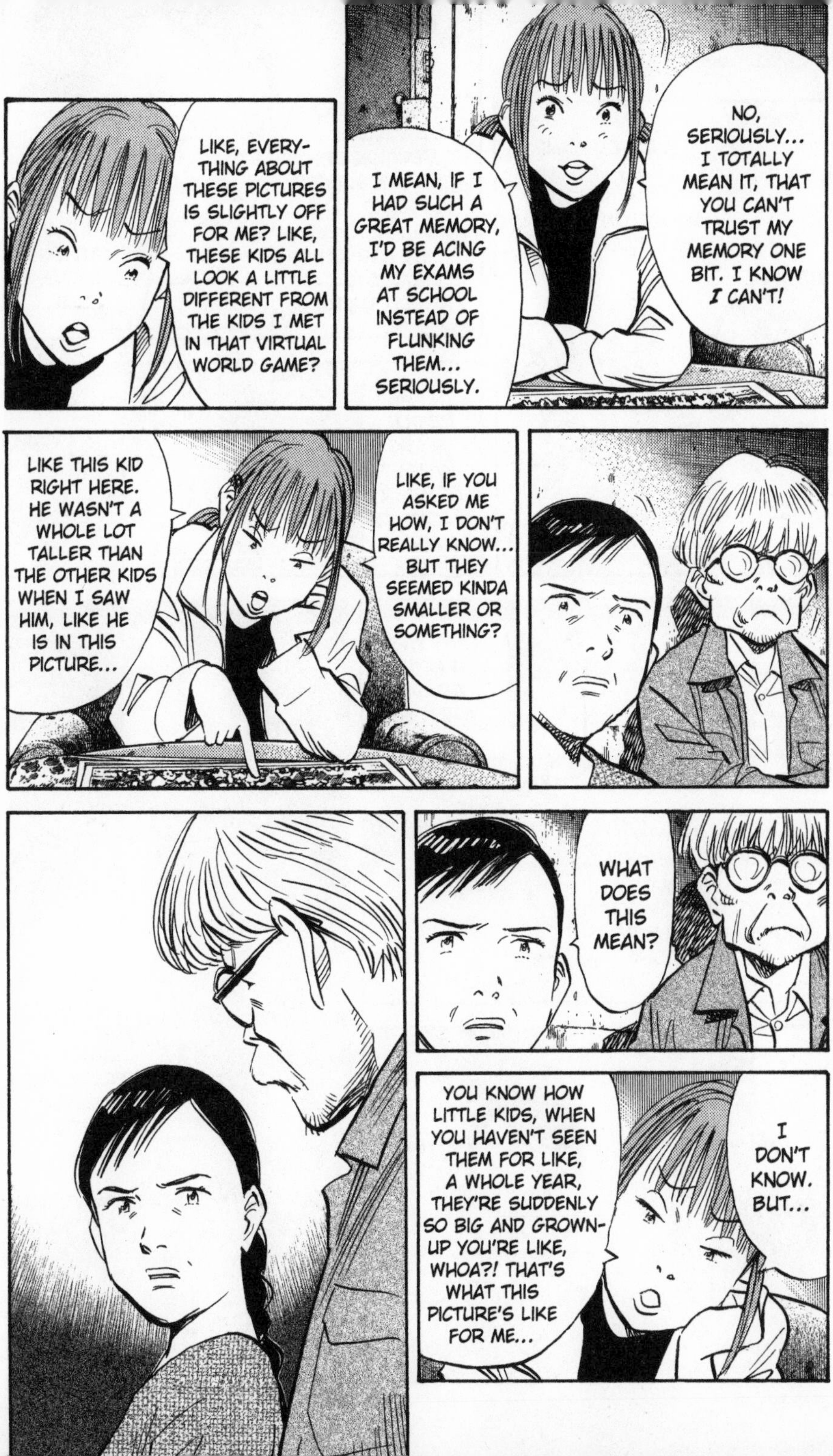
NO, SERIOUSLY... I TOTALLY MEAN IT, THAT YOU CAN'T TRUST MY MEMORY ONE BIT. I KNOW *I* CAN'T!
I MEAN, IF I HAD SUCH A GREAT MEMORY, I'D BE ACING MY EXAMS AT SCHOOL INSTEAD OF FLUNKING THEM... SERIOUSLY.
LIKE, EVERY-THING ABOUT THESE PICTURES IS SLIGHTLY OFF FOR ME? LIKE, THESE KIDS ALL LOOK A LITTLE DIFFERENT FROM THE KIDS I MET IN THAT VIRTUAL WORLD GAME?
LIKE, IF YOU ASKED ME HOW, I DON'T REALLY KNOW... BUT THEY SEEMED KINDA SMALLER OR SOMETHING?
LIKE THIS KID RIGHT HERE. HE WASN'T A WHOLE LOT TALLER THAN THE OTHER KIDS WHEN I SAW HIM, LIKE HE IS IN THIS PICTURE...
WHAT DOES THIS MEAN?
I DON'T KNOW. BUT...
YOU KNOW HOW LITTLE KIDS, WHEN YOU HAVEN'T SEEN THEM FOR LIKE, A WHOLE YEAR, THEY'RE SUDDENLY SO BIG AND GROWN-UP YOU'RE LIKE, WHOA?! THAT'S WHAT THIS PICTURE'S LIKE FOR ME...

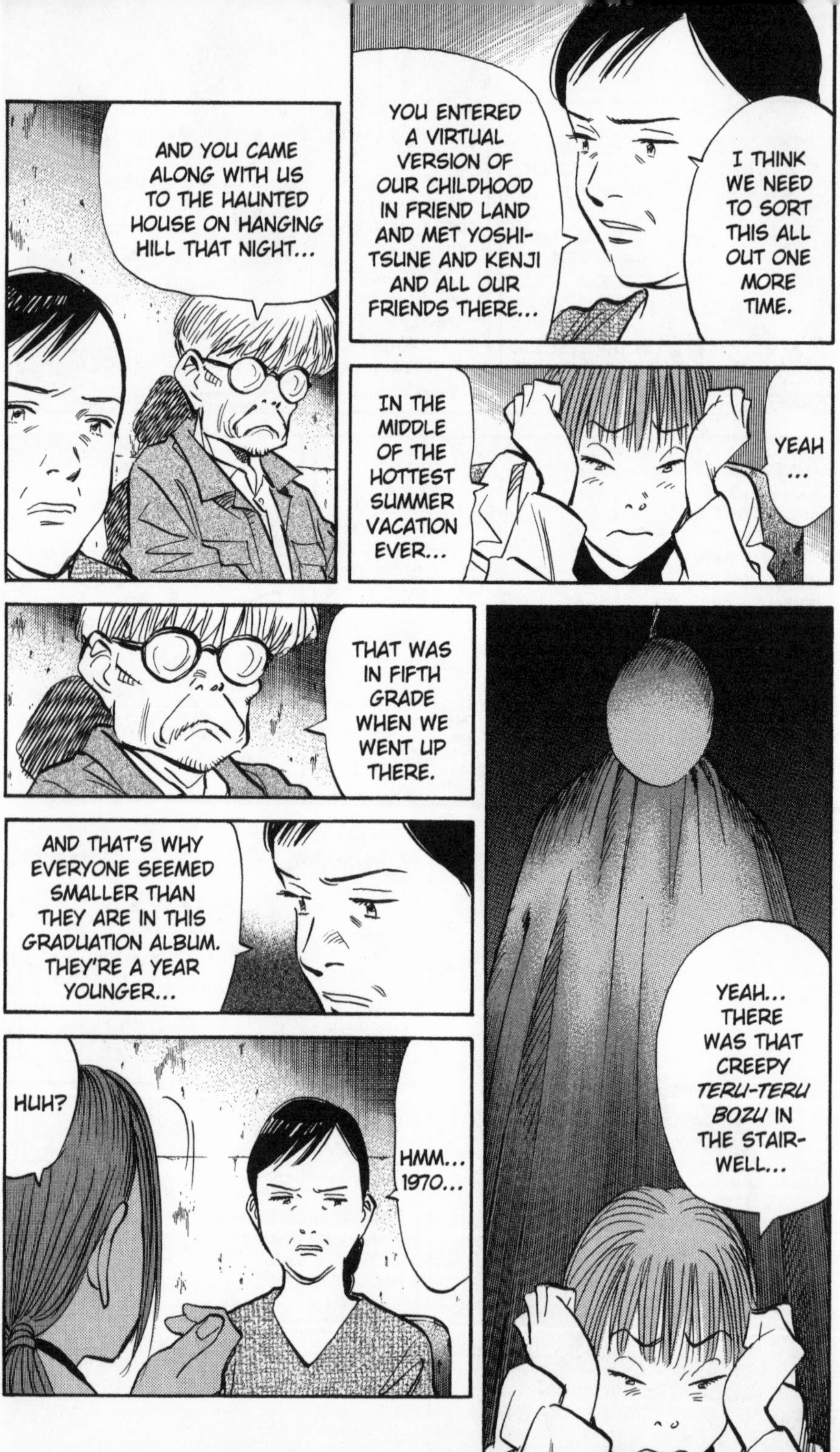
I THINK WE NEED TO SORT THIS ALL OUT ONE MORE TIME.
YOU ENTERED A VIRTUAL VERSION OF OUR CHILDHOOD IN FRIEND LAND AND MET YOSHI-TSUNE AND KENJI AND ALL OUR FRIENDS THERE...
YEAH ...
IN THE MIDDLE OF THE HOTTEST SUMMER VACATION EVER...
AND YOU CAME ALONG WITH US TO THE HAUNTED HOUSE ON HANGING HILL THAT NIGHT...
YEAH... THERE WAS THAT CREEPY *TERU-TERU BOZU* IN THE STAIR-WELL...
THAT WAS IN FIFTH GRADE WHEN WE WENT UP THERE.
AND THAT'S WHY EVERYONE SEEMED SMALLER THAN THEY ARE IN THIS GRADUATION ALBUM. THEY'RE A YEAR YOUNGER...
HMM... 1970...
HUH?

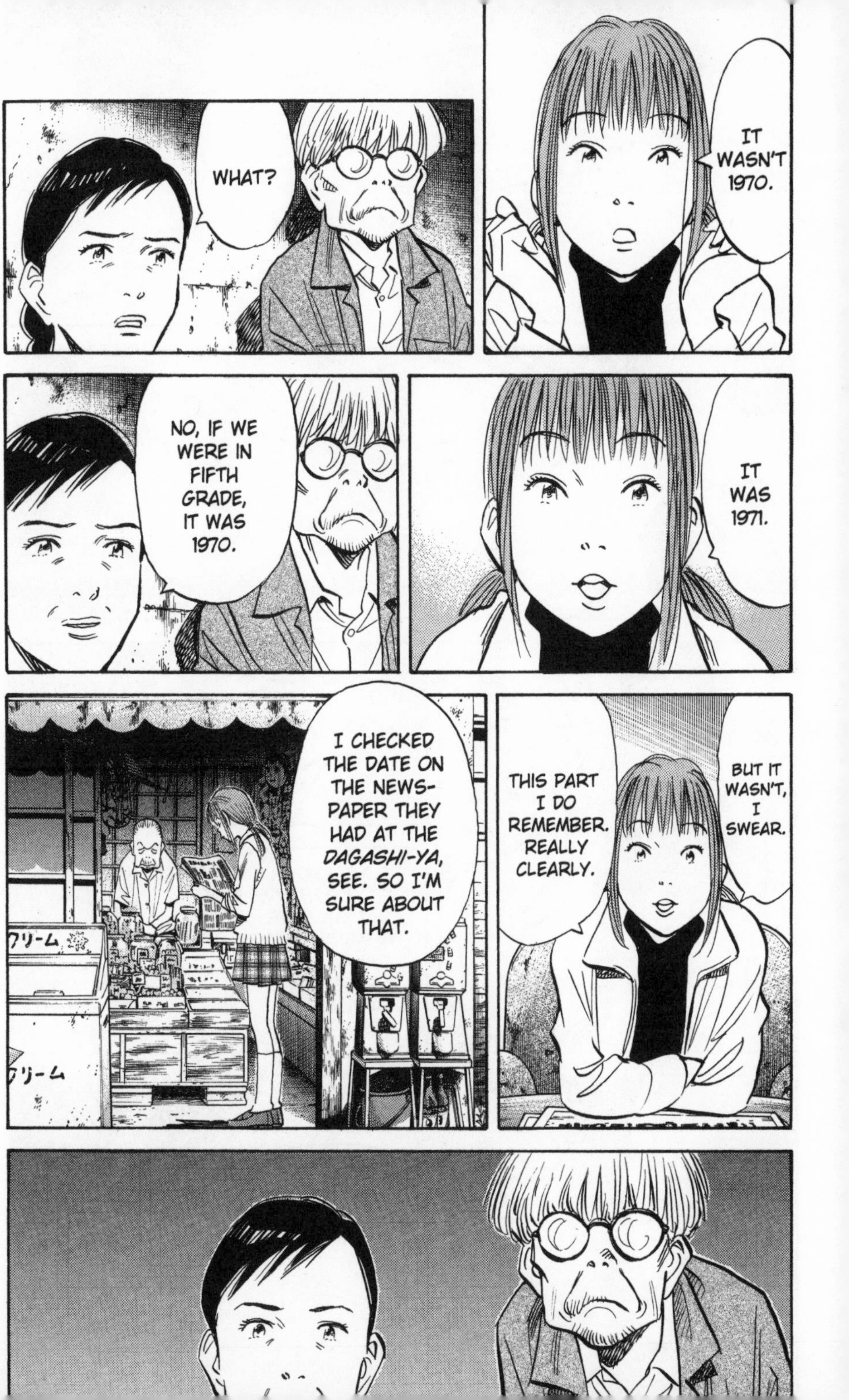
IT WASN'T 1970.
WHAT?
IT WAS 1971.
NO, IF WE WERE IN FIFTH GRADE, IT WAS 1970.
BUT IT WASN'T, I SWEAR.
THIS PART I DO REMEMBER. REALLY CLEARLY.
I CHECKED THE DATE ON THE NEWS-PAPER THEY HAD AT THE *DAGASHI-YA*, SEE. SO I'M SURE ABOUT THAT.

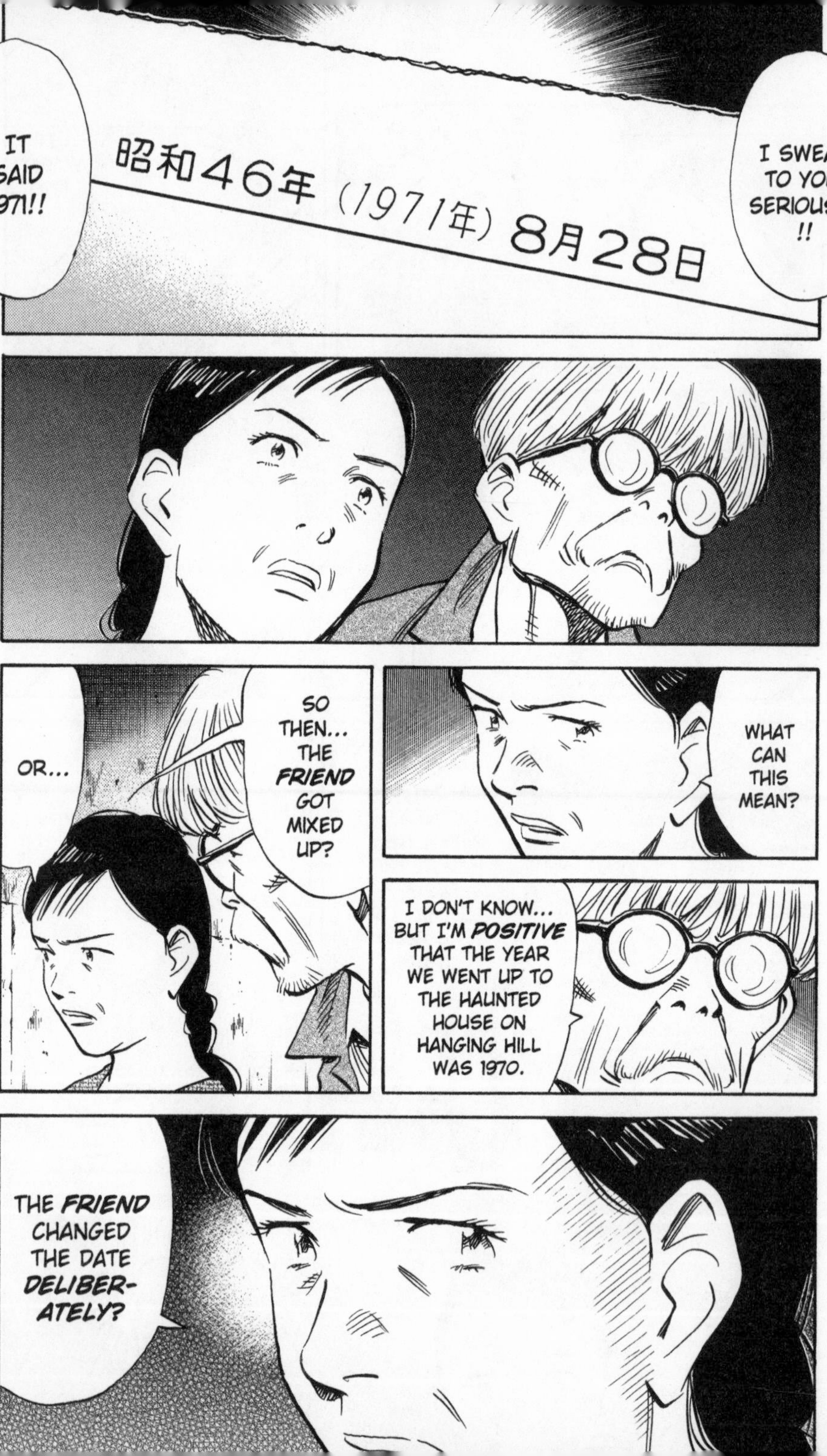
I SWEAR TO YOU, SERIOUSLY!!
昭和46年（1971年）8月28日
IT SAID 1971!!
WHAT CAN THIS MEAN?
I DON'T KNOW... BUT I'M *POSITIVE* THAT THE YEAR WE WENT UP TO THE HAUNTED HOUSE ON HANGING HILL WAS 1970.
SO THEN... THE *FRIEND* GOT MIXED UP?
OR...
THE *FRIEND* CHANGED THE DATE *DELIBER-ATELY?*

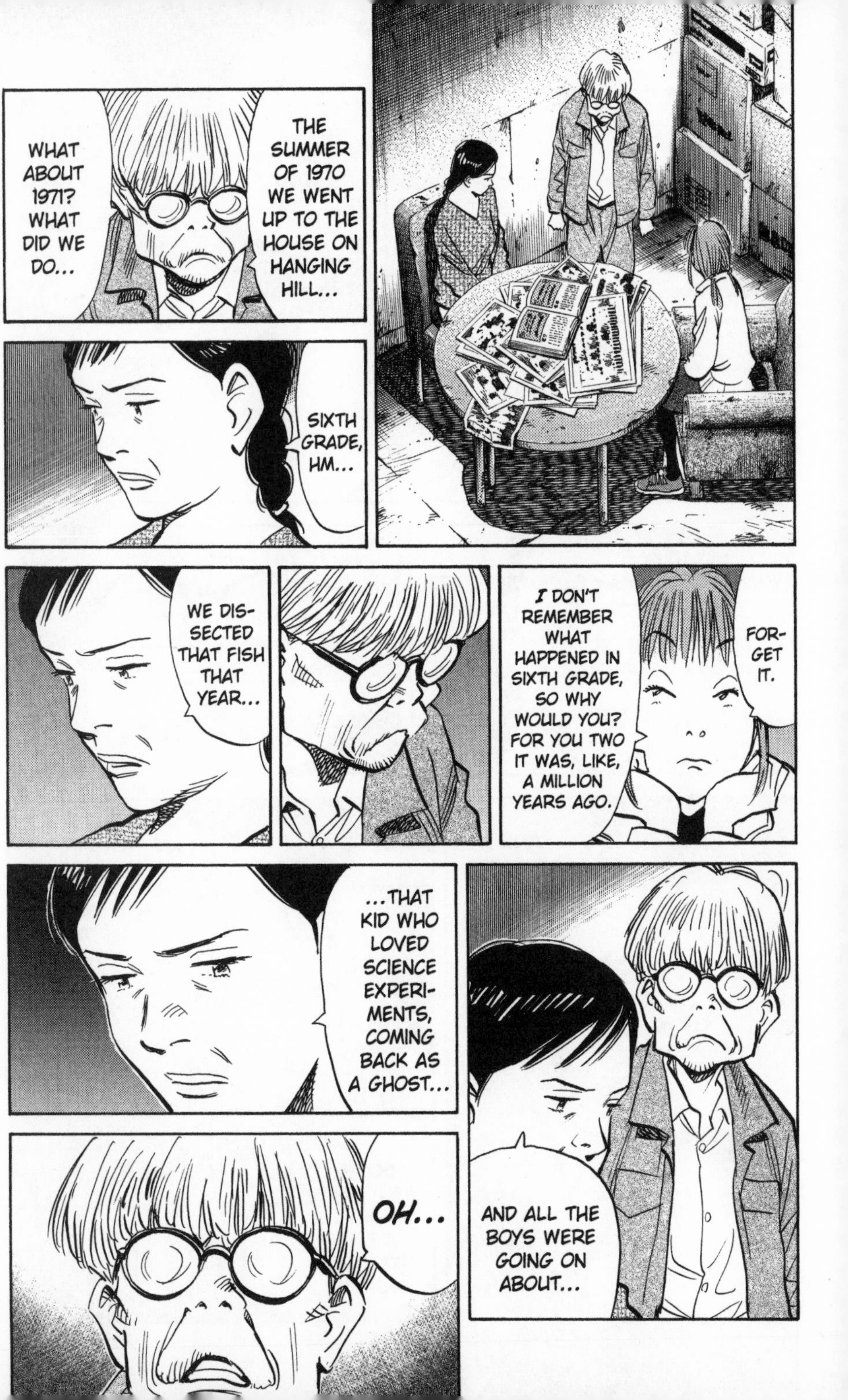
THE SUMMER OF 1970 WE WENT UP TO THE HOUSE ON HANGING HILL...
WHAT ABOUT 1971? WHAT DID WE DO...
SIXTH GRADE, HM...
FOR-GET IT.
I DON'T REMEMBER WHAT HAPPENED IN SIXTH GRADE, SO WHY WOULD YOU? FOR YOU TWO IT WAS, LIKE, A MILLION YEARS AGO.
WE DIS-SECTED THAT FISH THAT YEAR...
AND ALL THE BOYS WERE GOING ON ABOUT...
...THAT KID WHO LOVED SCIENCE EXPERI-MENTS, COMING BACK AS A GHOST...
OH...

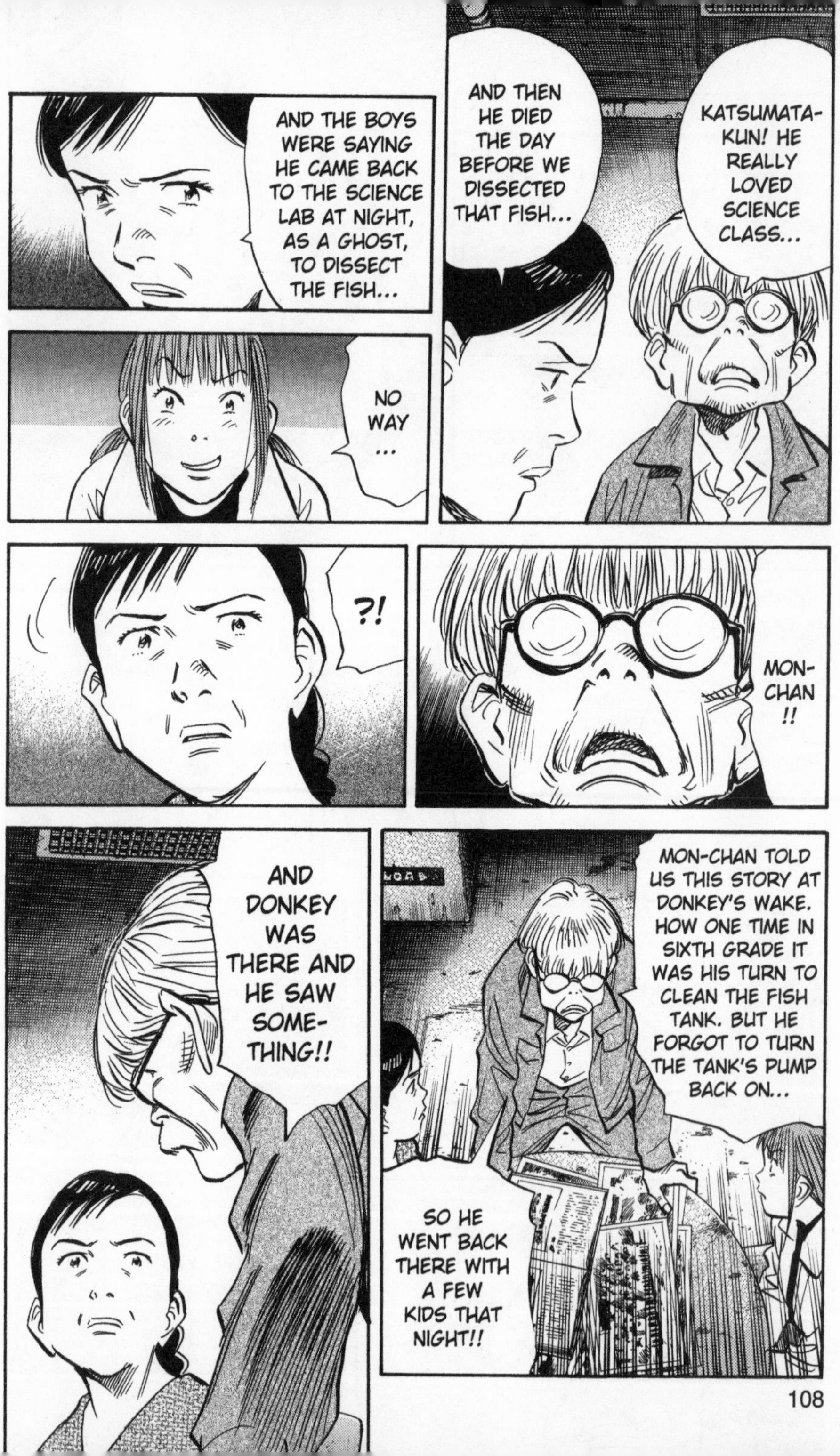
KATSUMATA-KUN! HE REALLY LOVED SCIENCE CLASS...
AND THEN HE DIED THE DAY BEFORE WE DISSECTED THAT FISH...
AND THE BOYS WERE SAYING HE CAME BACK TO THE SCIENCE LAB AT NIGHT, AS A GHOST, TO DISSECT THE FISH...
NO WAY ...
MON-CHAN !!
?!
MON-CHAN TOLD US THIS STORY AT DONKEY'S WAKE. HOW ONE TIME IN SIXTH GRADE IT WAS HIS TURN TO CLEAN THE FISH TANK. BUT HE FORGOT TO TURN THE TANK'S PUMP BACK ON...
SO HE WENT BACK THERE WITH A FEW KIDS THAT NIGHT!!
AND DONKEY WAS THERE AND HE SAW SOME-THING!!

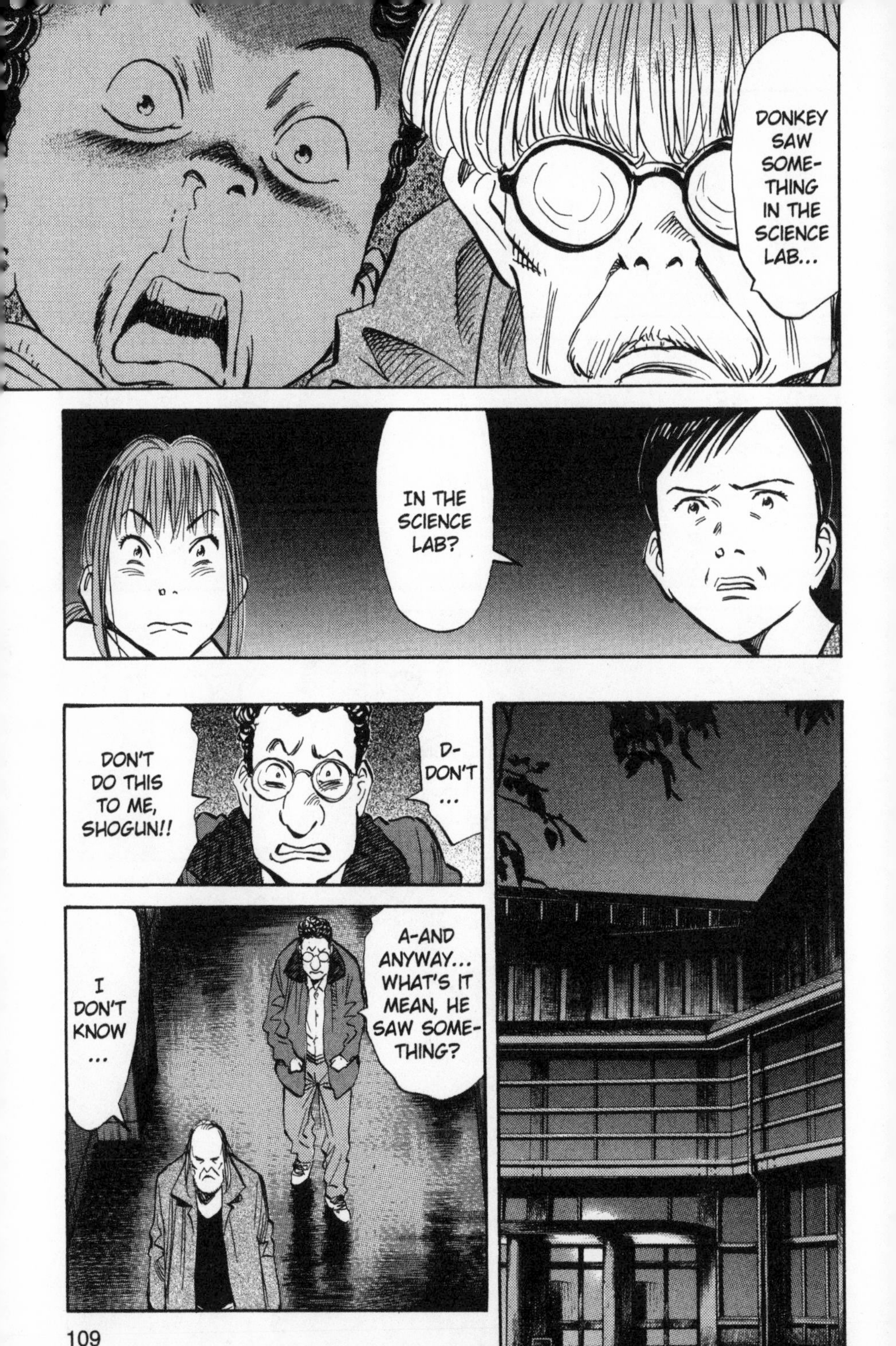
DONKEY SAW SOME-THING IN THE SCIENCE LAB...
IN THE SCIENCE LAB?
D- DON'T ...
DON'T DO THIS TO ME, SHOGUN!!
A-AND ANYWAY... WHAT'S IT MEAN, HE SAW SOME-THING?
I DON'T KNOW ...

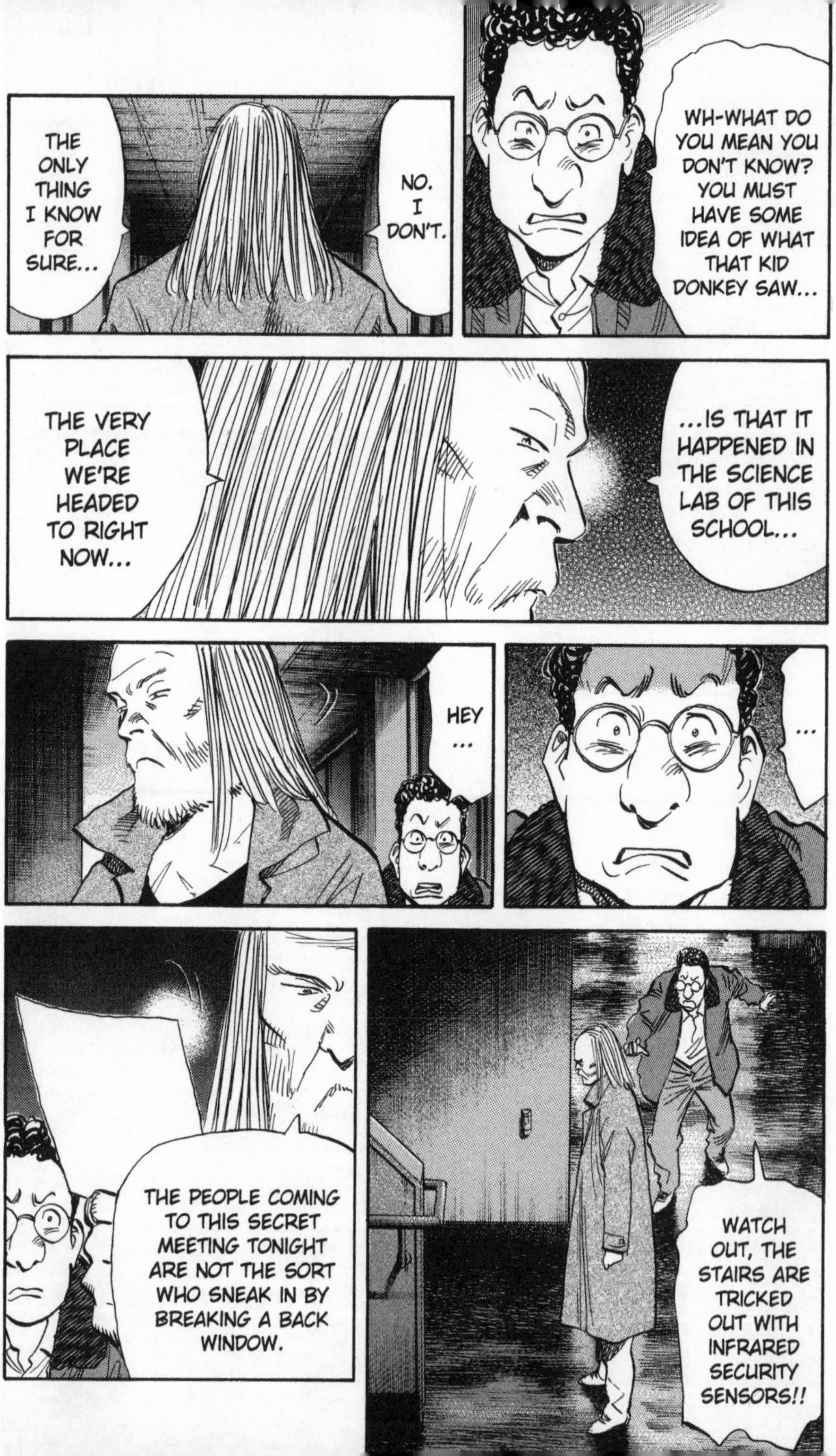
WH-WHAT DO YOU MEAN YOU DON'T KNOW? YOU MUST HAVE SOME IDEA OF WHAT THAT KID DONKEY SAW...
NO. I DON'T.
THE ONLY THING I KNOW FOR SURE...
...IS THAT IT HAPPENED IN THE SCIENCE LAB OF THIS SCHOOL...
THE VERY PLACE WE'RE HEADED TO RIGHT NOW...
...
HEY ...
WATCH OUT, THE STAIRS ARE TRICKED OUT WITH INFRARED SECURITY SENSORS!!
THE PEOPLE COMING TO THIS SECRET MEETING TONIGHT ARE NOT THE SORT WHO SNEAK IN BY BREAKING A BACK WINDOW.

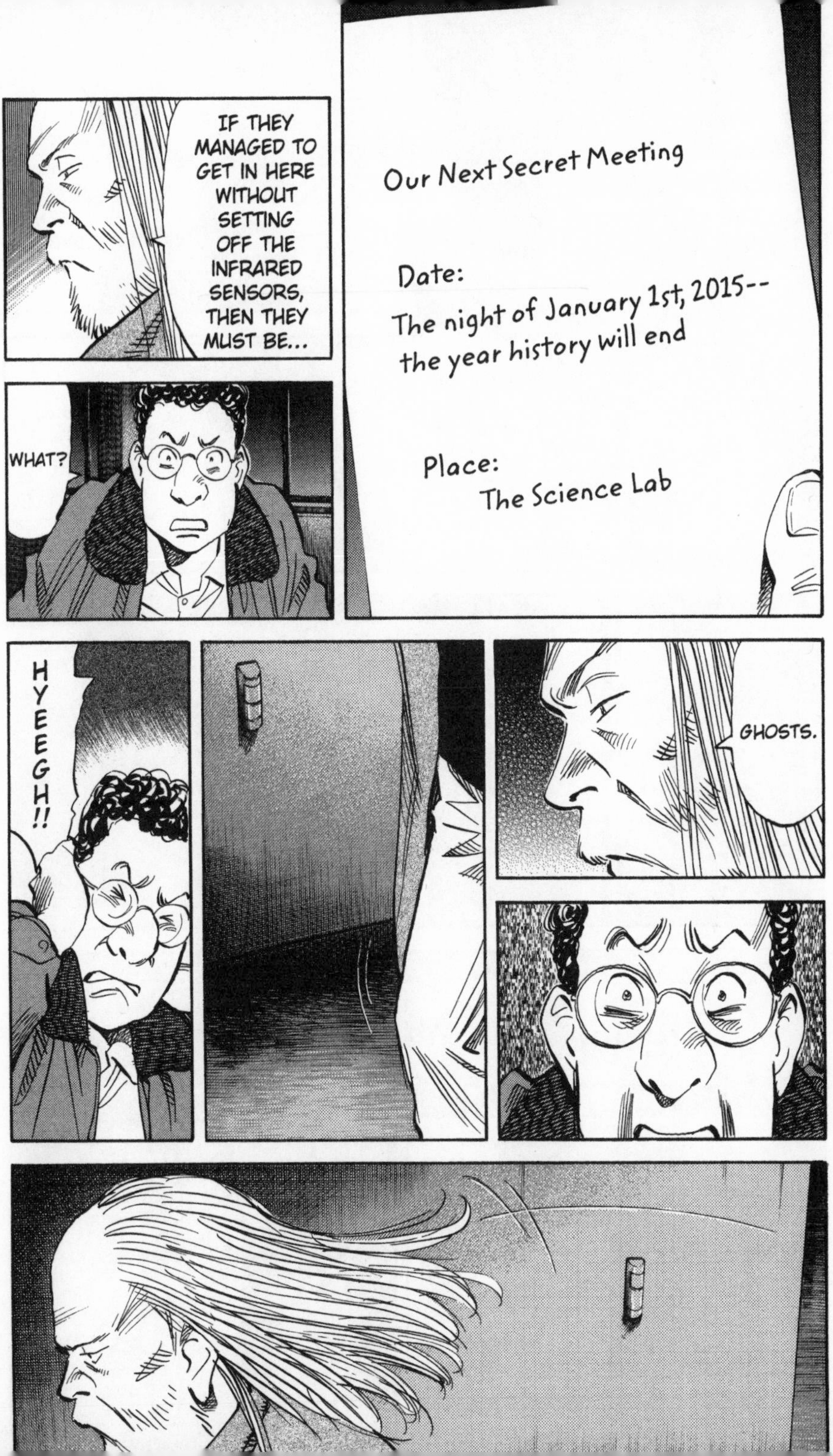
Our Next Secret Meeting
Date:
The night of January 1st, 2015--
the year history will end
Place:
The Science Lab
IF THEY MANAGED TO GET IN HERE WITHOUT SETTING OFF THE INFRARED SENSORS, THEN THEY MUST BE...
WHAT?
GHOSTS.
HYEEGH!!

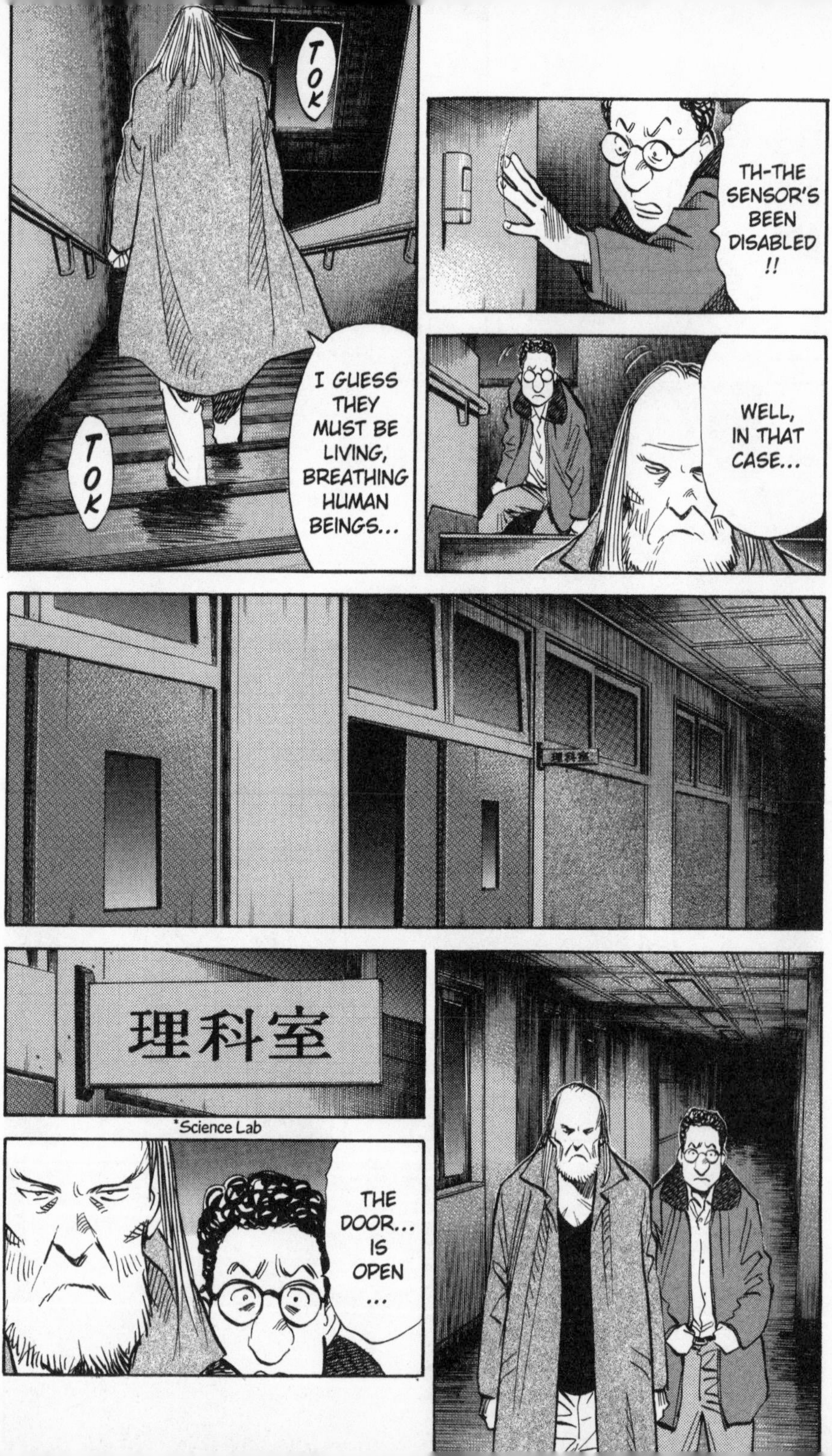
TH-THE SENSOR'S BEEN DISABLED !!
WELL, IN THAT CASE...
TOK
I GUESS THEY MUST BE LIVING, BREATHING HUMAN BEINGS...
TOK
理科室
*Science Lab
THE DOOR... IS OPEN ...

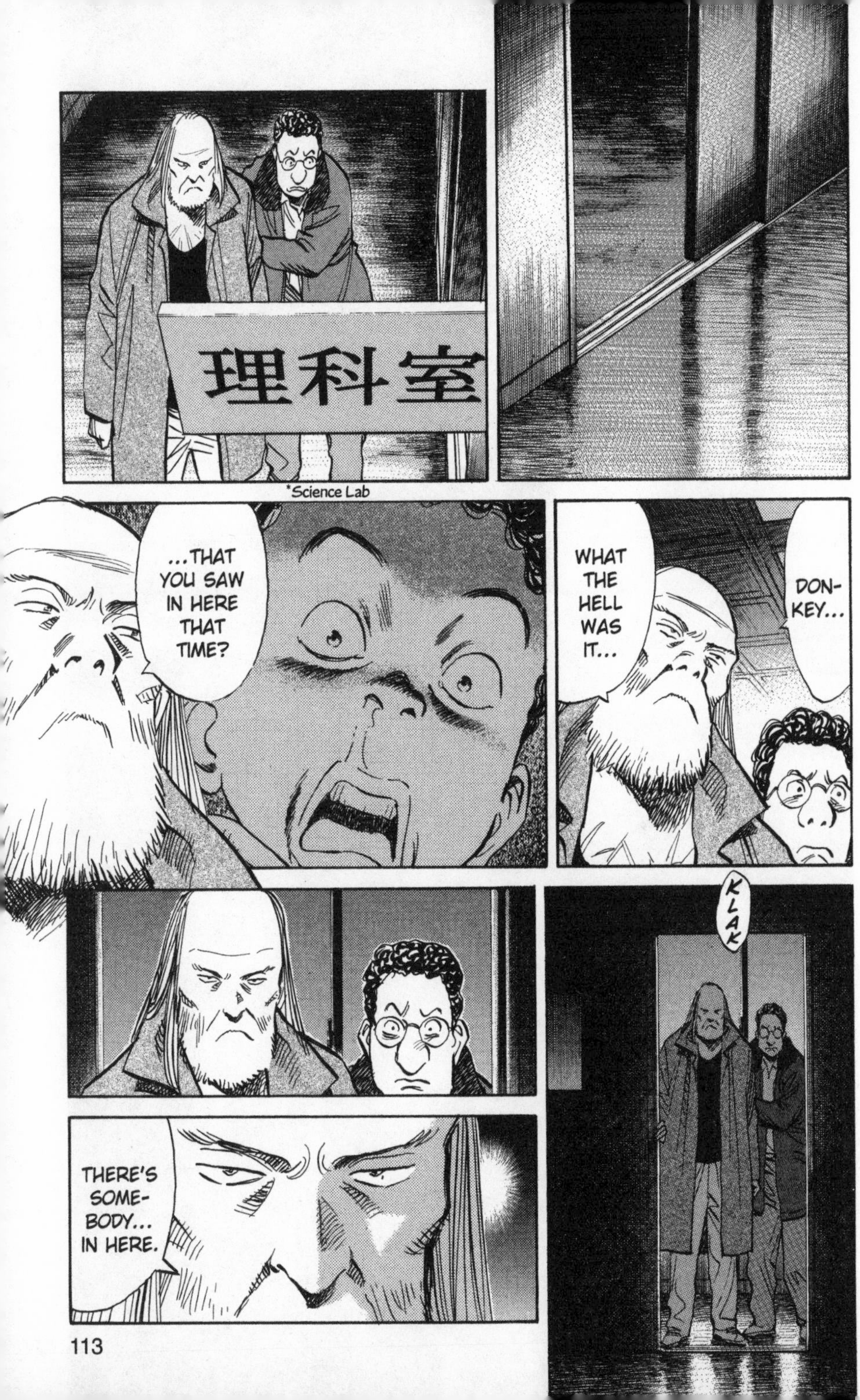
理科室
*Science Lab
DON-KEY...
WHAT THE HELL WAS IT...
...THAT YOU SAW IN HERE THAT TIME?
KLAK
THERE'S SOMEBODY... IN HERE.

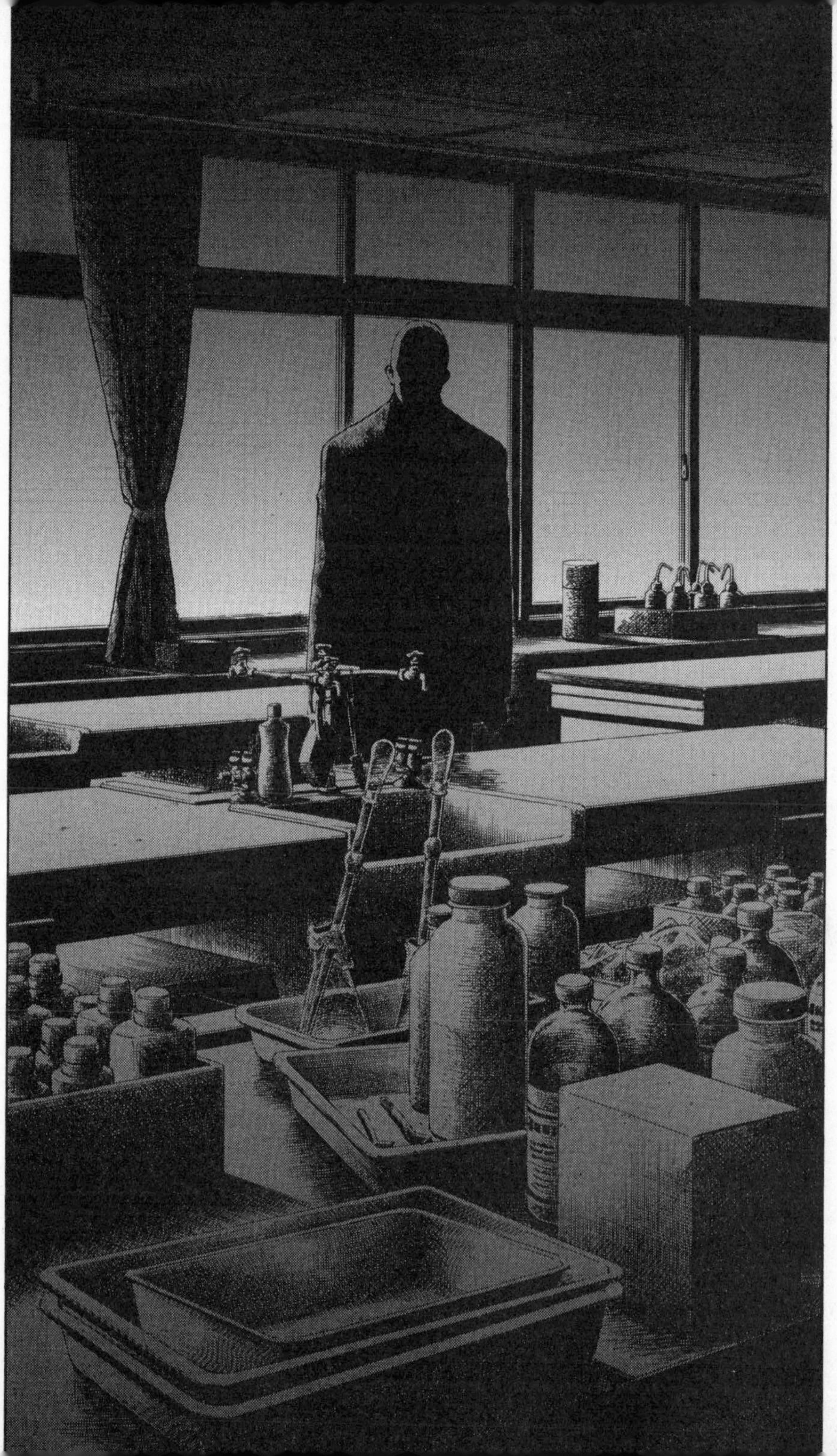

Chapter 7 By the Light of the Alcohol Lamp

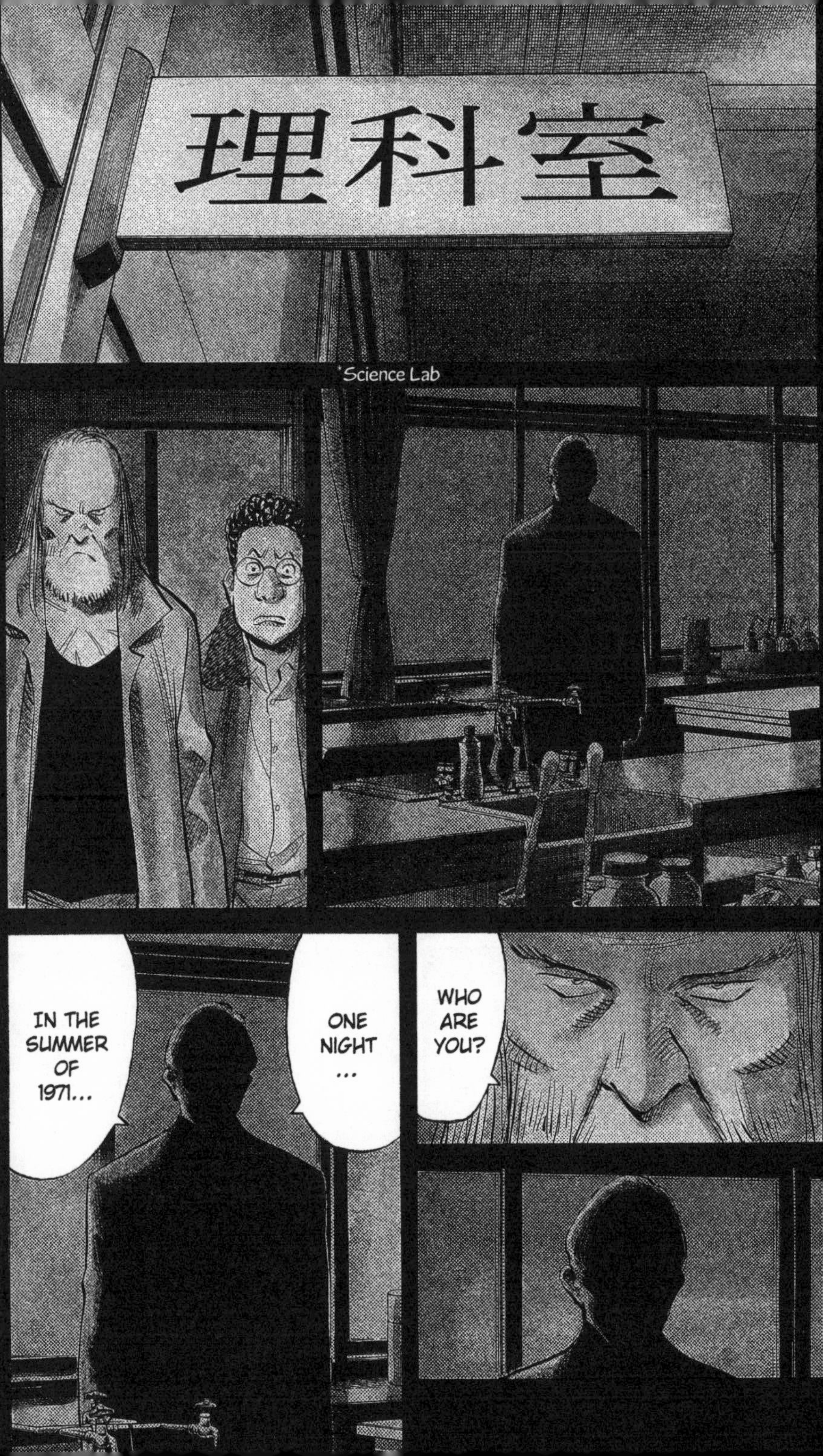
理科室
*Science Lab
WHO ARE YOU?
ONE NIGHT ...
IN THE SUMMER OF 1971...

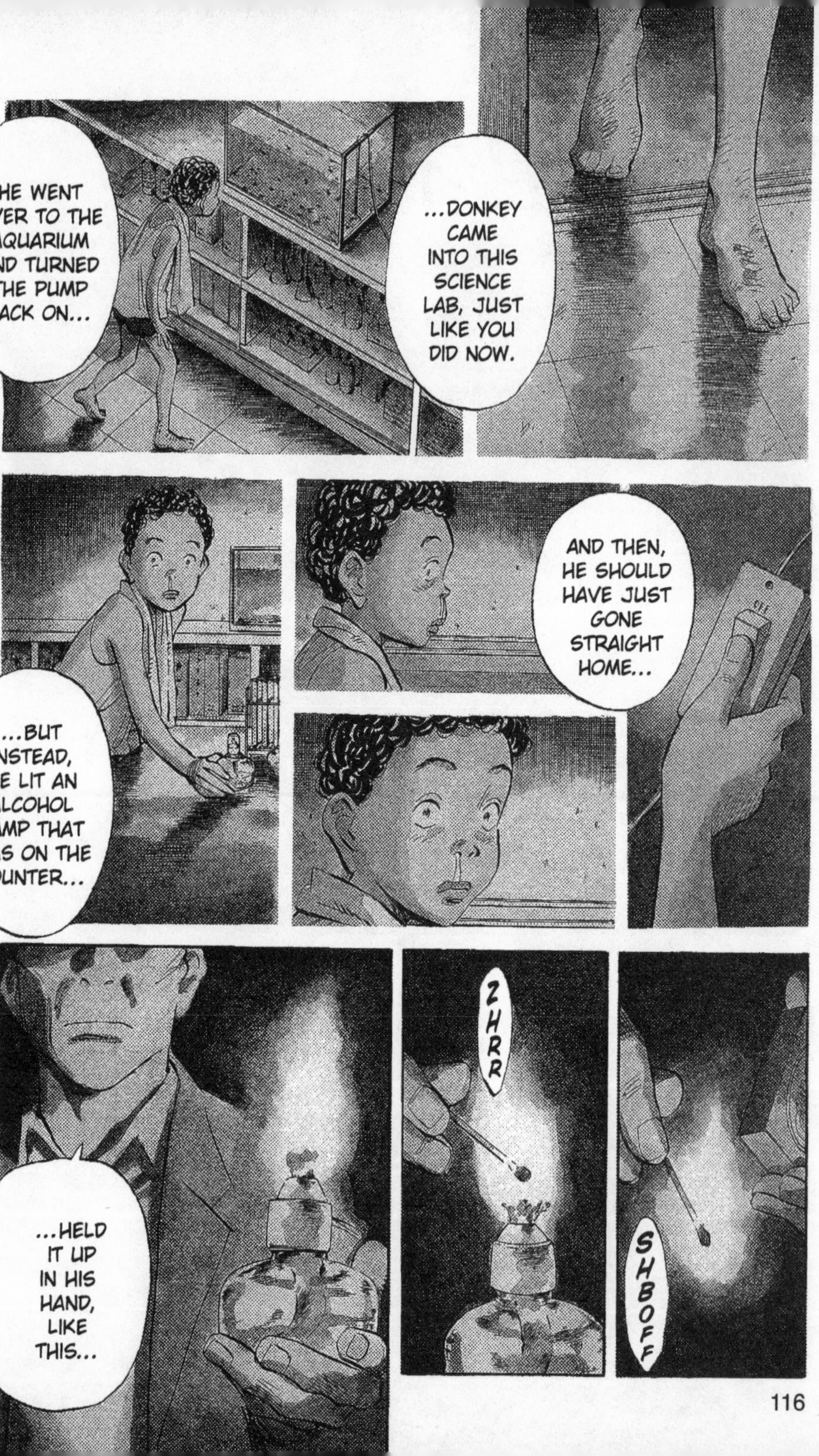
...DONKEY CAME INTO THIS SCIENCE LAB, JUST LIKE YOU DID NOW.
HE WENT OVER TO THE AQUARIUM AND TURNED THE PUMP BACK ON...
AND THEN, HE SHOULD HAVE JUST GONE STRAIGHT HOME...
...BUT INSTEAD, HE LIT AN ALCOHOL LAMP THAT WAS ON THE COUNTER...
SHBOFF
ZHRR
...HELD IT UP IN HIS HAND, LIKE THIS...

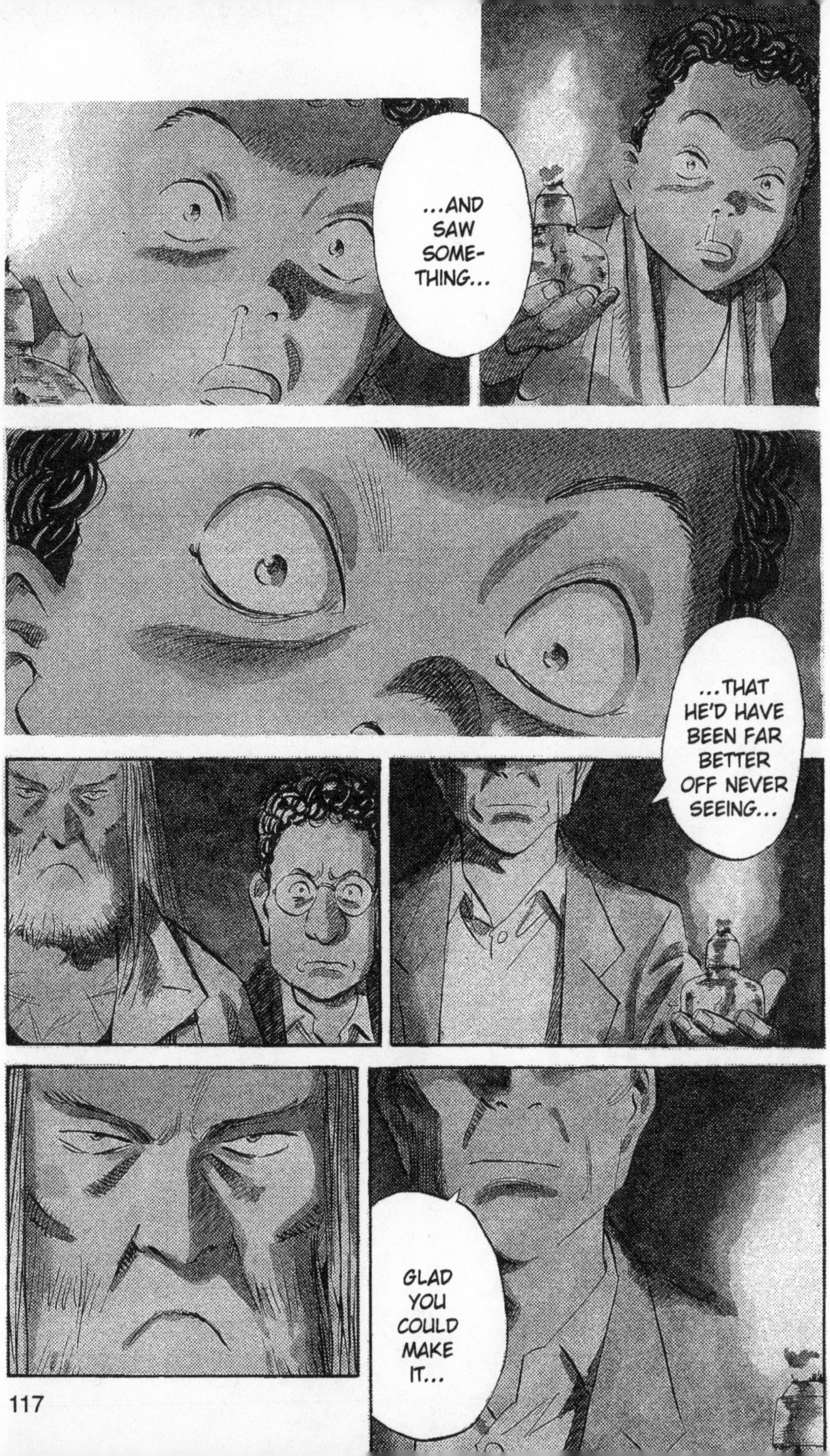
...AND SAW SOME-THING...
...THAT HE'D HAVE BEEN FAR BETTER OFF NEVER SEEING...
GLAD YOU COULD MAKE IT...

Chapter 7
By the Light of the Alcohol Lamp

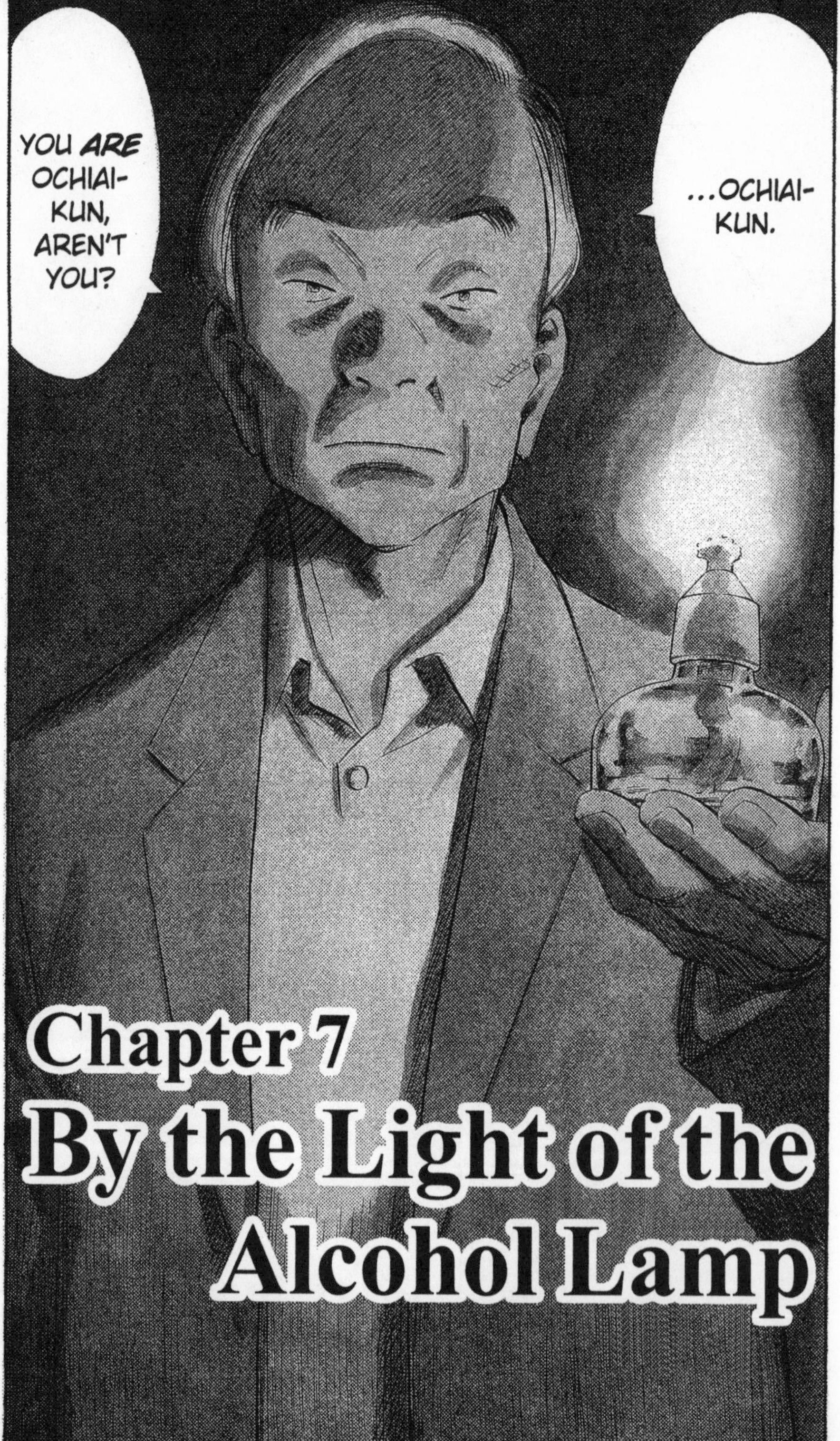

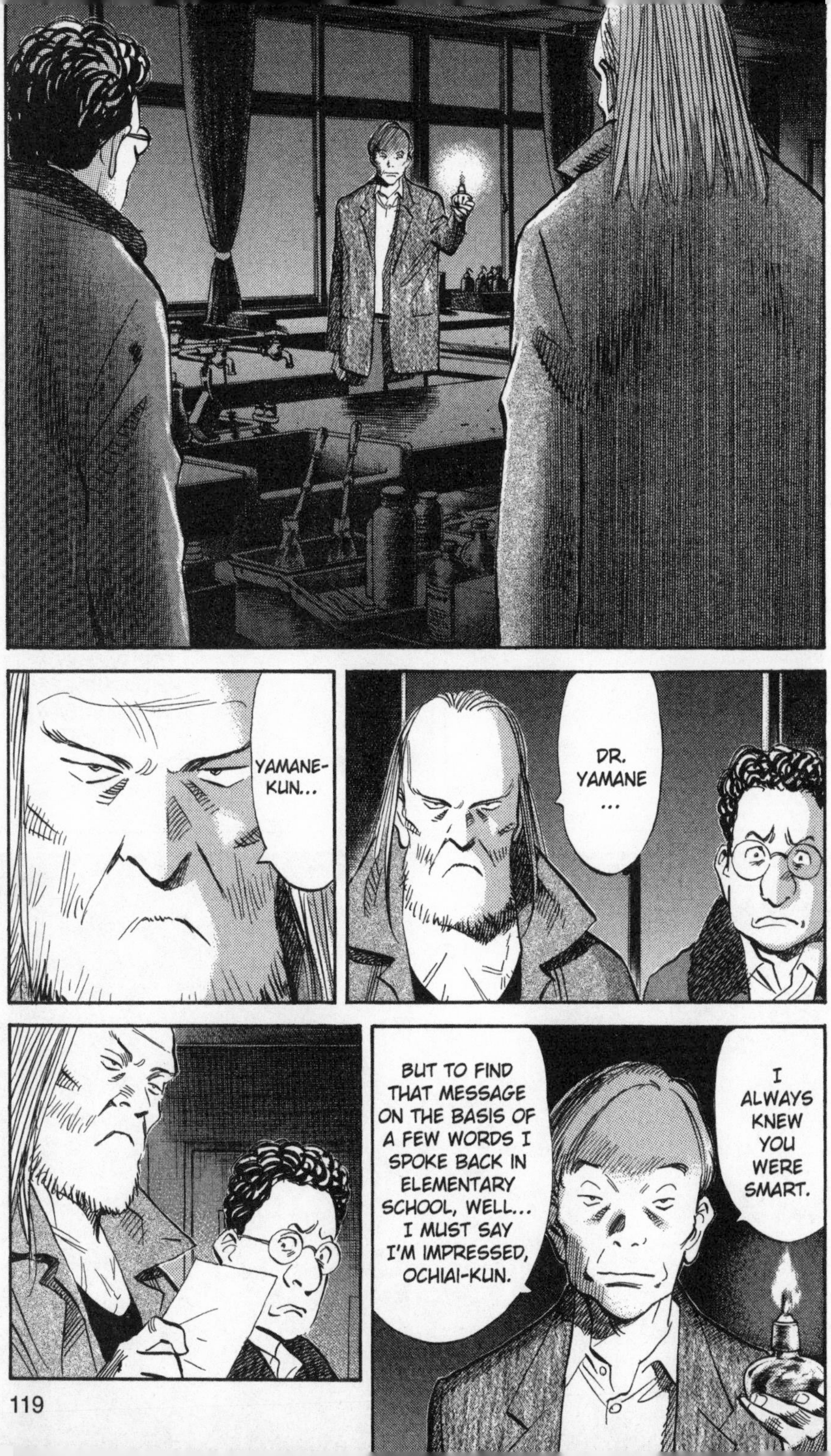
DR. YAMANE...
YAMANE-KUN...
I ALWAYS KNEW YOU WERE SMART.
BUT TO FIND THAT MESSAGE ON THE BASIS OF A FEW WORDS I SPOKE BACK IN ELEMENTARY SCHOOL, WELL... I MUST SAY I'M IMPRESSED, OCHIAI-KUN.

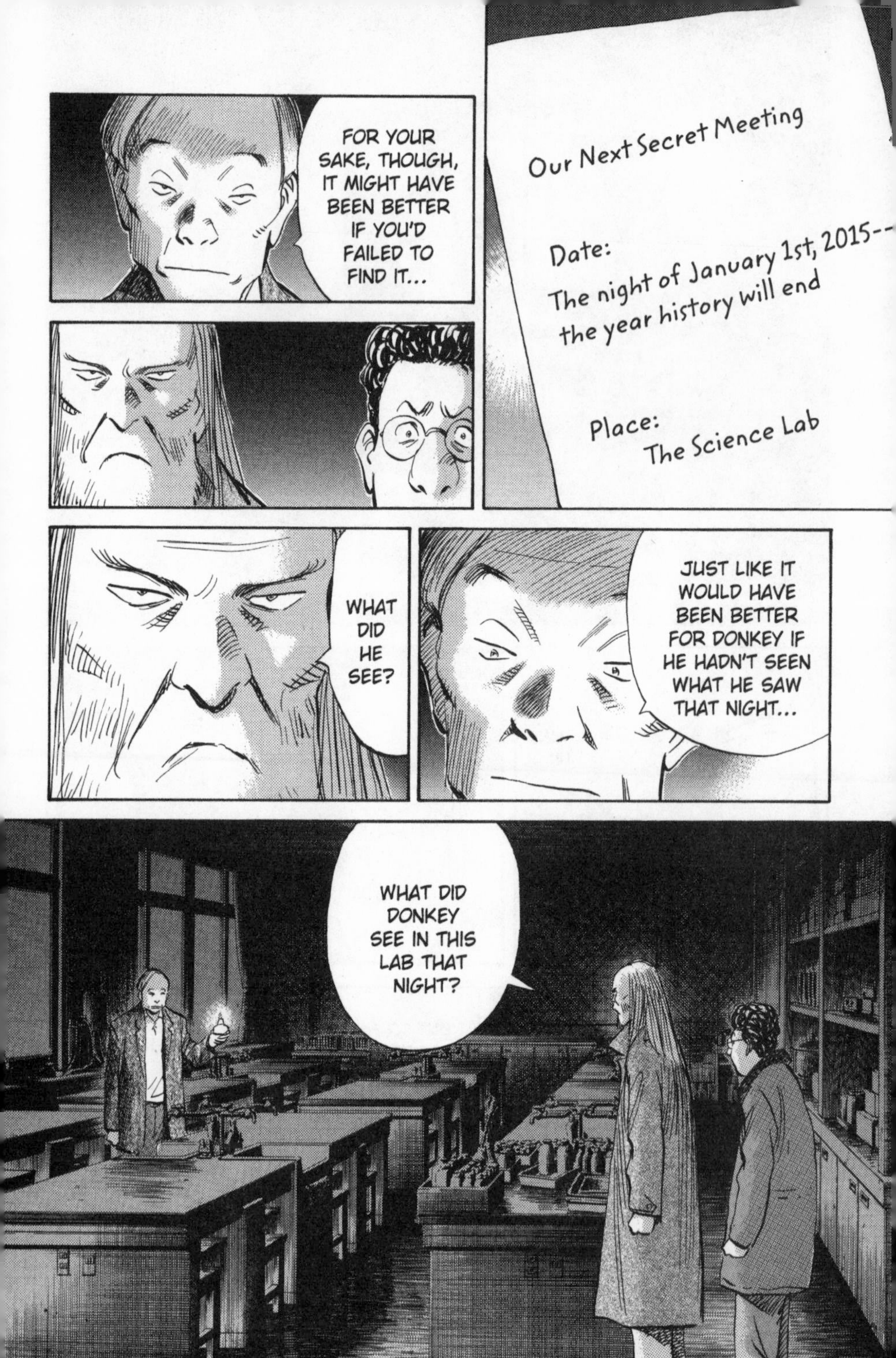
Our Next Secret Meeting
Date:
The night of January 1st, 2015--
the year history will end
Place:
The Science Lab
FOR YOUR SAKE, THOUGH, IT MIGHT HAVE BEEN BETTER IF YOU'D FAILED TO FIND IT...
JUST LIKE IT WOULD HAVE BEEN BETTER FOR DONKEY IF HE HADN'T SEEN WHAT HE SAW THAT NIGHT...
WHAT DID HE SEE?
WHAT DID DONKEY SEE IN THIS LAB THAT NIGHT?

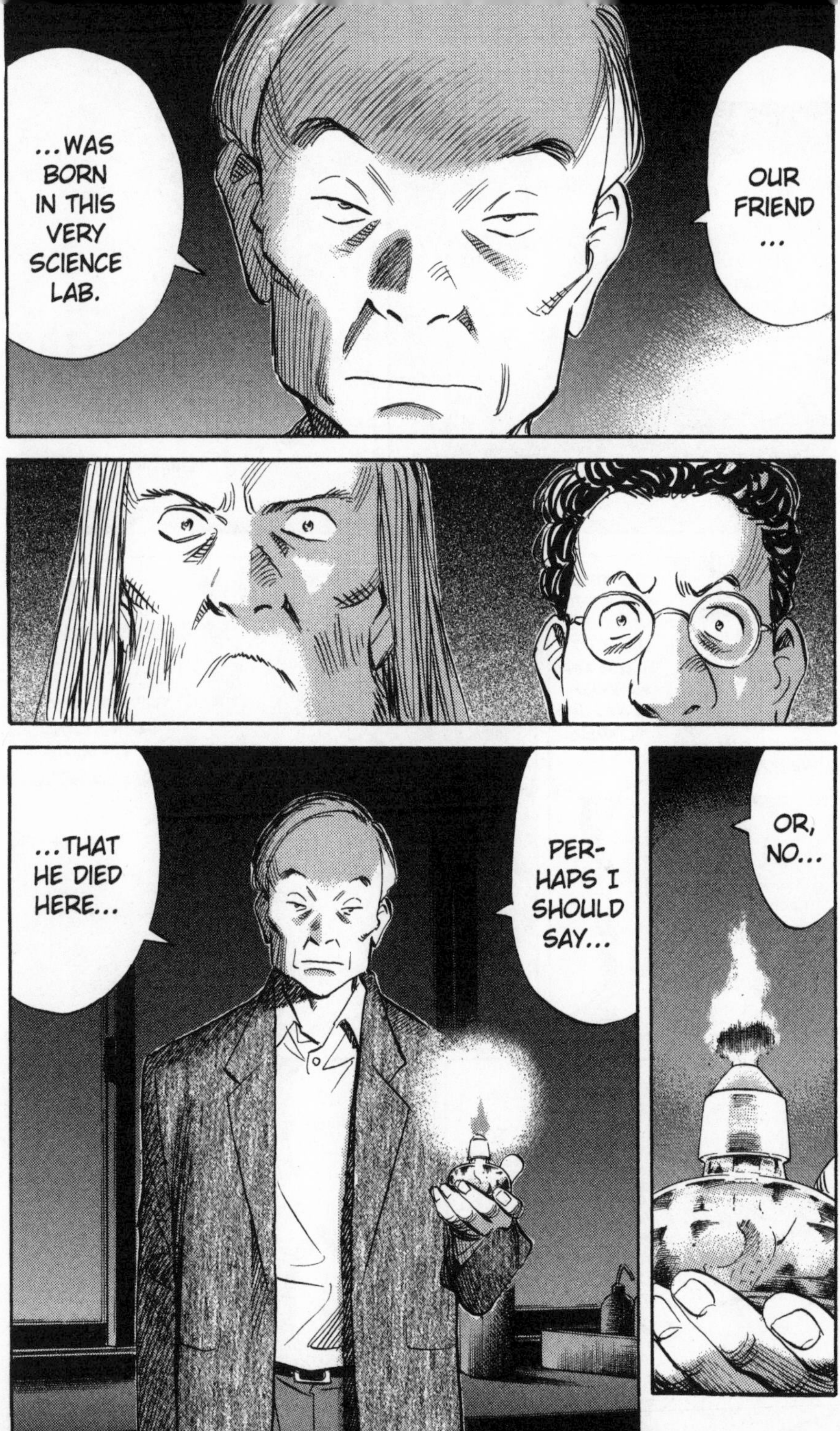
OUR FRIEND...
...WAS BORN IN THIS VERY SCIENCE LAB.
OR, NO...
PER-HAPS I SHOULD SAY...
...THAT HE DIED HERE...

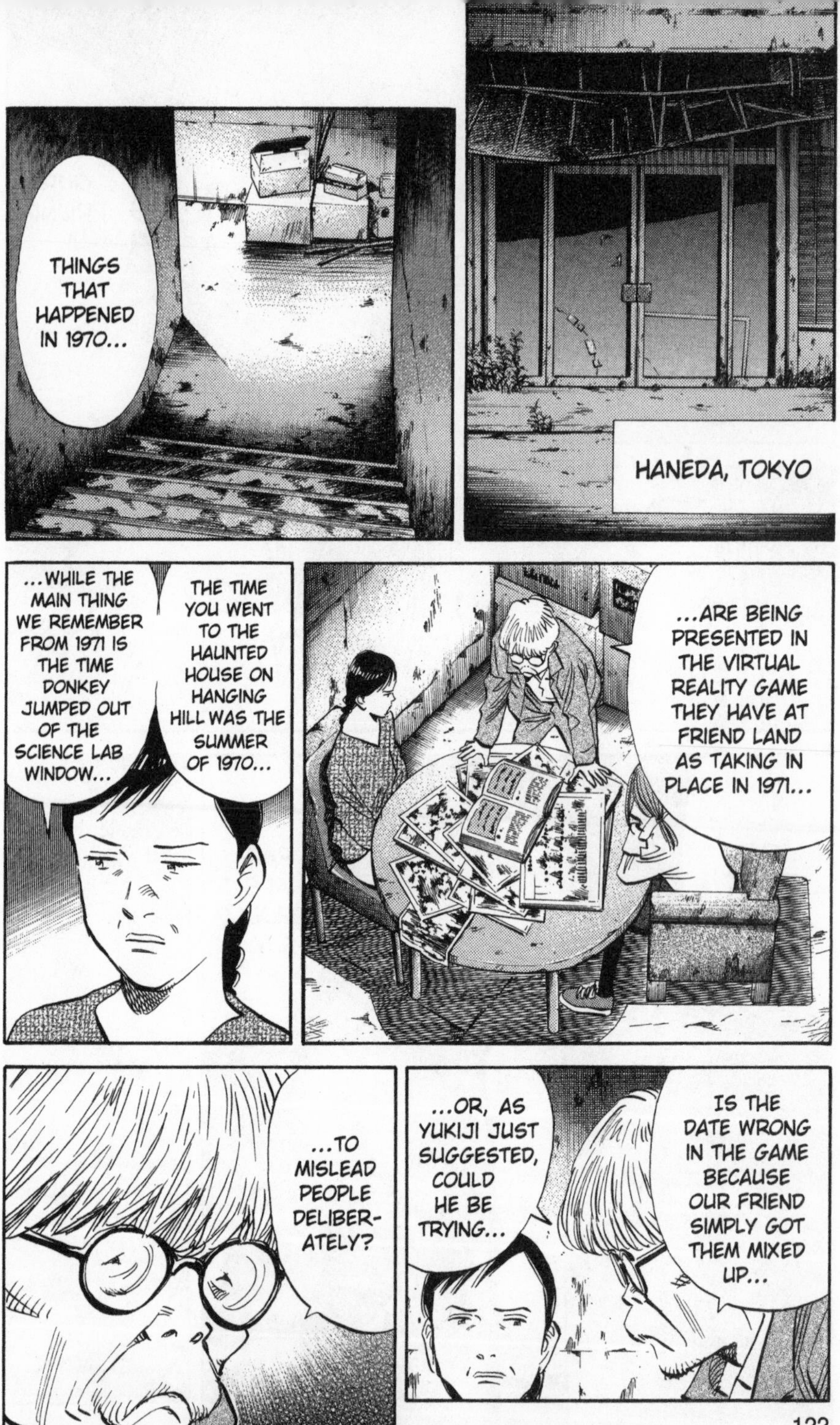
HANEDA, TOKYO
THINGS THAT HAPPENED IN 1970...
...ARE BEING PRESENTED IN THE VIRTUAL REALITY GAME THEY HAVE AT FRIEND LAND AS TAKING IN PLACE IN 1971...
THE TIME YOU WENT TO THE HAUNTED HOUSE ON HANGING HILL WAS THE SUMMER OF 1970...
...WHILE THE MAIN THING WE REMEMBER FROM 1971 IS THE TIME DONKEY JUMPED OUT OF THE SCIENCE LAB WINDOW...
IS THE DATE WRONG IN THE GAME BECAUSE OUR FRIEND SIMPLY GOT THEM MIXED UP...
...OR, AS YUKIJI JUST SUGGESTED, COULD HE BE TRYING...
...TO MISLEAD PEOPLE DELIBER-ATELY?

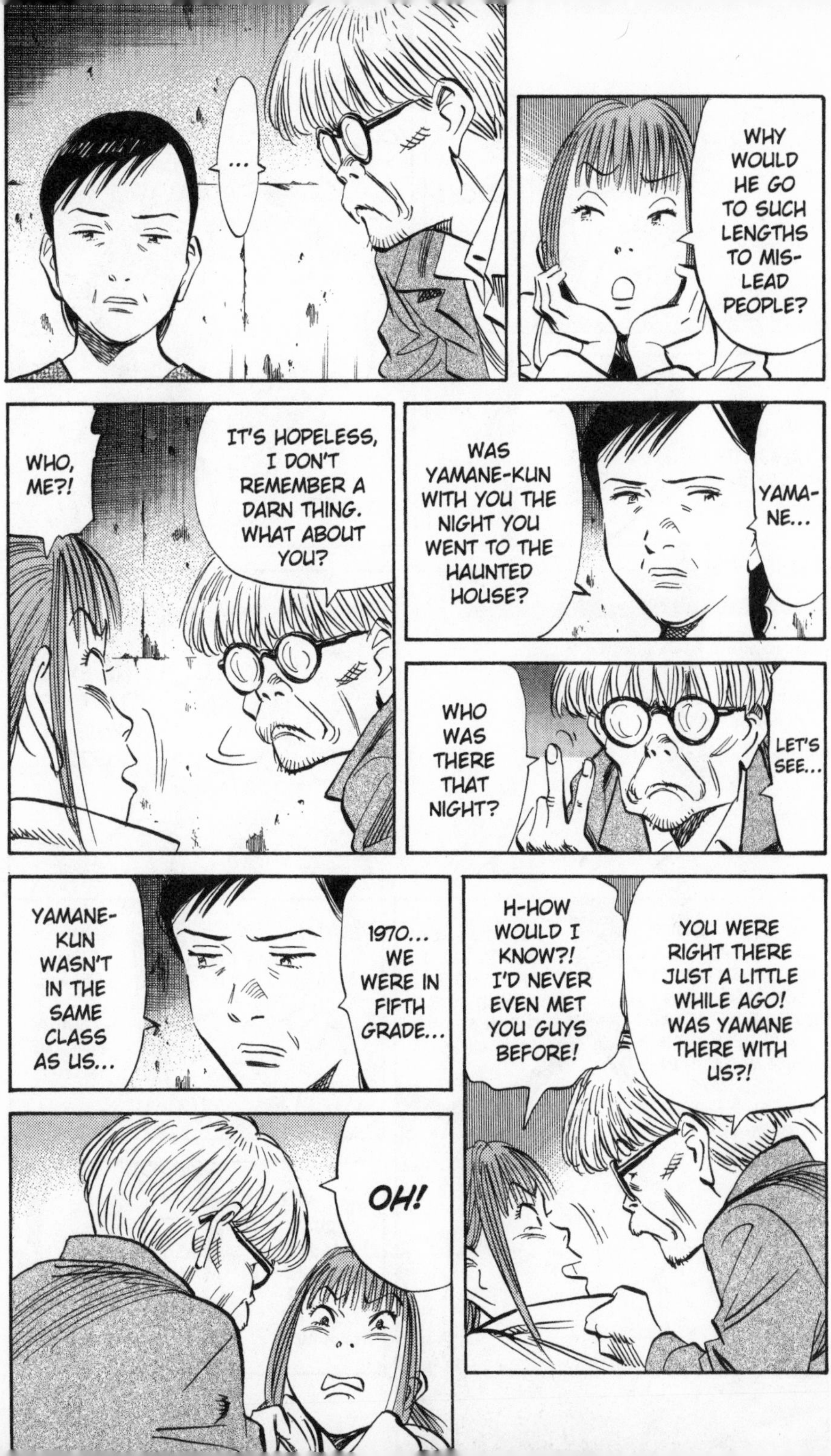
WHY WOULD HE GO TO SUCH LENGTHS TO MIS-LEAD PEOPLE?
...
YAMA-NE...
WAS YAMANE-KUN WITH YOU THE NIGHT YOU WENT TO THE HAUNTED HOUSE?
LET'S SEE...
WHO WAS THERE THAT NIGHT?
IT'S HOPELESS, I DON'T REMEMBER A DARN THING. WHAT ABOUT YOU?
WHO, ME?!
YOU WERE RIGHT THERE JUST A LITTLE WHILE AGO! WAS YAMANE THERE WITH US?!
H-HOW WOULD I KNOW?! I'D NEVER EVEN MET YOU GUYS BEFORE!
1970... WE WERE IN FIFTH GRADE...
YAMANE-KUN WASN'T IN THE SAME CLASS AS US...
OH!

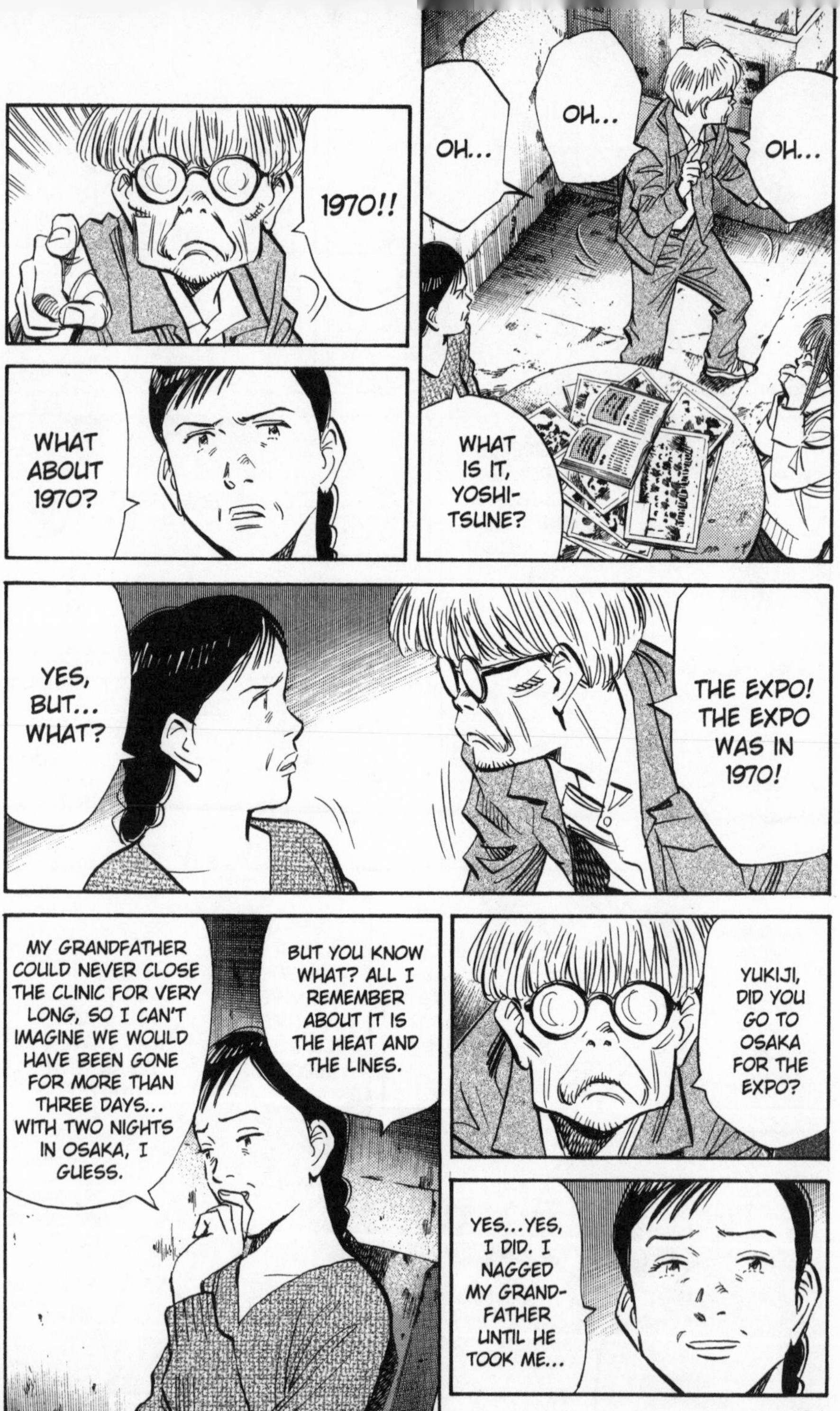
OH...
OH...
OH...
WHAT IS IT, YOSHI-TSUNE?
1970!!
WHAT ABOUT 1970?
THE EXPO! THE EXPO WAS IN 1970!
YES, BUT... WHAT?
YUKIJI, DID YOU GO TO OSAKA FOR THE EXPO?
YES...YES, I DID. I NAGGED MY GRAND-FATHER UNTIL HE TOOK ME...
BUT YOU KNOW WHAT? ALL I REMEMBER ABOUT IT IS THE HEAT AND THE LINES.
MY GRANDFATHER COULD NEVER CLOSE THE CLINIC FOR VERY LONG, SO I CAN'T IMAGINE WE WOULD HAVE BEEN GONE FOR MORE THAN THREE DAYS... WITH TWO NIGHTS IN OSAKA, I GUESS.

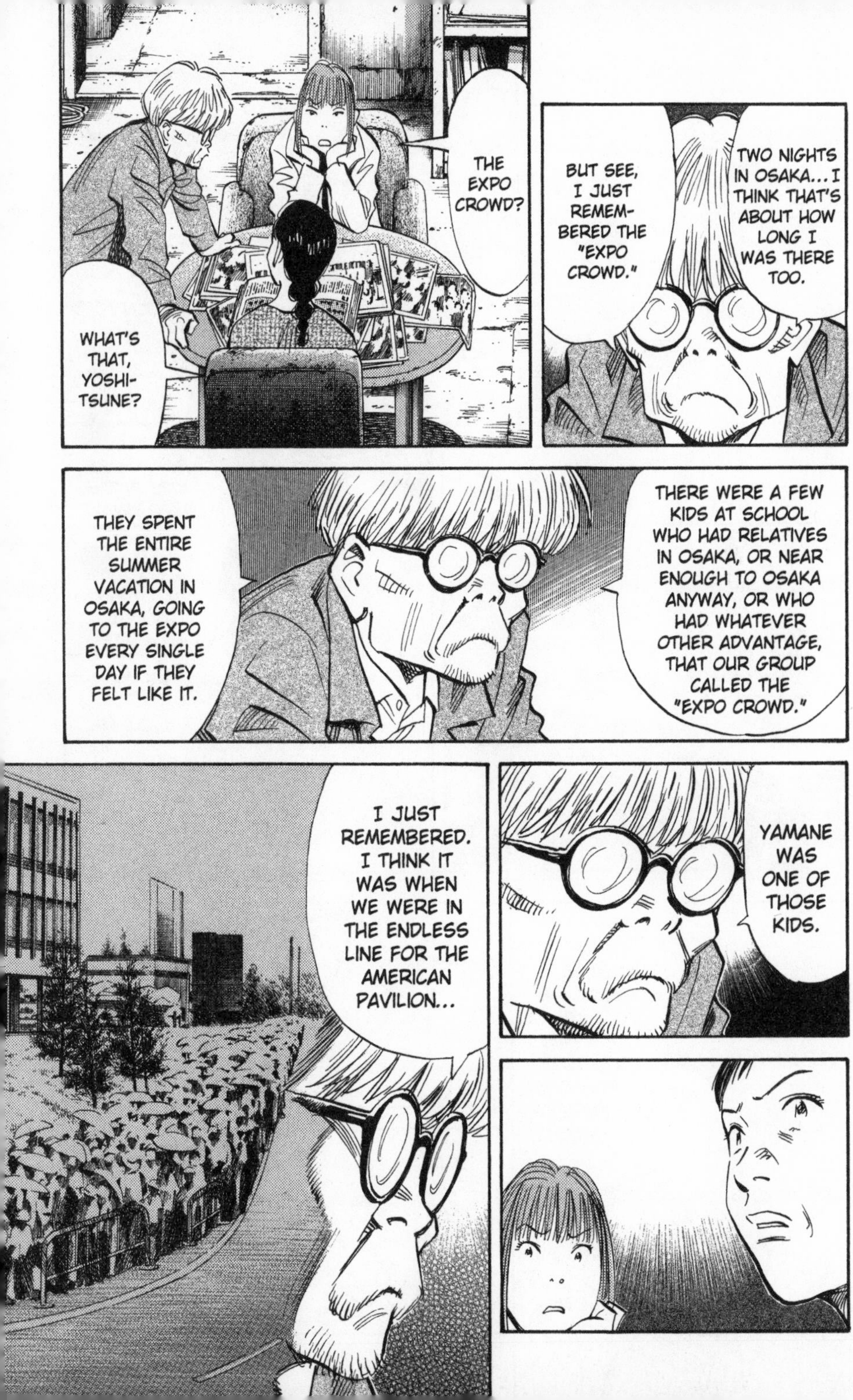
TWO NIGHTS IN OSAKA... I THINK THAT'S ABOUT HOW LONG I WAS THERE TOO.
BUT SEE, I JUST REMEMBERED THE "EXPO CROWD."
THE EXPO CROWD?
WHAT'S THAT, YOSHITSUNE?
THERE WERE A FEW KIDS AT SCHOOL WHO HAD RELATIVES IN OSAKA, OR NEAR ENOUGH TO OSAKA ANYWAY, OR WHO HAD WHATEVER OTHER ADVANTAGE, THAT OUR GROUP CALLED THE "EXPO CROWD."
THEY SPENT THE ENTIRE SUMMER VACATION IN OSAKA, GOING TO THE EXPO EVERY SINGLE DAY IF THEY FELT LIKE IT.
YAMANE WAS ONE OF THOSE KIDS.
I JUST REMEMBERED. I THINK IT WAS WHEN WE WERE IN THE ENDLESS LINE FOR THE AMERICAN PAVILION...

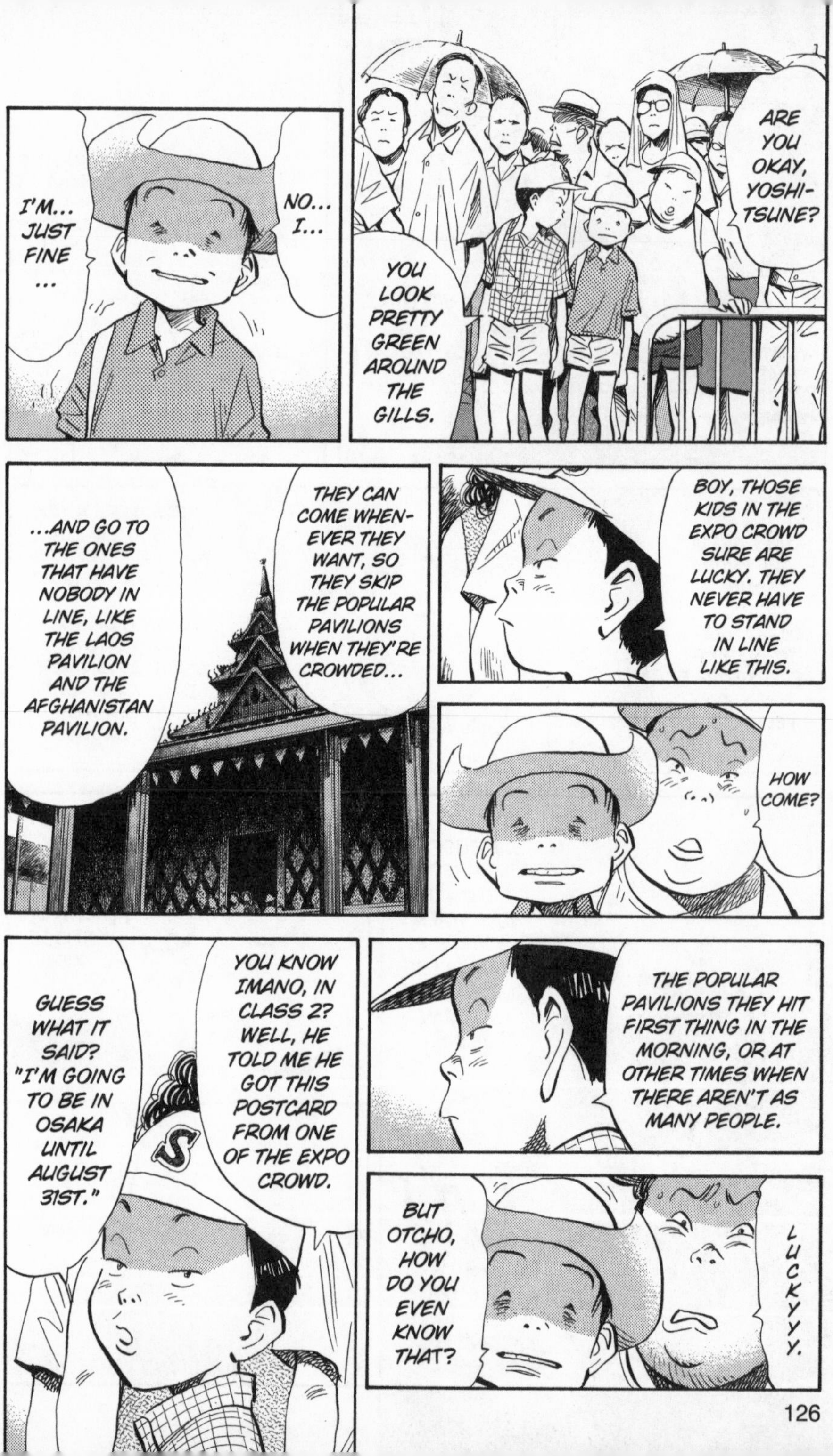
ARE YOU OKAY, YOSHITSUNE?
YOU LOOK PRETTY GREEN AROUND THE GILLS.
NO... I...
I'M... JUST FINE ...
BOY, THOSE KIDS IN THE EXPO CROWD SURE ARE LUCKY. THEY NEVER HAVE TO STAND IN LINE LIKE THIS.
HOW COME?
THEY CAN COME WHEN-EVER THEY WANT, SO THEY SKIP THE POPULAR PAVILIONS WHEN THEY'RE CROWDED...
...AND GO TO THE ONES THAT HAVE NOBODY IN LINE, LIKE THE LAOS PAVILION AND THE AFGHANISTAN PAVILION.
THE POPULAR PAVILIONS THEY HIT FIRST THING IN THE MORNING, OR AT OTHER TIMES WHEN THERE AREN'T AS MANY PEOPLE.
LUCKYYY.
BUT OTCHO, HOW DO YOU EVEN KNOW THAT?
YOU KNOW IMANO, IN CLASS 2? WELL, HE TOLD ME HE GOT THIS POSTCARD FROM ONE OF THE EXPO CROWD.
GUESS WHAT IT SAID? "I'M GOING TO BE IN OSAKA UNTIL AUGUST 31ST."

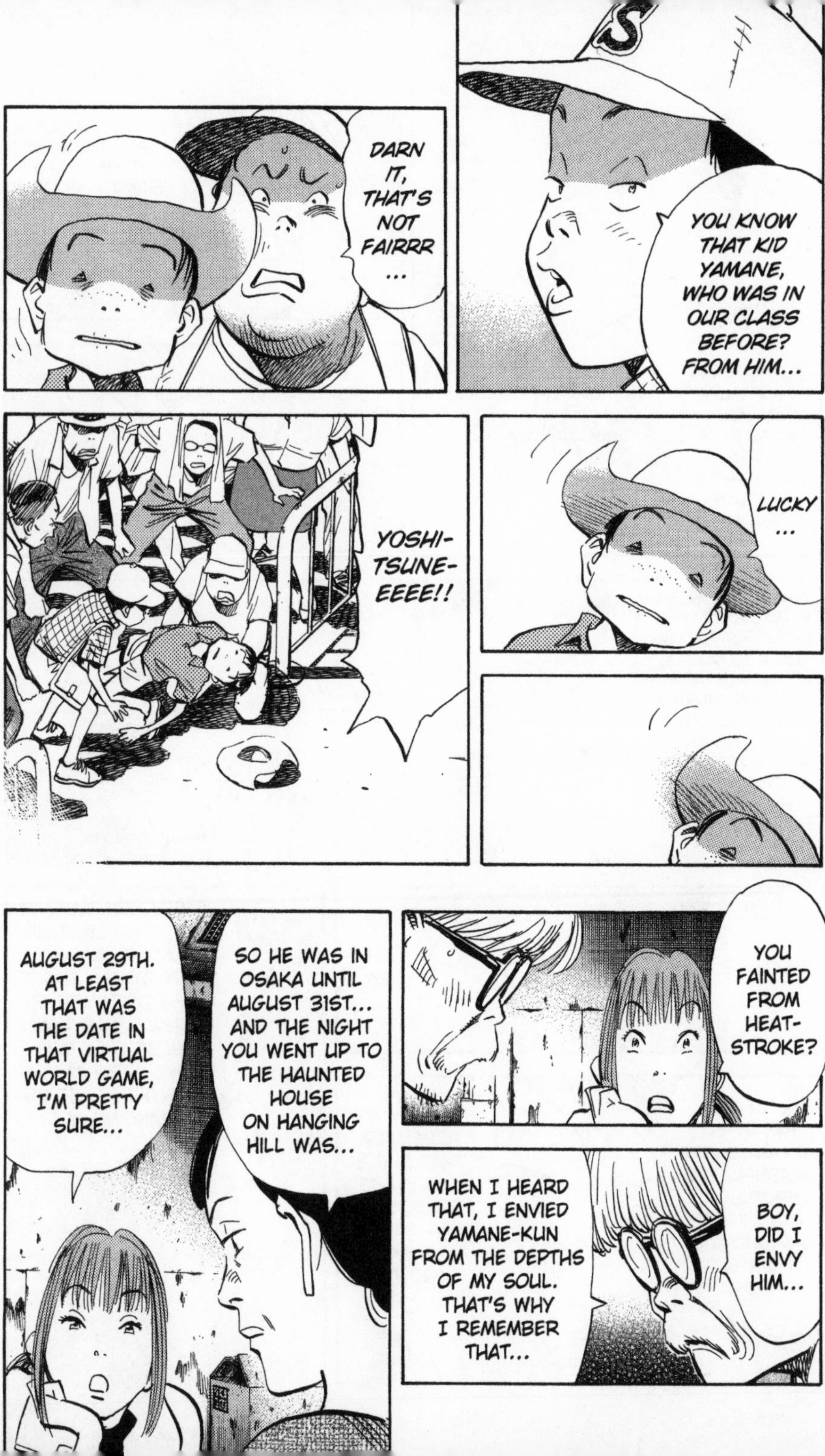
YOU KNOW THAT KID YAMANE, WHO WAS IN OUR CLASS BEFORE? FROM HIM...
DARN IT, THAT'S NOT FAIRRR ...
LUCKY ...
YOSHI-TSUNE-EEEE!!
YOU FAINTED FROM HEAT-STROKE?
BOY, DID I ENVY HIM...
WHEN I HEARD THAT, I ENVIED YAMANE-KUN FROM THE DEPTHS OF MY SOUL. THAT'S WHY I REMEMBER THAT...
SO HE WAS IN OSAKA UNTIL AUGUST 31ST... AND THE NIGHT YOU WENT UP TO THE HAUNTED HOUSE ON HANGING HILL WAS...
AUGUST 29TH. AT LEAST THAT WAS THE DATE IN THAT VIRTUAL WORLD GAME, I'M PRETTY SURE...

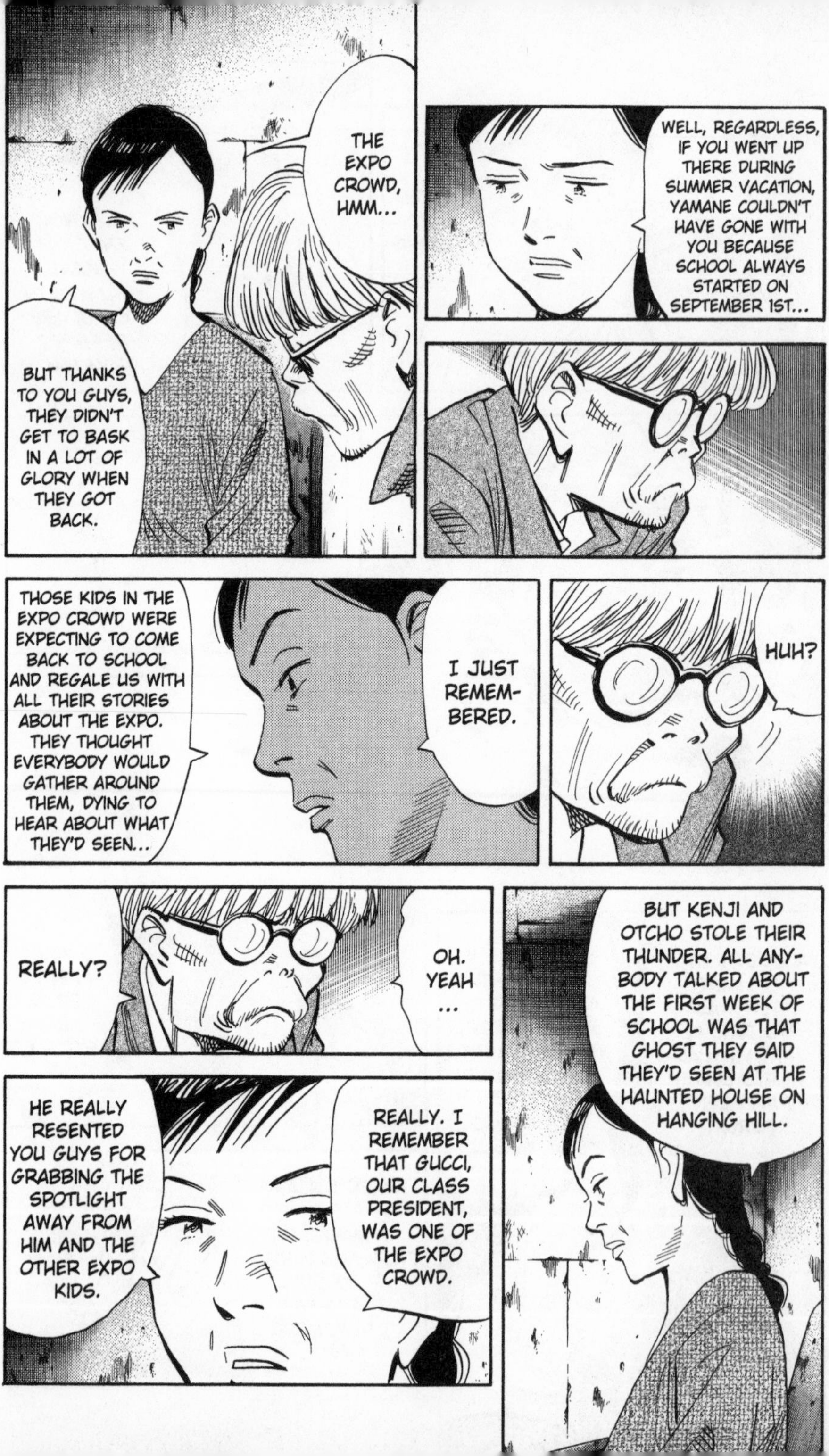
WELL, REGARDLESS, IF YOU WENT UP THERE DURING SUMMER VACATION, YAMANE COULDN'T HAVE GONE WITH YOU BECAUSE SCHOOL ALWAYS STARTED ON SEPTEMBER 1ST...
THE EXPO CROWD, HMM...
BUT THANKS TO YOU GUYS, THEY DIDN'T GET TO BASK IN A LOT OF GLORY WHEN THEY GOT BACK.
HUH?
I JUST REMEM-BERED.
THOSE KIDS IN THE EXPO CROWD WERE EXPECTING TO COME BACK TO SCHOOL AND REGALE US WITH ALL THEIR STORIES ABOUT THE EXPO. THEY THOUGHT EVERYBODY WOULD GATHER AROUND THEM, DYING TO HEAR ABOUT WHAT THEY'D SEEN...
BUT KENJI AND OTCHO STOLE THEIR THUNDER. ALL ANY-BODY TALKED ABOUT THE FIRST WEEK OF SCHOOL WAS THAT GHOST THEY SAID THEY'D SEEN AT THE HAUNTED HOUSE ON HANGING HILL.
OH. YEAH ...
REALLY?
REALLY. I REMEMBER THAT GUCCI, OUR CLASS PRESIDENT, WAS ONE OF THE EXPO CROWD.
HE REALLY RESENTED YOU GUYS FOR GRABBING THE SPOTLIGHT AWAY FROM HIM AND THE OTHER EXPO KIDS.

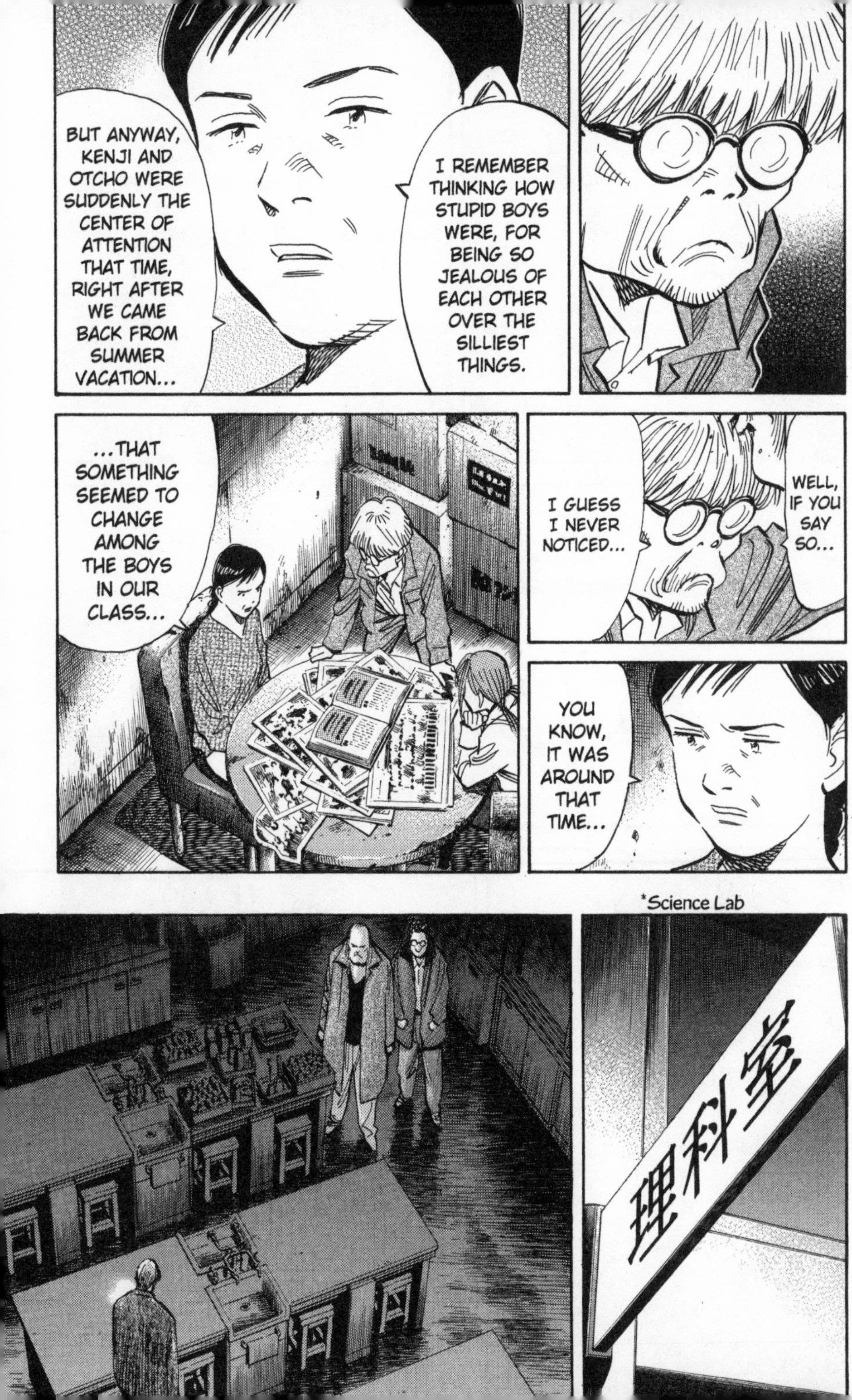
I REMEMBER THINKING HOW STUPID BOYS WERE, FOR BEING SO JEALOUS OF EACH OTHER OVER THE SILLIEST THINGS.
BUT ANYWAY, KENJI AND OTCHO WERE SUDDENLY THE CENTER OF ATTENTION THAT TIME, RIGHT AFTER WE CAME BACK FROM SUMMER VACATION...
WELL, IF YOU SAY SO...
I GUESS I NEVER NOTICED...
YOU KNOW, IT WAS AROUND THAT TIME...
...THAT SOMETHING SEEMED TO CHANGE AMONG THE BOYS IN OUR CLASS...
*Science Lab
理科室

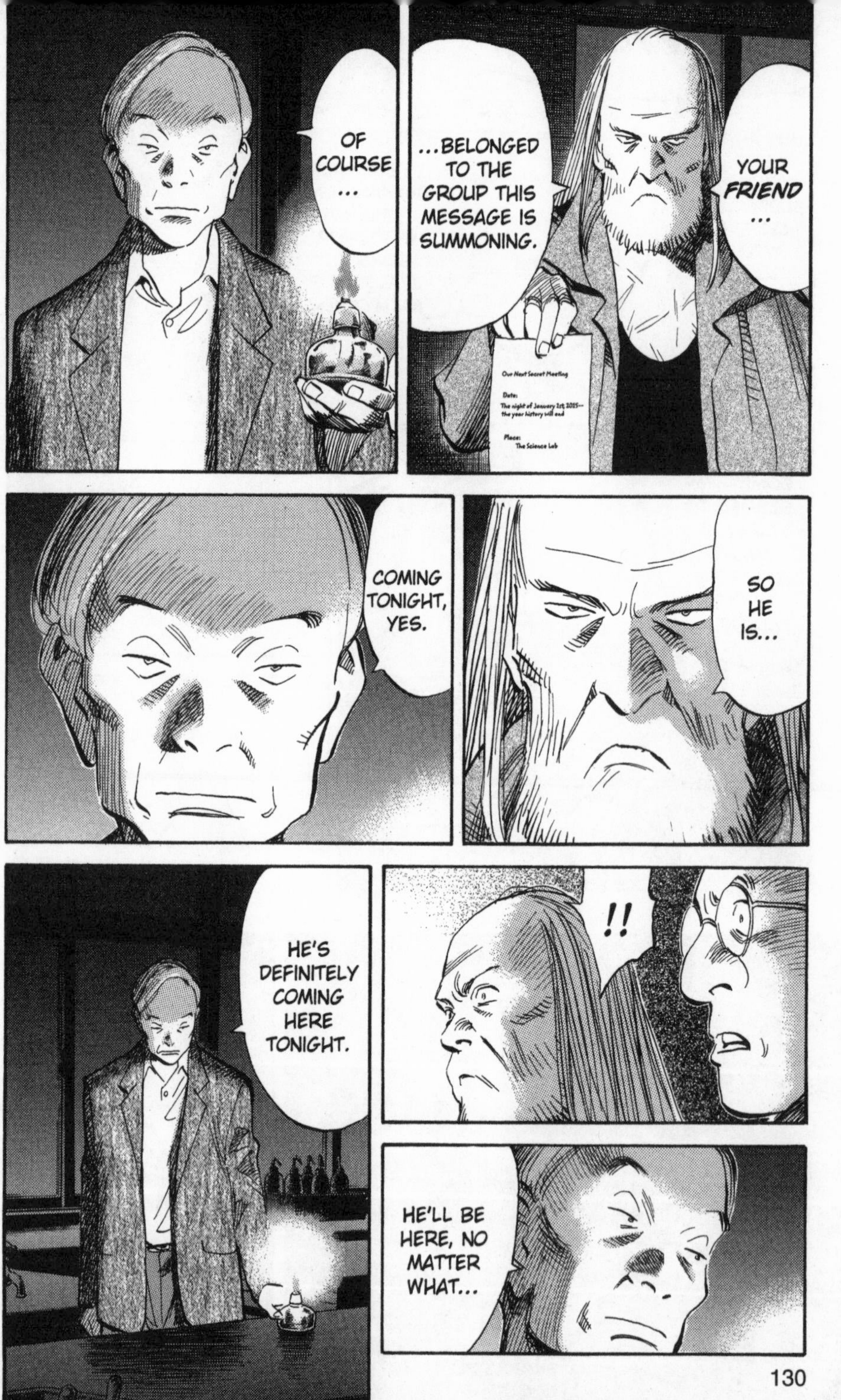
YOUR FRIEND...
...BELONGED TO THE GROUP THIS MESSAGE IS SUMMONING.
Our Next Secret Meeting
Date:
The night of January 1st, 2015-- the year history will end
Place:
The Science Lab
OF COURSE...
SO HE IS...
COMING TONIGHT, YES.
!!
HE'LL BE HERE, NO MATTER WHAT...
HE'S DEFINITELY COMING HERE TONIGHT.

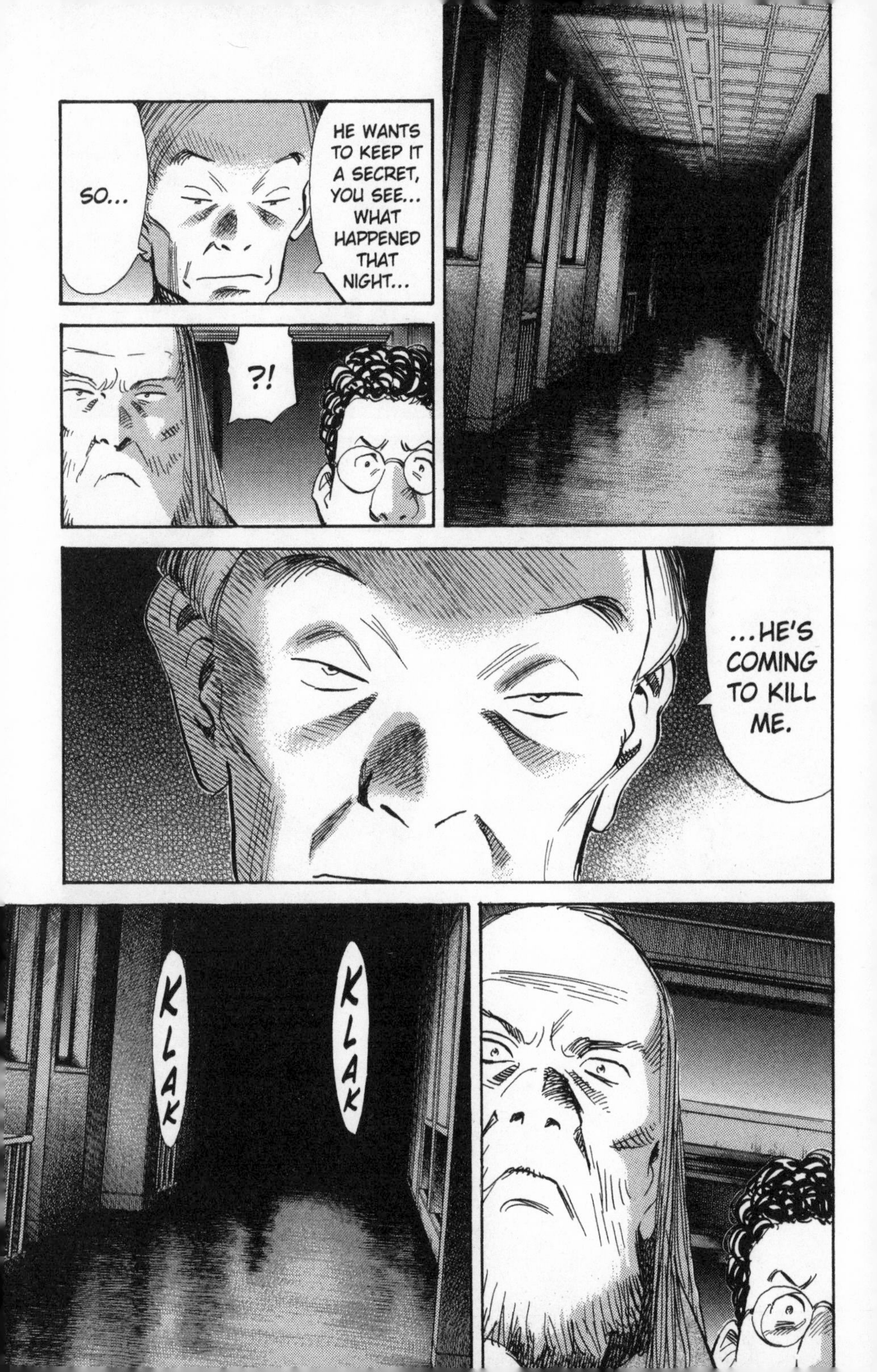
HE WANTS TO KEEP IT A SECRET, YOU SEE... WHAT HAPPENED THAT NIGHT...
SO...
?!
...HE'S COMING TO KILL ME.
KLAK
KLAK

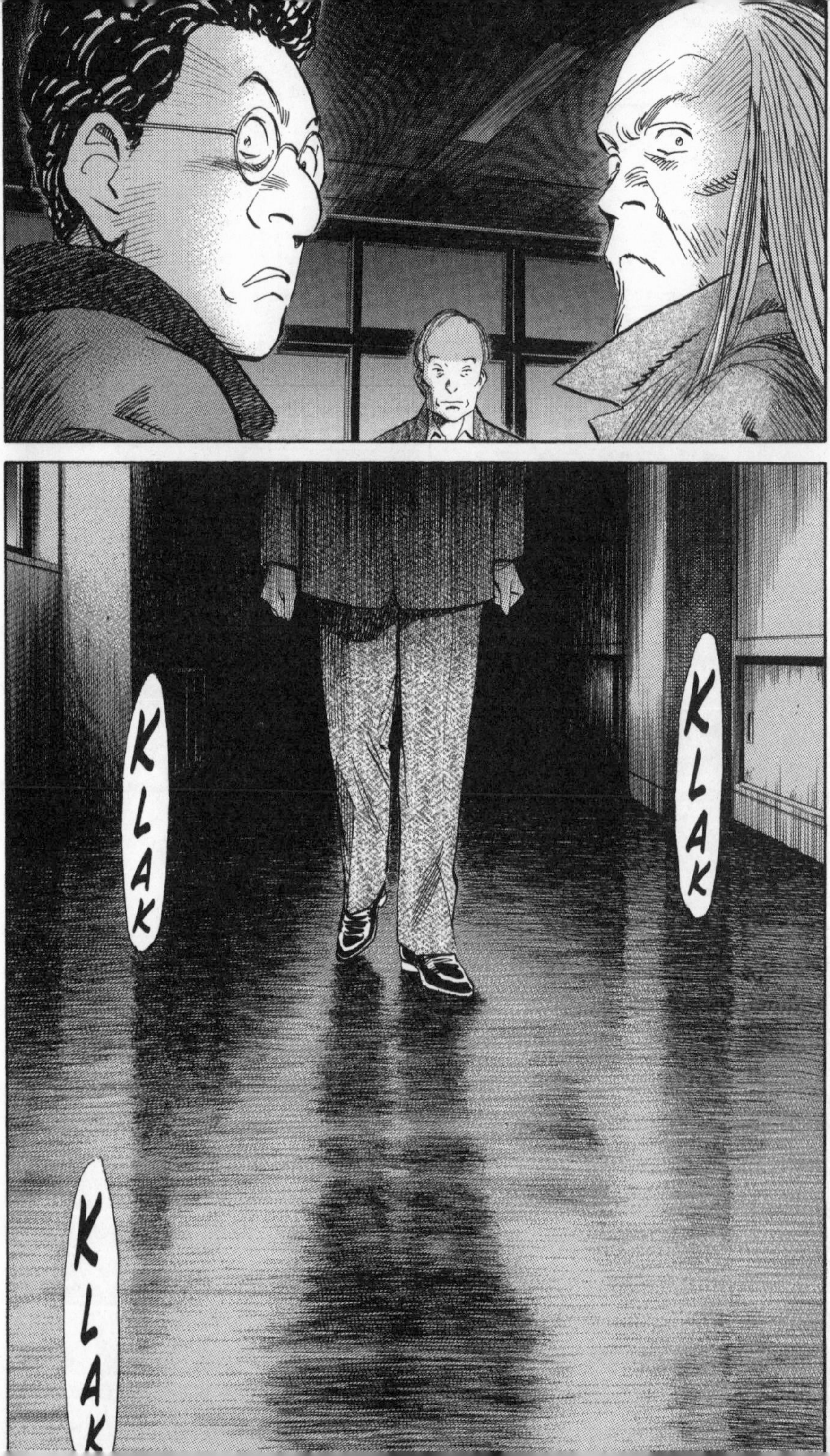
KLAK
KLAK
KLAK

Chapter 8 The Man Who…

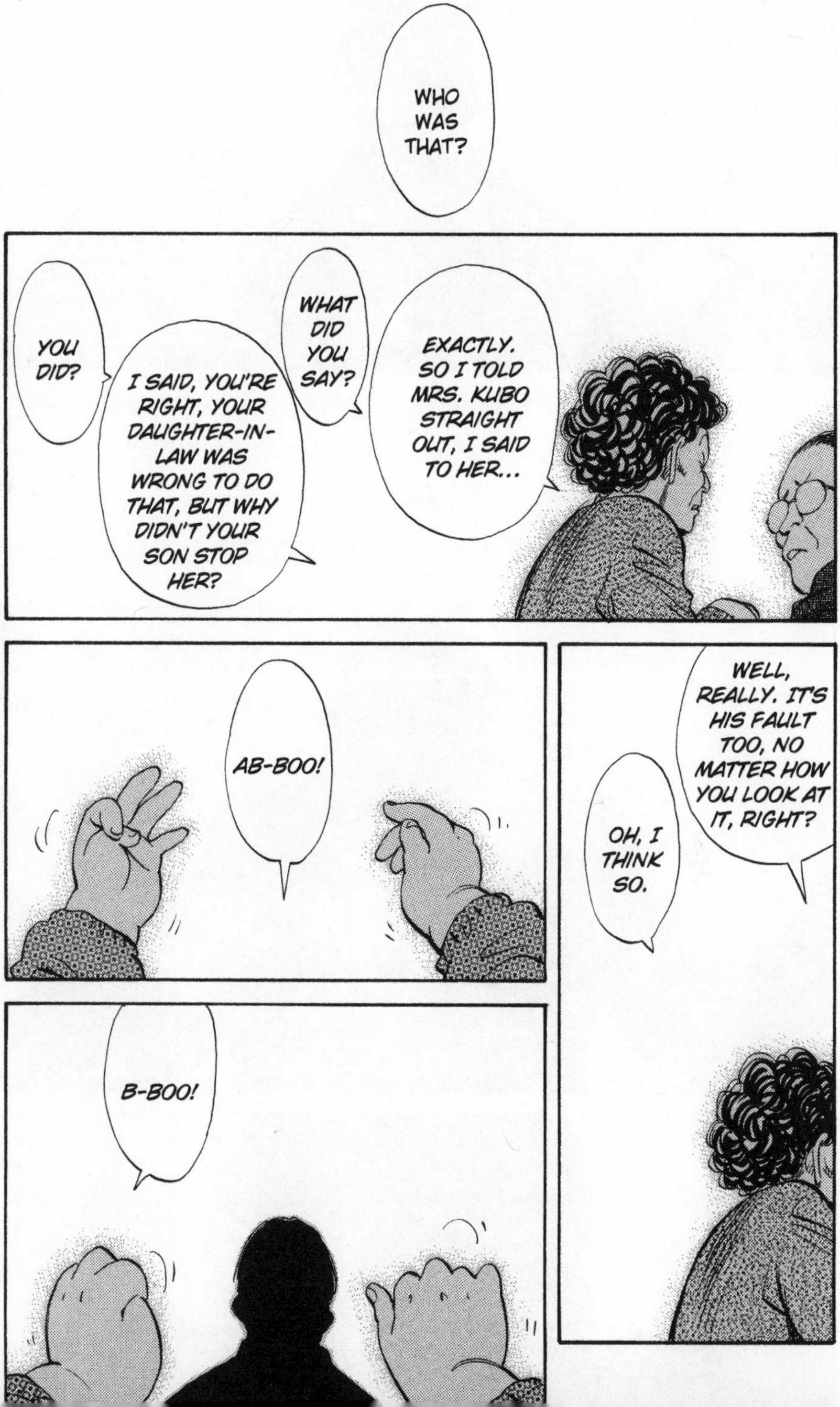
WHO WAS THAT?
EXACTLY. SO I TOLD MRS. KUBO STRAIGHT OUT, I SAID TO HER...
WHAT DID YOU SAY?
I SAID, YOU'RE RIGHT, YOUR DAUGHTER-IN-LAW WAS WRONG TO DO THAT, BUT WHY DIDN'T YOUR SON STOP HER?
YOU DID?
WELL, REALLY. IT'S HIS FAULT TOO, NO MATTER HOW YOU LOOK AT IT, RIGHT?
OH, I THINK SO.
AB-BOO!
B-BOO!

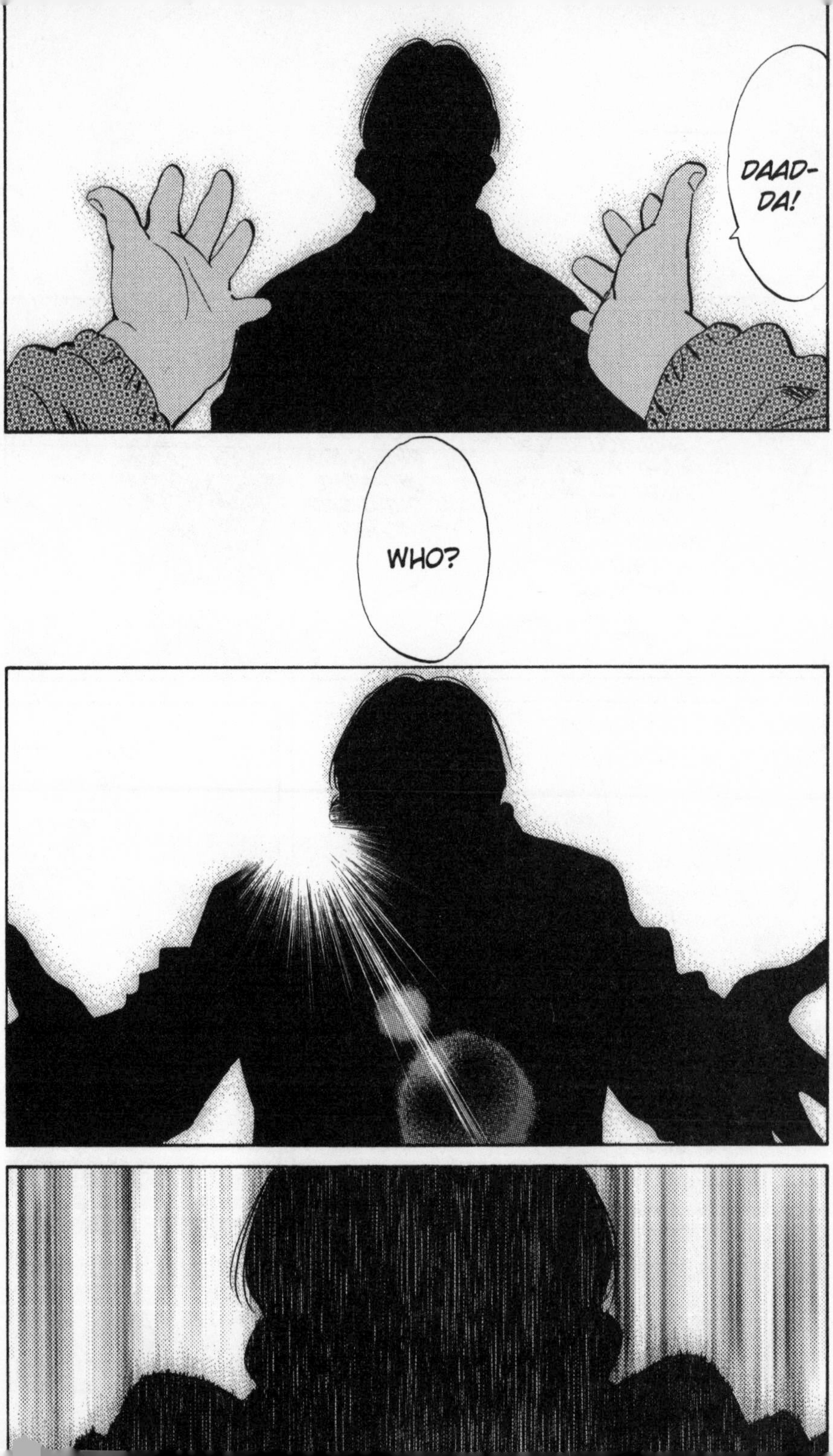
DAAD-
DA!
WHO?

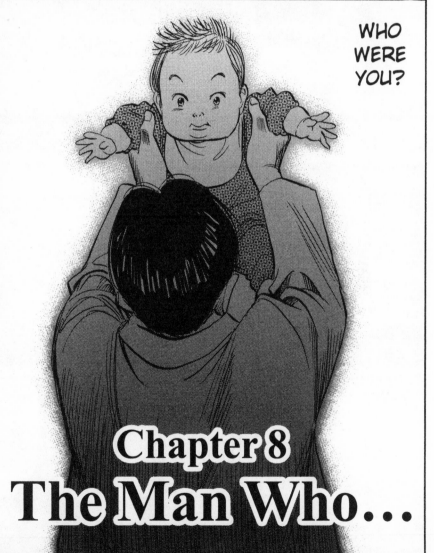

WHO
WERE
YOU?

Chapter 8
The Man Who...

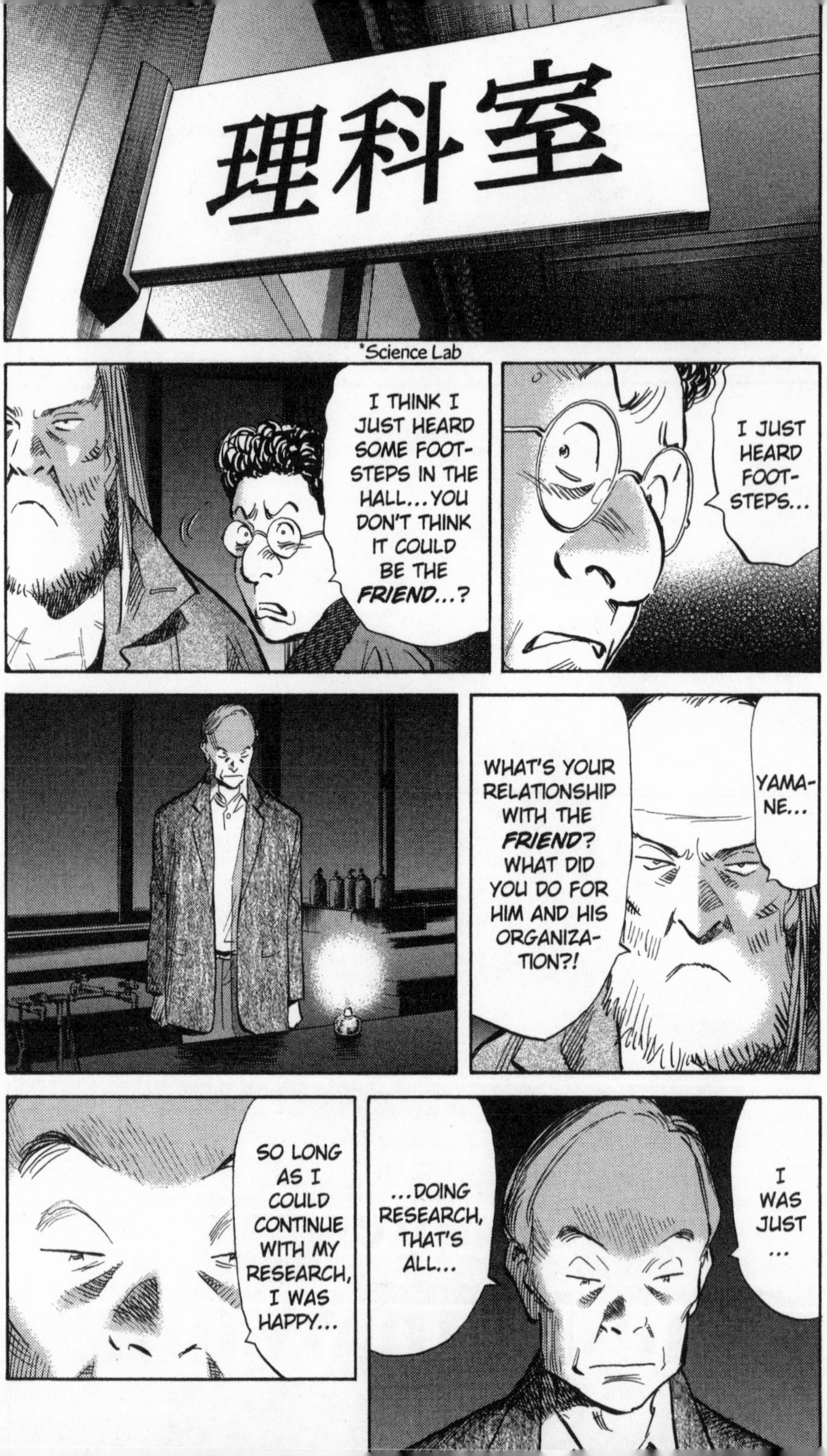
理科室
*Science Lab
I JUST HEARD FOOT-STEPS...
I THINK I JUST HEARD SOME FOOT-STEPS IN THE HALL...YOU DON'T THINK IT COULD BE THE FRIEND...?
YAMA-NE...
WHAT'S YOUR RELATIONSHIP WITH THE FRIEND? WHAT DID YOU DO FOR HIM AND HIS ORGANIZA-TION?!
I WAS JUST ...
...DOING RESEARCH, THAT'S ALL...
SO LONG AS I COULD CONTINUE WITH MY RESEARCH, I WAS HAPPY...

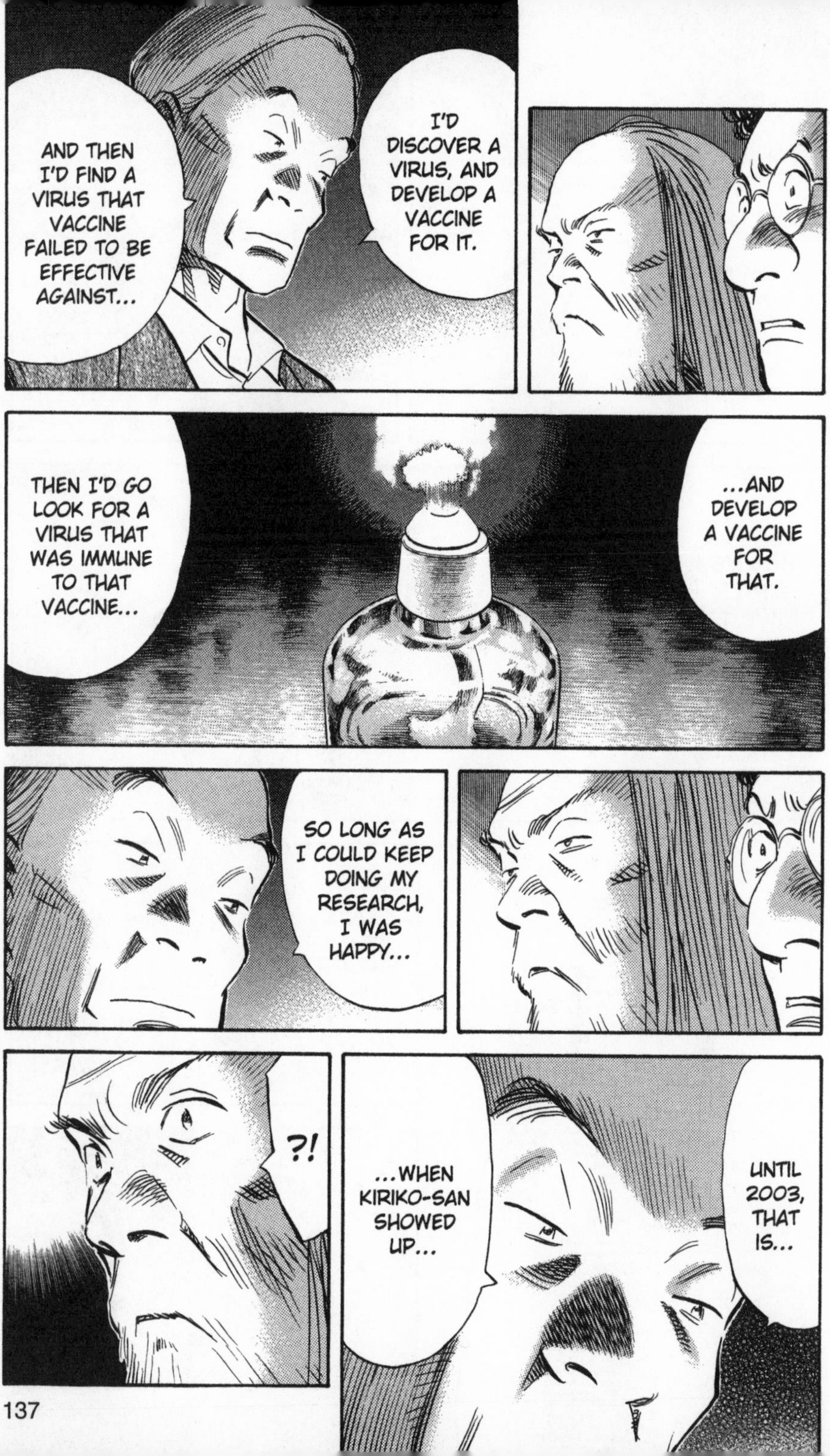
I'D DISCOVER A VIRUS, AND DEVELOP A VACCINE FOR IT.
AND THEN I'D FIND A VIRUS THAT VACCINE FAILED TO BE EFFECTIVE AGAINST...
THEN I'D GO LOOK FOR A VIRUS THAT WAS IMMUNE TO THAT VACCINE...
...AND DEVELOP A VACCINE FOR THAT.
SO LONG AS I COULD KEEP DOING MY RESEARCH, I WAS HAPPY...
UNTIL 2003, THAT IS...
...WHEN KIRIKO-SAN SHOWED UP...
?!

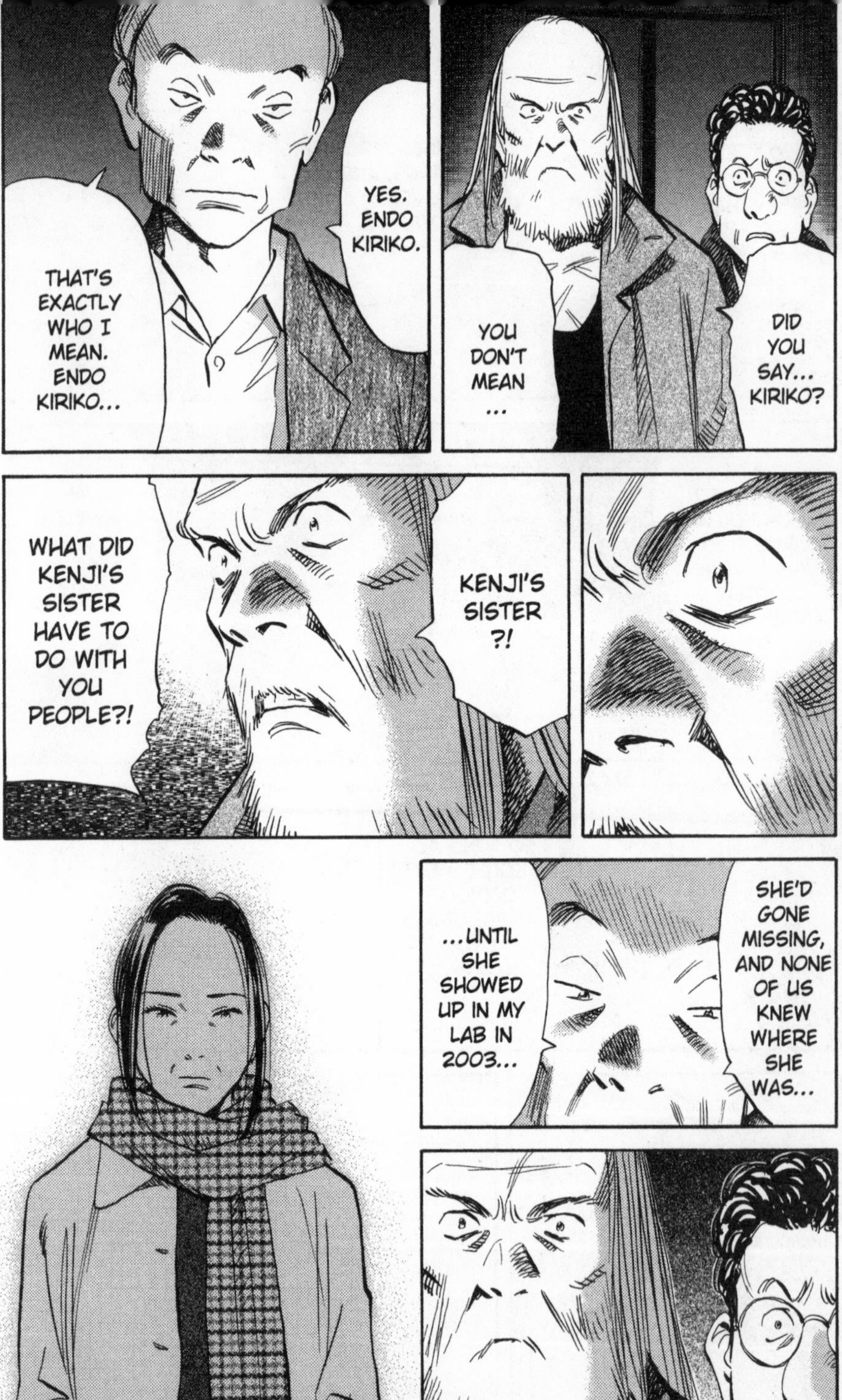
DID YOU SAY... KIRIKO?
YOU DON'T MEAN ...
YES. ENDO KIRIKO.
THAT'S EXACTLY WHO I MEAN. ENDO KIRIKO...
KENJI'S SISTER ?!
WHAT DID KENJI'S SISTER HAVE TO DO WITH YOU PEOPLE?!
SHE'D GONE MISSING, AND NONE OF US KNEW WHERE SHE WAS...
...UNTIL SHE SHOWED UP IN MY LAB IN 2003...

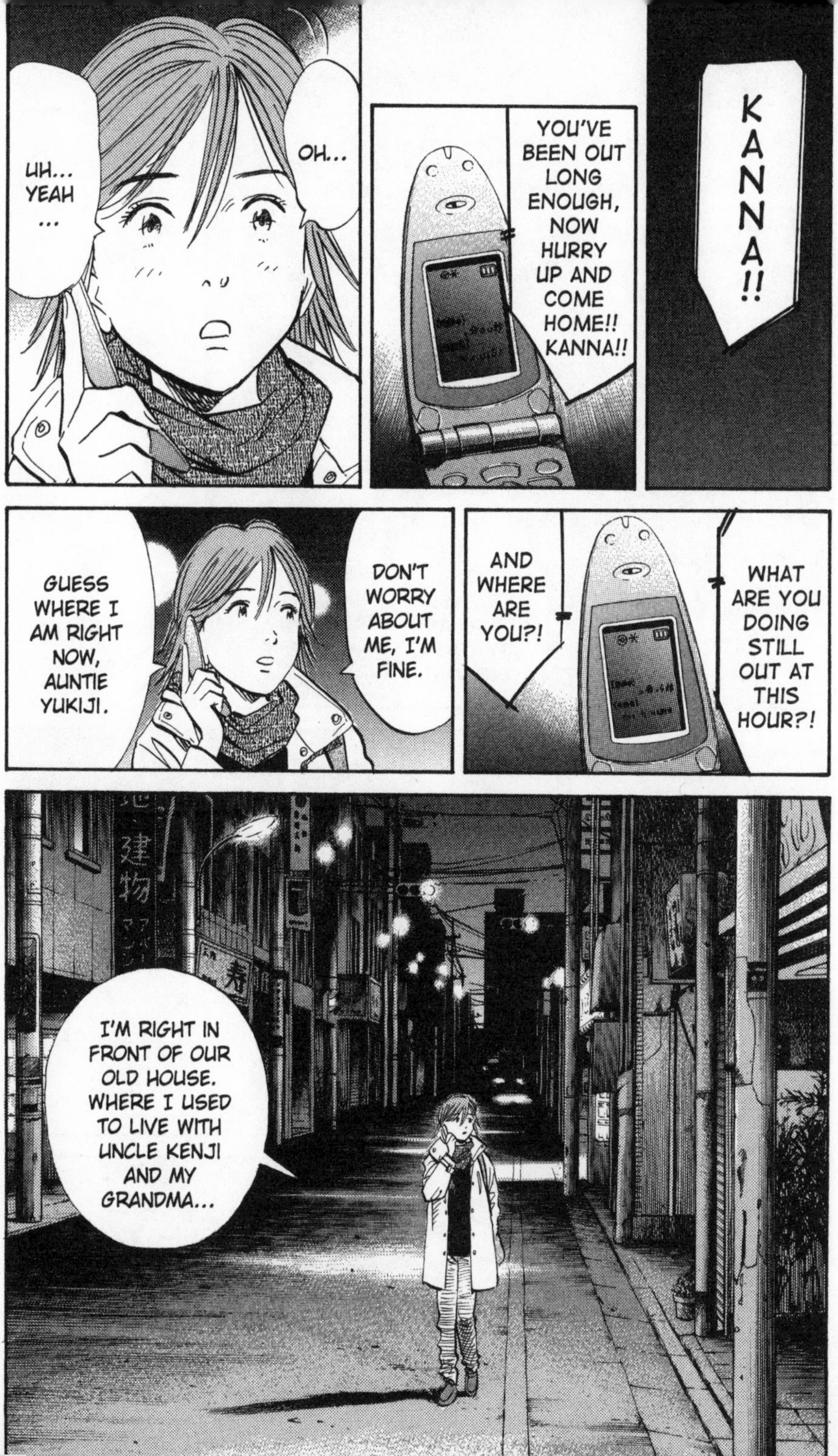
KANNA!!
YOU'VE BEEN OUT LONG ENOUGH, NOW HURRY UP AND COME HOME!! KANNA!!
OH...
UH... YEAH ...
WHAT ARE YOU DOING STILL OUT AT THIS HOUR?!
AND WHERE ARE YOU?!
DON'T WORRY ABOUT ME, I'M FINE.
GUESS WHERE I AM RIGHT NOW, AUNTIE YUKIJI.
I'M RIGHT IN FRONT OF OUR OLD HOUSE. WHERE I USED TO LIVE WITH UNCLE KENJI AND MY GRANDMA...

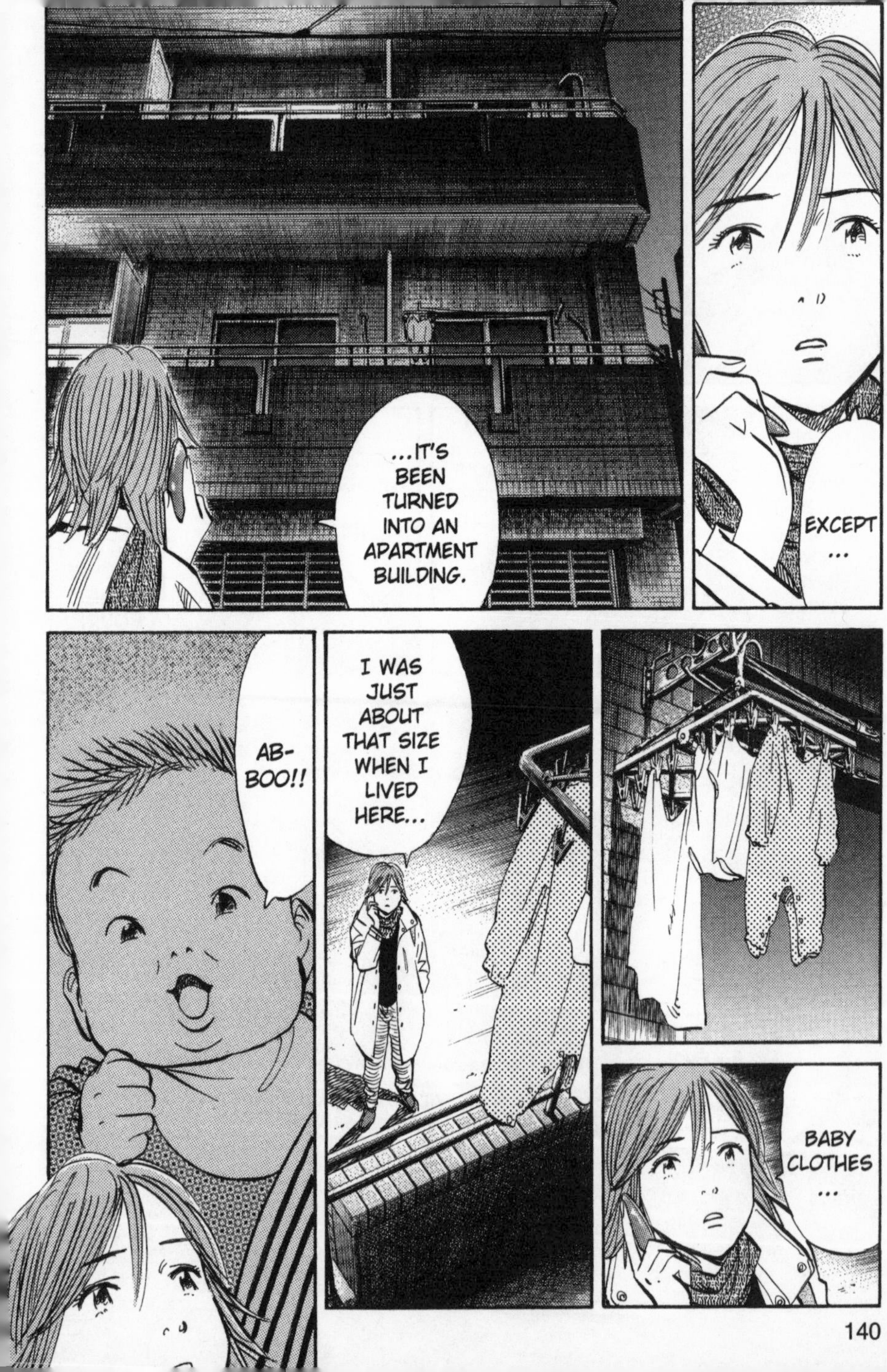
EXCEPT...
...IT'S BEEN TURNED INTO AN APARTMENT BUILDING.
BABY CLOTHES...
I WAS JUST ABOUT THAT SIZE WHEN I LIVED HERE...
AB-BOO!!

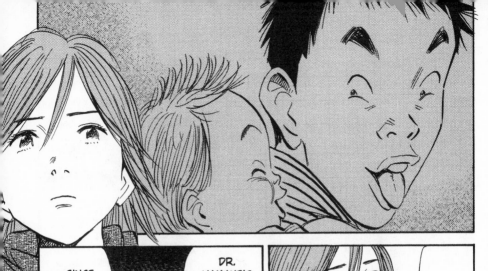

UNCLE KENJI ...
ENOUGH, KANNA. NOW PLEASE JUST COME HOME!!
DR. YAMANE'S OLD HOUSE WAS TURNED INTO A PARKING LOT, BUT...
...SINCE I'M HERE ANYWAY, I'D LIKE TO WALK AROUND THE NEIGHBORHOOD A LITTLE LONGER.
THIS IS WHERE IT ALL STARTED, RIGHT? MAYBE THERE MIGHT BE SOME OTHER CLUES...
KANNA, YOU NEED TO GET SOME REST OR YOU'LL GET SICK.
YOU'VE HARDLY SLEPT AT ALL THE PAST FEW DAYS!!
I'M FINE, AUNTIE YUKIJI.
KANNA, YOU...

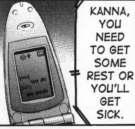

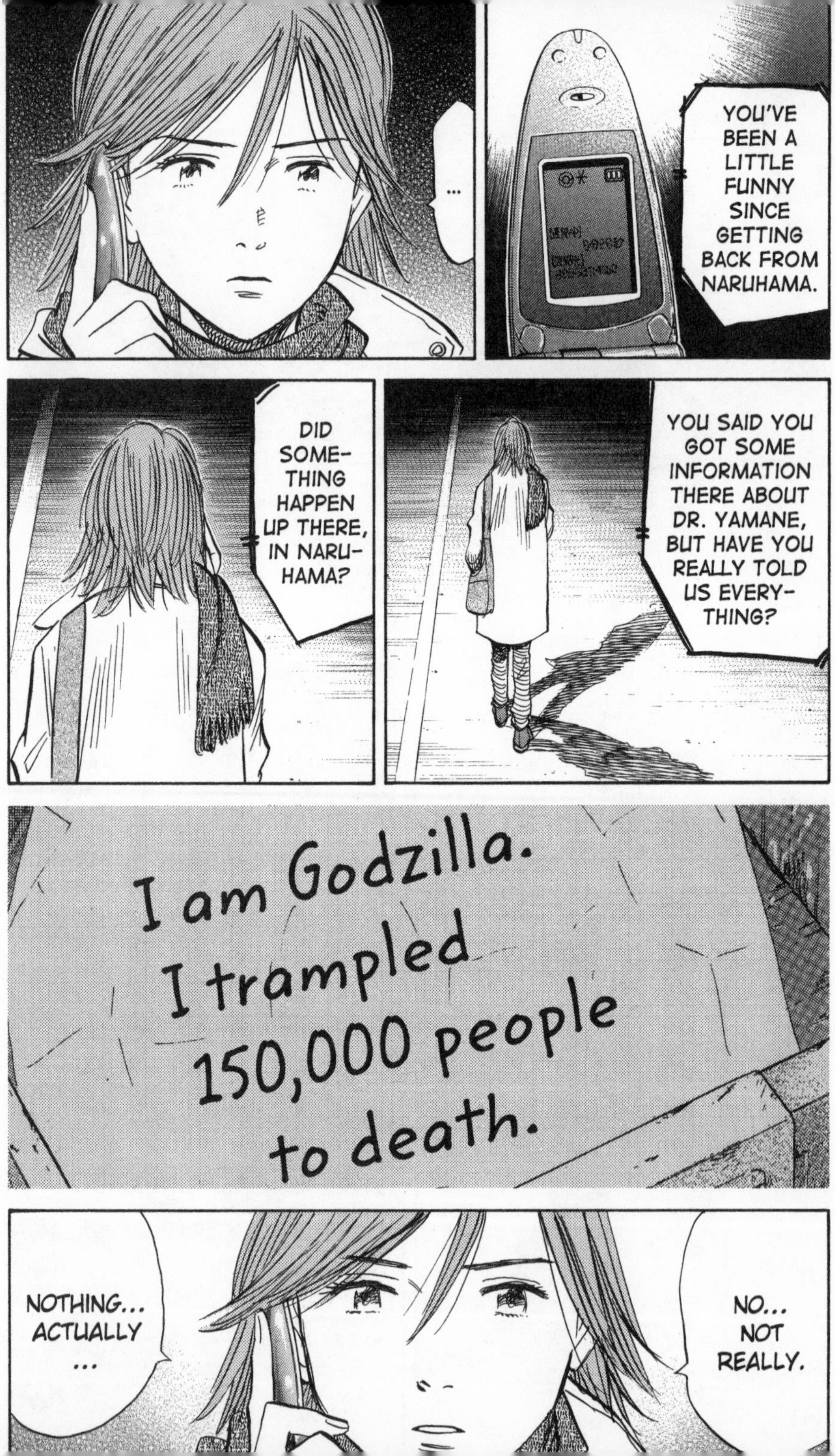
YOU'VE BEEN A LITTLE FUNNY SINCE GETTING BACK FROM NARUHAMA.
...
YOU SAID YOU GOT SOME INFORMATION THERE ABOUT DR. YAMANE, BUT HAVE YOU REALLY TOLD US EVERY-THING?
DID SOME-THING HAPPEN UP THERE, IN NARU-HAMA?
I am Godzilla. I trampled 150,000 people to death.
NO... NOT REALLY.
NOTHING... ACTUALLY ...

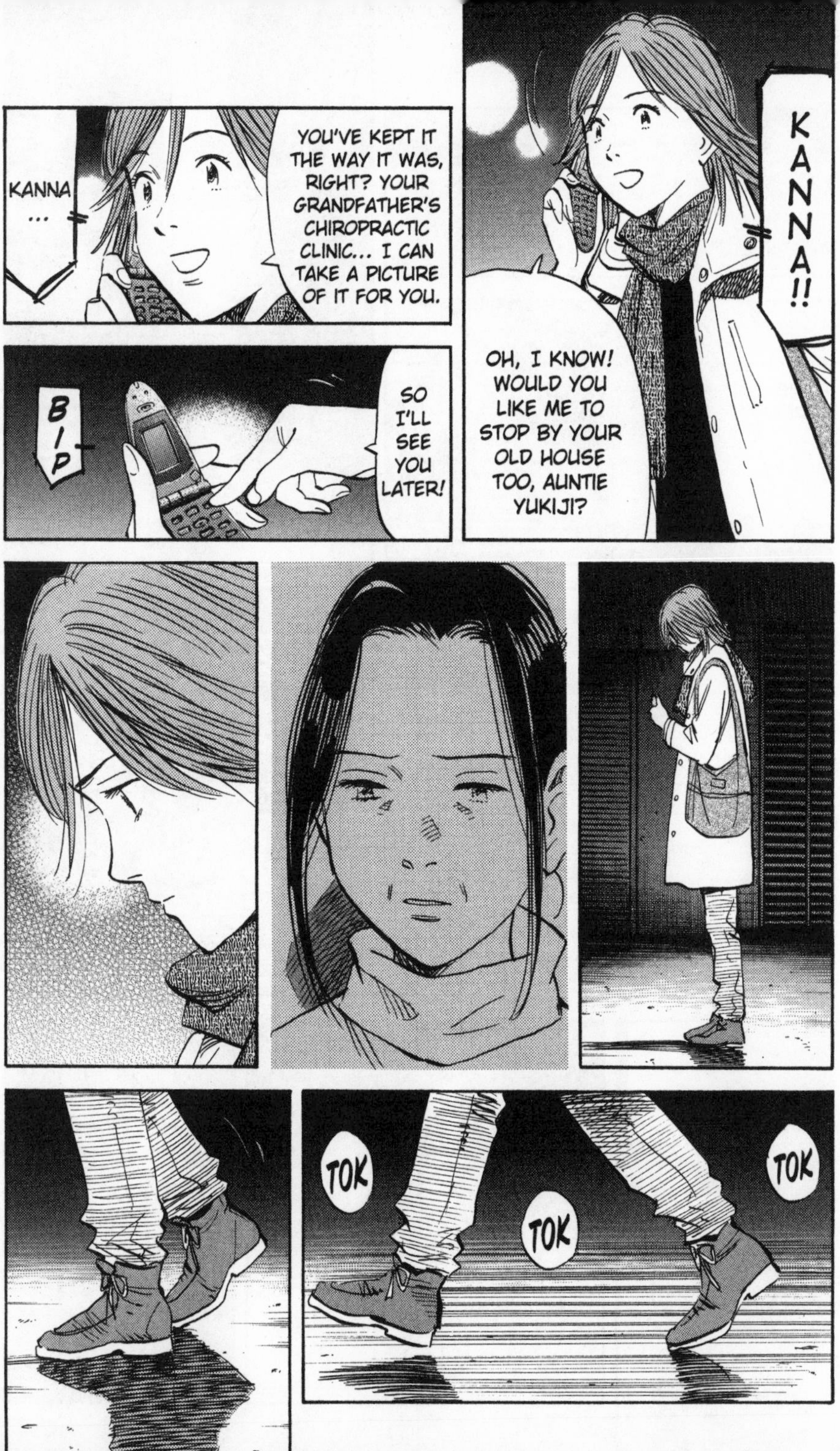
KANNA!!
OH, I KNOW! WOULD YOU LIKE ME TO STOP BY YOUR OLD HOUSE TOO, AUNTIE YUKIJI?
YOU'VE KEPT IT THE WAY IT WAS, RIGHT? YOUR GRANDFATHER'S CHIROPRACTIC CLINIC... I CAN TAKE A PICTURE OF IT FOR YOU.
KANNA ...
SO I'LL SEE YOU LATER!
BIP
TOK
TOK
TOK

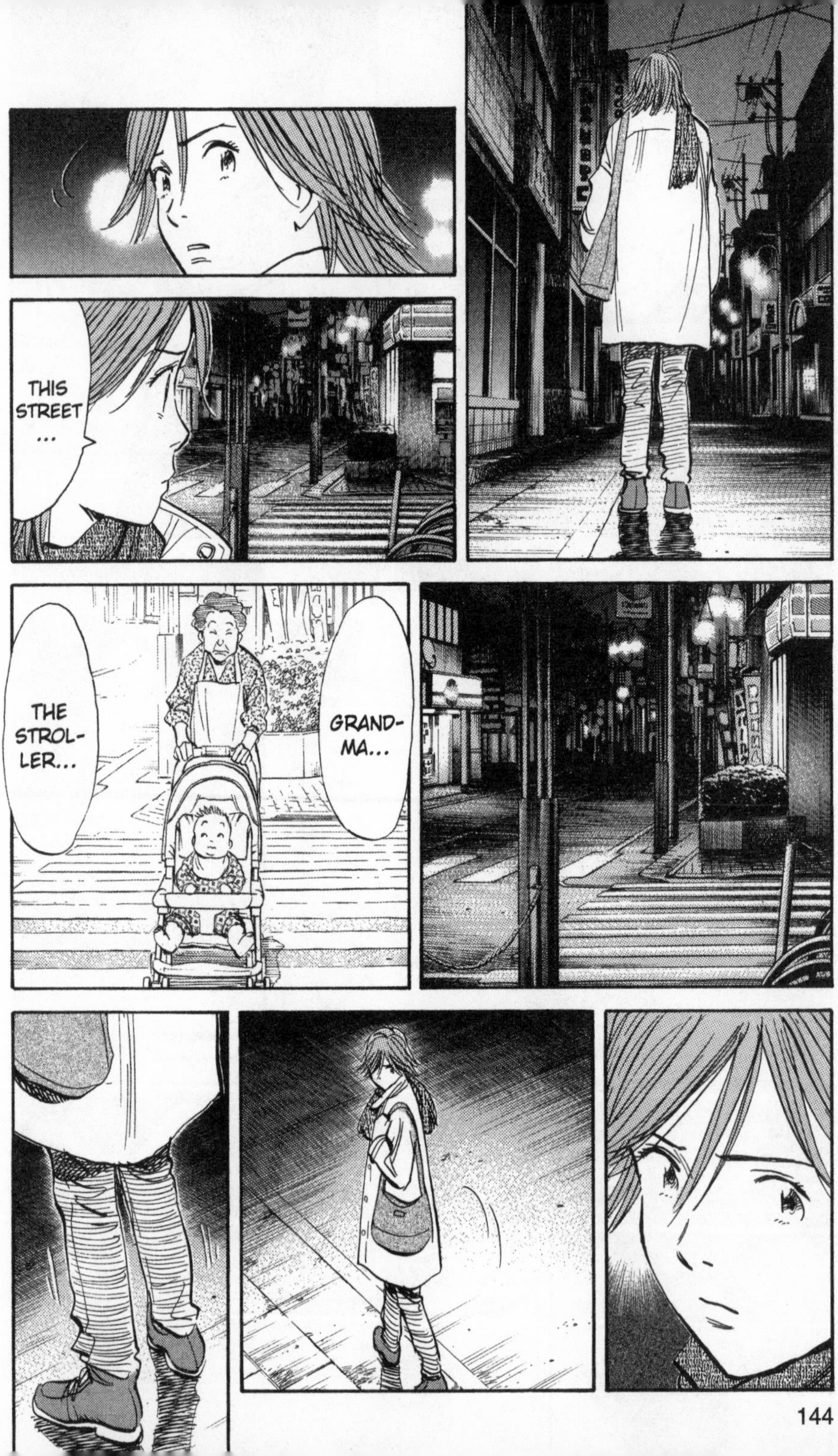
THIS STREET ...
GRAND-MA...
THE STROL-LER...

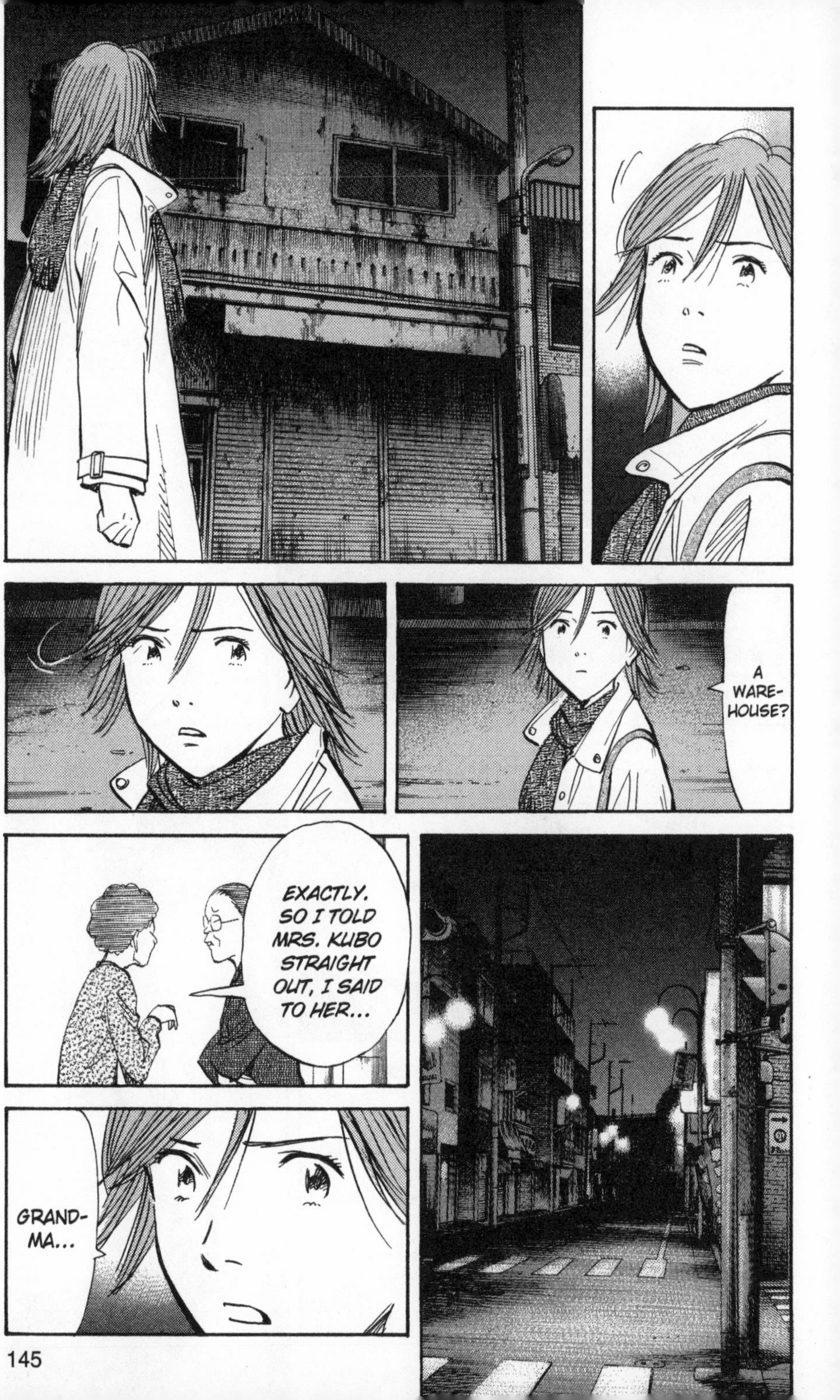

A WARE-HOUSE?
EXACTLY. SO I TOLD MRS. KUBO STRAIGHT OUT, I SAID TO HER...
GRAND-MA...

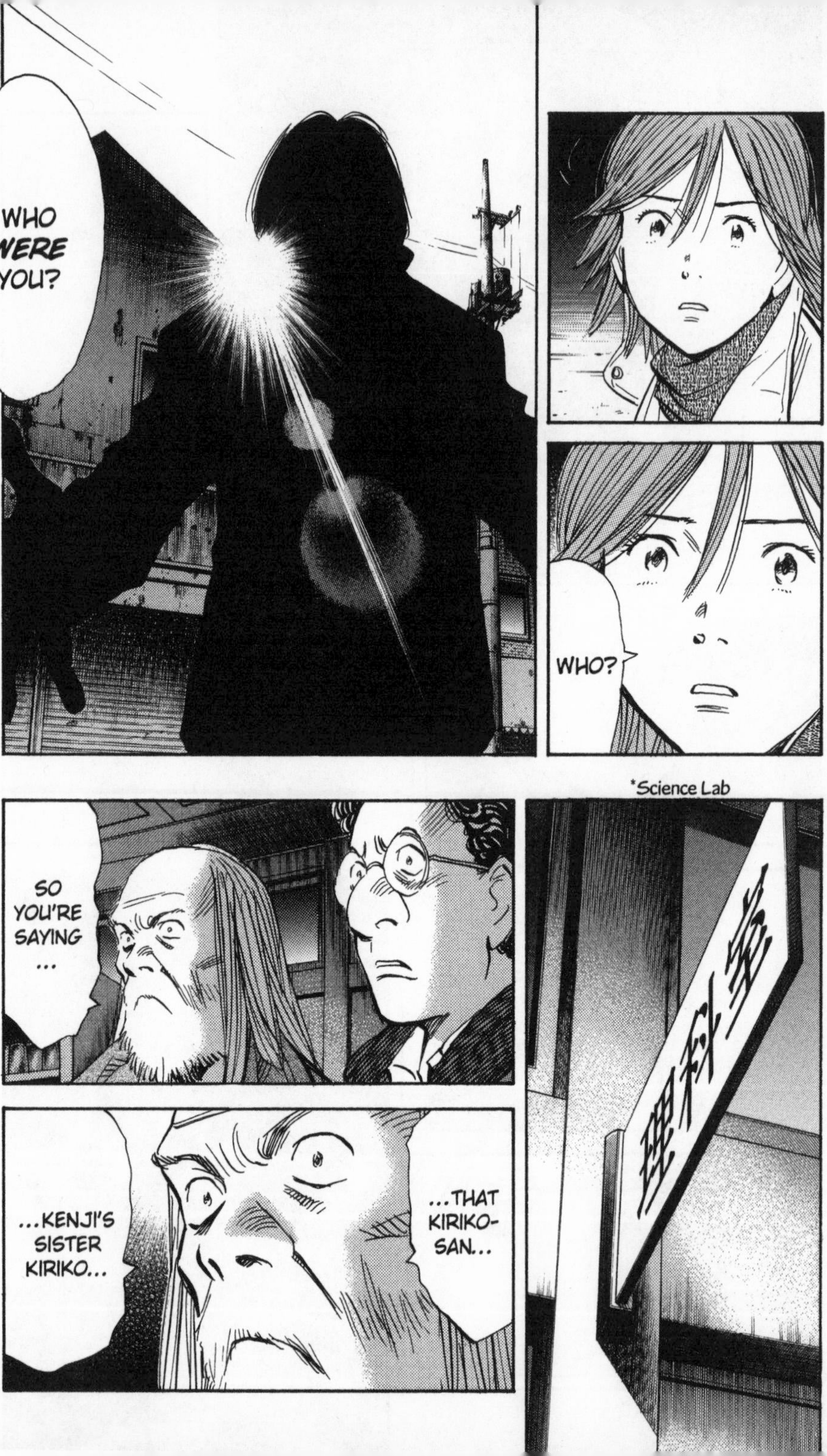
WHO?
WHO WERE YOU?
*Science Lab
理科室
SO YOU'RE SAYING ...
...THAT KIRIKO-SAN...
...KENJI'S SISTER KIRIKO...

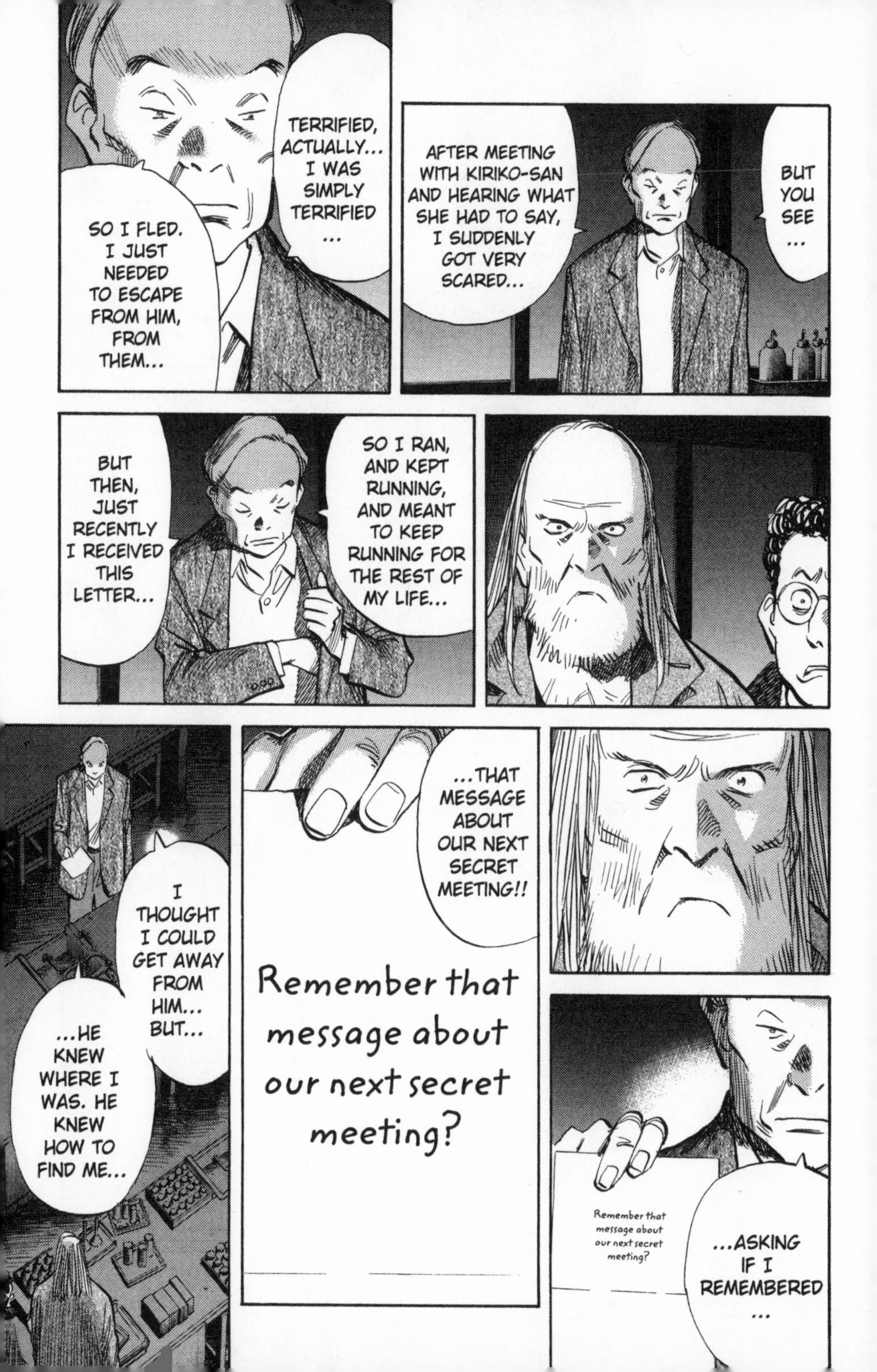
BUT YOU SEE...
AFTER MEETING WITH KIRIKO-SAN AND HEARING WHAT SHE HAD TO SAY, I SUDDENLY GOT VERY SCARED...
TERRIFIED, ACTUALLY... I WAS SIMPLY TERRIFIED...
SO I FLED. I JUST NEEDED TO ESCAPE FROM HIM, FROM THEM...
SO I RAN, AND KEPT RUNNING, AND MEANT TO KEEP RUNNING FOR THE REST OF MY LIFE...
BUT THEN, JUST RECENTLY I RECEIVED THIS LETTER...
Remember that message about our next secret meeting?
...ASKING IF I REMEMBERED...
...THAT MESSAGE ABOUT OUR NEXT SECRET MEETING!!
Remember that message about our next secret meeting?
I THOUGHT I COULD GET AWAY FROM HIM... BUT...
...HE KNEW WHERE I WAS. HE KNEW HOW TO FIND ME...

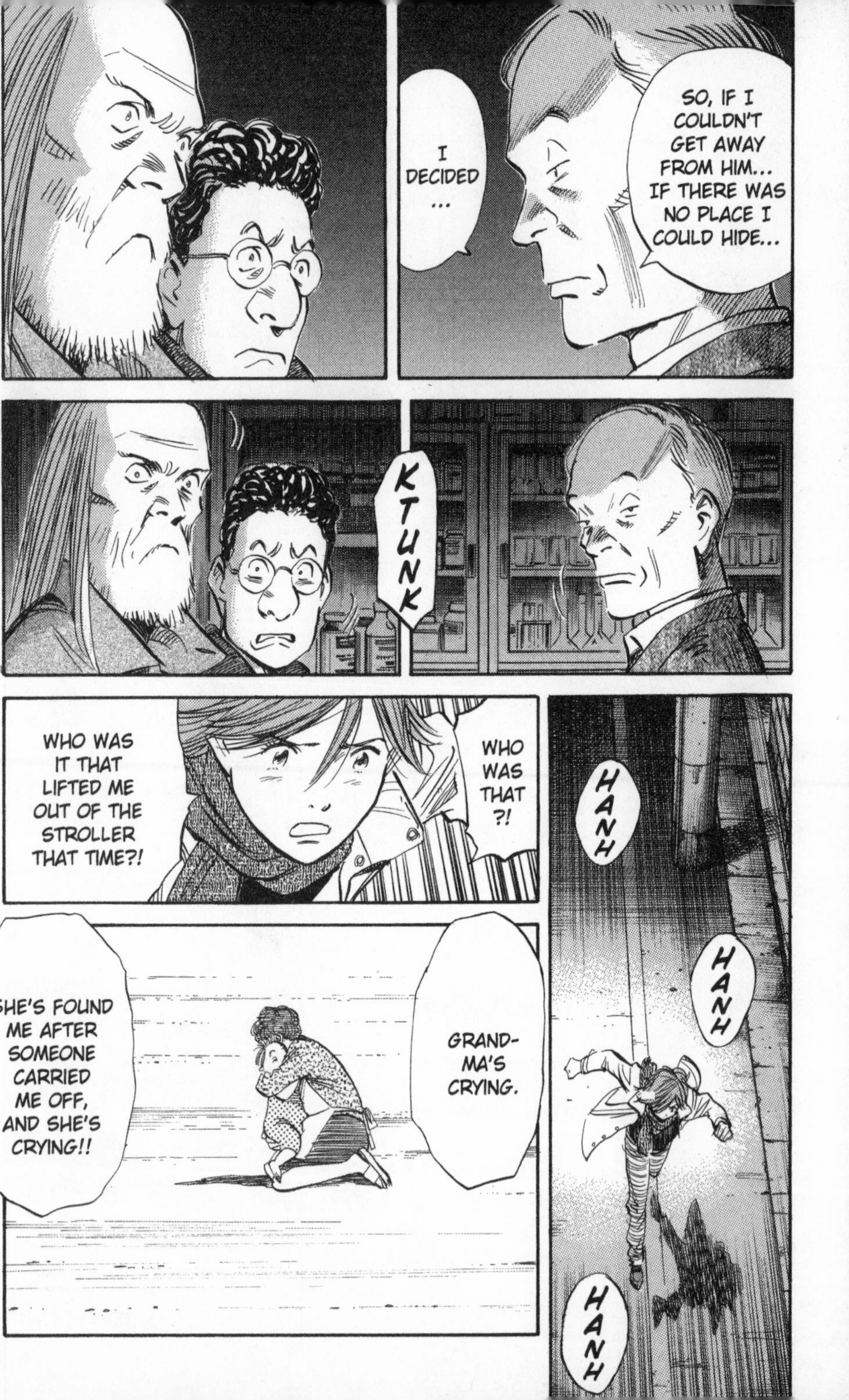
SO, IF I COULDN'T GET AWAY FROM HIM... IF THERE WAS NO PLACE I COULD HIDE...
I DECIDED ...
KTUNK
HANH
HANH
HANH
WHO WAS THAT ?!
WHO WAS IT THAT LIFTED ME OUT OF THE STROLLER THAT TIME?!
GRAND-MA'S CRYING.
SHE'S FOUND ME AFTER SOMEONE CARRIED ME OFF, AND SHE'S CRYING!!

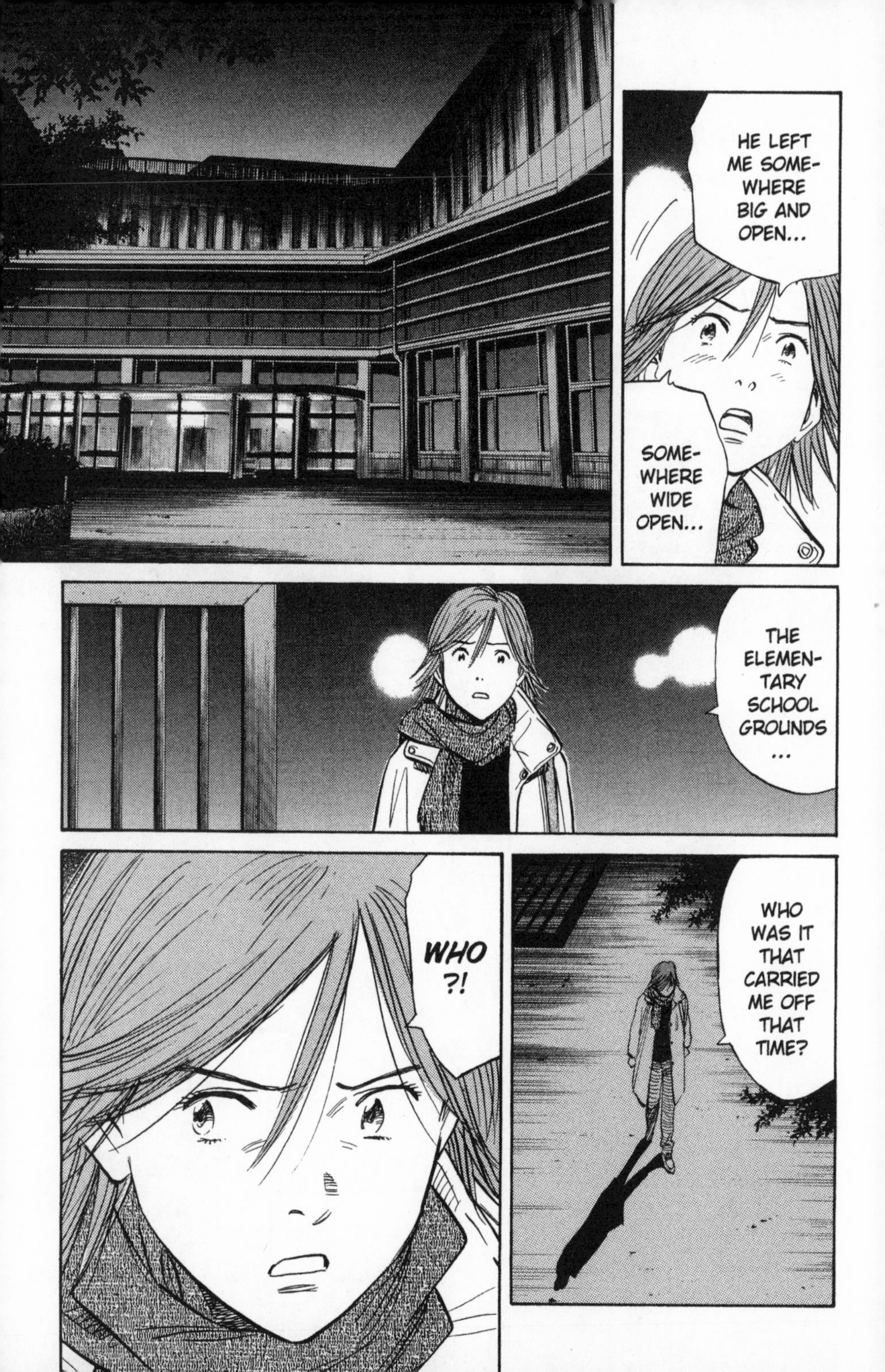
HE LEFT ME SOME-WHERE BIG AND OPEN...
SOME-WHERE WIDE OPEN...
THE ELEMEN-TARY SCHOOL GROUNDS...
WHO WAS IT THAT CARRIED ME OFF THAT TIME?
WHO ?!

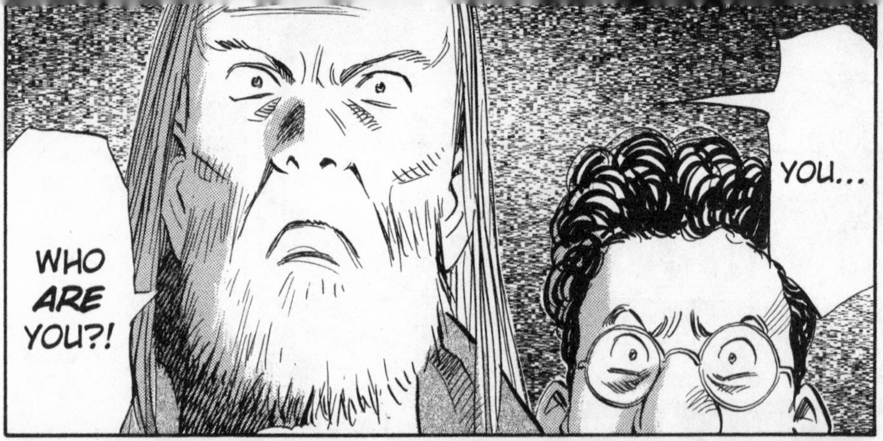
YOU...
WHO ARE YOU?!
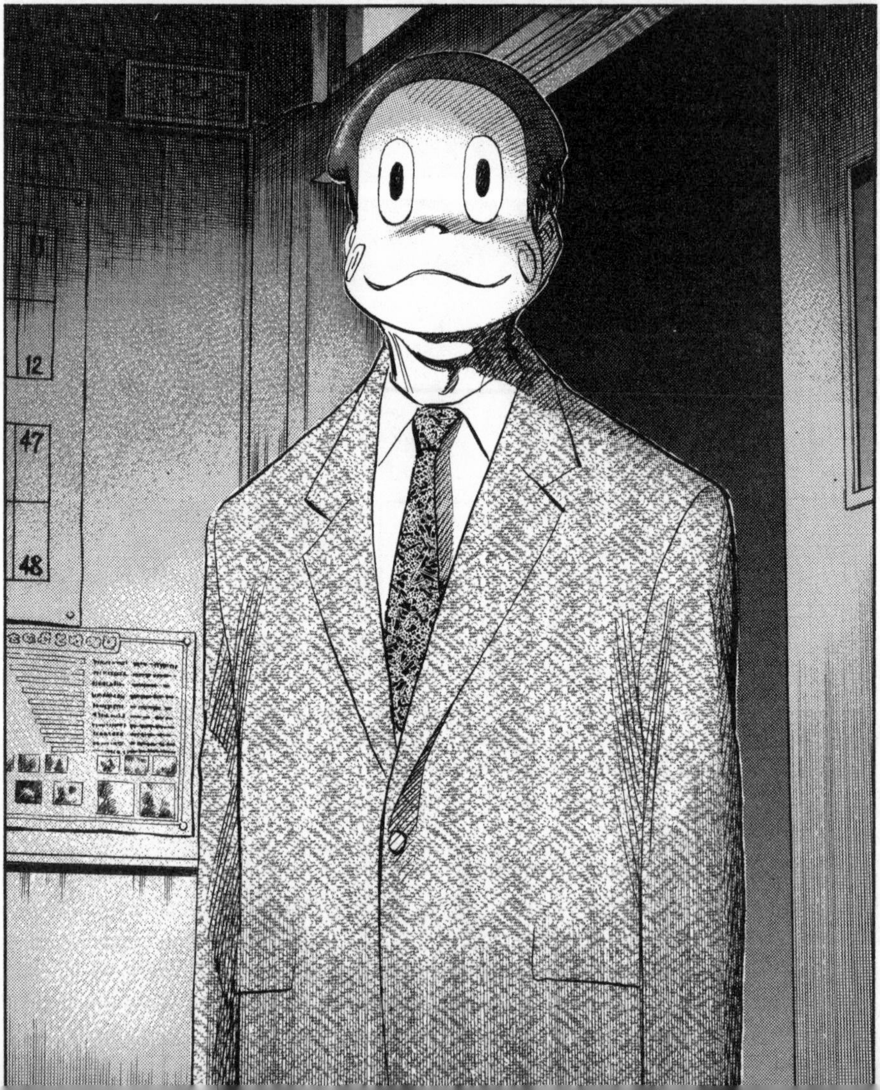
12
47
48

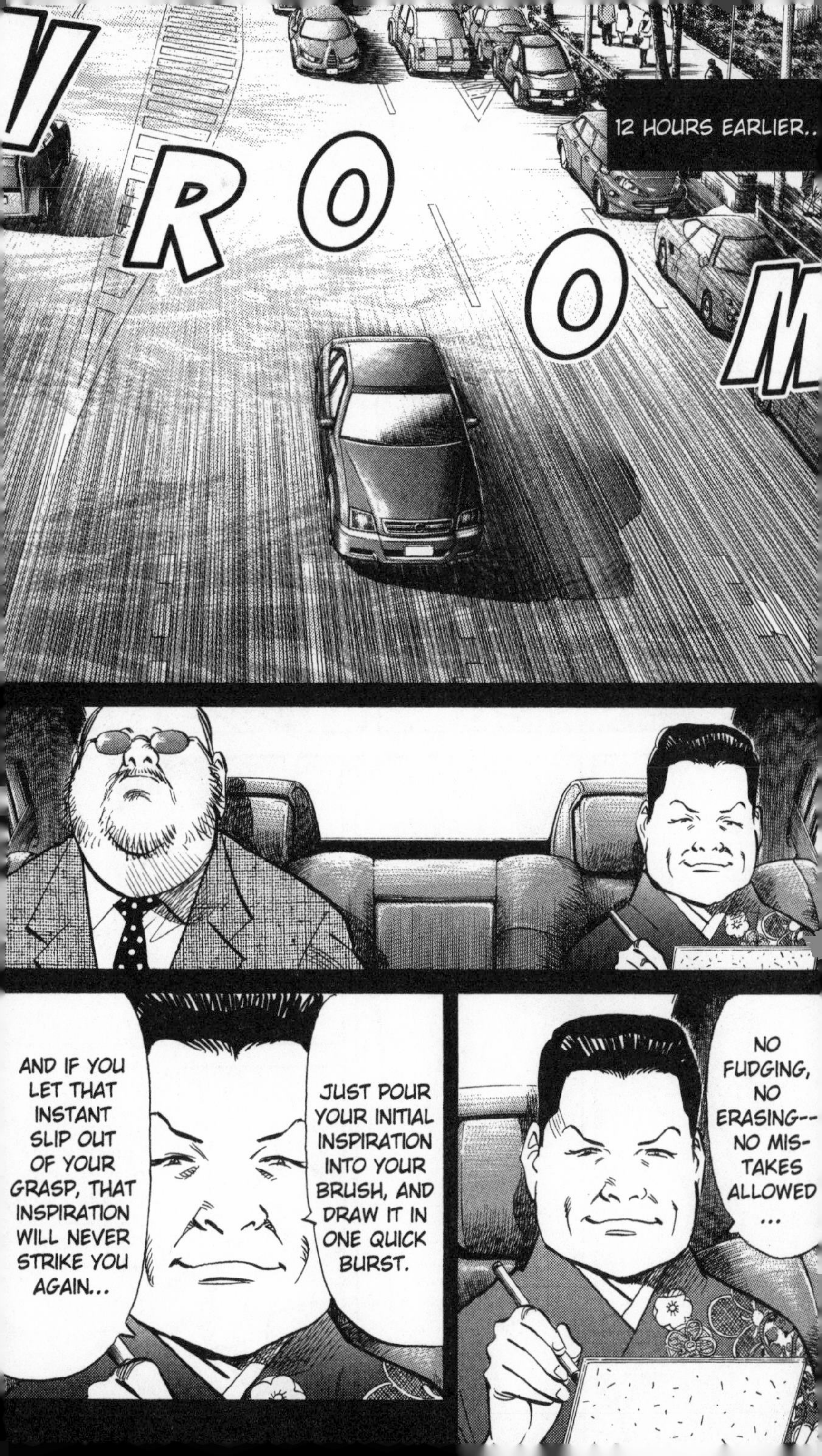
12 HOURS EARLIER..
VROOM
NO FUDGING, NO ERASING-- NO MISTAKES ALLOWED ...
JUST POUR YOUR INITIAL INSPIRATION INTO YOUR BRUSH, AND DRAW IT IN ONE QUICK BURST.
AND IF YOU LET THAT INSTANT SLIP OUT OF YOUR GRASP, THAT INSPIRATION WILL NEVER STRIKE YOU AGAIN...

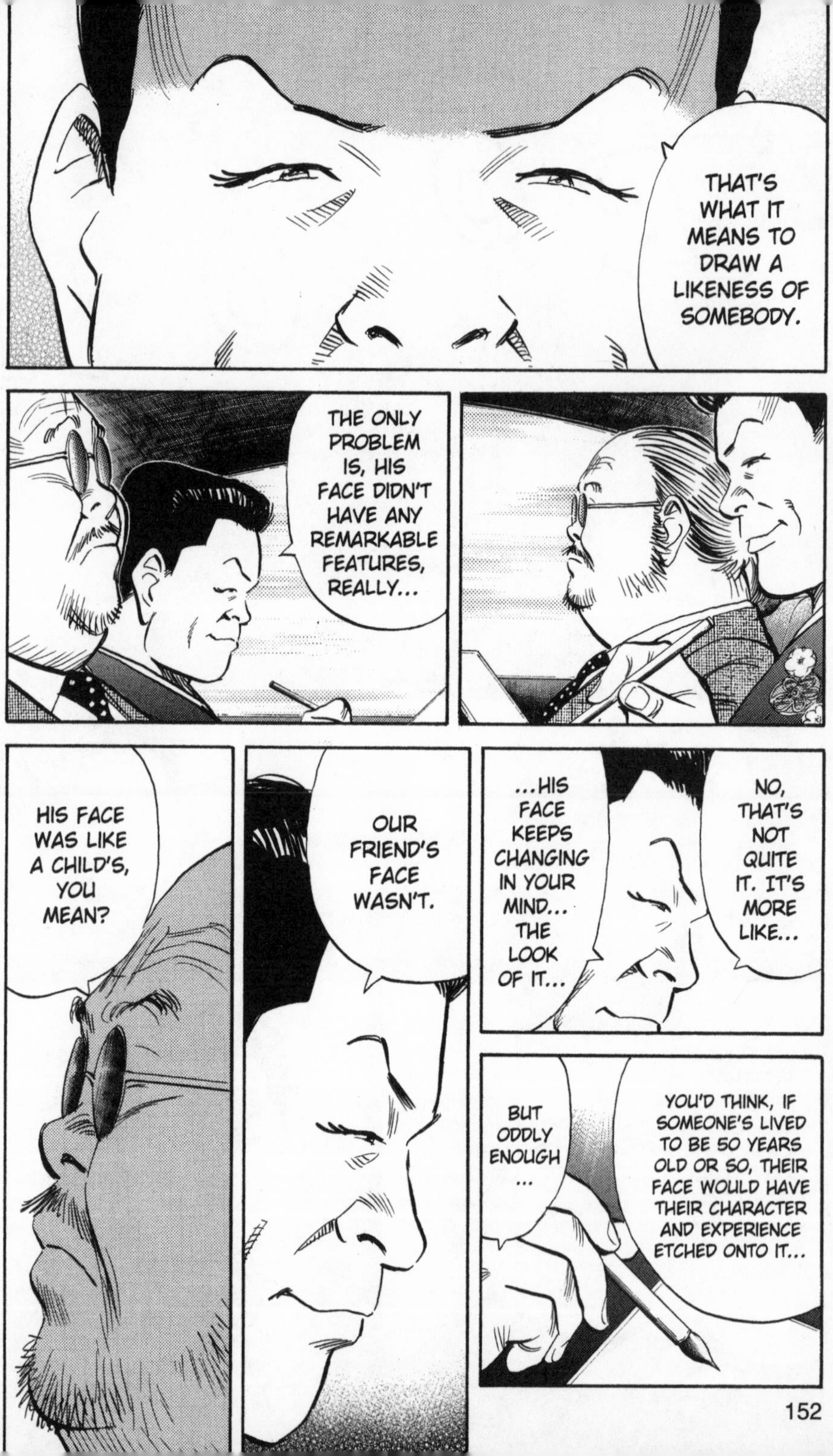
THAT'S WHAT IT MEANS TO DRAW A LIKENESS OF SOMEBODY.
THE ONLY PROBLEM IS, HIS FACE DIDN'T HAVE ANY REMARKABLE FEATURES, REALLY...
NO, THAT'S NOT QUITE IT. IT'S MORE LIKE...
...HIS FACE KEEPS CHANGING IN YOUR MIND... THE LOOK OF IT...
YOU'D THINK, IF SOMEONE'S LIVED TO BE 50 YEARS OLD OR SO, THEIR FACE WOULD HAVE THEIR CHARACTER AND EXPERIENCE ETCHED ONTO IT...
BUT ODDLY ENOUGH ...
OUR FRIEND'S FACE WASN'T.
HIS FACE WAS LIKE A CHILD'S, YOU MEAN?

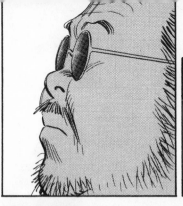

I COULDN'T HAVE PUT IT BETTER, MARUO.

VWUM

SHWIP SHWASH

UMPH!

FWAP

ZIP ZIP

FWAP

VWUM VWUM

THWIK

VAV-WUM VAV-WUM

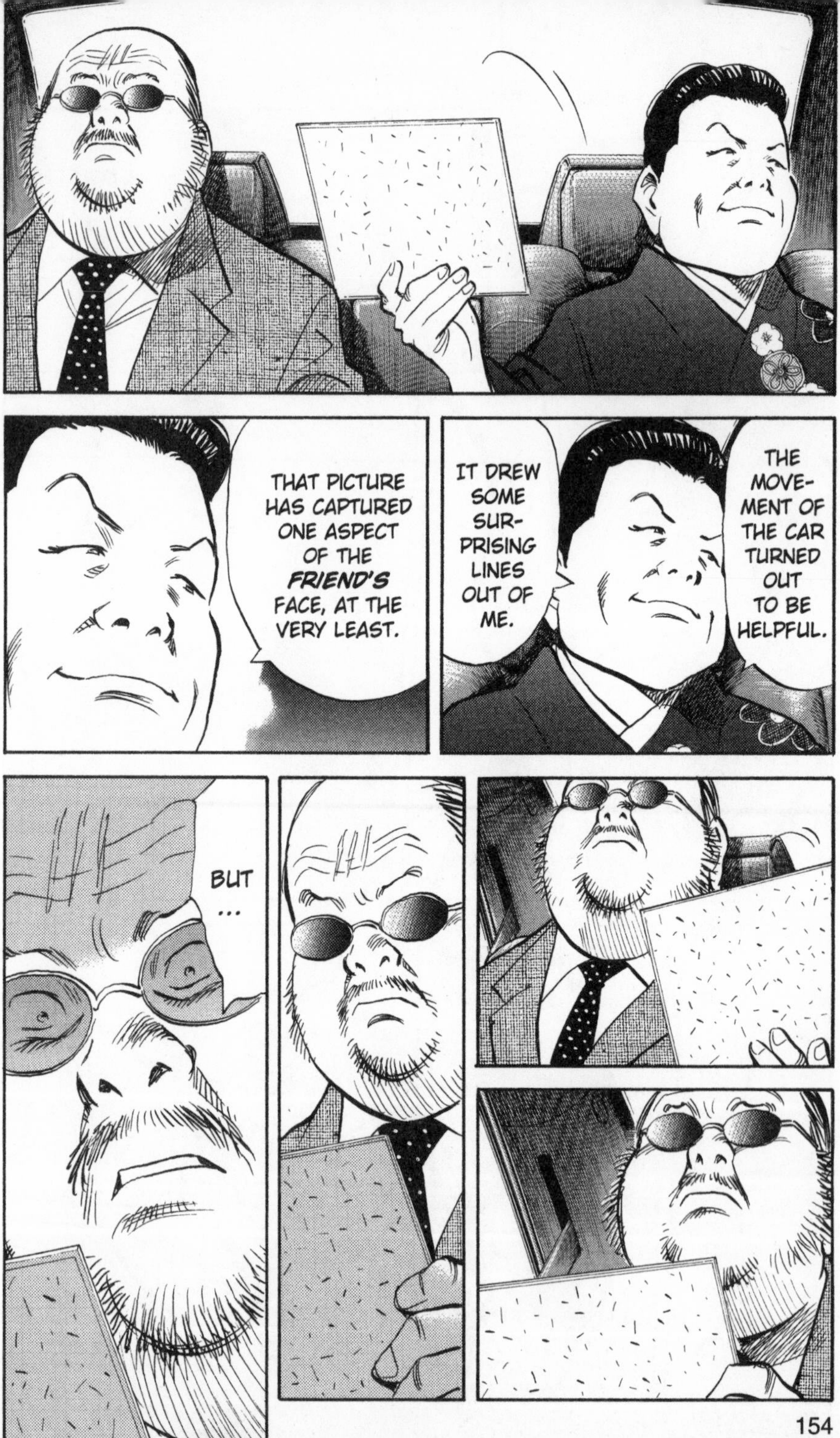

THE MOVEMENT OF THE CAR TURNED OUT TO BE HELPFUL.
IT DREW SOME SURPRISING LINES OUT OF ME.
THAT PICTURE HAS CAPTURED ONE ASPECT OF THE *FRIEND'S* FACE, AT THE VERY LEAST.
BUT ...

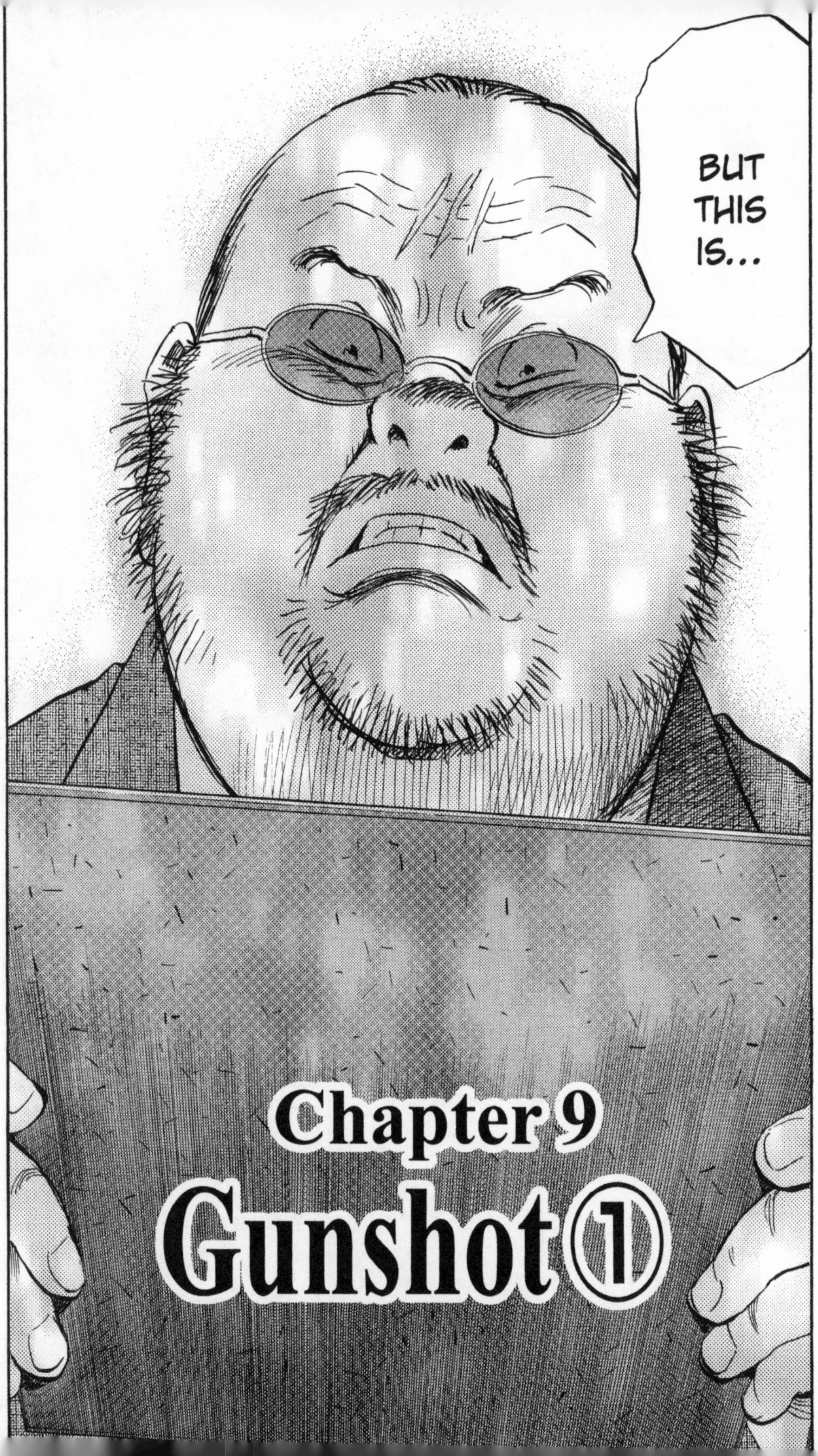
BUT THIS IS...
Chapter 9
Gunshot ①

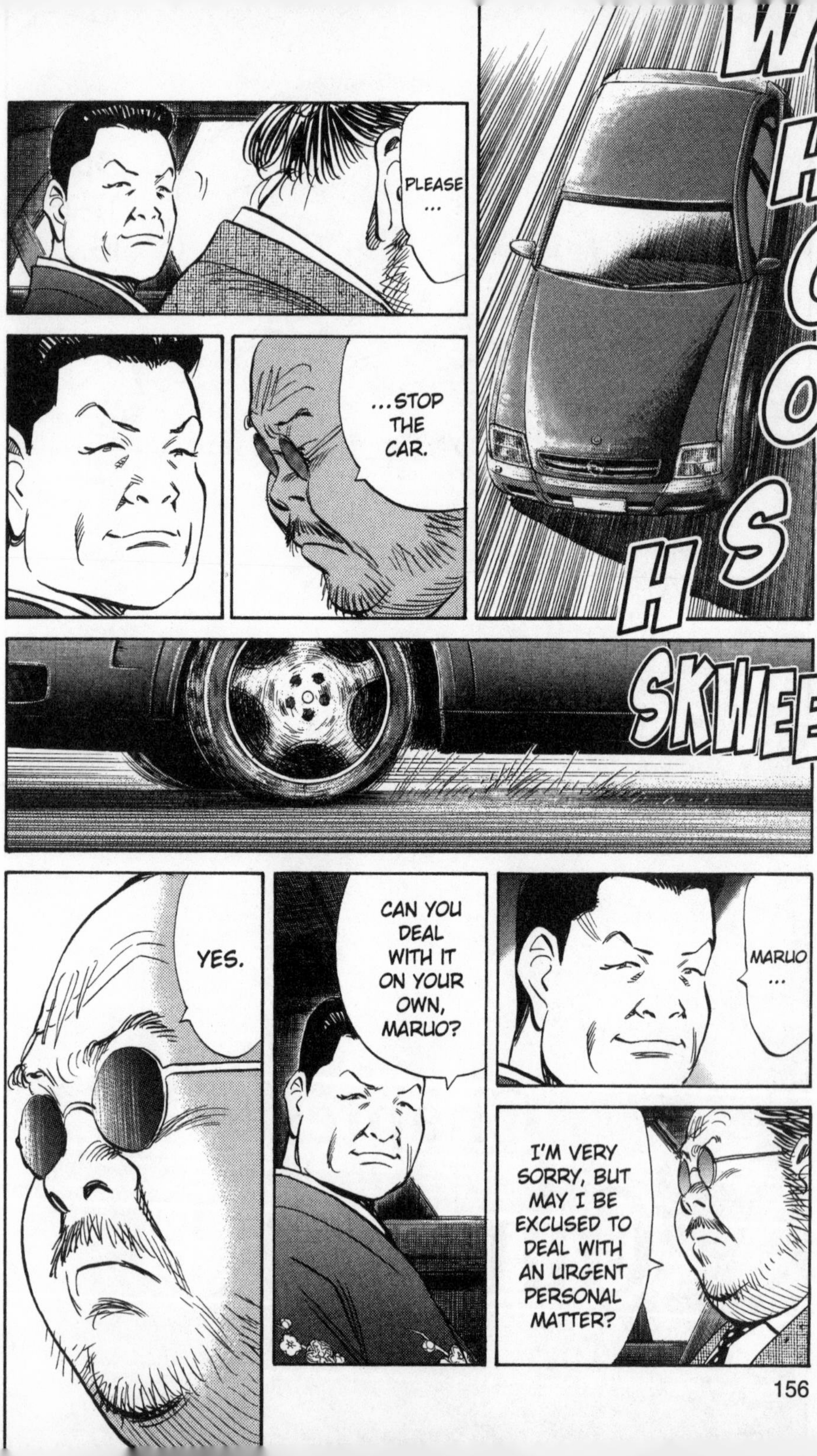
WHOOOSH
PLEASE ...
...STOP THE CAR.
SKWEE
MARUO ...
I'M VERY SORRY, BUT MAY I BE EXCUSED TO DEAL WITH AN URGENT PERSONAL MATTER?
CAN YOU DEAL WITH IT ON YOUR OWN, MARUO?
YES.

KRNCH

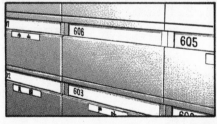

606 605

603

606

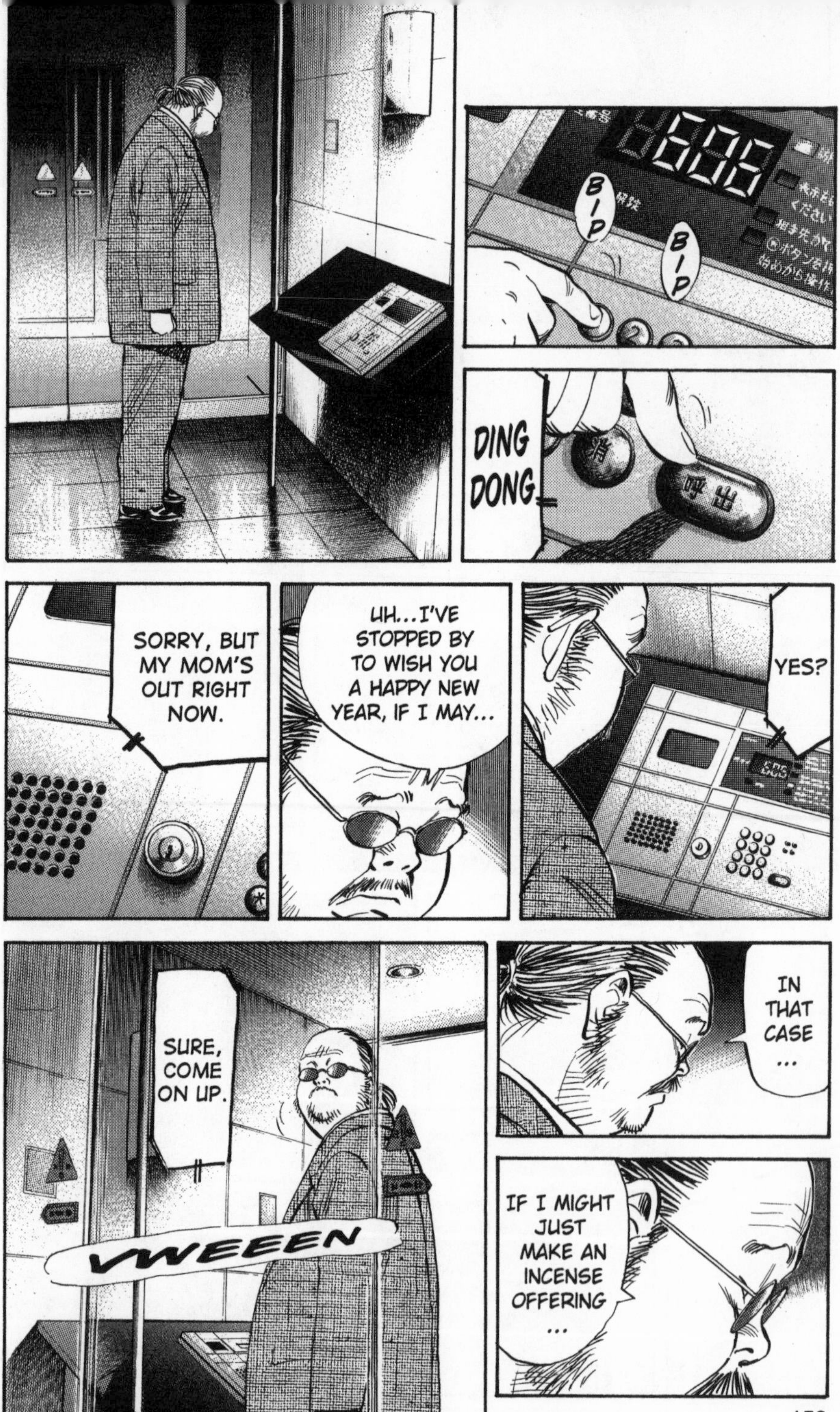
BIP
BIP
DING DONG
YES?
UH...I'VE STOPPED BY TO WISH YOU A HAPPY NEW YEAR, IF I MAY...
SORRY, BUT MY MOM'S OUT RIGHT NOW.
IN THAT CASE...
IF I MIGHT JUST MAKE AN INCENSE OFFERING...
SURE, COME ON UP.
VWEEEN

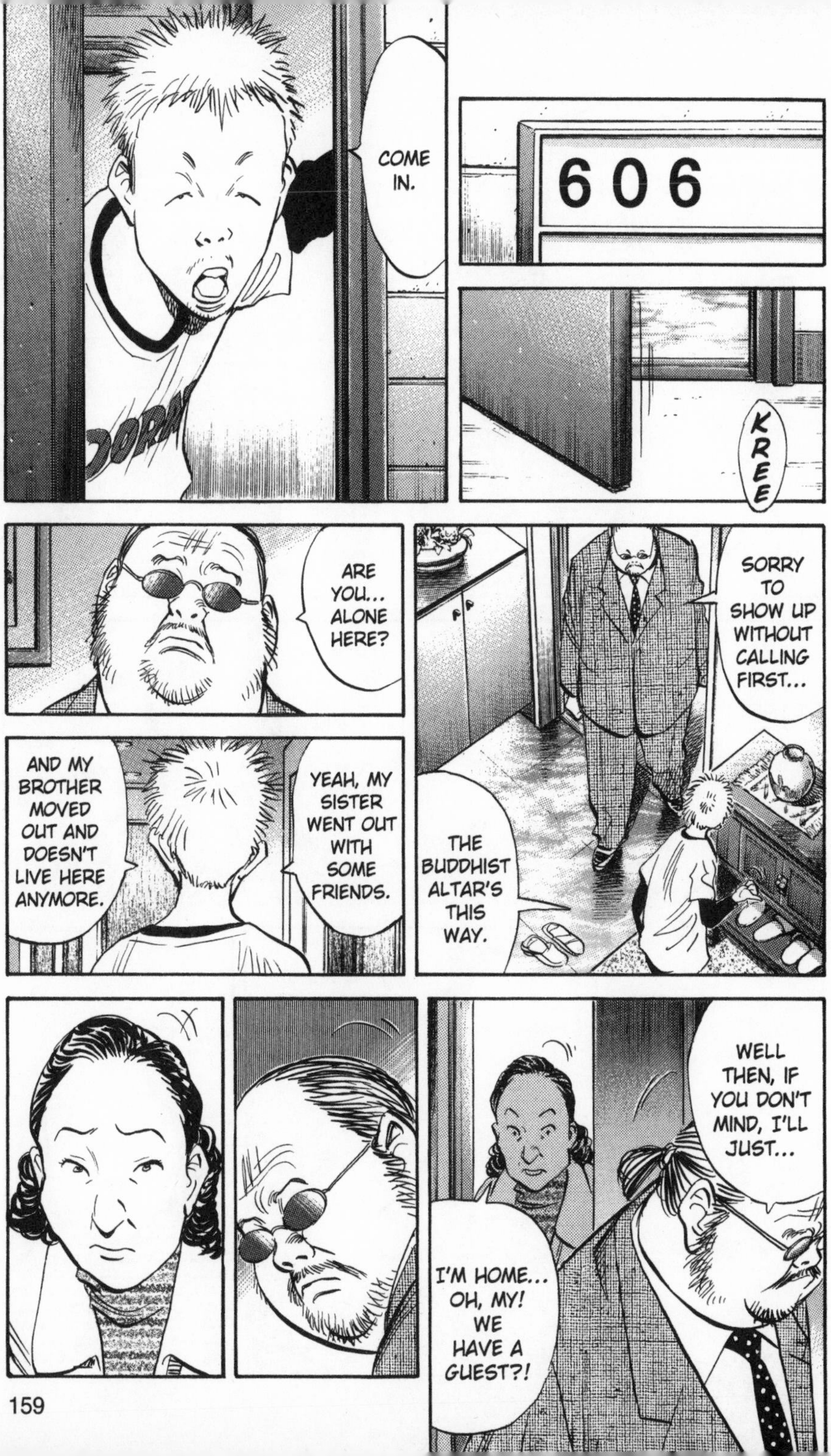
606
KREE
COME IN.
SORRY TO SHOW UP WITHOUT CALLING FIRST...
THE BUDDHIST ALTAR'S THIS WAY.
ARE YOU... ALONE HERE?
YEAH, MY SISTER WENT OUT WITH SOME FRIENDS.
AND MY BROTHER MOVED OUT AND DOESN'T LIVE HERE ANYMORE.
WELL THEN, IF YOU DON'T MIND, I'LL JUST...
I'M HOME... OH, MY! WE HAVE A GUEST?!

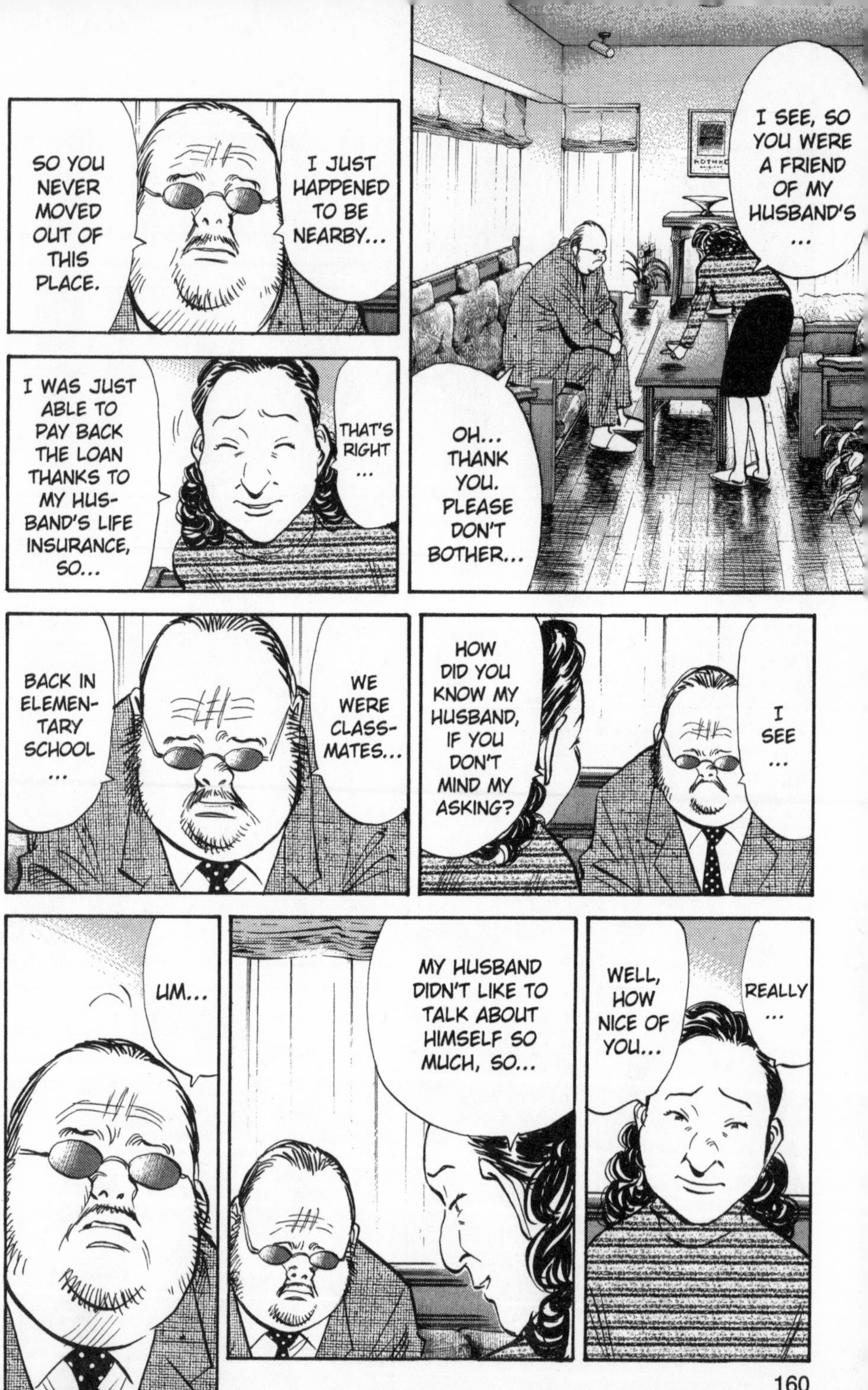
I SEE, SO YOU WERE A FRIEND OF MY HUSBAND'S ...
OH... THANK YOU. PLEASE DON'T BOTHER...
I JUST HAPPENED TO BE NEARBY...
SO YOU NEVER MOVED OUT OF THIS PLACE.
THAT'S RIGHT ...
I WAS JUST ABLE TO PAY BACK THE LOAN THANKS TO MY HUSBAND'S LIFE INSURANCE, SO...
I SEE ...
HOW DID YOU KNOW MY HUSBAND, IF YOU DON'T MIND MY ASKING?
WE WERE CLASSMATES...
BACK IN ELEMENTARY SCHOOL ...
REALLY ...
WELL, HOW NICE OF YOU...
MY HUSBAND DIDN'T LIKE TO TALK ABOUT HIMSELF SO MUCH, SO...
UM...

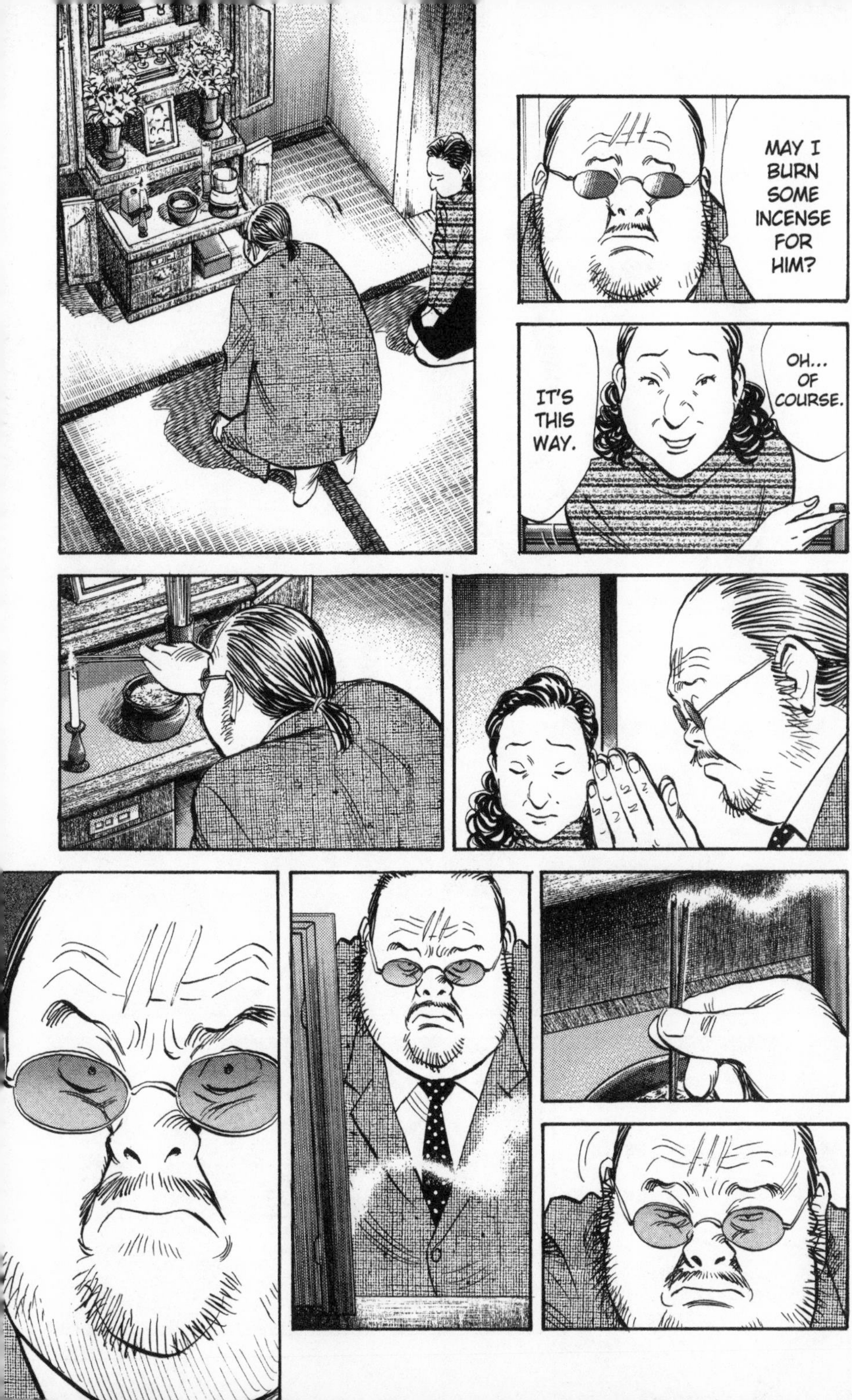

MAY I BURN SOME INCENSE FOR HIM?
OH... OF COURSE.
IT'S THIS WAY.

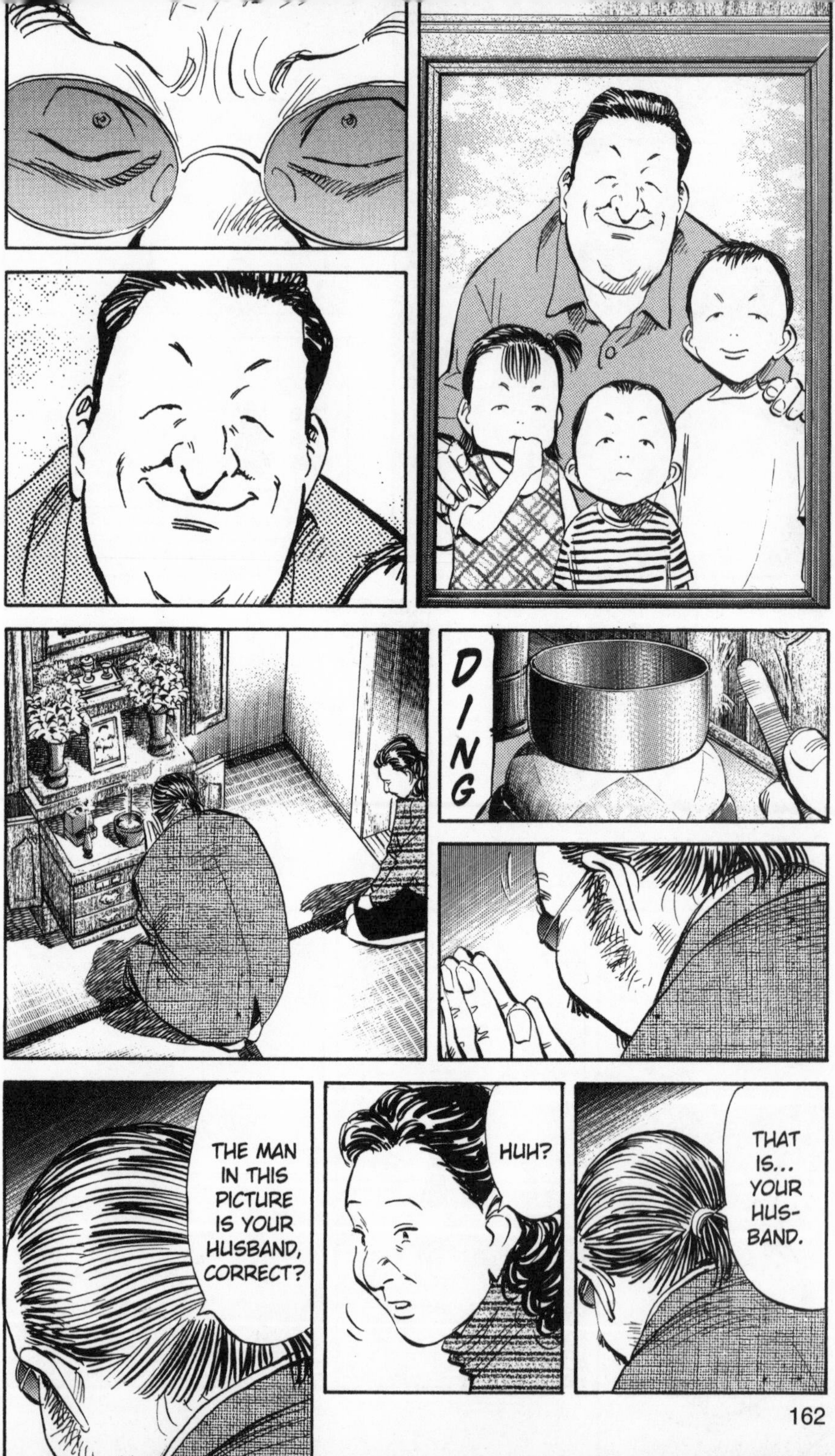
DING
THAT IS... YOUR HUS-BAND.
HUH?
THE MAN IN THIS PICTURE IS YOUR HUSBAND, CORRECT?

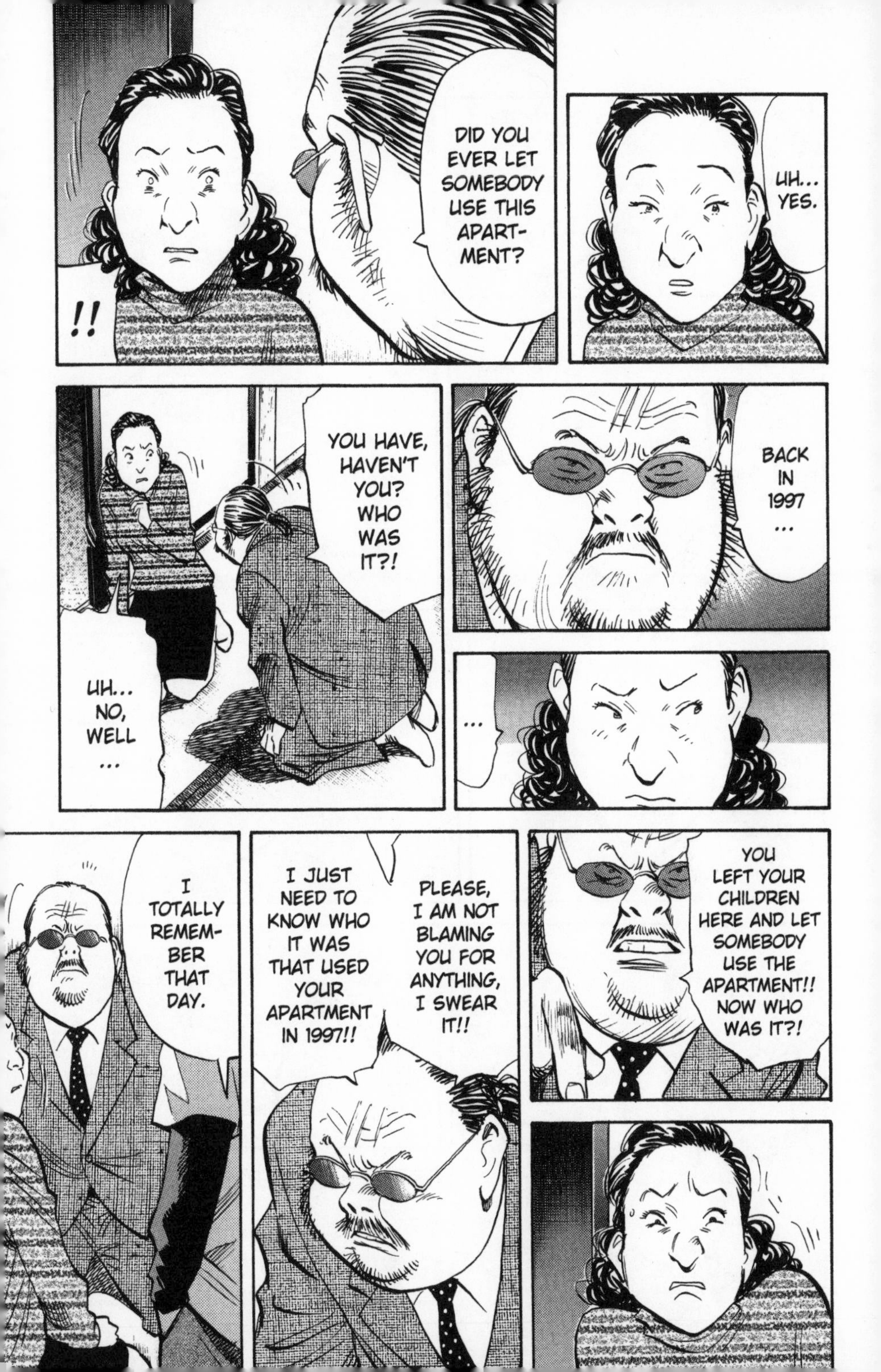
UH... YES.
DID YOU EVER LET SOMEBODY USE THIS APART-MENT?
!!
BACK IN 1997 ...
...
YOU HAVE, HAVEN'T YOU? WHO WAS IT?!
UH... NO, WELL ...
YOU LEFT YOUR CHILDREN HERE AND LET SOMEBODY USE THE APARTMENT!! NOW WHO WAS IT?!
PLEASE, I AM NOT BLAMING YOU FOR ANYTHING, I SWEAR IT!!
I JUST NEED TO KNOW WHO IT WAS THAT USED YOUR APARTMENT IN 1997!!
I TOTALLY REMEM-BER THAT DAY.

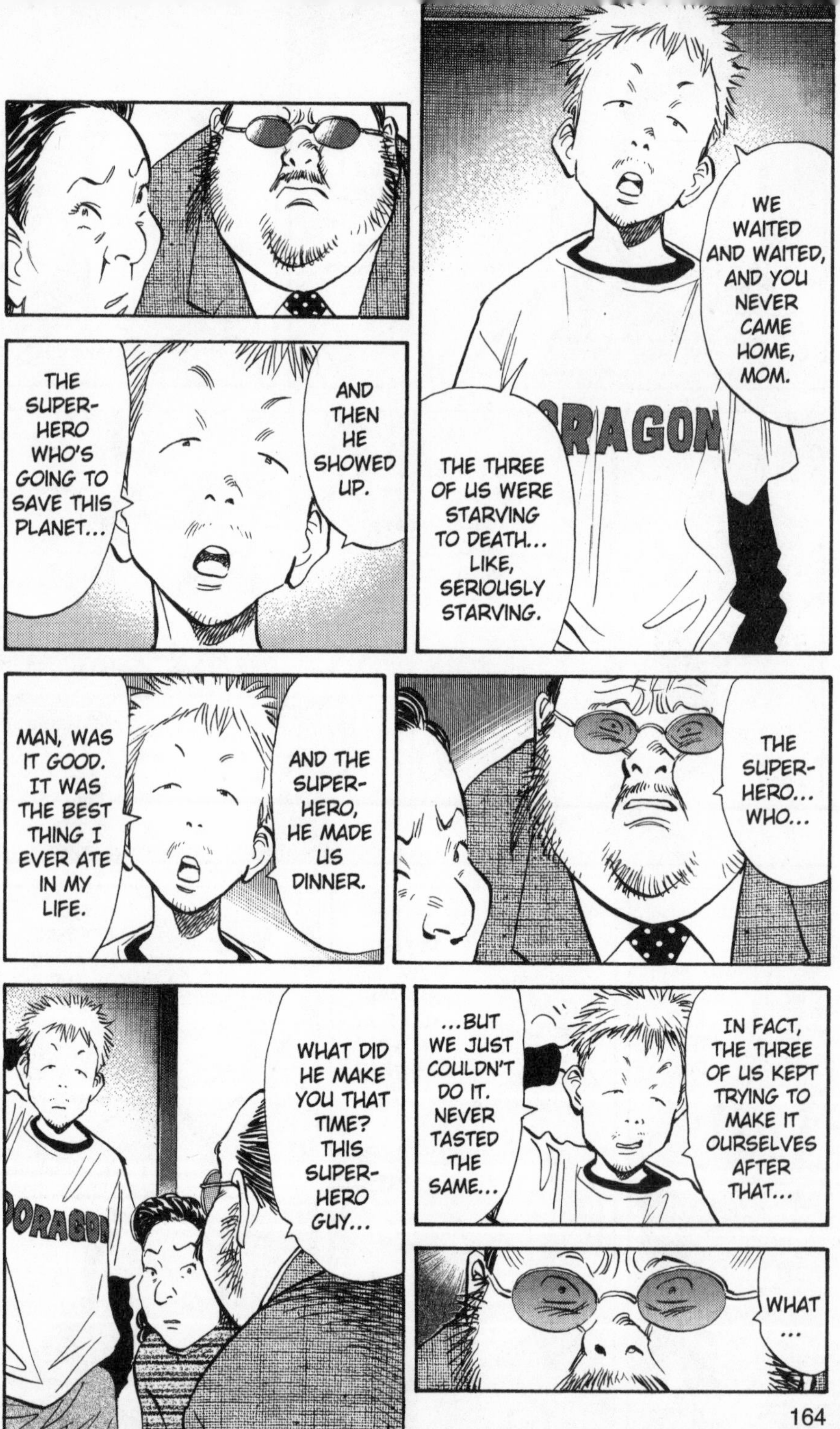
WE WAITED AND WAITED, AND YOU NEVER CAME HOME, MOM.
THE THREE OF US WERE STARVING TO DEATH... LIKE, SERIOUSLY STARVING.
DRAGON
AND THEN HE SHOWED UP.
THE SUPER-HERO WHO'S GOING TO SAVE THIS PLANET...
THE SUPER-HERO... WHO...
AND THE SUPER-HERO, HE MADE US DINNER.
MAN, WAS IT GOOD. IT WAS THE BEST THING I EVER ATE IN MY LIFE.
IN FACT, THE THREE OF US KEPT TRYING TO MAKE IT OURSELVES AFTER THAT...
...BUT WE JUST COULDN'T DO IT. NEVER TASTED THE SAME...
WHAT ...
WHAT DID HE MAKE YOU THAT TIME? THIS SUPER-HERO GUY...

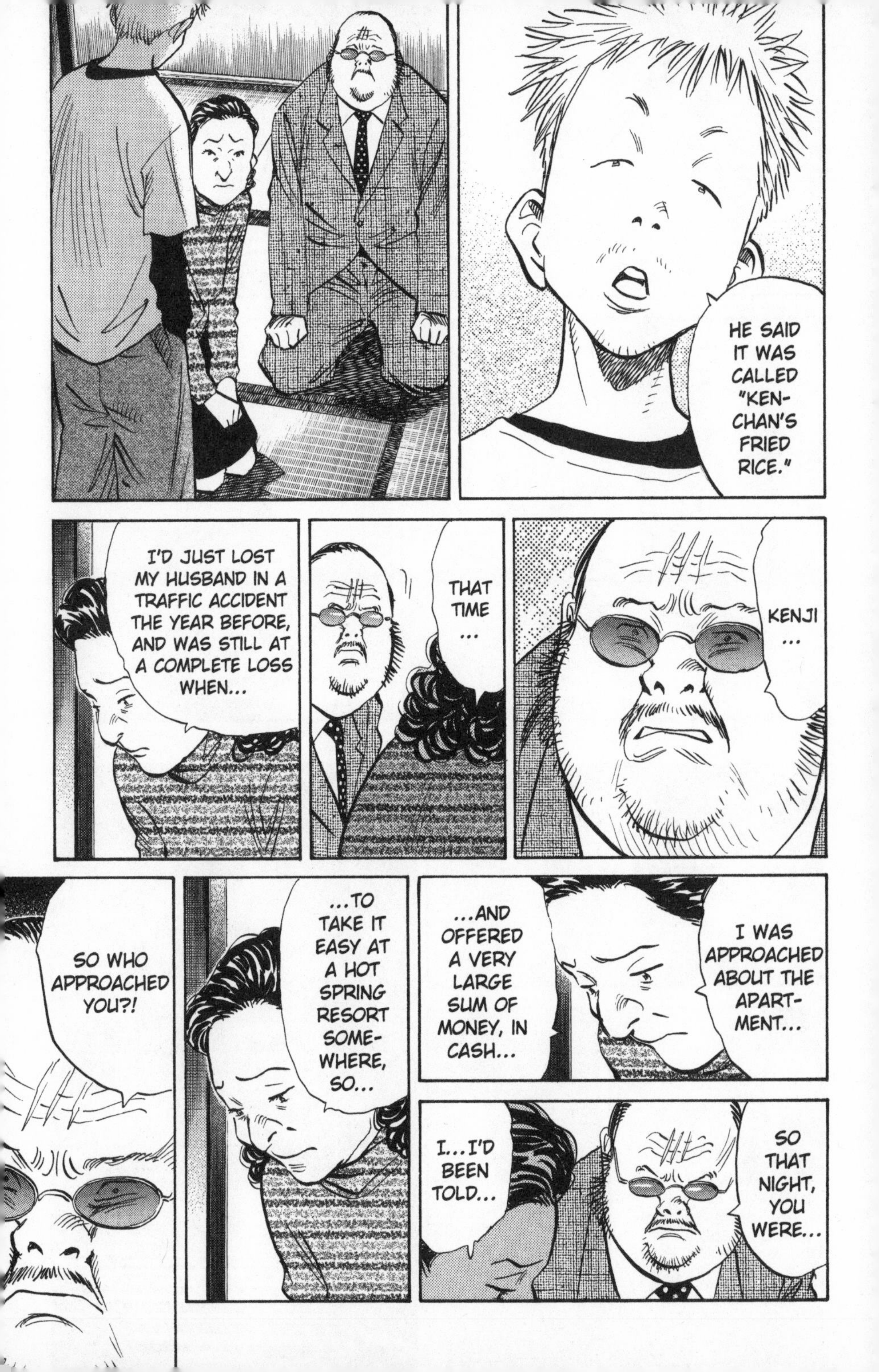
HE SAID IT WAS CALLED "KEN-CHAN'S FRIED RICE."
KENJI...
THAT TIME...
I'D JUST LOST MY HUSBAND IN A TRAFFIC ACCIDENT THE YEAR BEFORE, AND WAS STILL AT A COMPLETE LOSS WHEN...
I WAS APPROACHED ABOUT THE APARTMENT...
...AND OFFERED A VERY LARGE SUM OF MONEY, IN CASH...
SO THAT NIGHT, YOU WERE...
I...I'D BEEN TOLD...
...TO TAKE IT EASY AT A HOT SPRING RESORT SOMEWHERE, SO...
SO WHO APPROACHED YOU?!

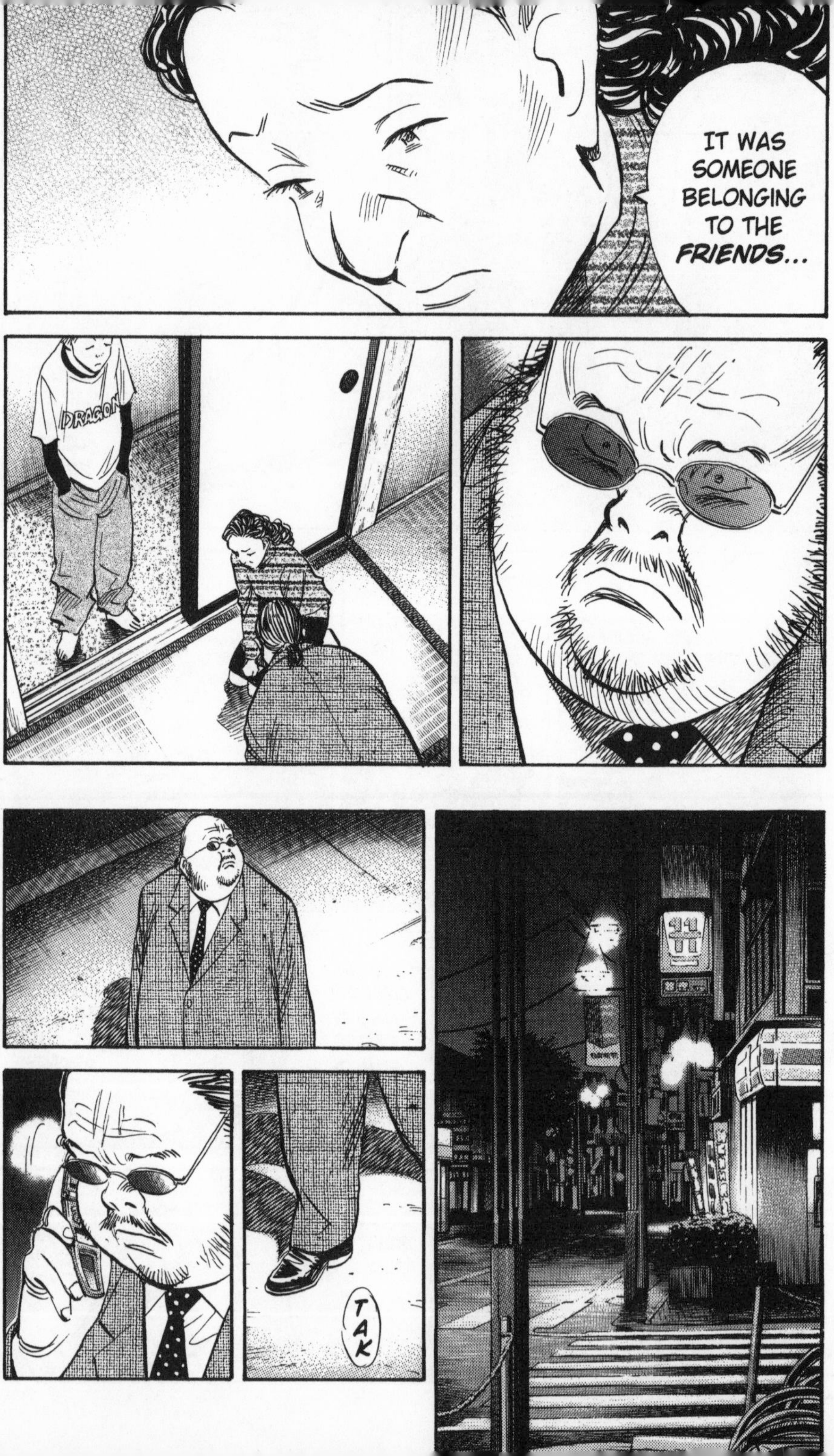
IT WAS SOMEONE BELONGING TO THE FRIENDS...
DRAGON
TAK

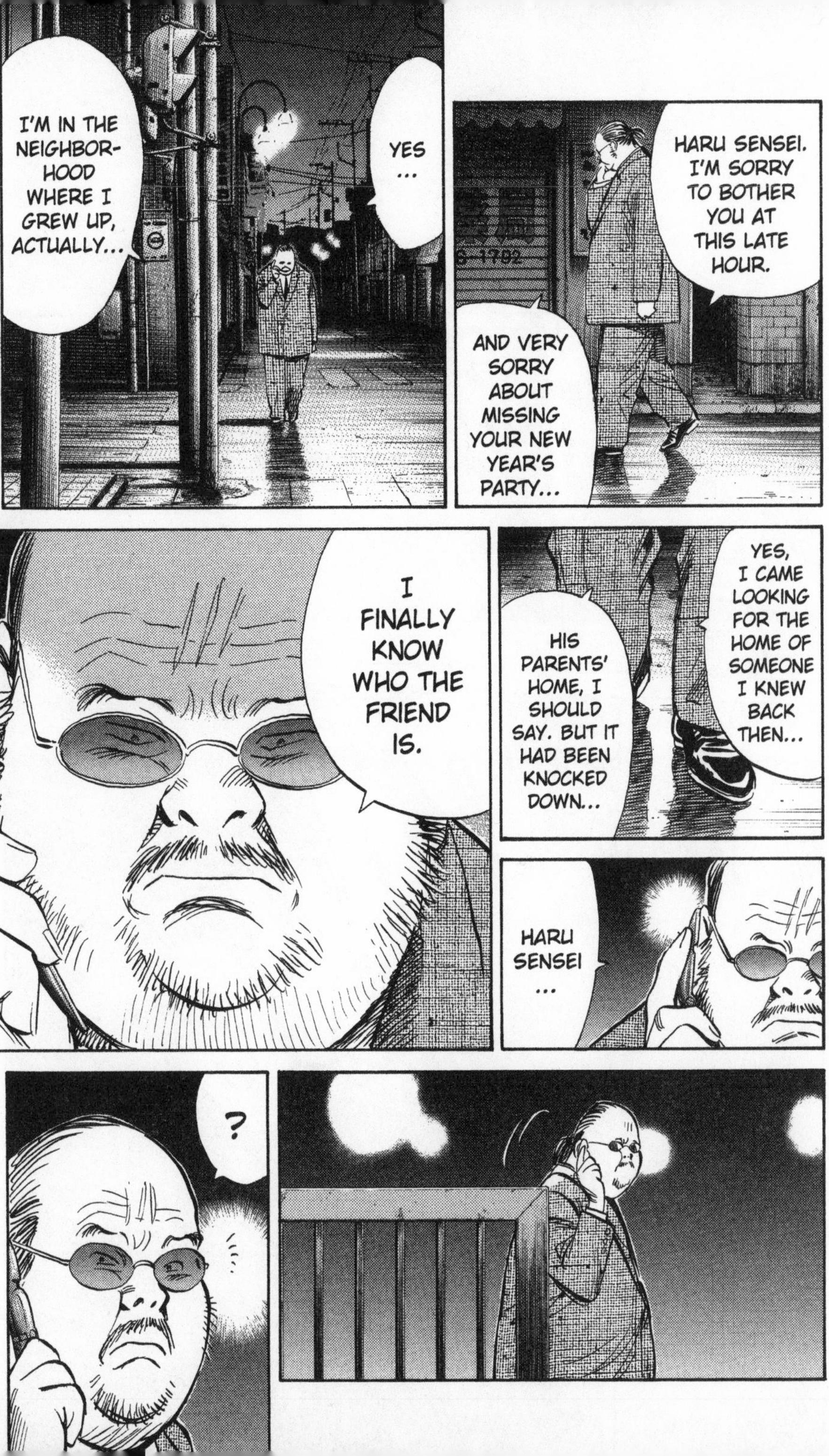
HARU SENSEI. I'M SORRY TO BOTHER YOU AT THIS LATE HOUR.
AND VERY SORRY ABOUT MISSING YOUR NEW YEAR'S PARTY...
YES ...
I'M IN THE NEIGHBOR-HOOD WHERE I GREW UP, ACTUALLY...
YES, I CAME LOOKING FOR THE HOME OF SOMEONE I KNEW BACK THEN...
HIS PARENTS' HOME, I SHOULD SAY. BUT IT HAD BEEN KNOCKED DOWN...
HARU SENSEI ...
I FINALLY KNOW WHO THE FRIEND IS.
?
...

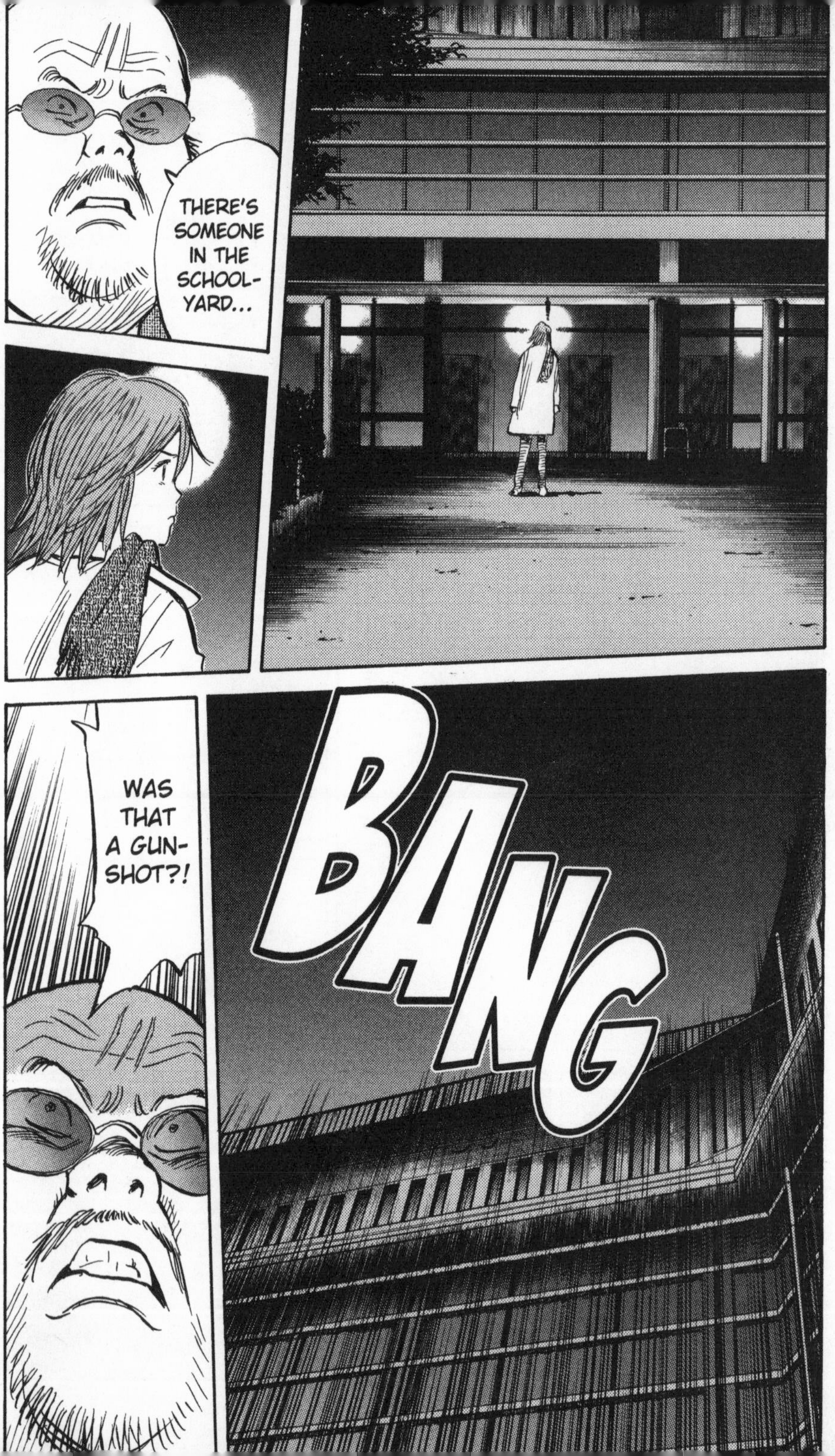
!
THERE'S SOMEONE IN THE SCHOOL-YARD...
BANG
WAS THAT A GUN-SHOT?!

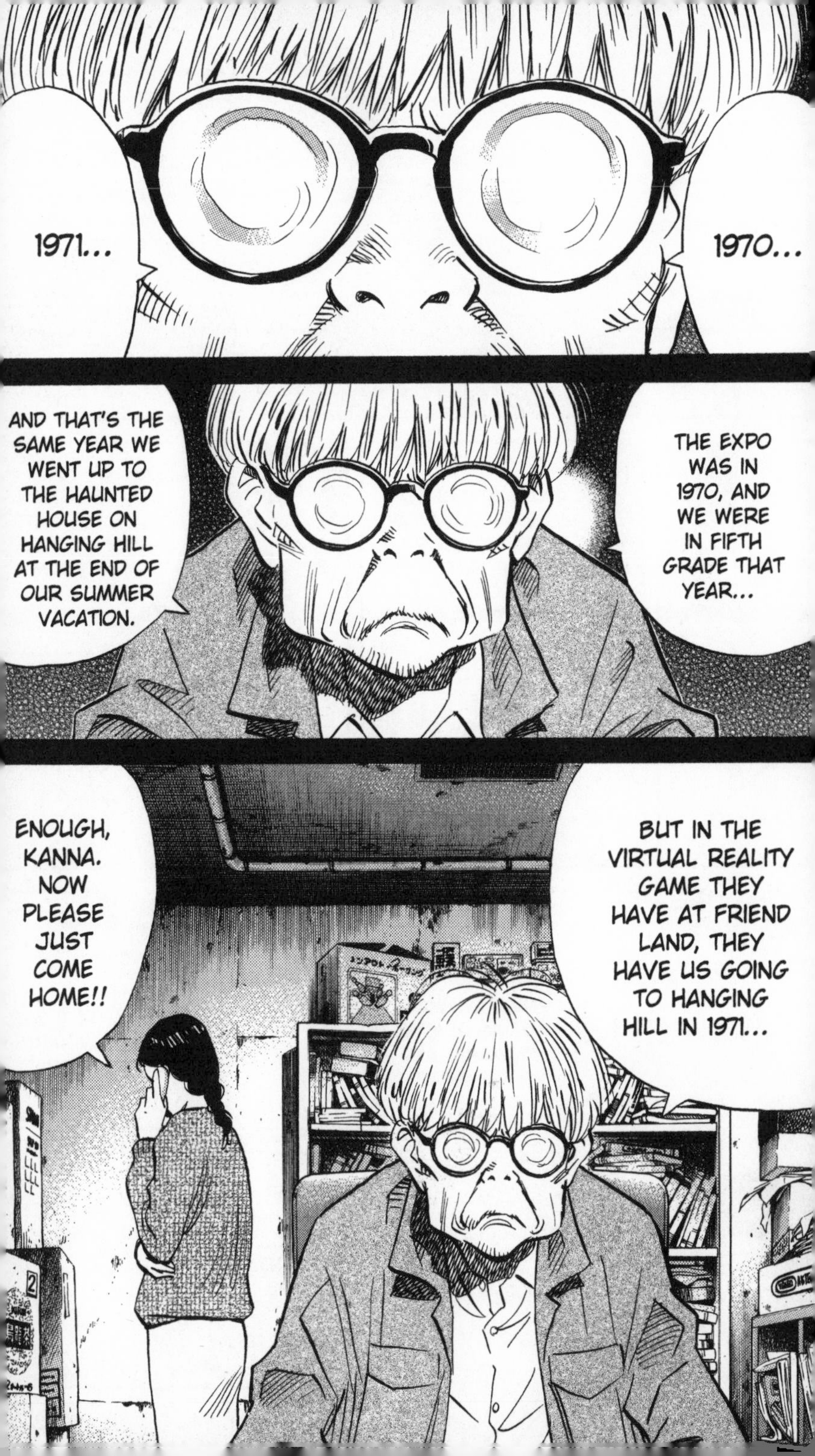
1970...
1971...
THE EXPO WAS IN 1970, AND WE WERE IN FIFTH GRADE THAT YEAR...
AND THAT'S THE SAME YEAR WE WENT UP TO THE HAUNTED HOUSE ON HANGING HILL AT THE END OF OUR SUMMER VACATION.
BUT IN THE VIRTUAL REALITY GAME THEY HAVE AT FRIEND LAND, THEY HAVE US GOING TO HANGING HILL IN 1971...
ENOUGH, KANNA. NOW PLEASE JUST COME HOME!!

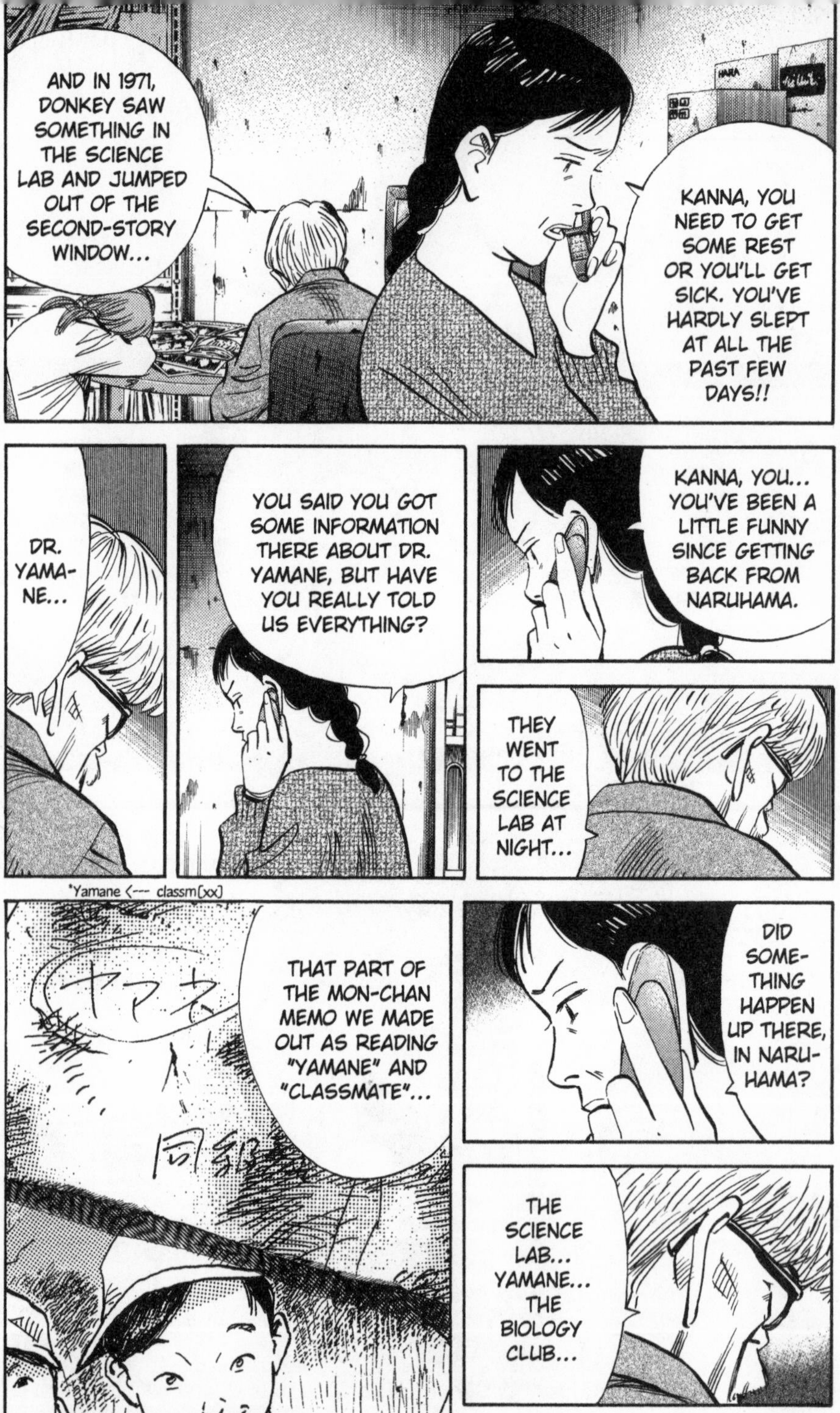
KANNA, YOU NEED TO GET SOME REST OR YOU'LL GET SICK. YOU'VE HARDLY SLEPT AT ALL THE PAST FEW DAYS!!
AND IN 1971, DONKEY SAW SOMETHING IN THE SCIENCE LAB AND JUMPED OUT OF THE SECOND-STORY WINDOW...
KANNA, YOU... YOU'VE BEEN A LITTLE FUNNY SINCE GETTING BACK FROM NARUHAMA.
THEY WENT TO THE SCIENCE LAB AT NIGHT...
YOU SAID YOU GOT SOME INFORMATION THERE ABOUT DR. YAMANE, BUT HAVE YOU REALLY TOLD US EVERYTHING?
DR. YAMANE...
*Yamane <--- classm[xx]
DID SOMETHING HAPPEN UP THERE, IN NARUHAMA?
THE SCIENCE LAB... YAMANE... THE BIOLOGY CLUB...
THAT PART OF THE MON-CHAN MEMO WE MADE OUT AS READING "YAMANE" AND "CLASSMATE"...

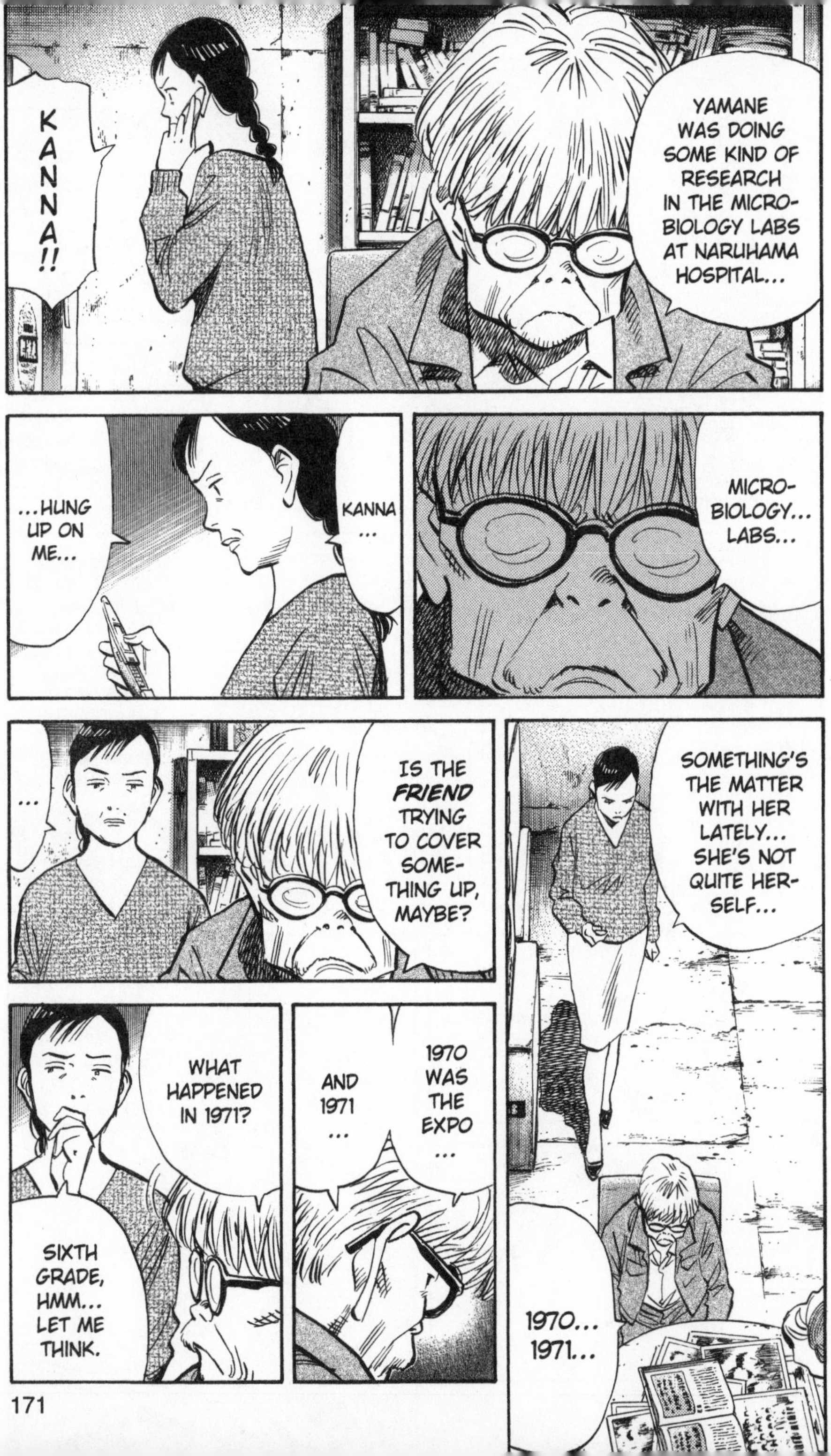

YAMANE WAS DOING SOME KIND OF RESEARCH IN THE MICRO-BIOLOGY LABS AT NARUHAMA HOSPITAL...
KANNA!!
MICRO-BIOLOGY... LABS...
KANNA ...
...HUNG UP ON ME...
SOMETHING'S THE MATTER WITH HER LATELY... SHE'S NOT QUITE HER-SELF...
1970... 1971...
IS THE *FRIEND* TRYING TO COVER SOME-THING UP, MAYBE?
...
1970 WAS THE EXPO ...
AND 1971 ...
WHAT HAPPENED IN 1971?
SIXTH GRADE, HMM... LET ME THINK.

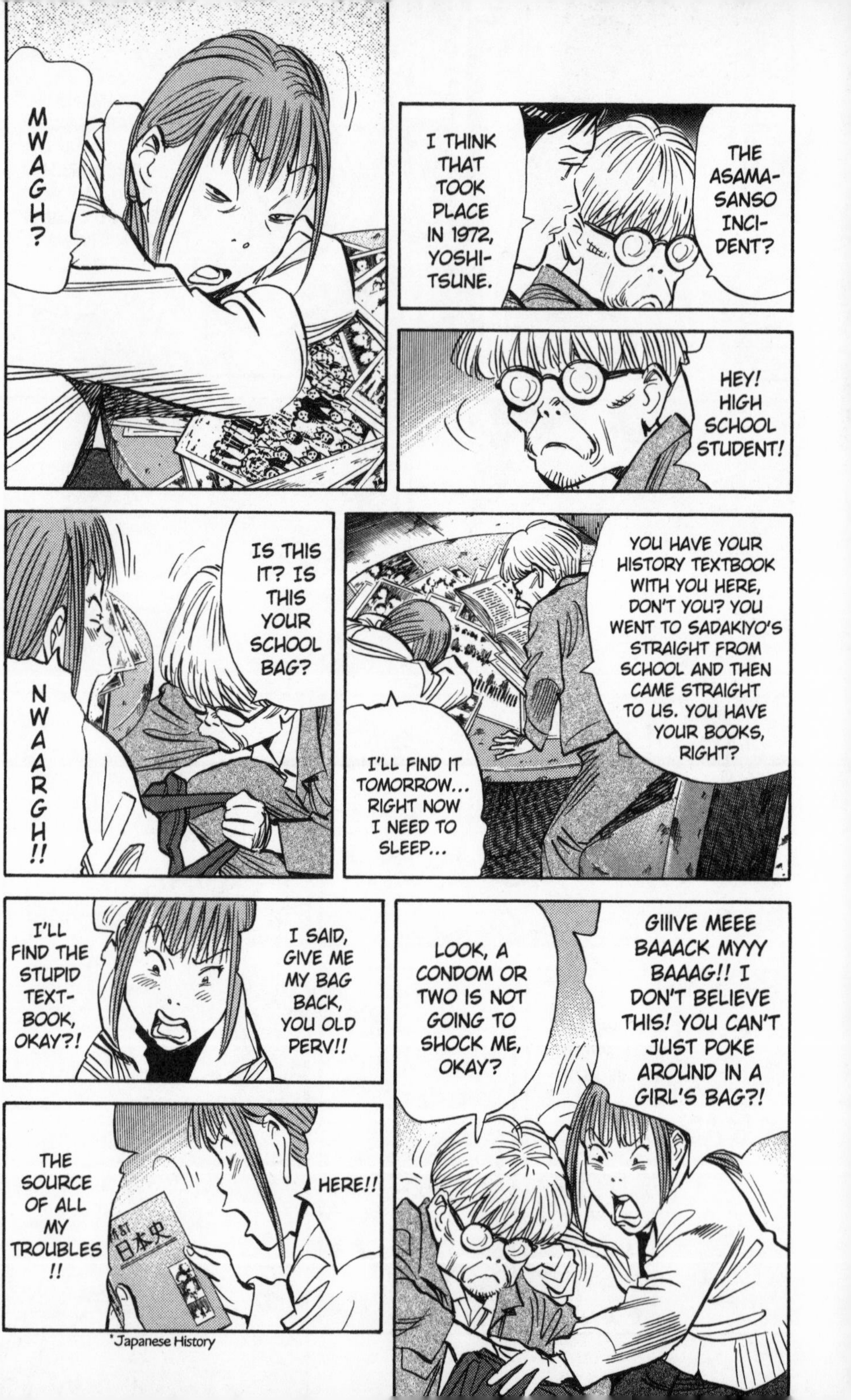
THE ASAMA-SANSO INCIDENT?
I THINK THAT TOOK PLACE IN 1972, YOSHITSUNE.
HEY! HIGH SCHOOL STUDENT!
MWAGH?
YOU HAVE YOUR HISTORY TEXTBOOK WITH YOU HERE, DON'T YOU? YOU WENT TO SADAKIYO'S STRAIGHT FROM SCHOOL AND THEN CAME STRAIGHT TO US. YOU HAVE YOUR BOOKS, RIGHT?
I'LL FIND IT TOMORROW... RIGHT NOW I NEED TO SLEEP...
IS THIS IT? IS THIS YOUR SCHOOL BAG?
NWAAARGH!!
GIIIVE MEEE BAAACK MYYY BAAAG!! I DON'T BELIEVE THIS! YOU CAN'T JUST POKE AROUND IN A GIRL'S BAG?!
LOOK, A CONDOM OR TWO IS NOT GOING TO SHOCK ME, OKAY?
I SAID, GIVE ME MY BAG BACK, YOU OLD PERV!!
I'LL FIND THE STUPID TEXT-BOOK, OKAY?!
HERE!!
日本史
THE SOURCE OF ALL MY TROUBLES!!
*Japanese History

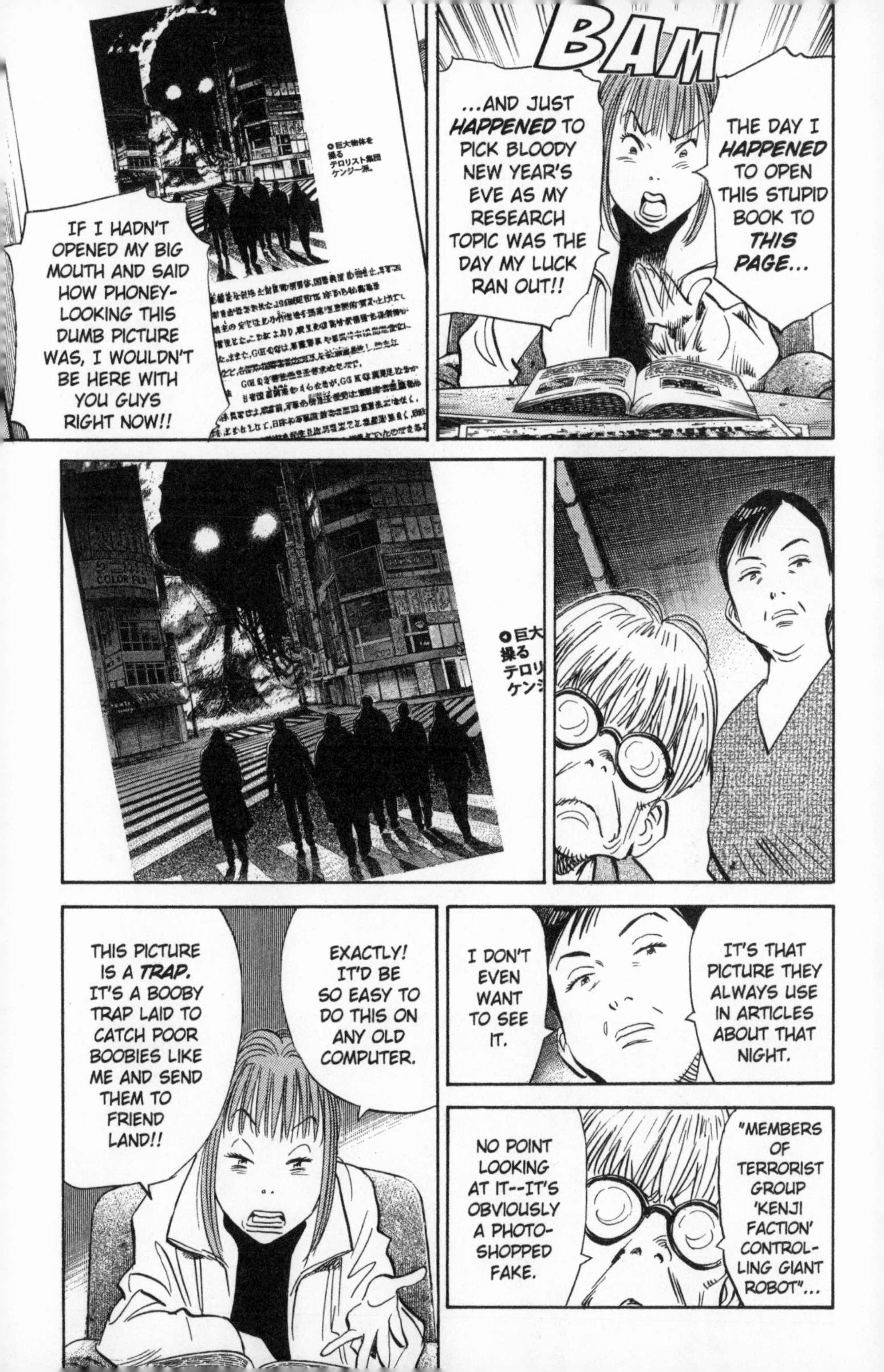
BAM
THE DAY I *HAPPENED* TO OPEN THIS STUPID BOOK TO *THIS PAGE*...
...AND JUST *HAPPENED* TO PICK BLOODY NEW YEAR'S EVE AS MY RESEARCH TOPIC WAS THE DAY MY LUCK RAN OUT!!
巨大物体を操るテロリスト集団ケンジ一派。
IF I HADN'T OPENED MY BIG MOUTH AND SAID HOW PHONEY-LOOKING THIS DUMB PICTURE WAS, I WOULDN'T BE HERE WITH YOU GUYS RIGHT NOW!!
COLOR FILM
IT'S THAT PICTURE THEY ALWAYS USE IN ARTICLES ABOUT THAT NIGHT.
I DON'T EVEN WANT TO SEE IT.
"MEMBERS OF TERRORIST GROUP 'KENJI FACTION' CONTROLLING GIANT ROBOT"...
NO POINT LOOKING AT IT--IT'S OBVIOUSLY A PHOTO-SHOPPED FAKE.
EXACTLY! IT'D BE SO EASY TO DO THIS ON ANY OLD COMPUTER.
THIS PICTURE IS A *TRAP.* IT'S A BOOBY TRAP LAID TO CATCH POOR BOOBIES LIKE ME AND SEND THEM TO FRIEND LAND!!

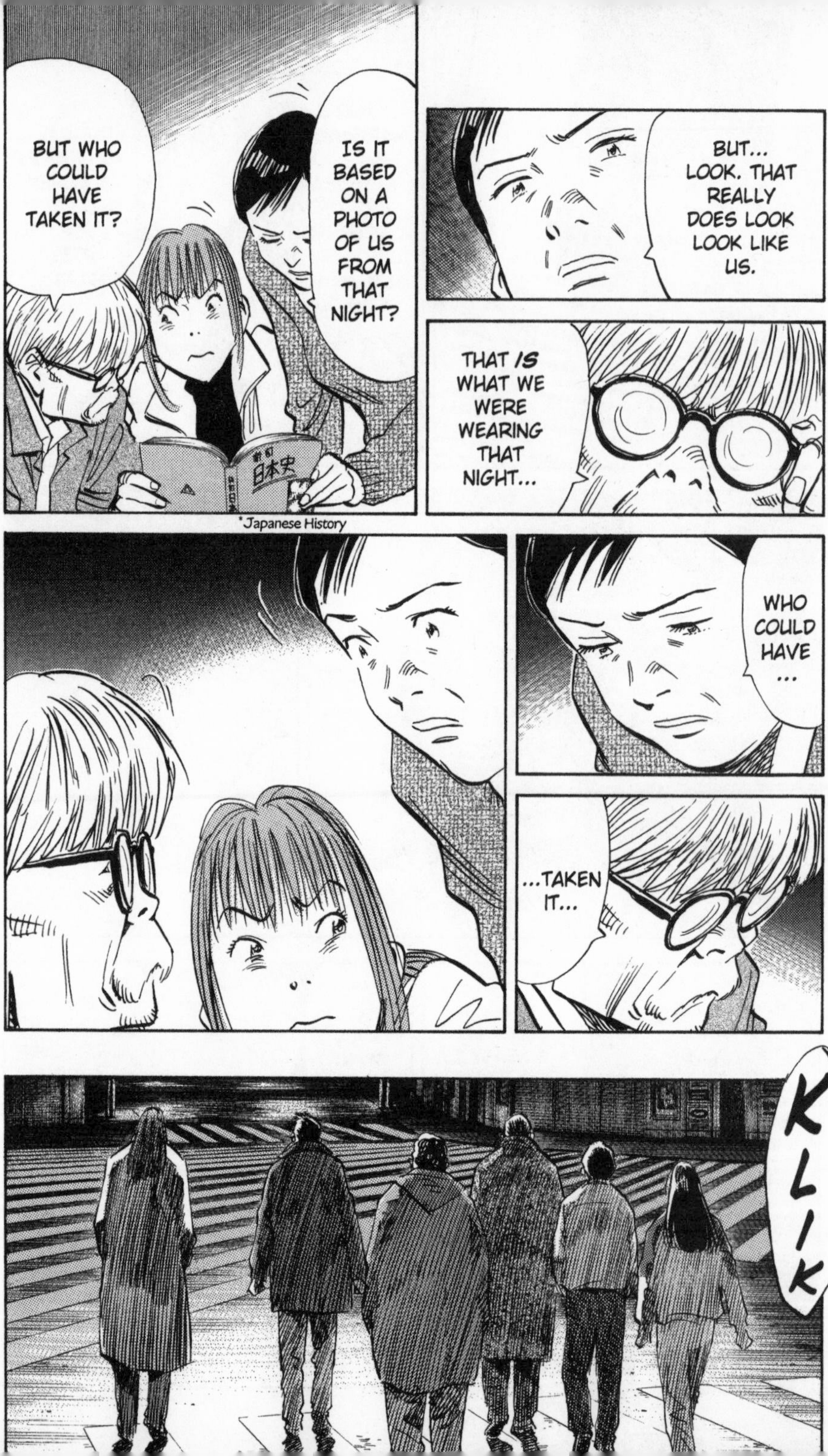
BUT... LOOK. THAT REALLY DOES LOOK LOOK LIKE US.
THAT *IS* WHAT WE WERE WEARING THAT NIGHT...
IS IT BASED ON A PHOTO OF US FROM THAT NIGHT?
BUT WHO COULD HAVE TAKEN IT?
日本史
*Japanese History
WHO COULD HAVE ...
...TAKEN IT...
KLIK

...WANTED TO RECORD THIS HISTORIC MOMENT...

OH... I JUST ...

Chapter 10
Gunshot②

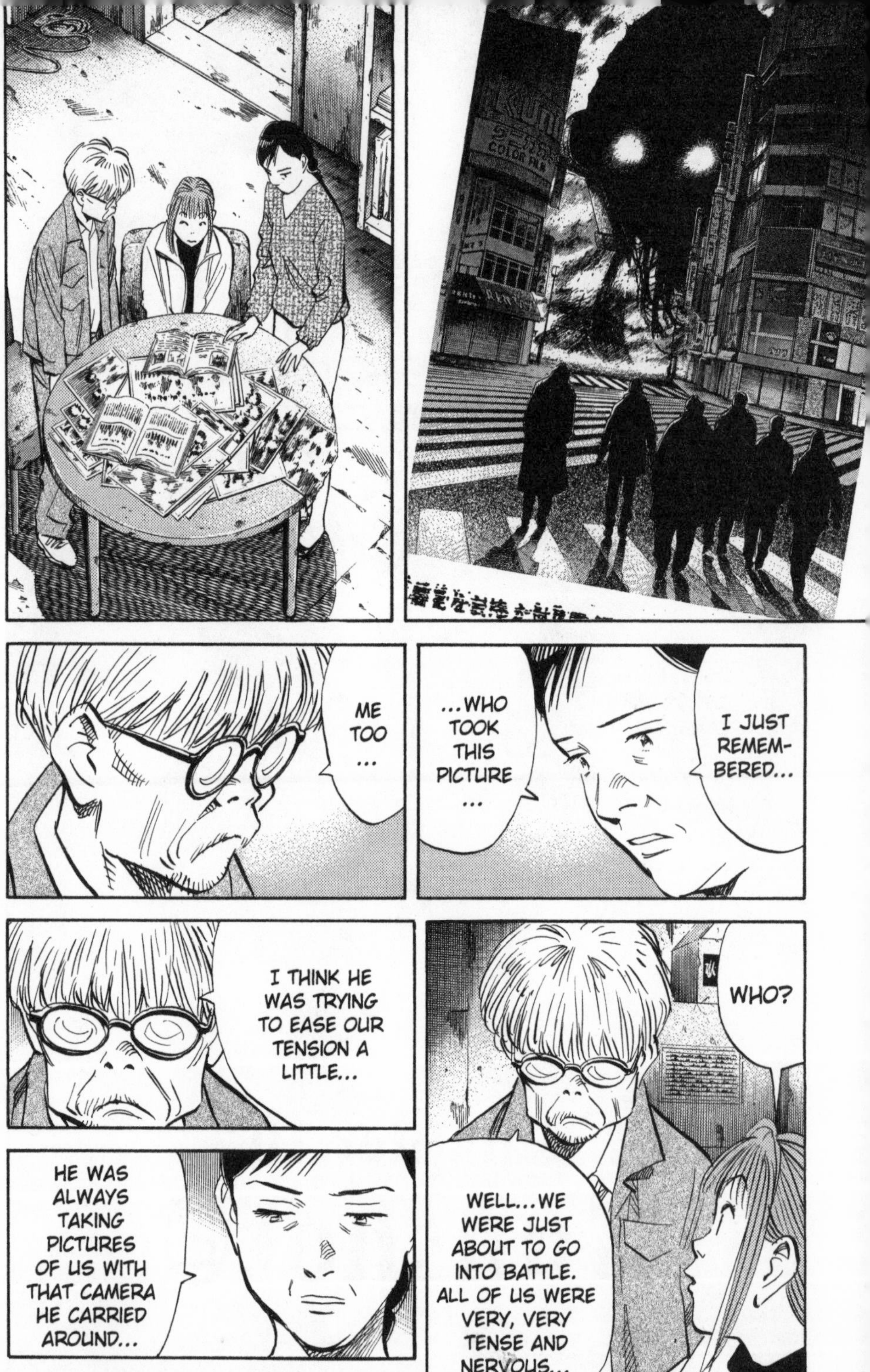
COLOR FILM
I JUST REMEMBERED...
...WHO TOOK THIS PICTURE...
ME TOO...
WHO?
WELL...WE WERE JUST ABOUT TO GO INTO BATTLE. ALL OF US WERE VERY, VERY TENSE AND NERVOUS...
I THINK HE WAS TRYING TO EASE OUR TENSION A LITTLE...
HE WAS ALWAYS TAKING PICTURES OF US WITH THAT CAMERA HE CARRIED AROUND...

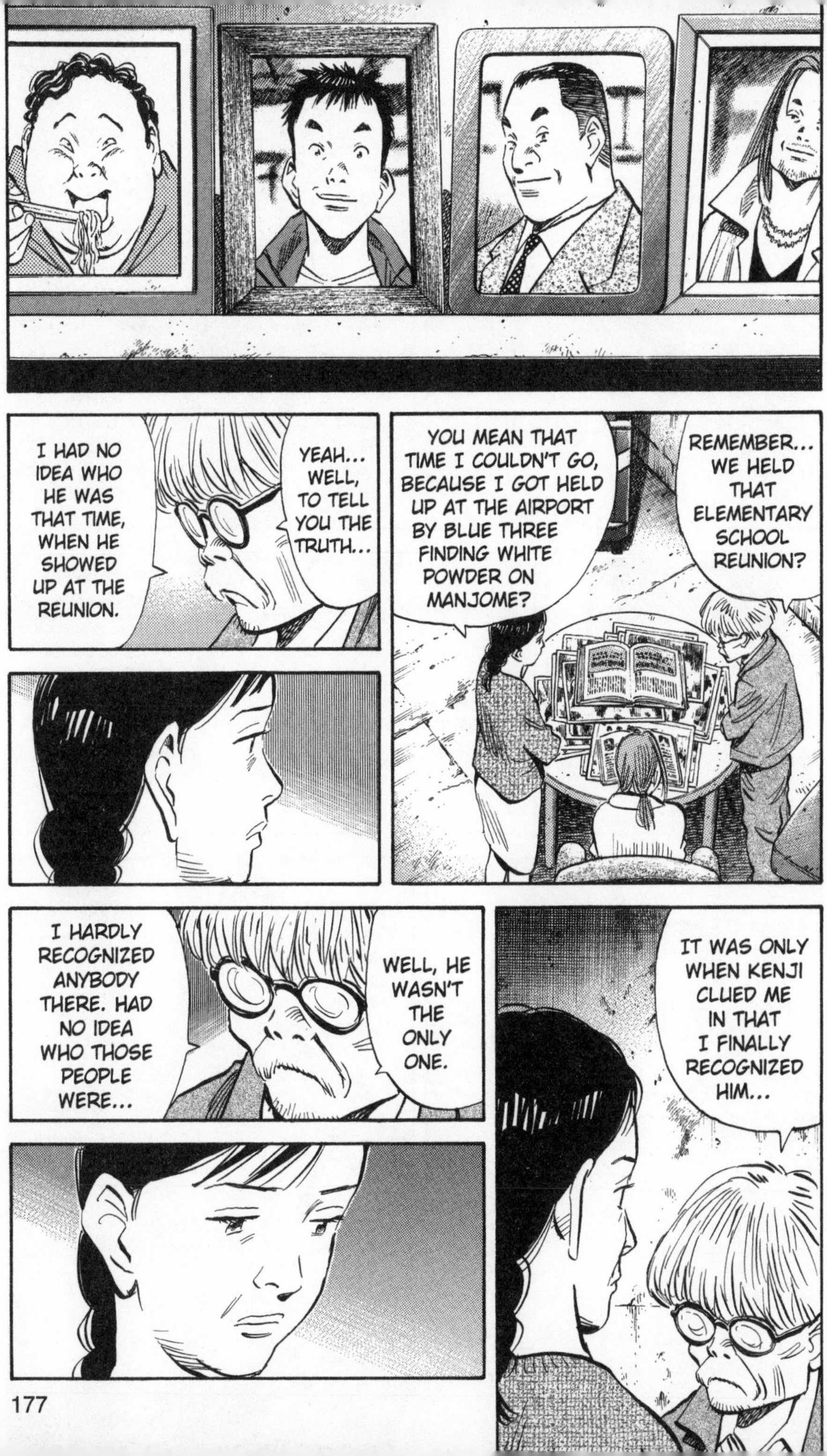

REMEMBER... WE HELD THAT ELEMENTARY SCHOOL REUNION?
YOU MEAN THAT TIME I COULDN'T GO, BECAUSE I GOT HELD UP AT THE AIRPORT BY BLUE THREE FINDING WHITE POWDER ON MANJOME?
YEAH... WELL, TO TELL YOU THE TRUTH...
I HAD NO IDEA WHO HE WAS THAT TIME, WHEN HE SHOWED UP AT THE REUNION.
IT WAS ONLY WHEN KENJI CLUED ME IN THAT I FINALLY RECOGNIZED HIM...
WELL, HE WASN'T THE ONLY ONE.
I HARDLY RECOGNIZED ANYBODY THERE. HAD NO IDEA WHO THOSE PEOPLE WERE...

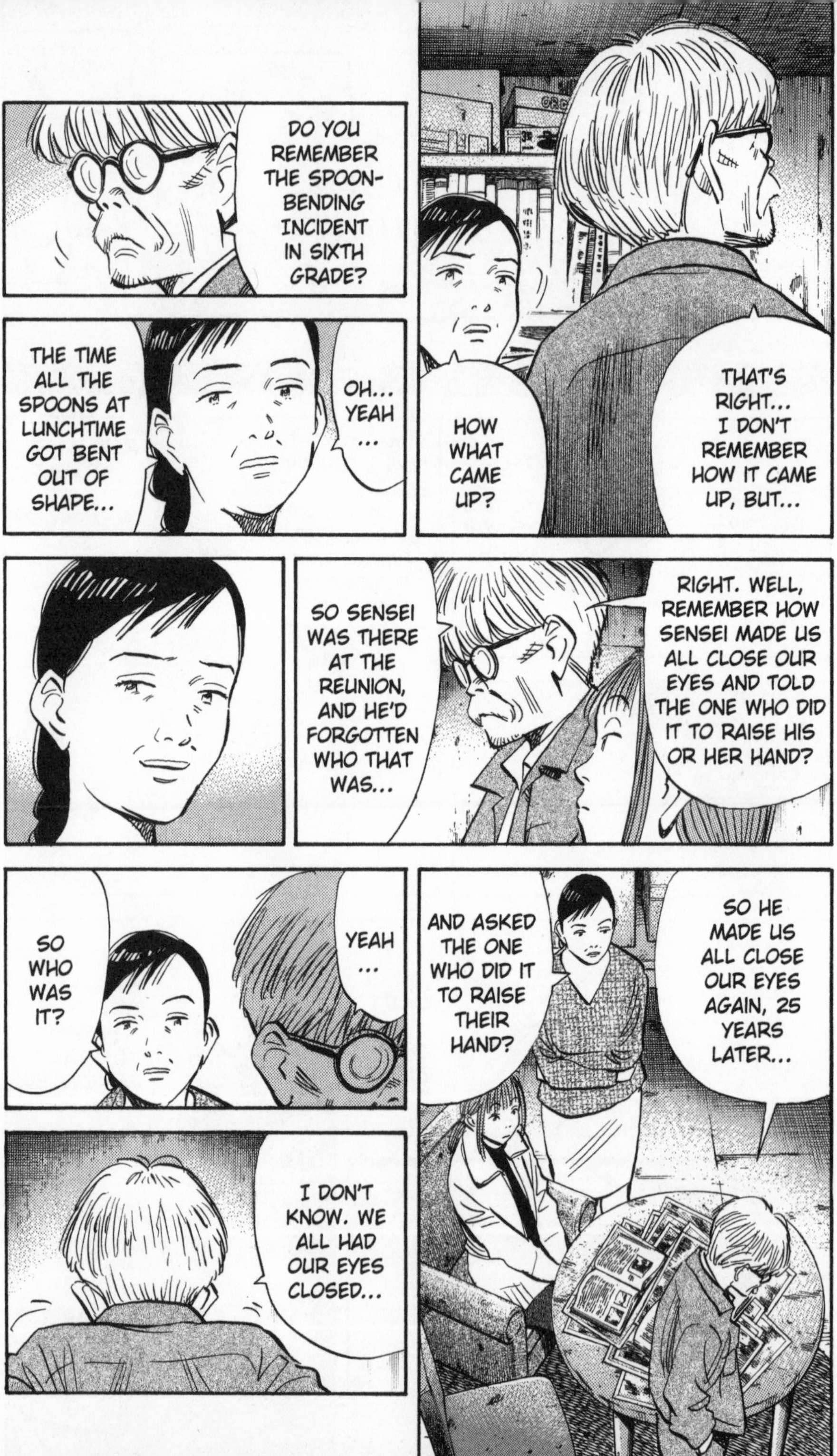
THAT'S RIGHT... I DON'T REMEMBER HOW IT CAME UP, BUT...
HOW WHAT CAME UP?
DO YOU REMEMBER THE SPOON-BENDING INCIDENT IN SIXTH GRADE?
OH... YEAH...
THE TIME ALL THE SPOONS AT LUNCHTIME GOT BENT OUT OF SHAPE...
RIGHT. WELL, REMEMBER HOW SENSEI MADE US ALL CLOSE OUR EYES AND TOLD THE ONE WHO DID IT TO RAISE HIS OR HER HAND?
SO SENSEI WAS THERE AT THE REUNION, AND HE'D FORGOTTEN WHO THAT WAS...
SO HE MADE US ALL CLOSE OUR EYES AGAIN, 25 YEARS LATER...
AND ASKED THE ONE WHO DID IT TO RAISE THEIR HAND?
YEAH...
SO WHO WAS IT?
I DON'T KNOW. WE ALL HAD OUR EYES CLOSED...

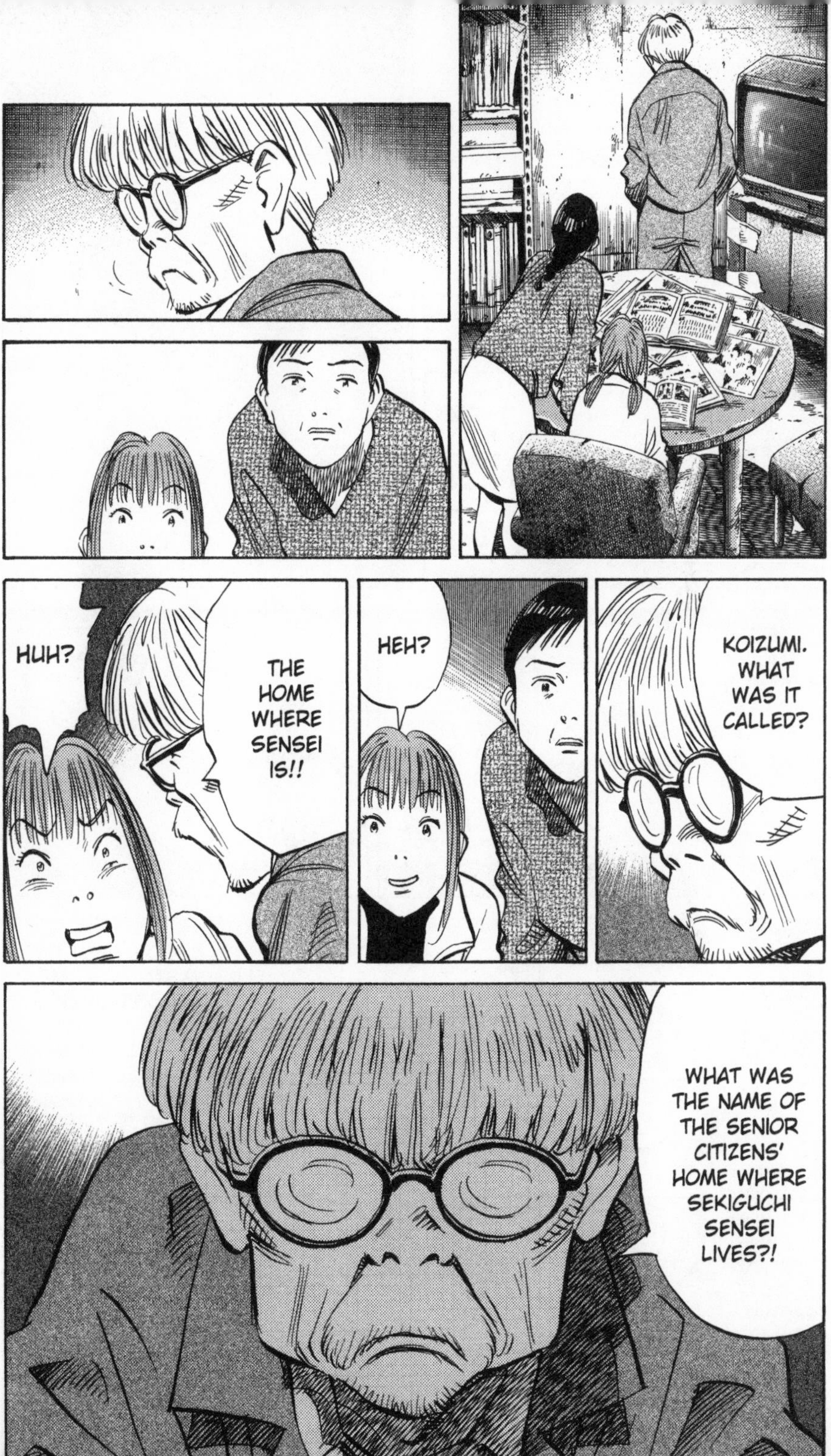
KOIZUMI. WHAT WAS IT CALLED?
HEH?
THE HOME WHERE SENSEI IS!!
HUH?
WHAT WAS THE NAME OF THE SENIOR CITIZENS' HOME WHERE SEKIGUCHI SENSEI LIVES?!

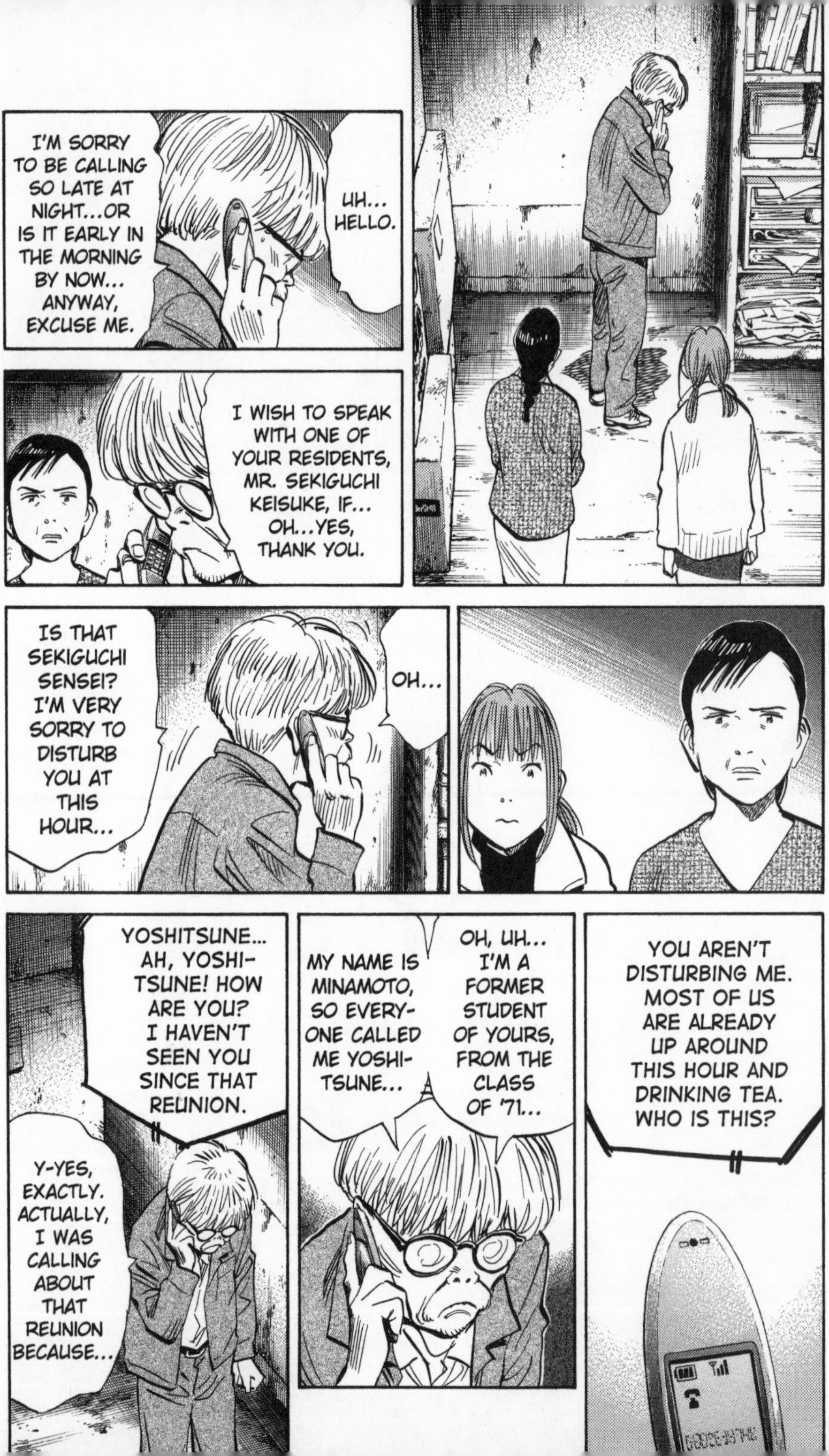
UH... HELLO.
I'M SORRY TO BE CALLING SO LATE AT NIGHT...OR IS IT EARLY IN THE MORNING BY NOW... ANYWAY, EXCUSE ME.
I WISH TO SPEAK WITH ONE OF YOUR RESIDENTS, MR. SEKIGUCHI KEISUKE, IF... OH...YES, THANK YOU.
OH...
IS THAT SEKIGUCHI SENSEI? I'M VERY SORRY TO DISTURB YOU AT THIS HOUR...
YOU AREN'T DISTURBING ME. MOST OF US ARE ALREADY UP AROUND THIS HOUR AND DRINKING TEA. WHO IS THIS?
OH, UH... I'M A FORMER STUDENT OF YOURS, FROM THE CLASS OF '71...
MY NAME IS MINAMOTO, SO EVERY-ONE CALLED ME YOSHI-TSUNE...
YOSHITSUNE... AH, YOSHI-TSUNE! HOW ARE YOU? I HAVEN'T SEEN YOU SINCE THAT REUNION.
Y-YES, EXACTLY. ACTUALLY, I WAS CALLING ABOUT THAT REUNION BECAUSE...

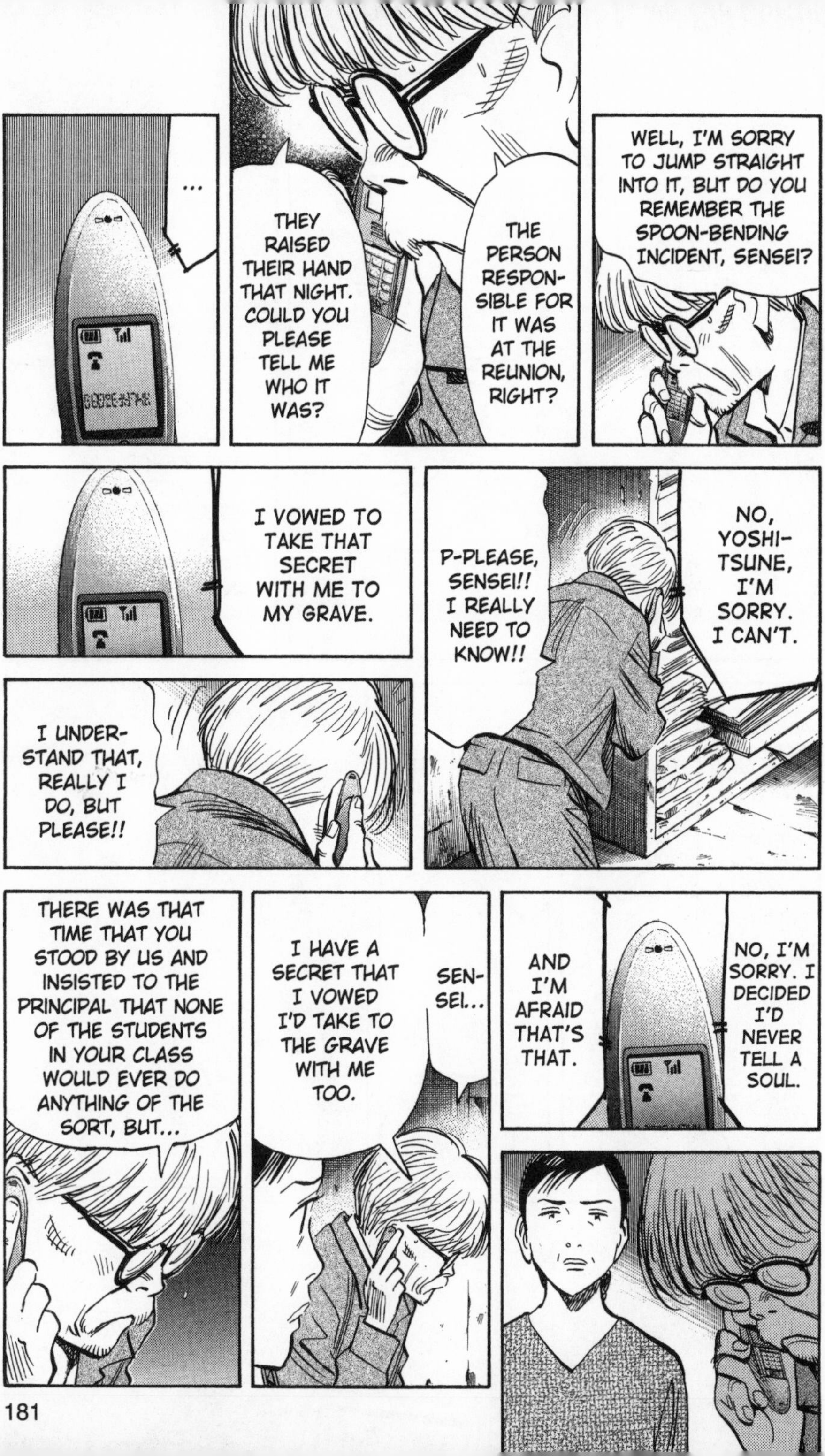
WELL, I'M SORRY TO JUMP STRAIGHT INTO IT, BUT DO YOU REMEMBER THE SPOON-BENDING INCIDENT, SENSEI?
THE PERSON RESPONSIBLE FOR IT WAS AT THE REUNION, RIGHT?
THEY RAISED THEIR HAND THAT NIGHT. COULD YOU PLEASE TELL ME WHO IT WAS?
...
NO, YOSHITSUNE, I'M SORRY. I CAN'T.
P-PLEASE, SENSEI!! I REALLY NEED TO KNOW!!
I VOWED TO TAKE THAT SECRET WITH ME TO MY GRAVE.
I UNDERSTAND THAT, REALLY I DO, BUT PLEASE!!
NO, I'M SORRY. I DECIDED I'D NEVER TELL A SOUL.
AND I'M AFRAID THAT'S THAT.
SENSEI...
I HAVE A SECRET THAT I VOWED I'D TAKE TO THE GRAVE WITH ME TOO.
THERE WAS THAT TIME THAT YOU STOOD BY US AND INSISTED TO THE PRINCIPAL THAT NONE OF THE STUDENTS IN YOUR CLASS WOULD EVER DO ANYTHING OF THE SORT, BUT...

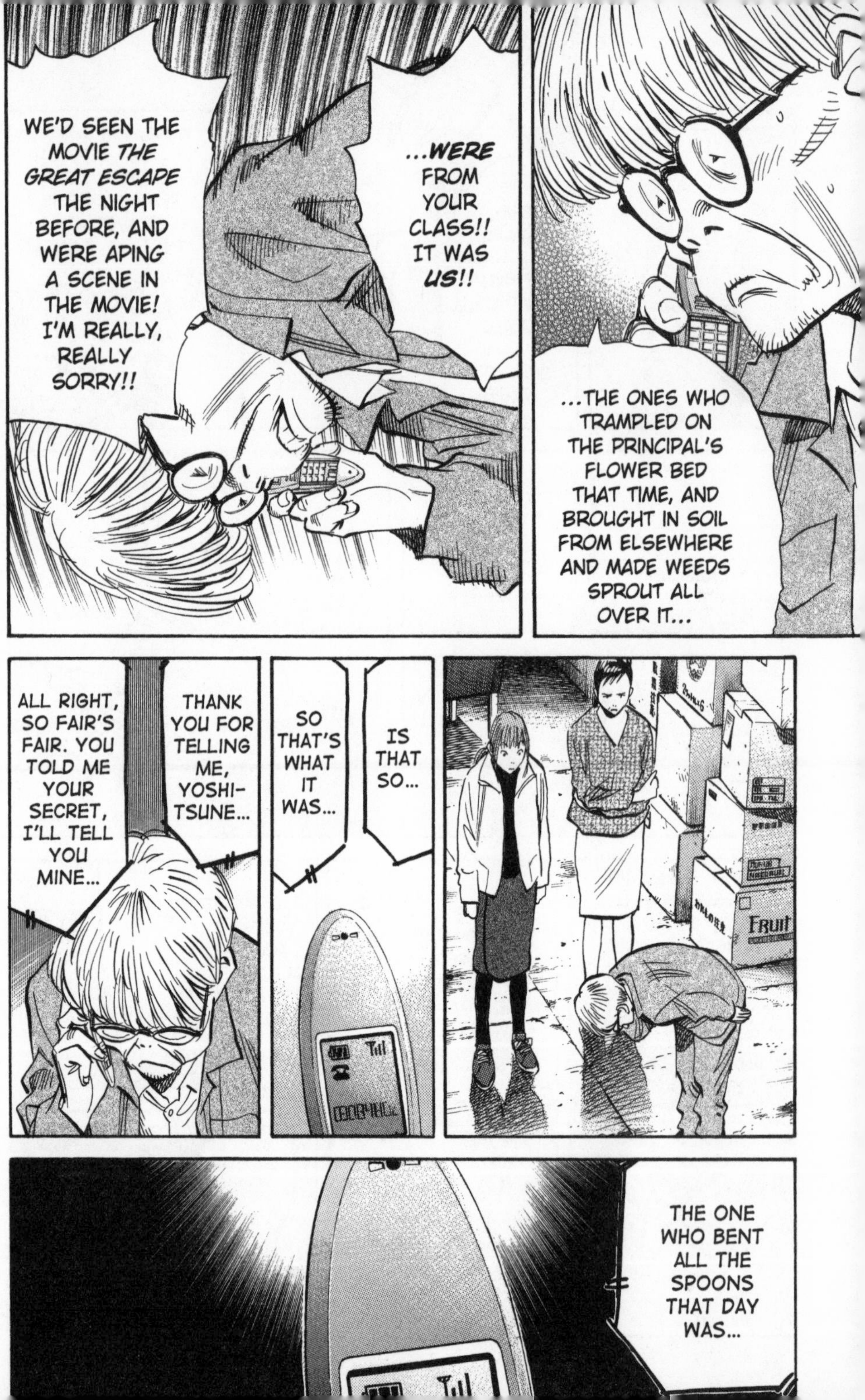
...THE ONES WHO TRAMPLED ON THE PRINCIPAL'S FLOWER BED THAT TIME, AND BROUGHT IN SOIL FROM ELSEWHERE AND MADE WEEDS SPROUT ALL OVER IT...
...*WERE* FROM YOUR CLASS!! IT WAS *US*!!
WE'D SEEN THE MOVIE *THE GREAT ESCAPE* THE NIGHT BEFORE, AND WERE APING A SCENE IN THE MOVIE! I'M REALLY, REALLY SORRY!!
Fruit
IS THAT SO...
SO THAT'S WHAT IT WAS...
THANK YOU FOR TELLING ME, YOSHITSUNE...
ALL RIGHT, SO FAIR'S FAIR. YOU TOLD ME YOUR SECRET, I'LL TELL YOU MINE...
THE ONE WHO BENT ALL THE SPOONS THAT DAY WAS...

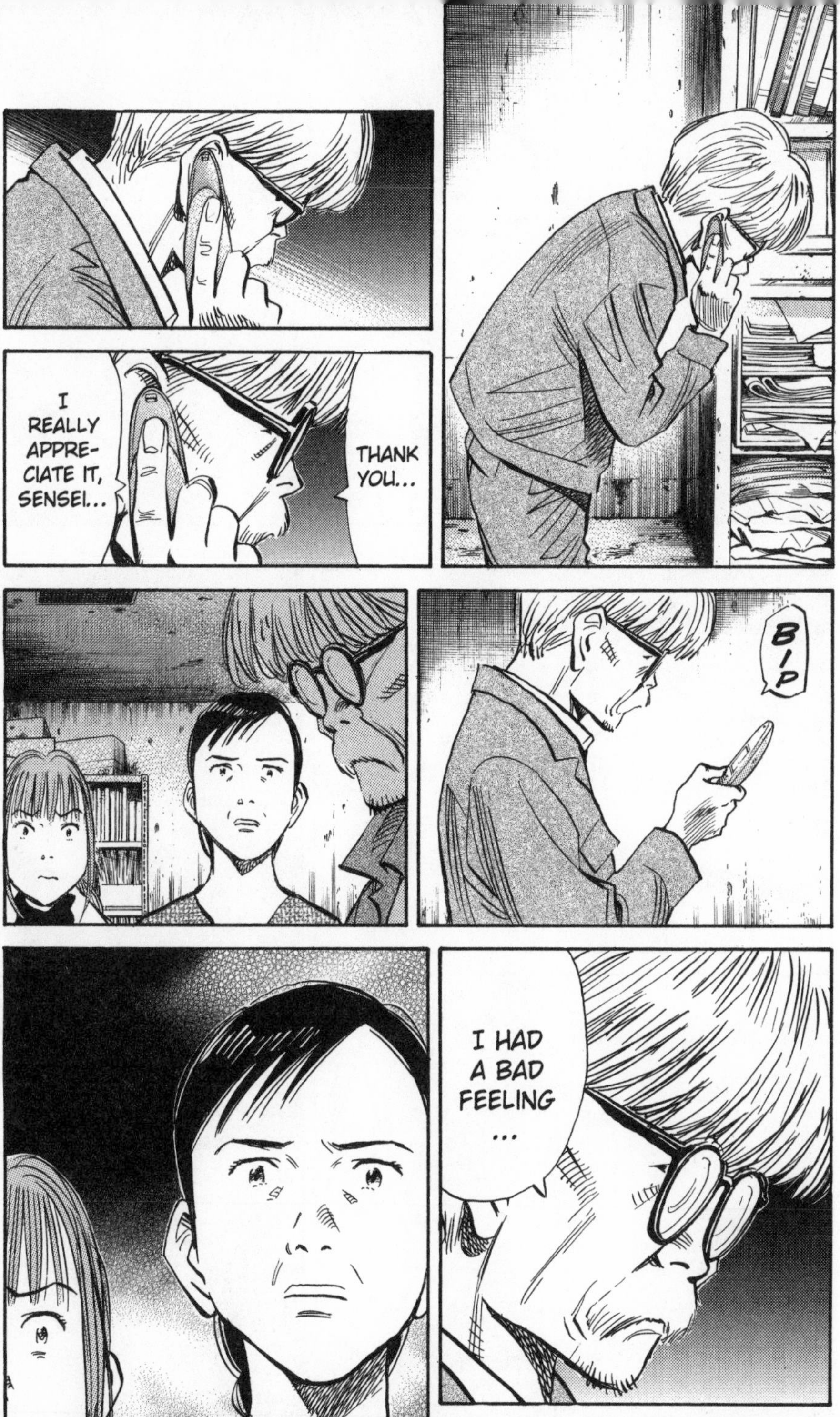
THANK YOU...
I REALLY APPRECIATE IT, SENSEI...
BIP
I HAD A BAD FEELING ...

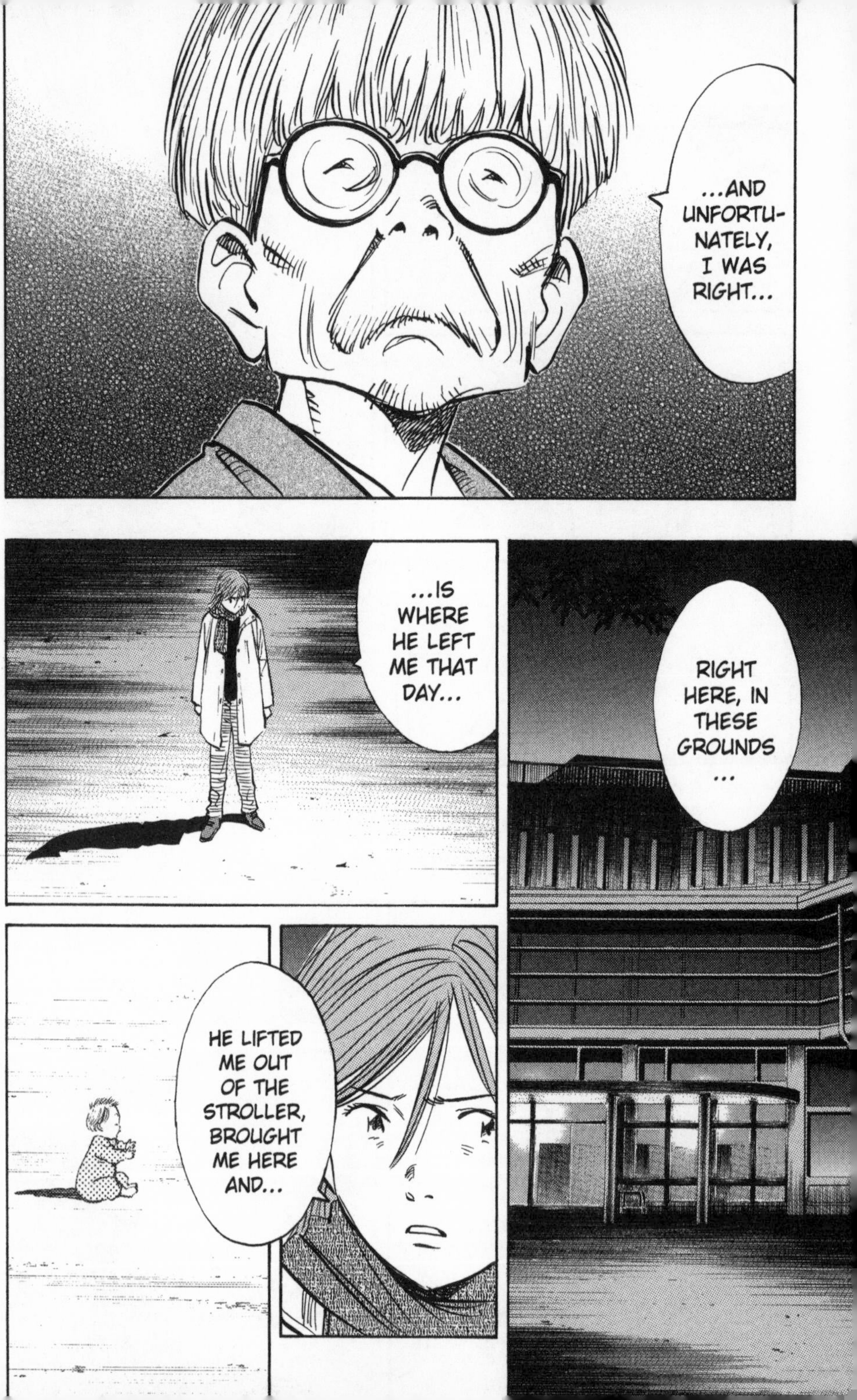
...AND UNFORTU-NATELY, I WAS RIGHT...
RIGHT HERE, IN THESE GROUNDS ...
...IS WHERE HE LEFT ME THAT DAY...
HE LIFTED ME OUT OF THE STROLLER, BROUGHT ME HERE AND...

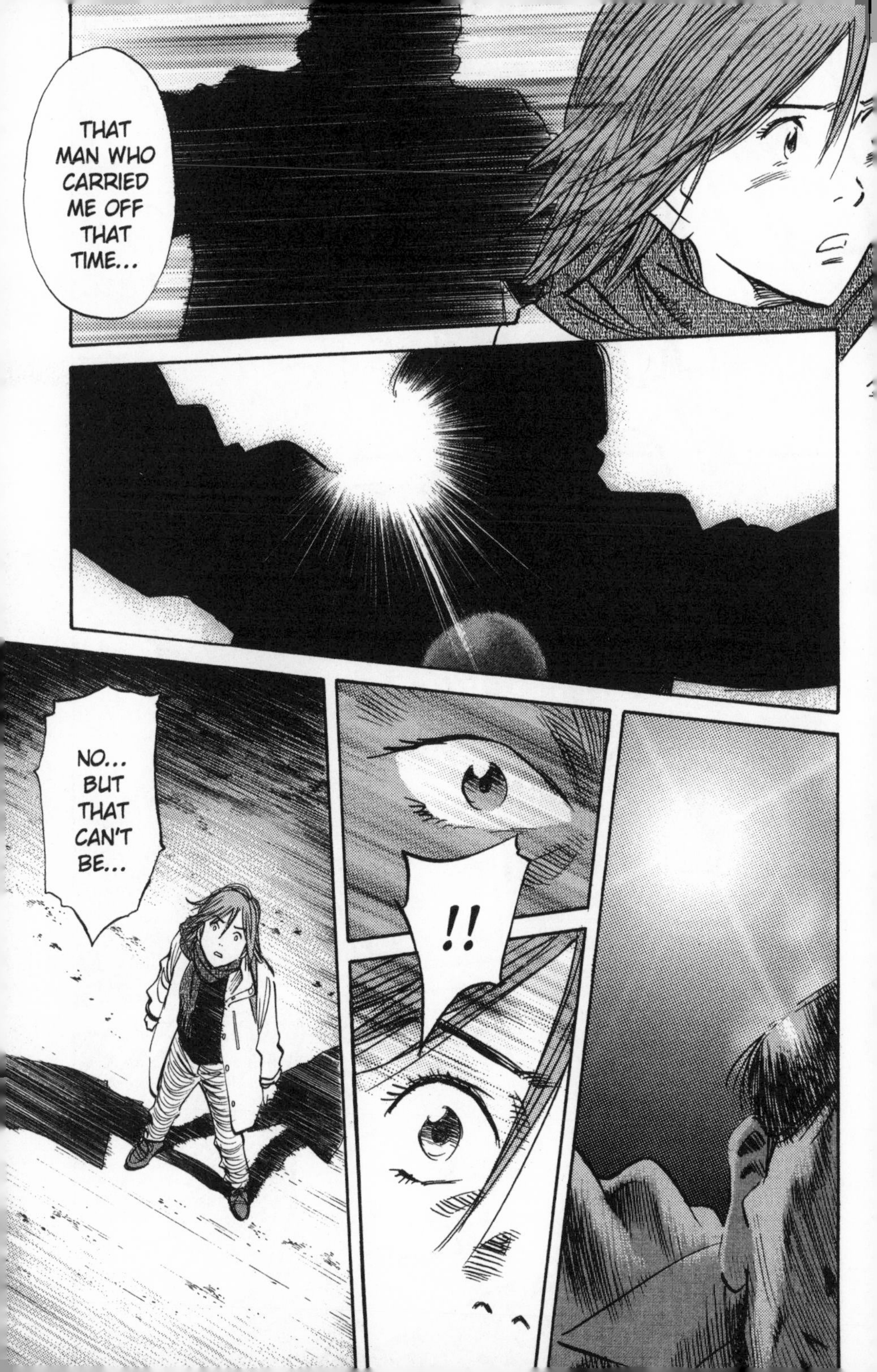
THAT MAN WHO CARRIED ME OFF THAT TIME...
NO... BUT THAT CAN'T BE...
!!

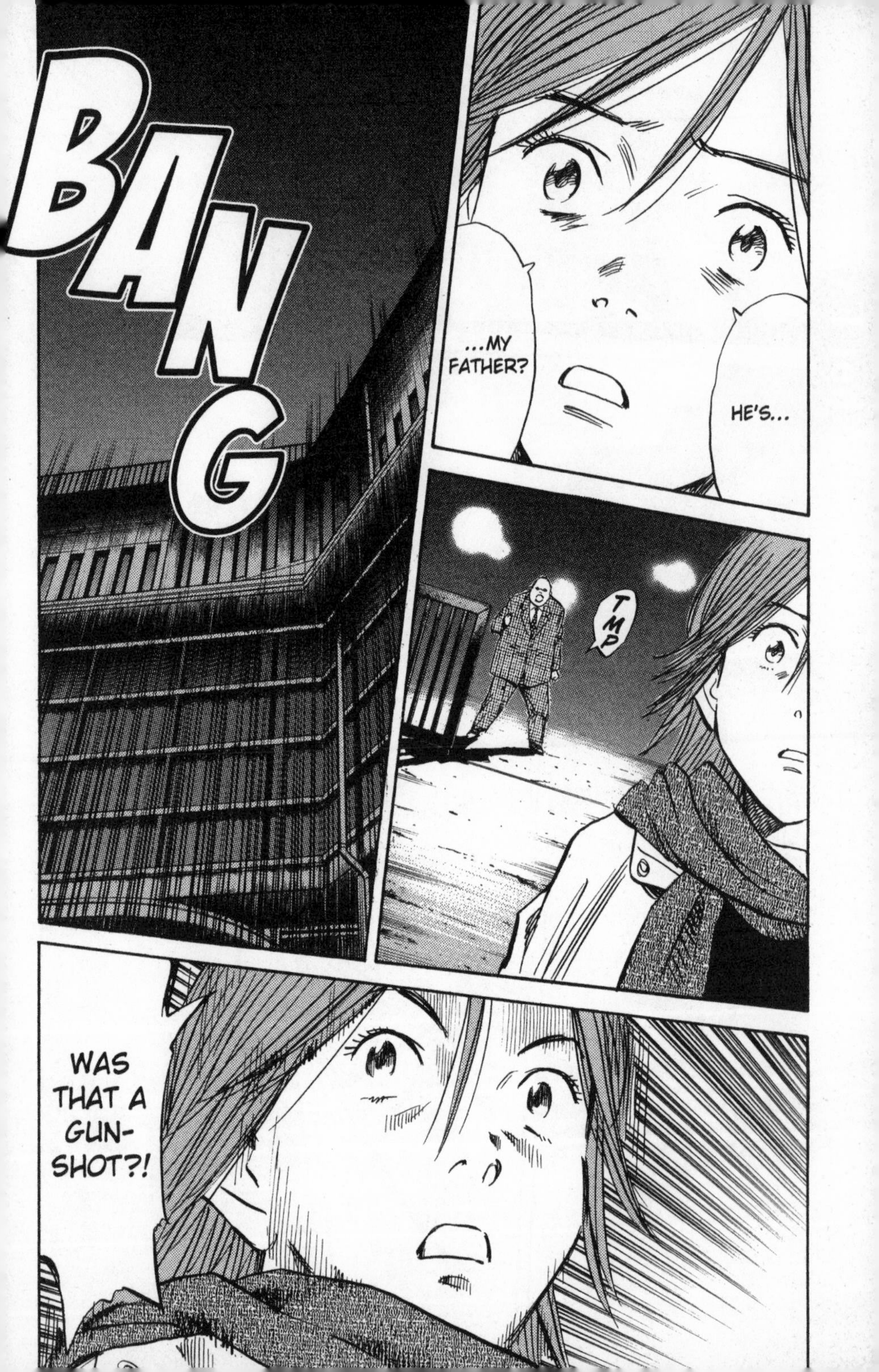
...MY FATHER?
HE'S...
TMP
BANG
WAS THAT A GUN-SHOT?!

Chapter 11 Gunshot Explained

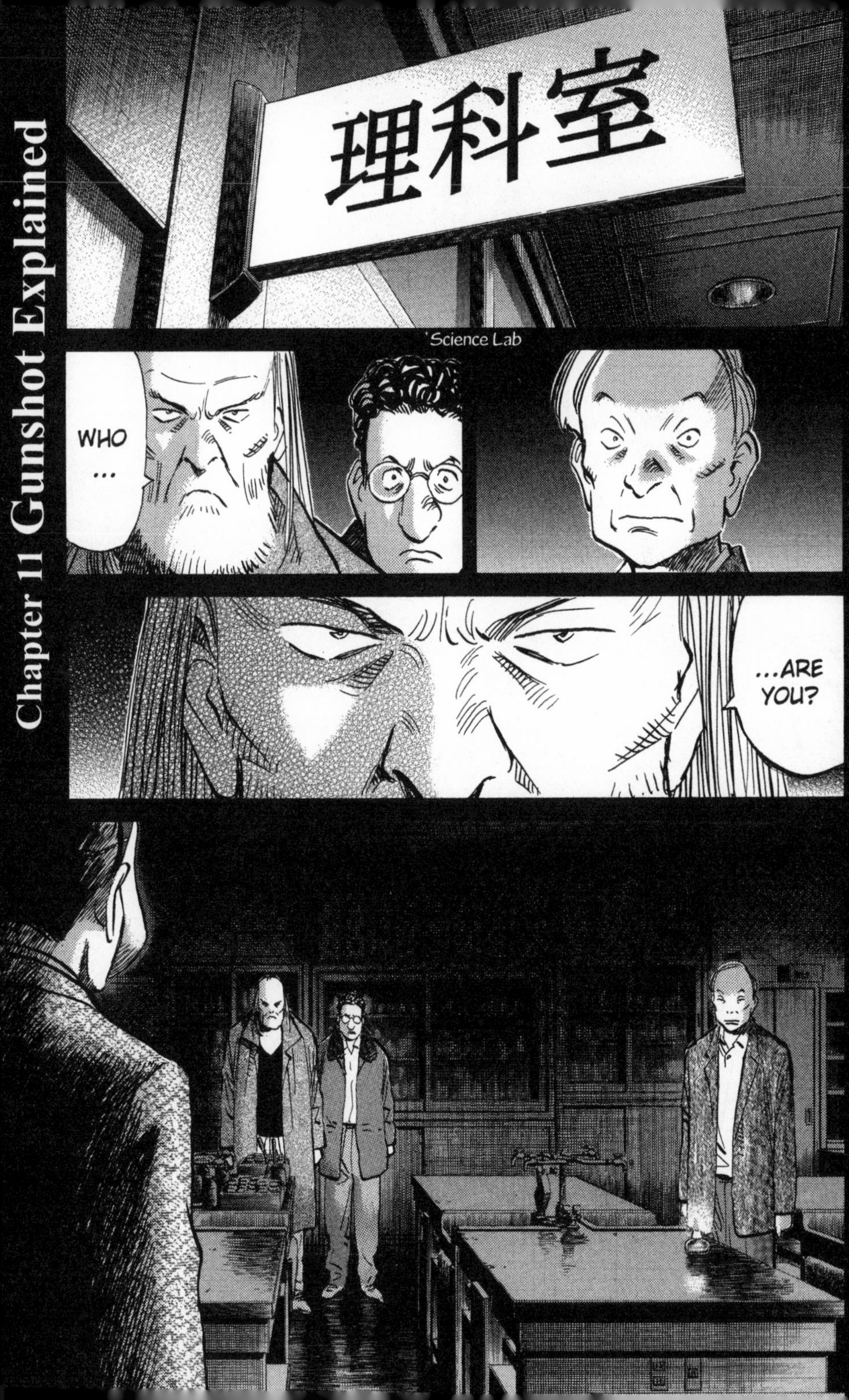
理科室
*Science Lab
WHO ...
...ARE YOU?

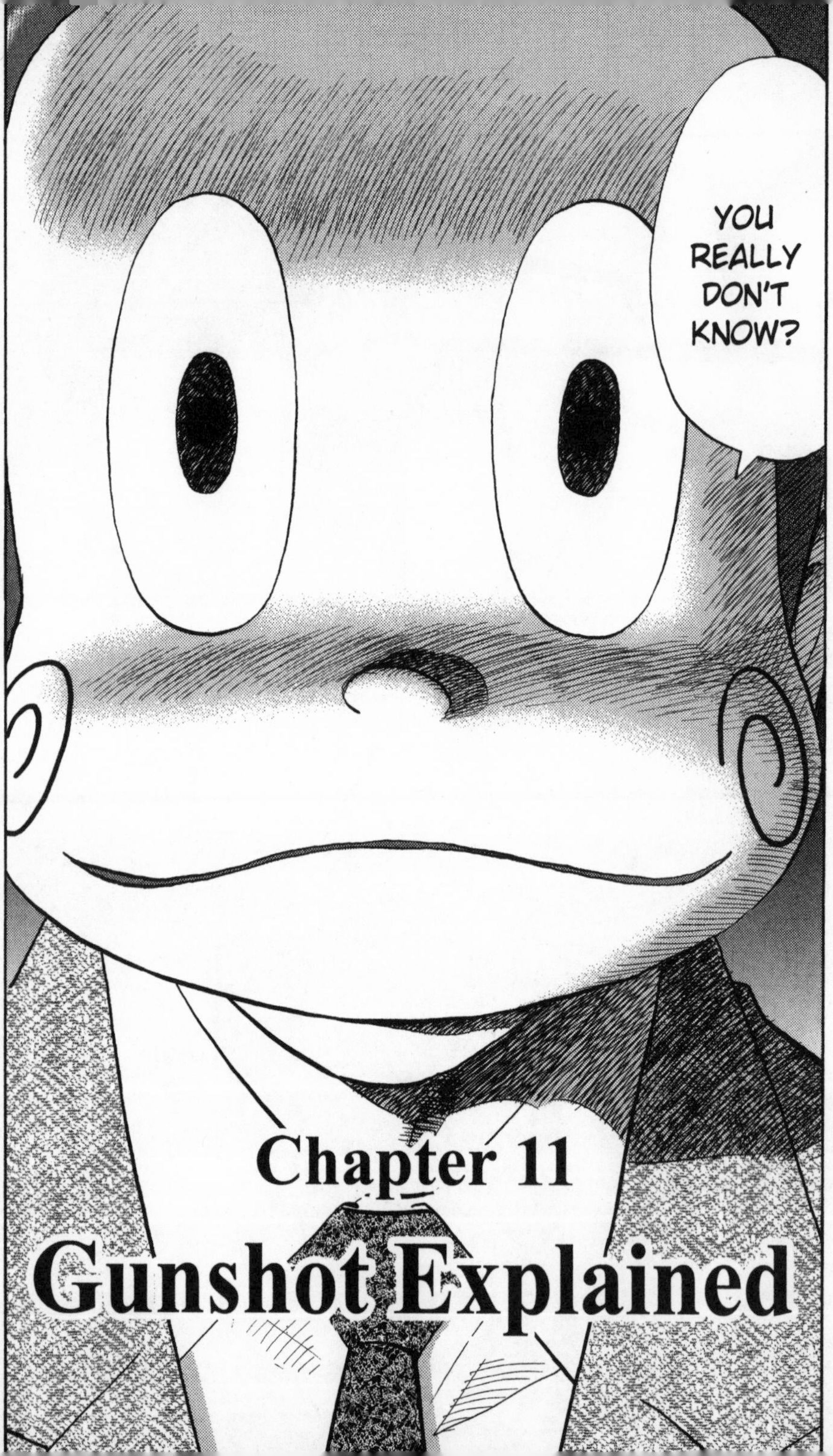
YOU REALLY DON'T KNOW?

Chapter 11

Gunshot Explained

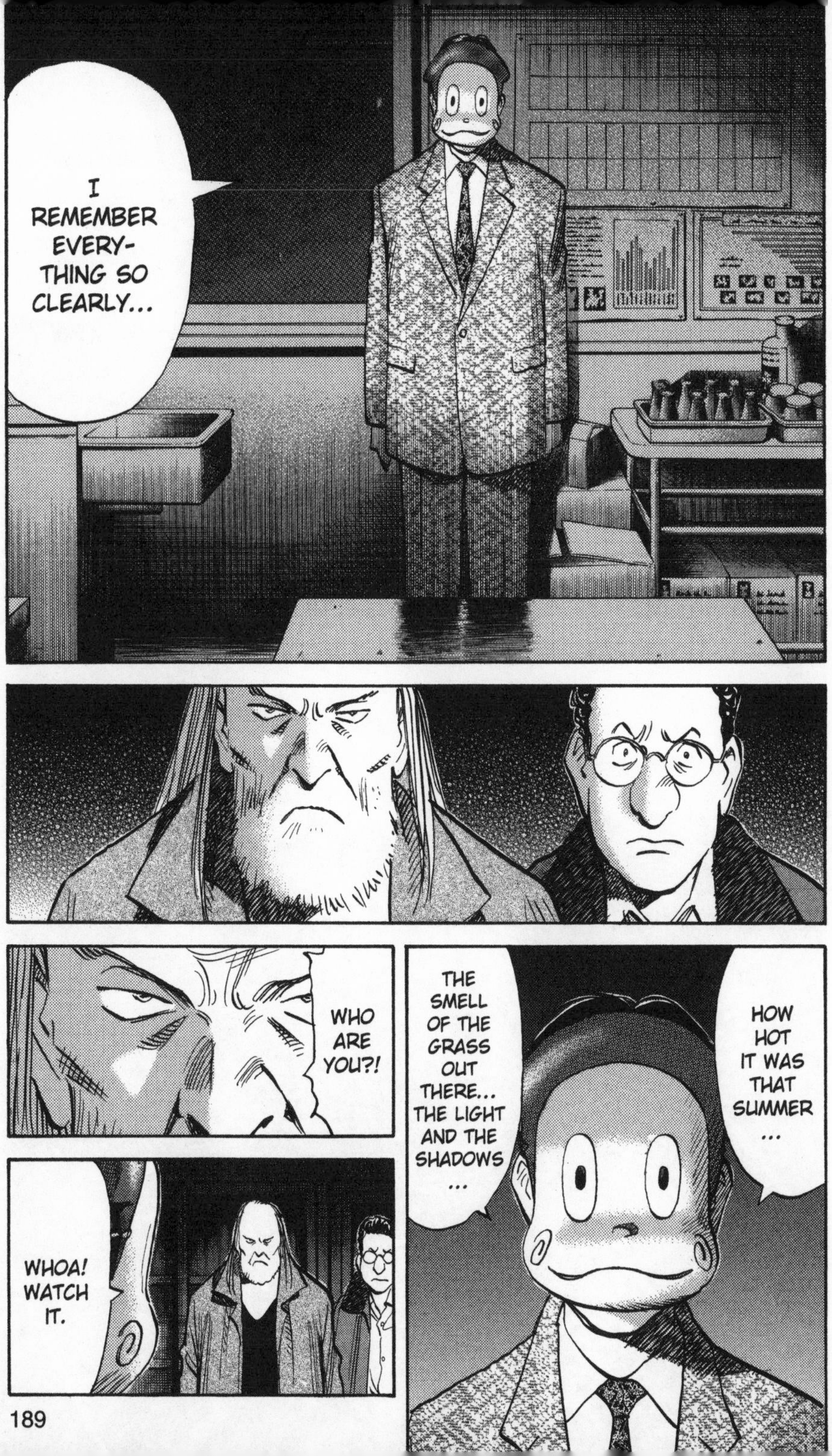
I REMEMBER EVERY-THING SO CLEARLY...
HOW HOT IT WAS THAT SUMMER...
THE SMELL OF THE GRASS OUT THERE... THE LIGHT AND THE SHADOWS...
WHO ARE YOU?!
WHOA! WATCH IT.

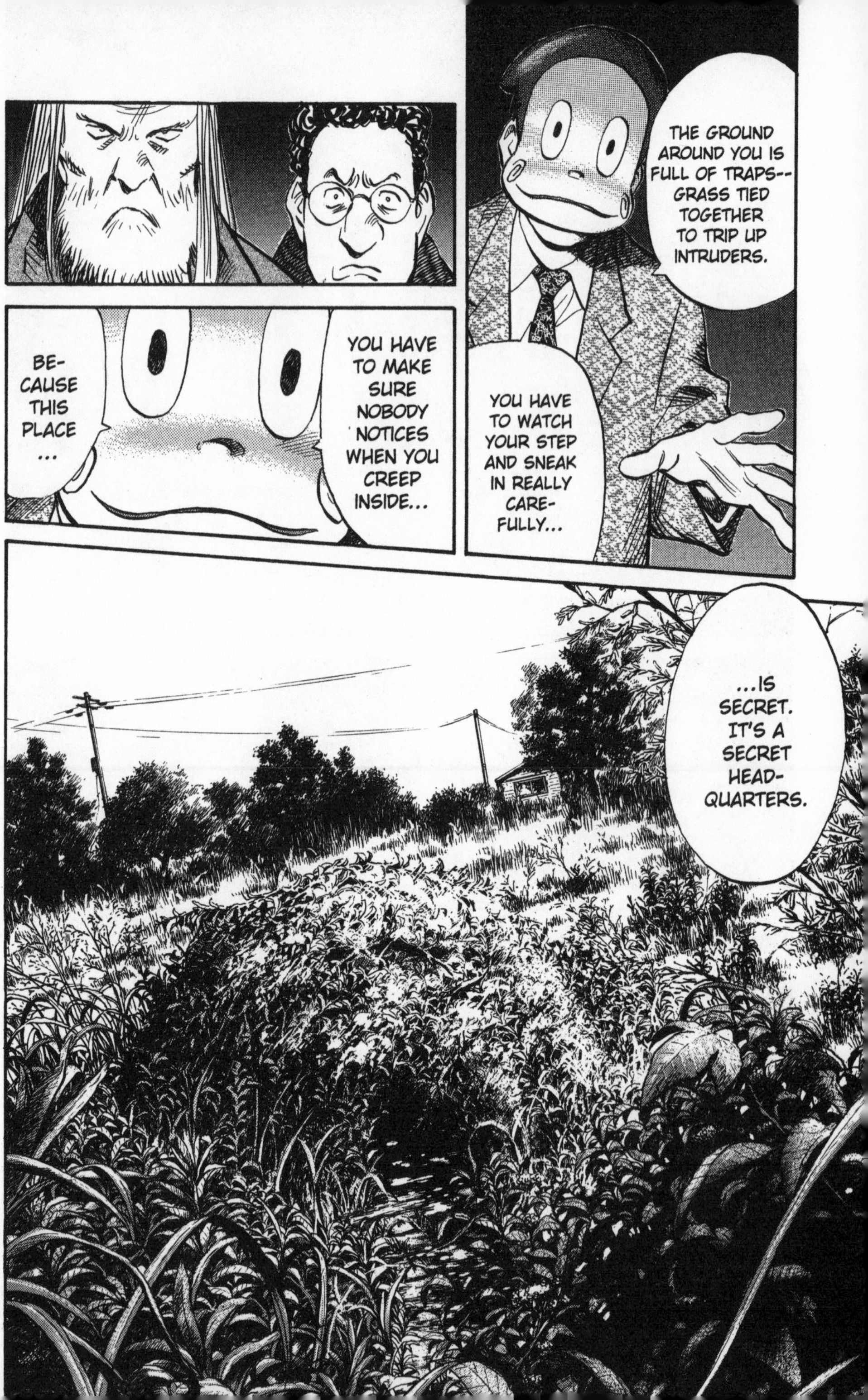
THE GROUND AROUND YOU IS FULL OF TRAPS-- GRASS TIED TOGETHER TO TRIP UP INTRUDERS.
YOU HAVE TO WATCH YOUR STEP AND SNEAK IN REALLY CARE-FULLY...
YOU HAVE TO MAKE SURE NOBODY NOTICES WHEN YOU CREEP INSIDE...
BE-CAUSE THIS PLACE ...
...IS SECRET. IT'S A SECRET HEAD-QUARTERS.

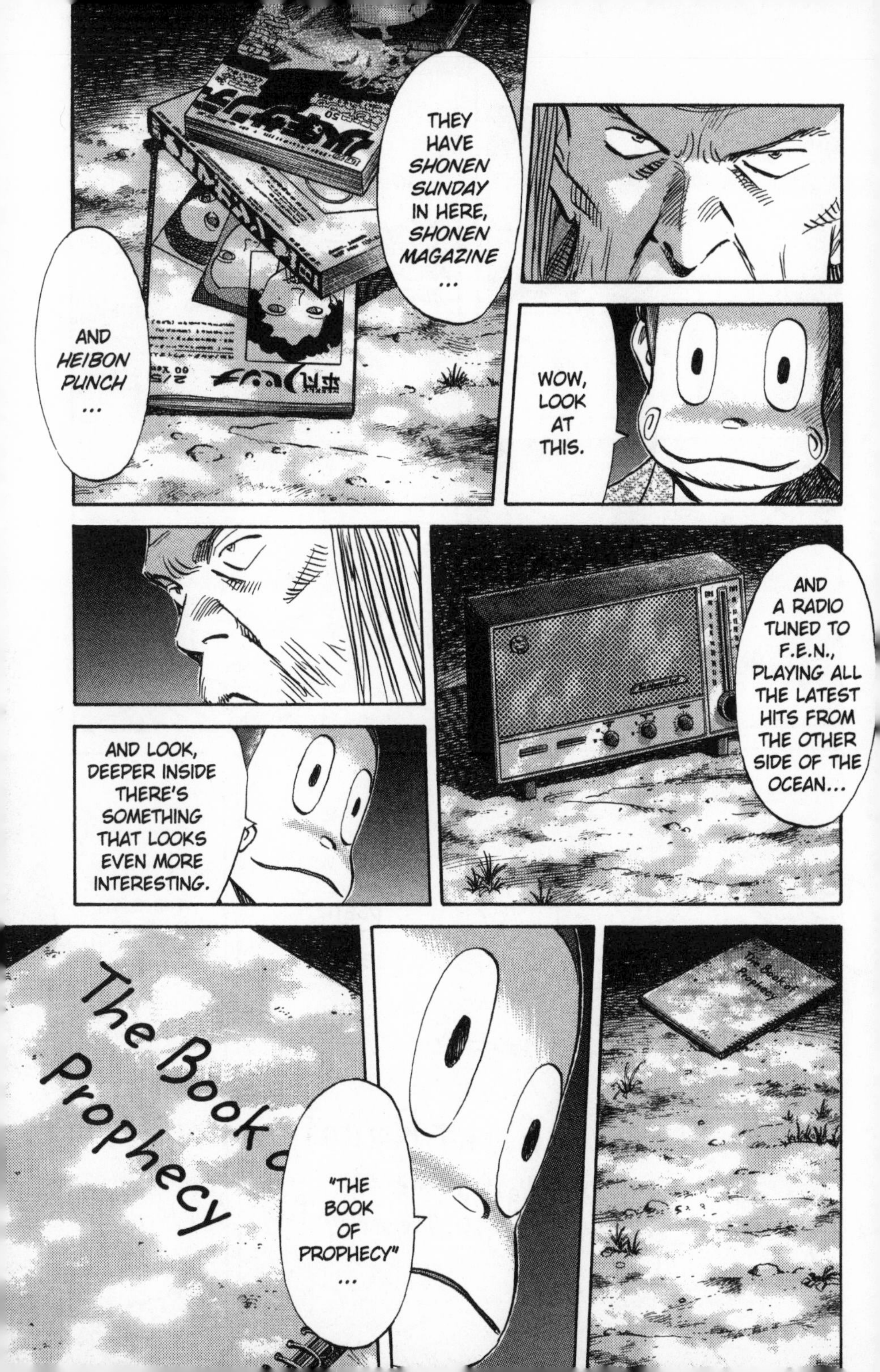
WOW, LOOK AT THIS.
THEY HAVE SHONEN SUNDAY IN HERE, SHONEN MAGAZINE ...
AND HEIBON PUNCH ...
AND A RADIO TUNED TO F.E.N., PLAYING ALL THE LATEST HITS FROM THE OTHER SIDE OF THE OCEAN...
AND LOOK, DEEPER INSIDE THERE'S SOMETHING THAT LOOKS EVEN MORE INTERESTING.
The Book of Prophecy
"THE BOOK OF PROPHECY" ...
The Book
Prophecy

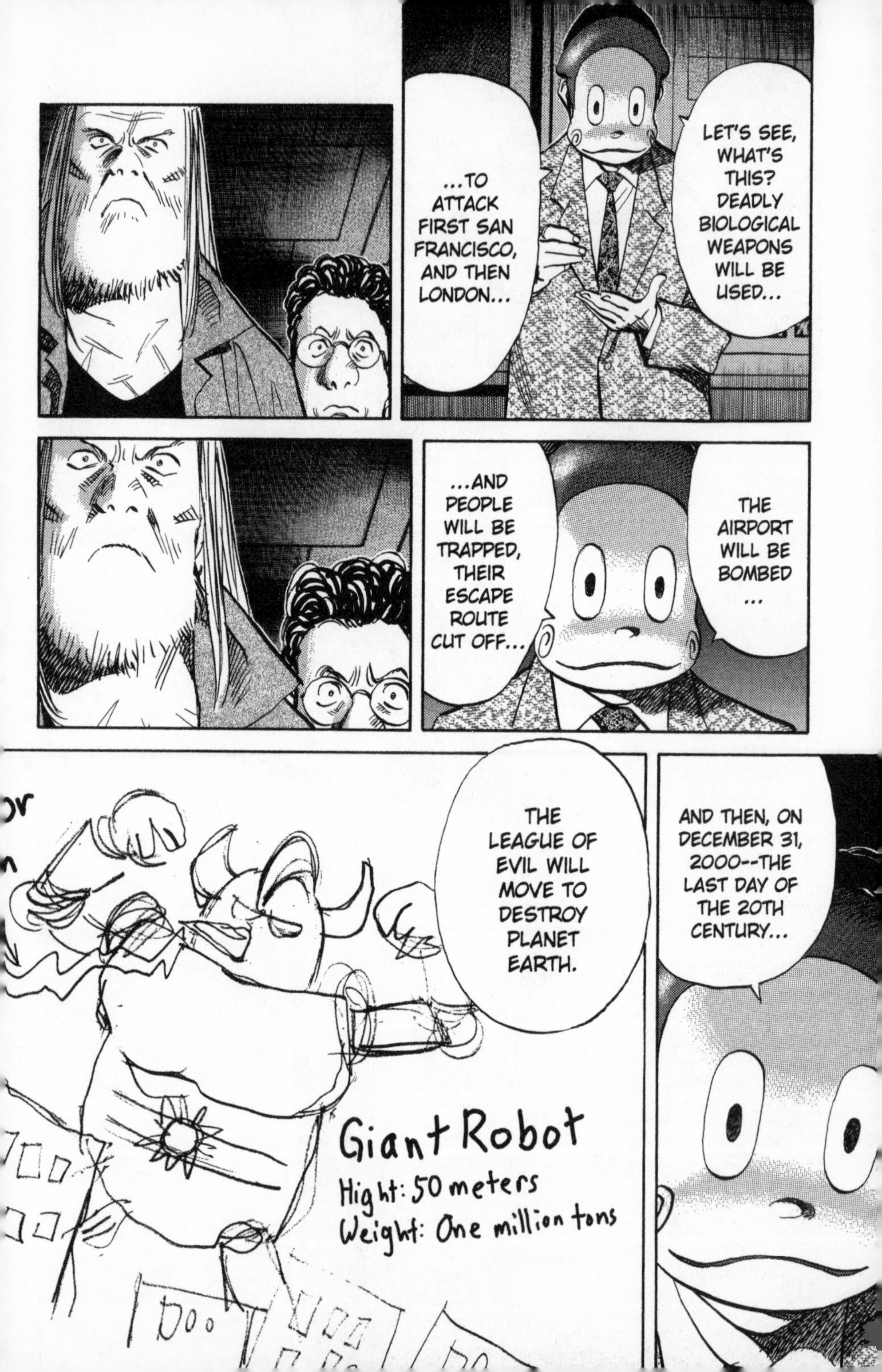
LET'S SEE, WHAT'S THIS? DEADLY BIOLOGICAL WEAPONS WILL BE USED...
...TO ATTACK FIRST SAN FRANCISCO, AND THEN LONDON...
THE AIRPORT WILL BE BOMBED ...
...AND PEOPLE WILL BE TRAPPED, THEIR ESCAPE ROUTE CUT OFF...
AND THEN, ON DECEMBER 31, 2000--THE LAST DAY OF THE 20TH CENTURY...
THE LEAGUE OF EVIL WILL MOVE TO DESTROY PLANET EARTH.
Giant Robot
Hight: 50 meters
Weight: One million tons

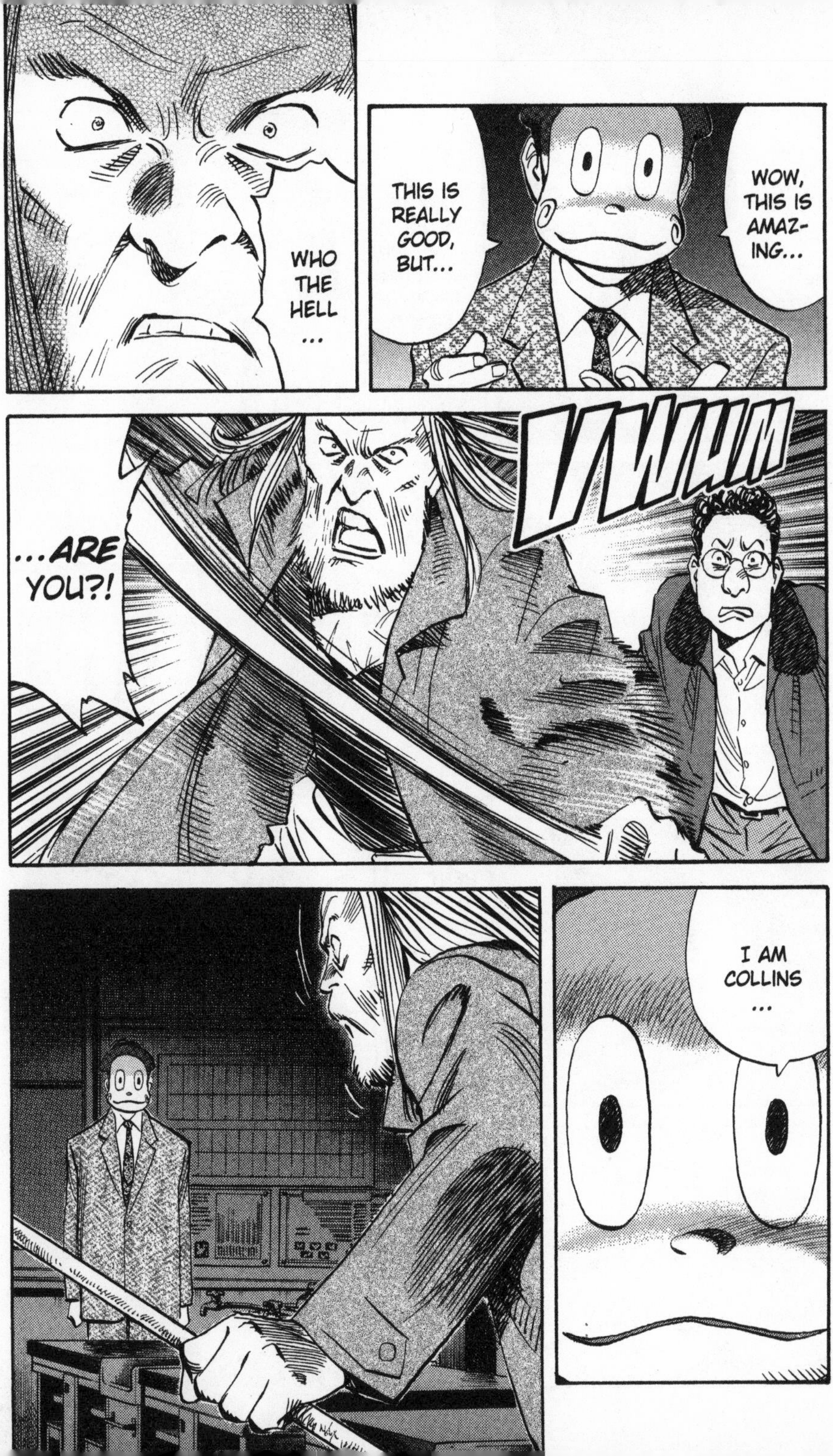
WOW, THIS IS AMAZ-ING...
THIS IS REALLY GOOD, BUT...
WHO THE HELL ...
VWUM
...ARE YOU?!
I AM COLLINS ...

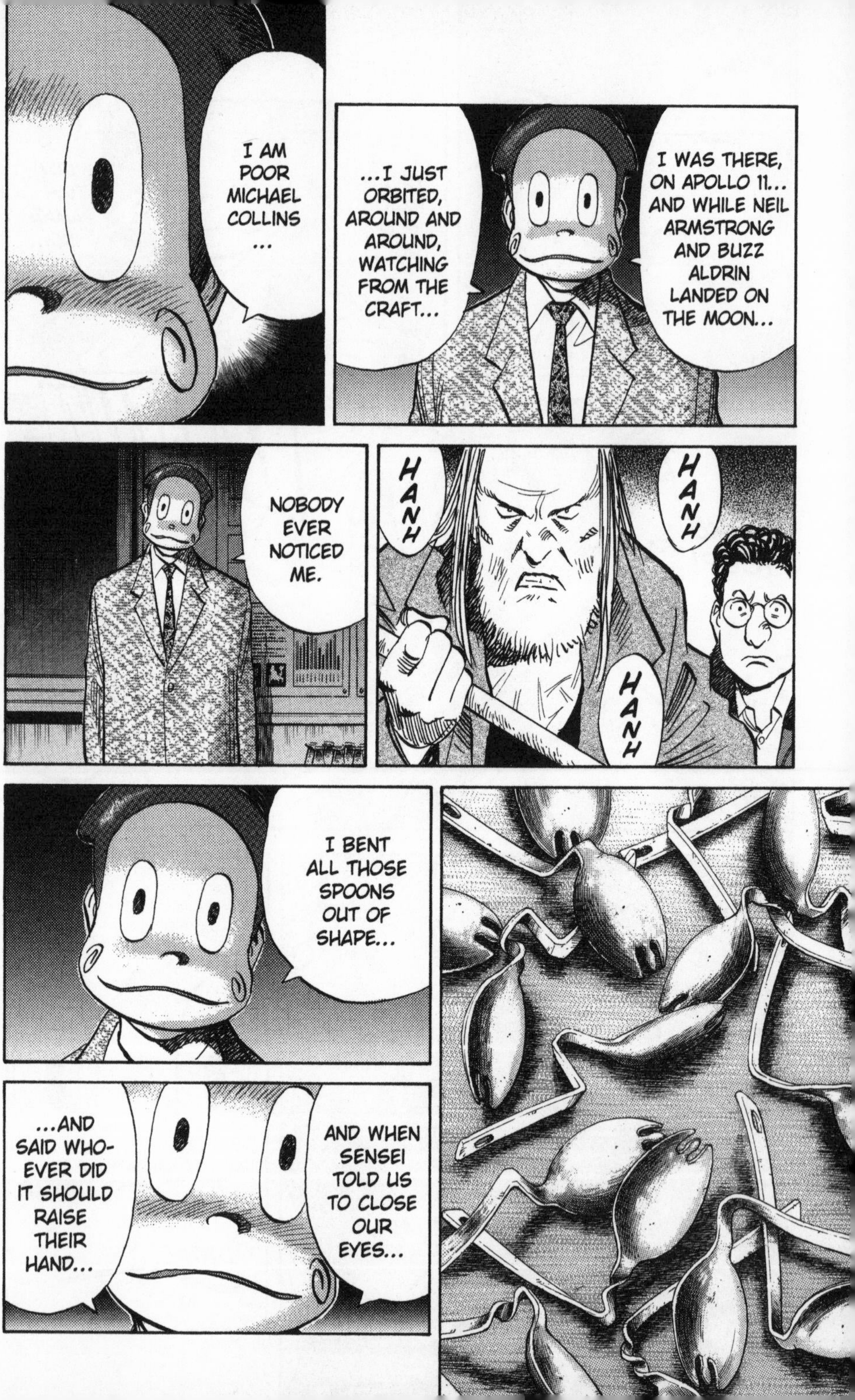
I WAS THERE, ON APOLLO 11... AND WHILE NEIL ARMSTRONG AND BUZZ ALDRIN LANDED ON THE MOON...
...I JUST ORBITED, AROUND AND AROUND, WATCHING FROM THE CRAFT...
I AM POOR MICHAEL COLLINS ...
HANH
HANH
HANH
NOBODY EVER NOTICED ME.
I BENT ALL THOSE SPOONS OUT OF SHAPE...
AND WHEN SENSEI TOLD US TO CLOSE OUR EYES...
...AND SAID WHO-EVER DID IT SHOULD RAISE THEIR HAND...

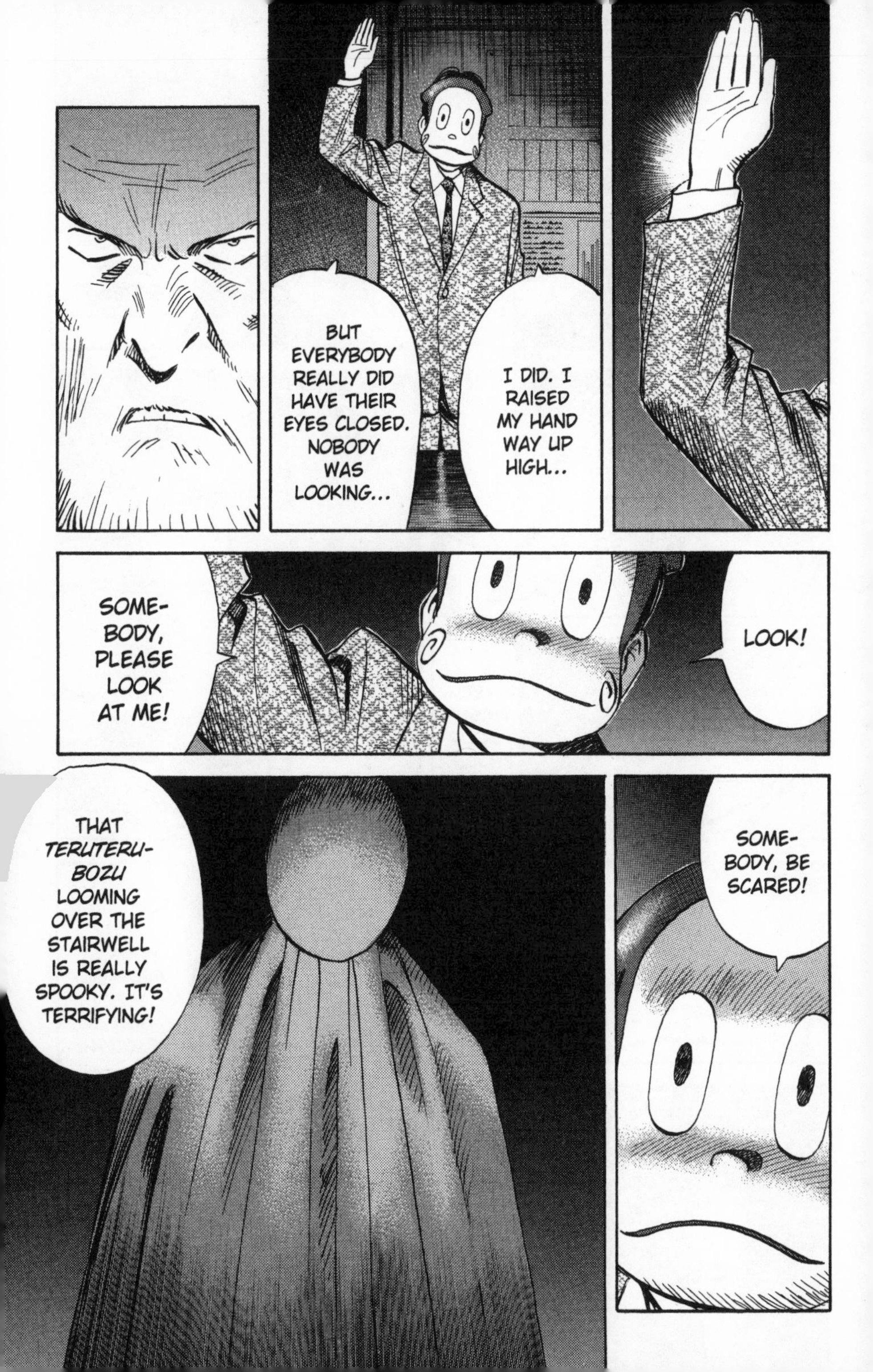
I DID. I RAISED MY HAND WAY UP HIGH...
BUT EVERYBODY REALLY DID HAVE THEIR EYES CLOSED. NOBODY WAS LOOKING...
LOOK!
SOME-BODY, PLEASE LOOK AT ME!
SOME-BODY, BE SCARED!
THAT *TERUTERU-BOZU* LOOMING OVER THE STAIRWELL IS REALLY SPOOKY. IT'S TERRIFYING!

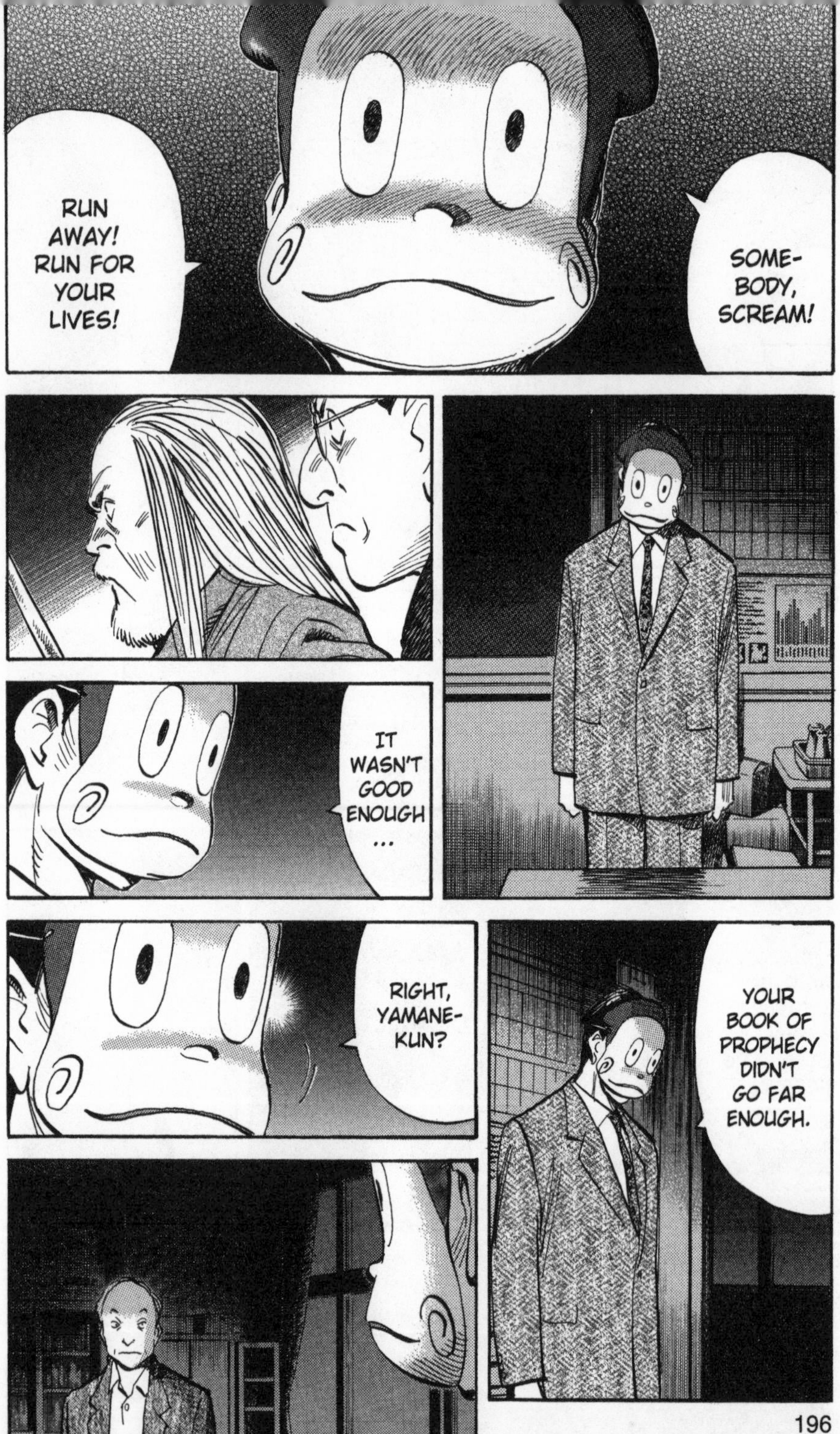
SOME-BODY, SCREAM!
RUN AWAY! RUN FOR YOUR LIVES!
IT WASN'T GOOD ENOUGH...
YOUR BOOK OF PROPHECY DIDN'T GO FAR ENOUGH.
RIGHT, YAMANE-KUN?

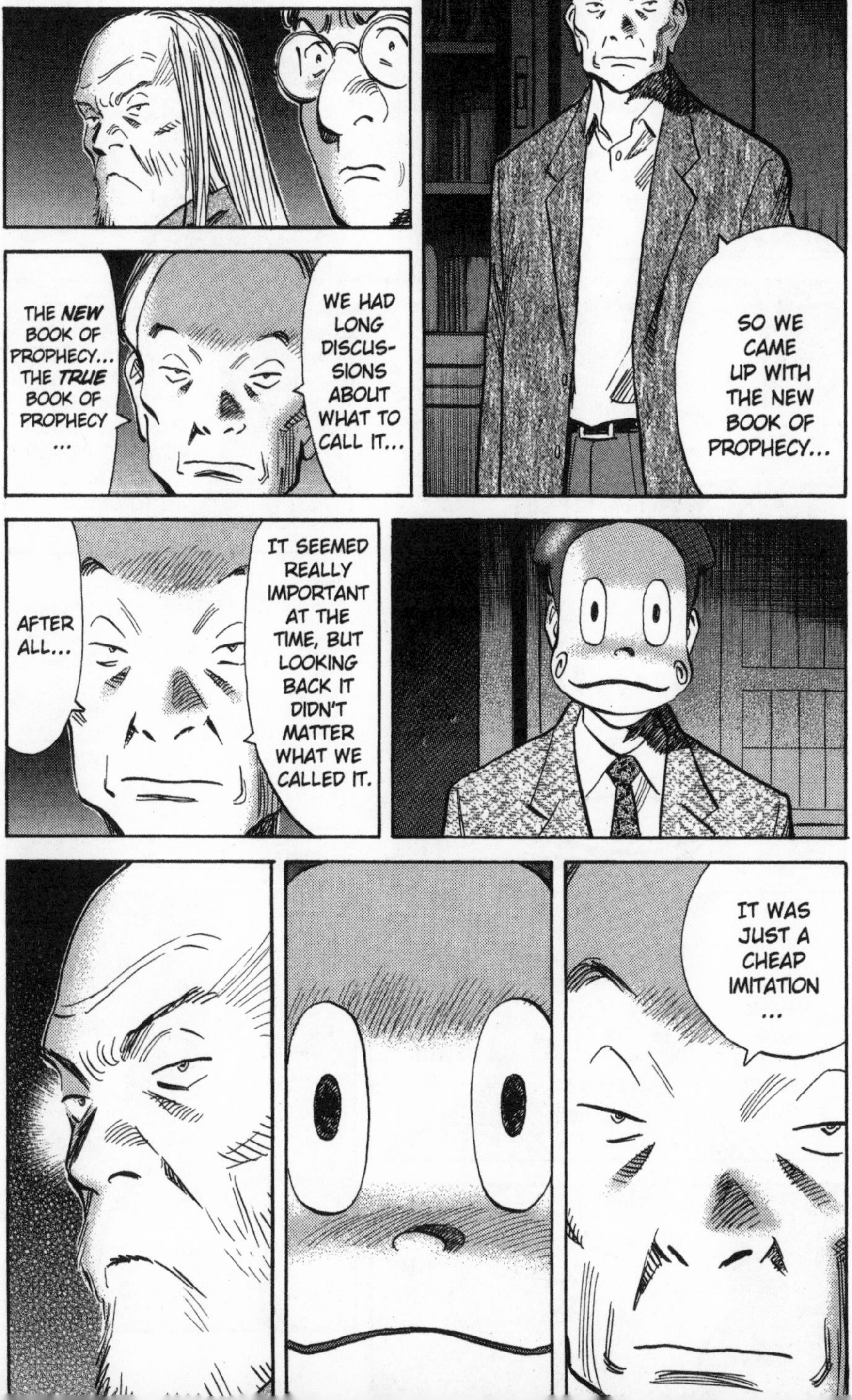
SO WE CAME UP WITH THE NEW BOOK OF PROPHECY...
WE HAD LONG DISCUS- SIONS ABOUT WHAT TO CALL IT...
THE *NEW* BOOK OF PROPHECY... THE *TRUE* BOOK OF PROPHECY ...
IT SEEMED REALLY IMPORTANT AT THE TIME, BUT LOOKING BACK IT DIDN'T MATTER WHAT WE CALLED IT.
AFTER ALL...
IT WAS JUST A CHEAP IMITATION ...

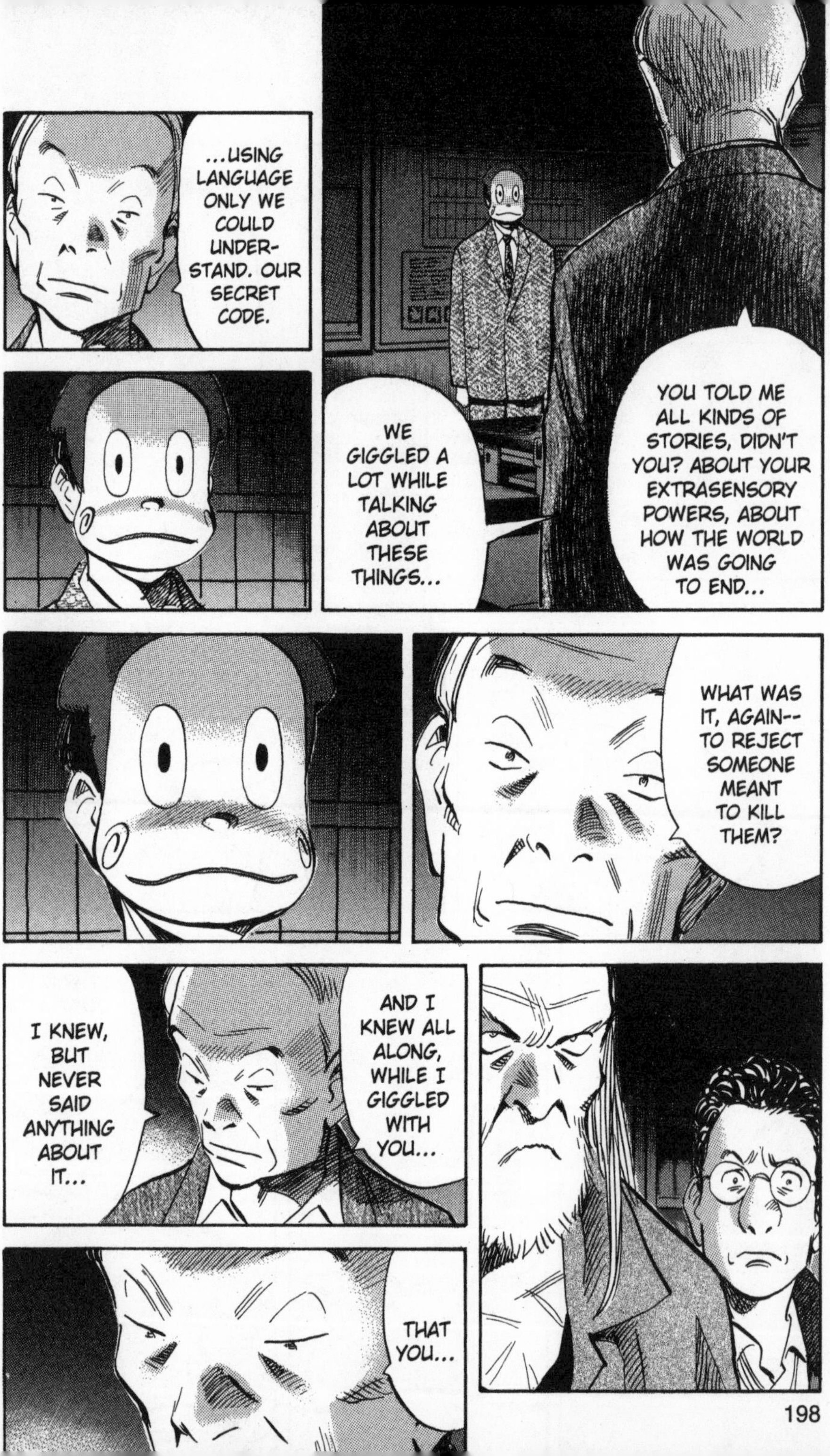
YOU TOLD ME ALL KINDS OF STORIES, DIDN'T YOU? ABOUT YOUR EXTRASENSORY POWERS, ABOUT HOW THE WORLD WAS GOING TO END...
WE GIGGLED A LOT WHILE TALKING ABOUT THESE THINGS...
...USING LANGUAGE ONLY WE COULD UNDER-STAND. OUR SECRET CODE.
WHAT WAS IT, AGAIN-- TO REJECT SOMEONE MEANT TO KILL THEM?
AND I KNEW ALL ALONG, WHILE I GIGGLED WITH YOU...
I KNEW, BUT NEVER SAID ANYTHING ABOUT IT...
THAT YOU...

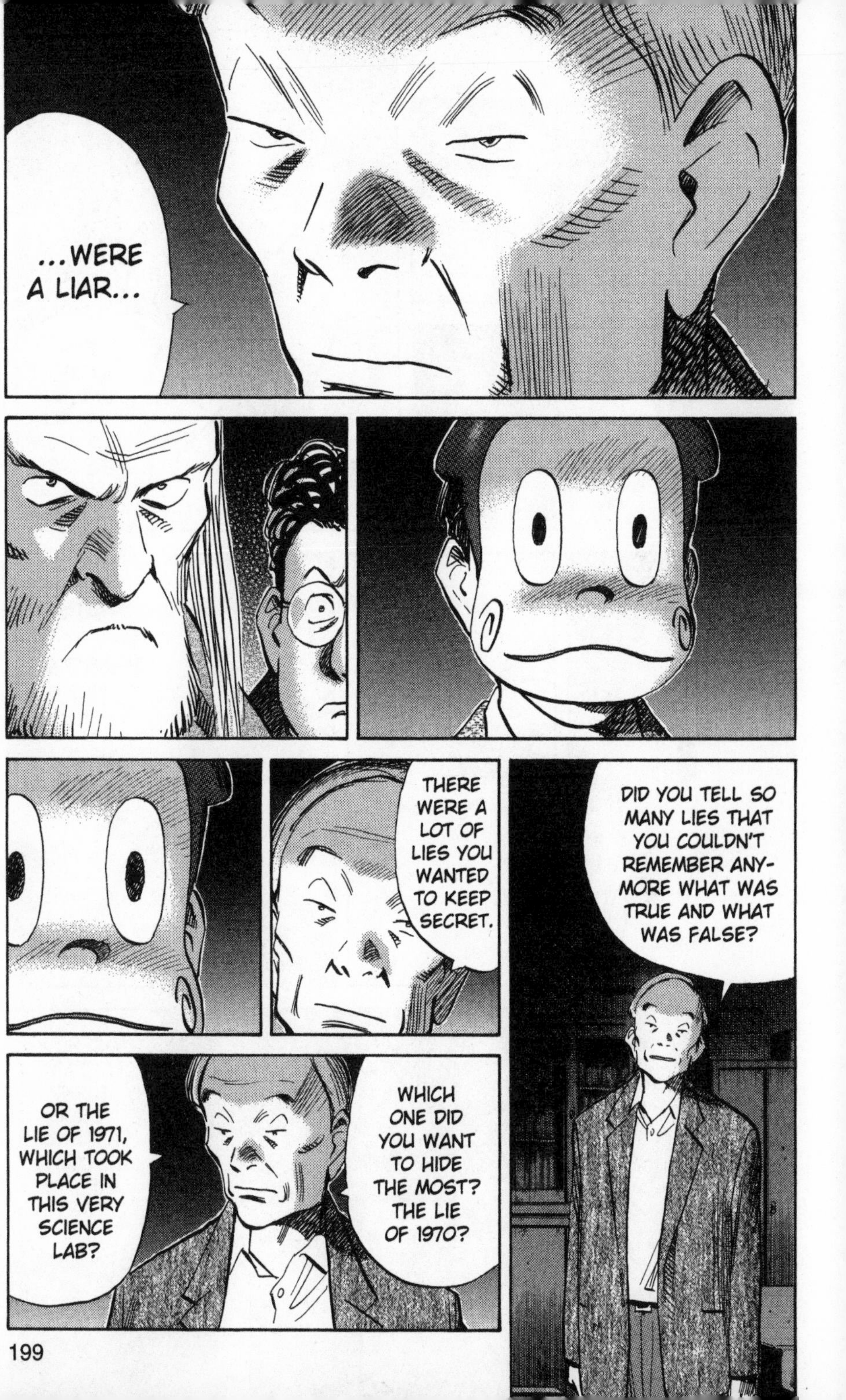
...WERE A LIAR...
DID YOU TELL SO MANY LIES THAT YOU COULDN'T REMEMBER ANY-MORE WHAT WAS TRUE AND WHAT WAS FALSE?
THERE WERE A LOT OF LIES YOU WANTED TO KEEP SECRET.
WHICH ONE DID YOU WANT TO HIDE THE MOST? THE LIE OF 1970?
OR THE LIE OF 1971, WHICH TOOK PLACE IN THIS VERY SCIENCE LAB?

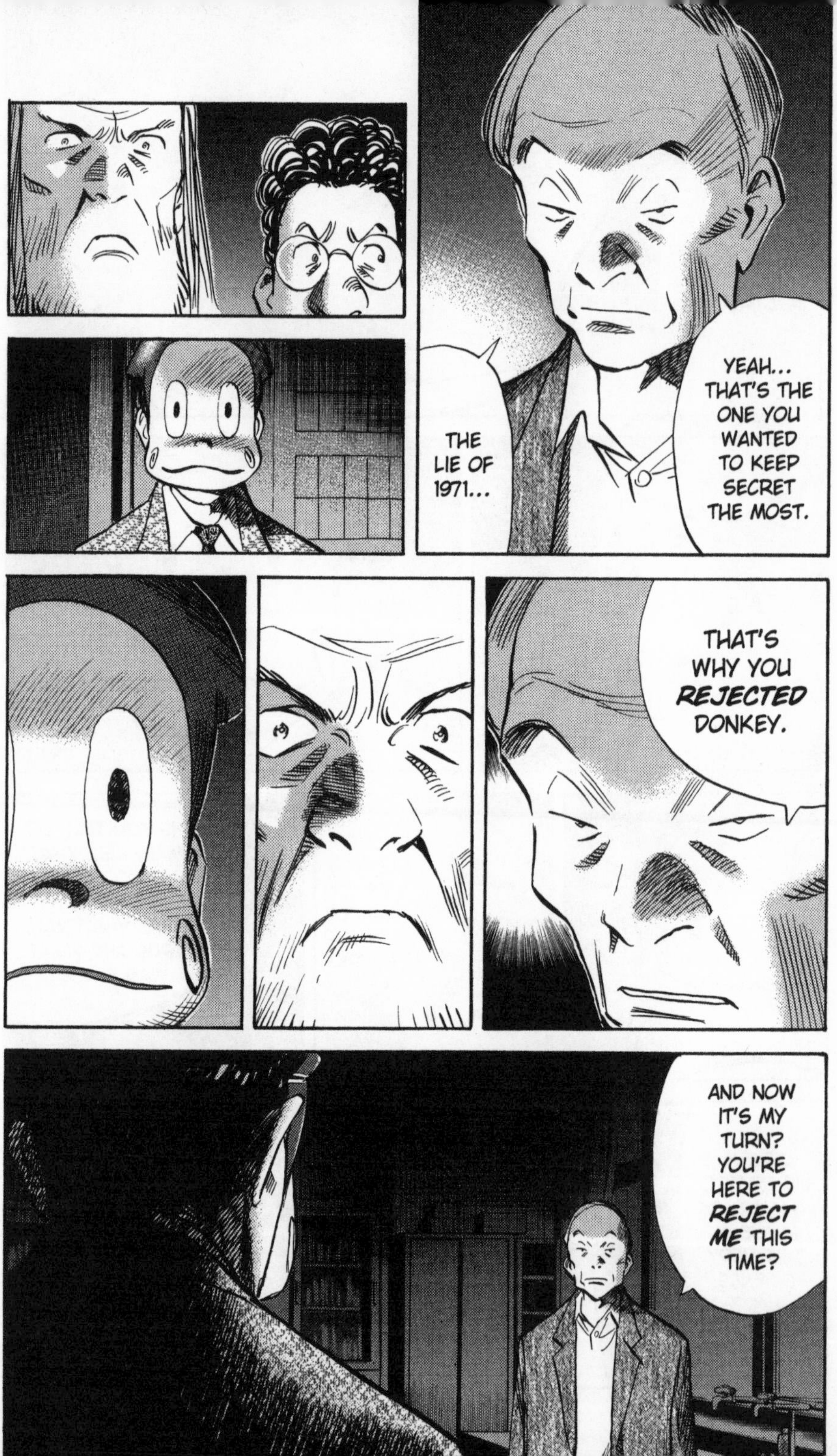
YEAH... THAT'S THE ONE YOU WANTED TO KEEP SECRET THE MOST.
THE LIE OF 1971...
THAT'S WHY YOU *REJECTED* DONKEY.
AND NOW IT'S MY TURN? YOU'RE HERE TO *REJECT ME* THIS TIME?

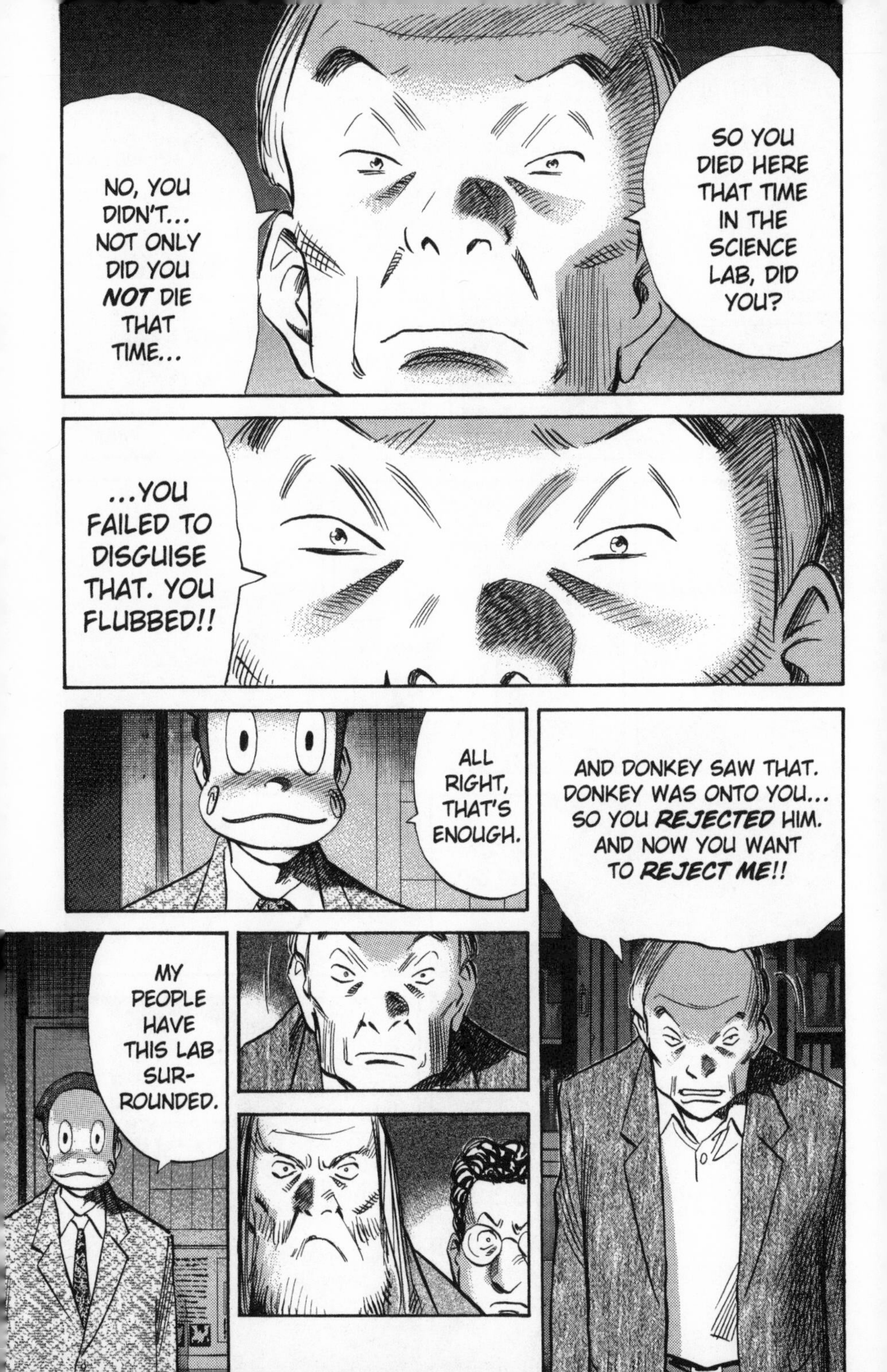
SO YOU DIED HERE THAT TIME IN THE SCIENCE LAB, DID YOU?
NO, YOU DIDN'T... NOT ONLY DID YOU NOT DIE THAT TIME...
...YOU FAILED TO DISGUISE THAT. YOU FLUBBED!!
AND DONKEY SAW THAT. DONKEY WAS ONTO YOU... SO YOU REJECTED HIM. AND NOW YOU WANT TO REJECT ME!!
ALL RIGHT, THAT'S ENOUGH.
MY PEOPLE HAVE THIS LAB SUR-ROUNDED.

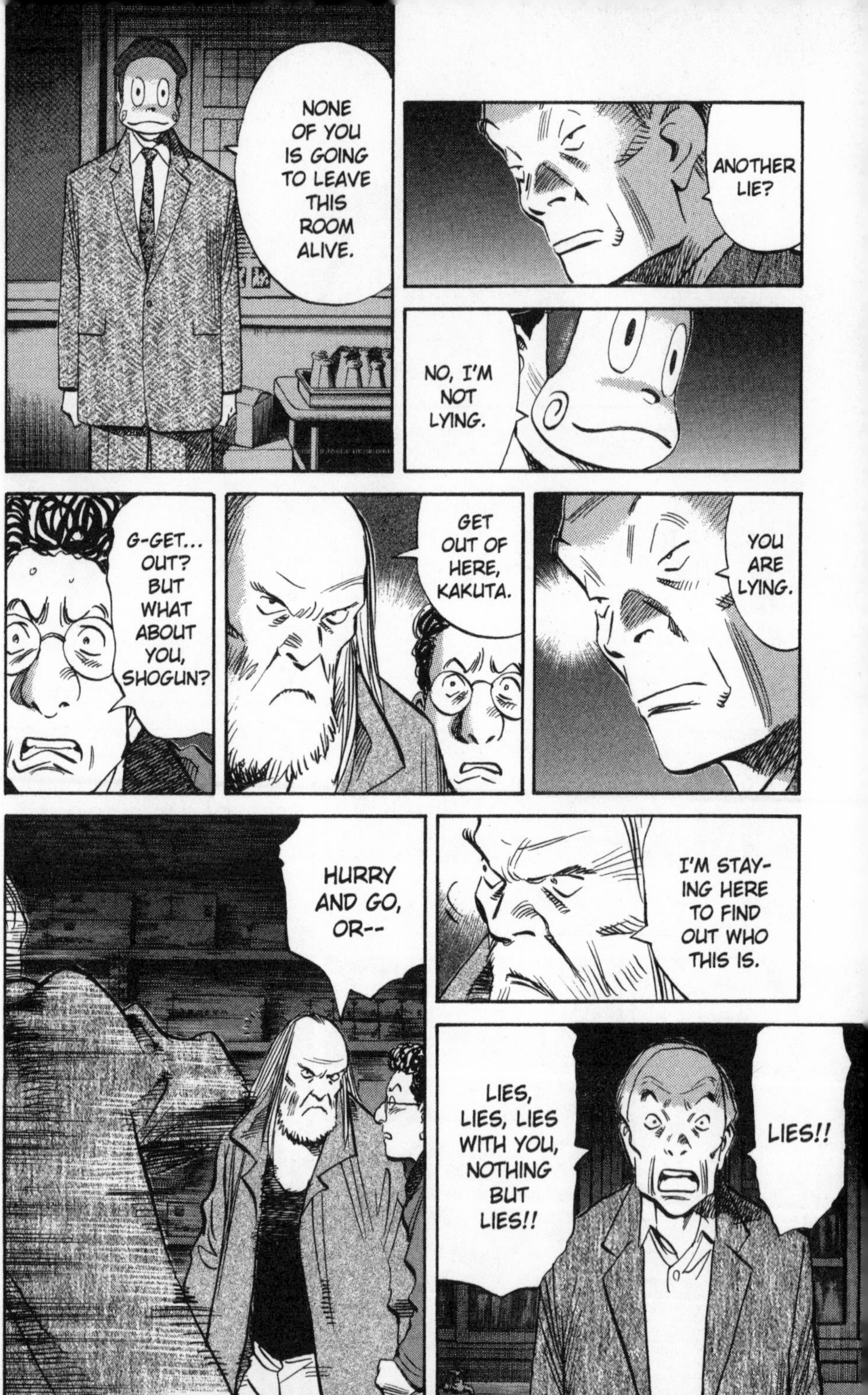
ANOTHER LIE?
NO, I'M NOT LYING.
NONE OF YOU IS GOING TO LEAVE THIS ROOM ALIVE.
YOU ARE LYING.
GET OUT OF HERE, KAKUTA.
G-GET... OUT? BUT WHAT ABOUT YOU, SHOGUN?
I'M STAY-ING HERE TO FIND OUT WHO THIS IS.
LIES!!
LIES, LIES, LIES WITH YOU, NOTHING BUT LIES!!
HURRY AND GO, OR--

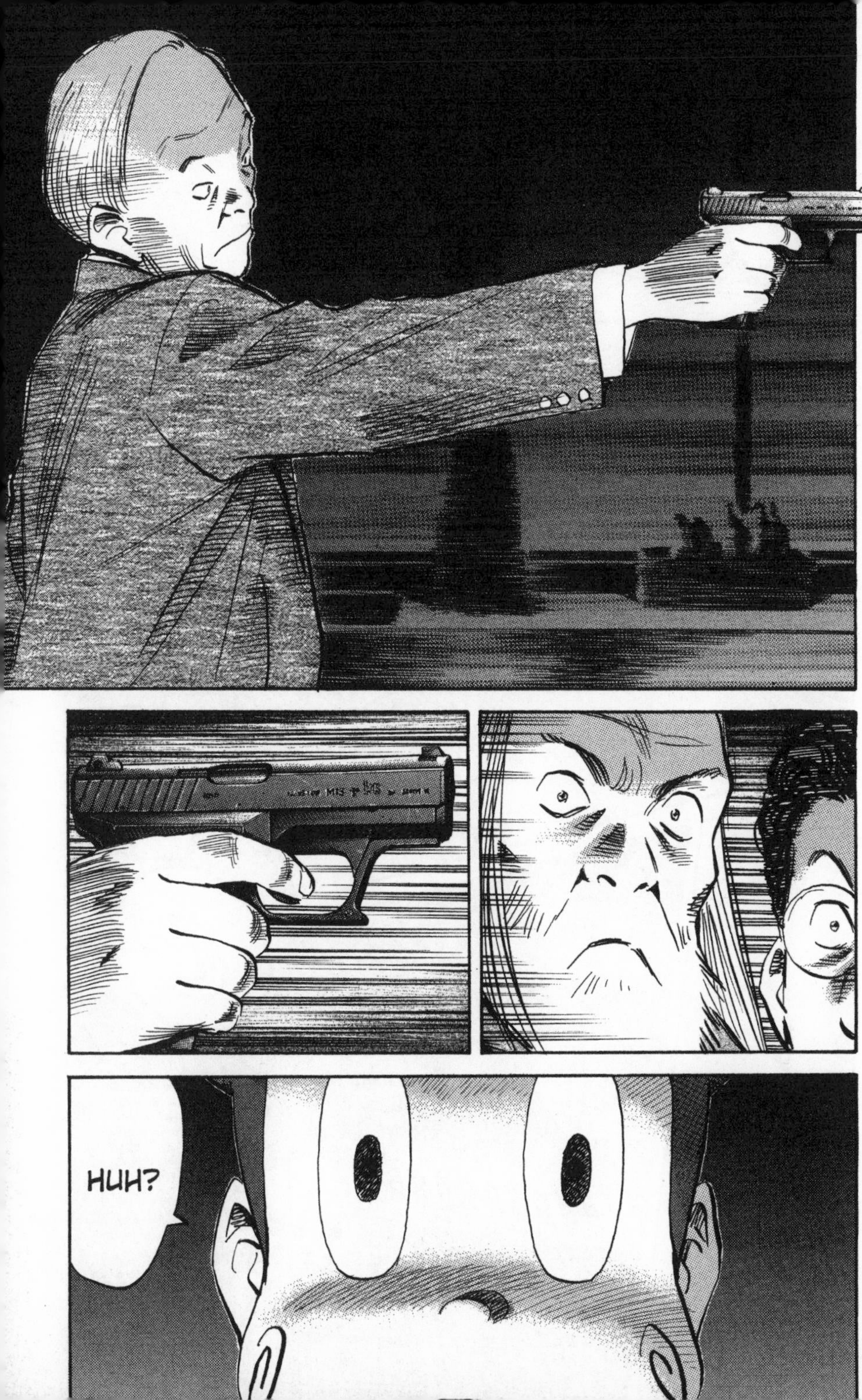
HUH?

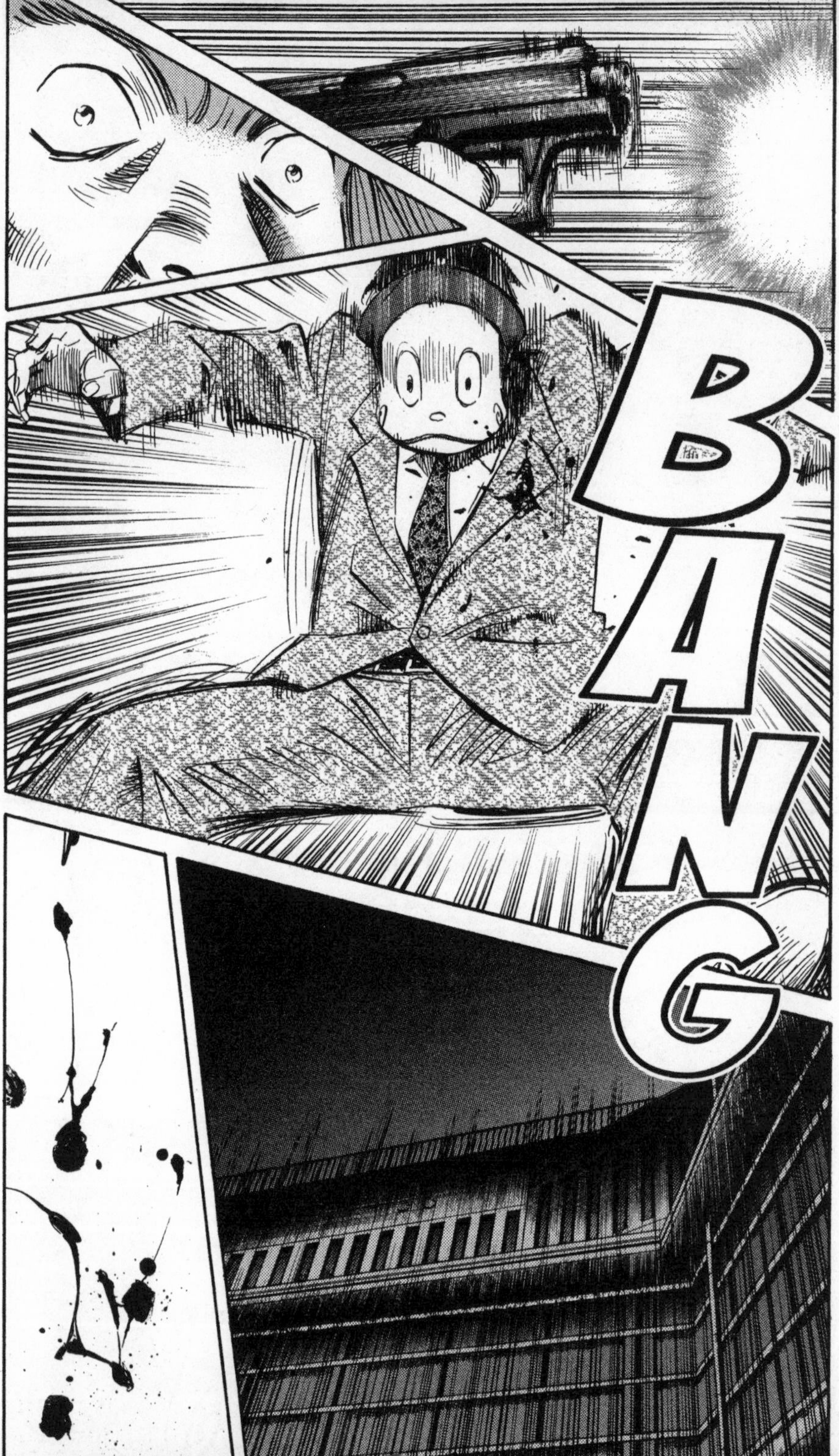
BANG

Chapter 12 Friend's Face

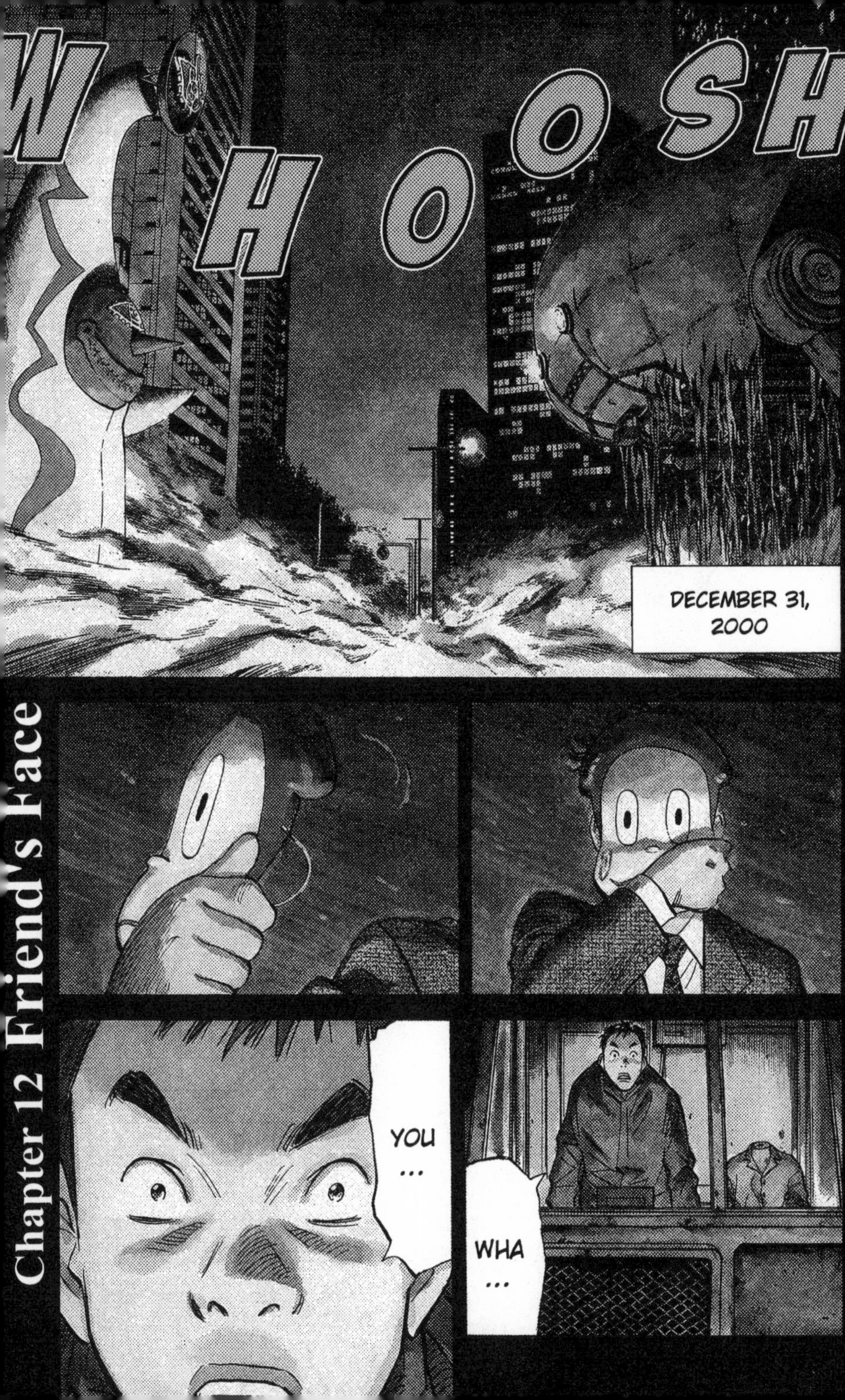

WHOOSH
DECEMBER 31, 2000
WHA ...
YOU ...

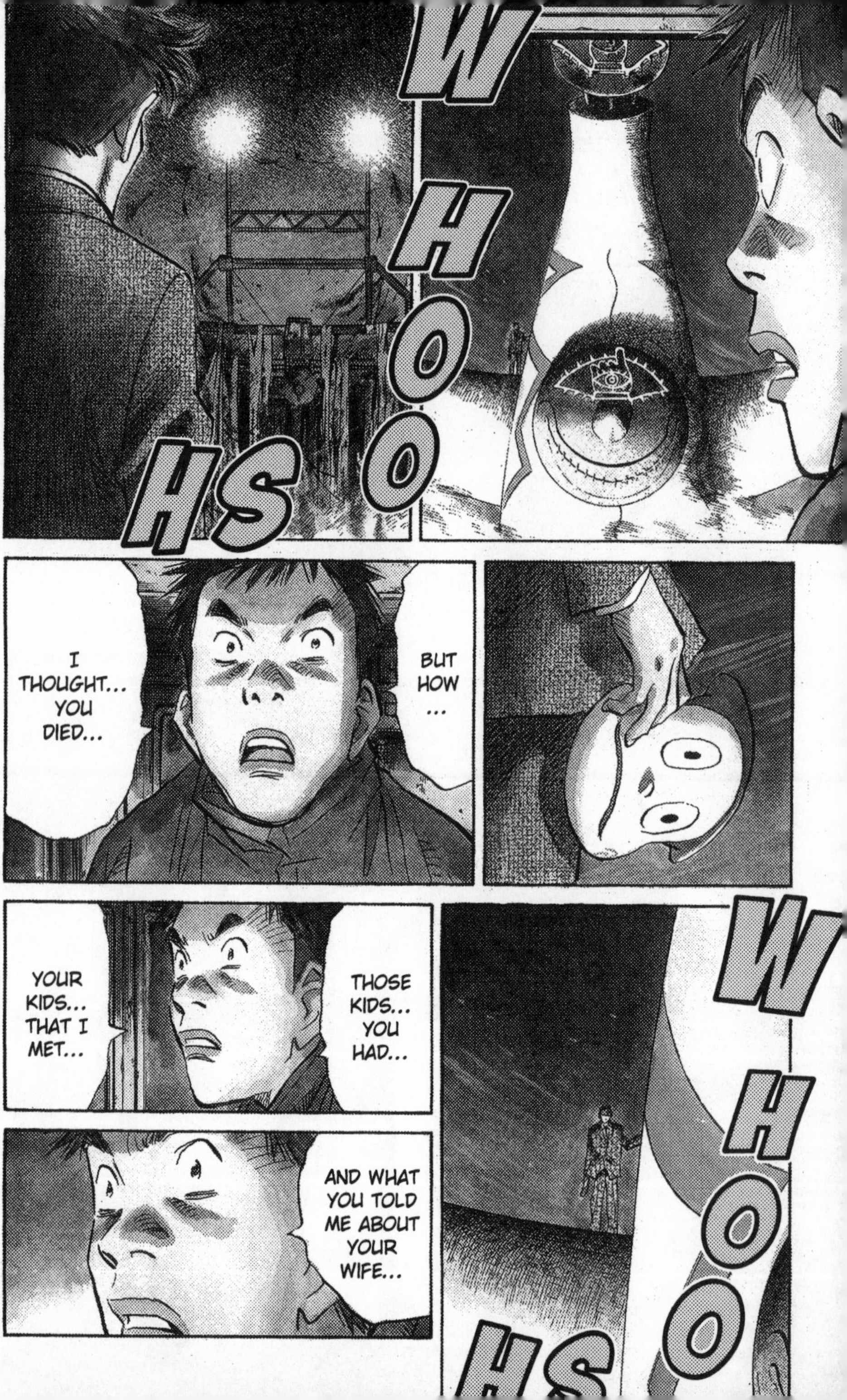
WHOOSH
BUT HOW...
I THOUGHT... YOU DIED...
WHOOSH
THOSE KIDS... YOU HAD...
YOUR KIDS... THAT I MET...
AND WHAT YOU TOLD ME ABOUT YOUR WIFE...

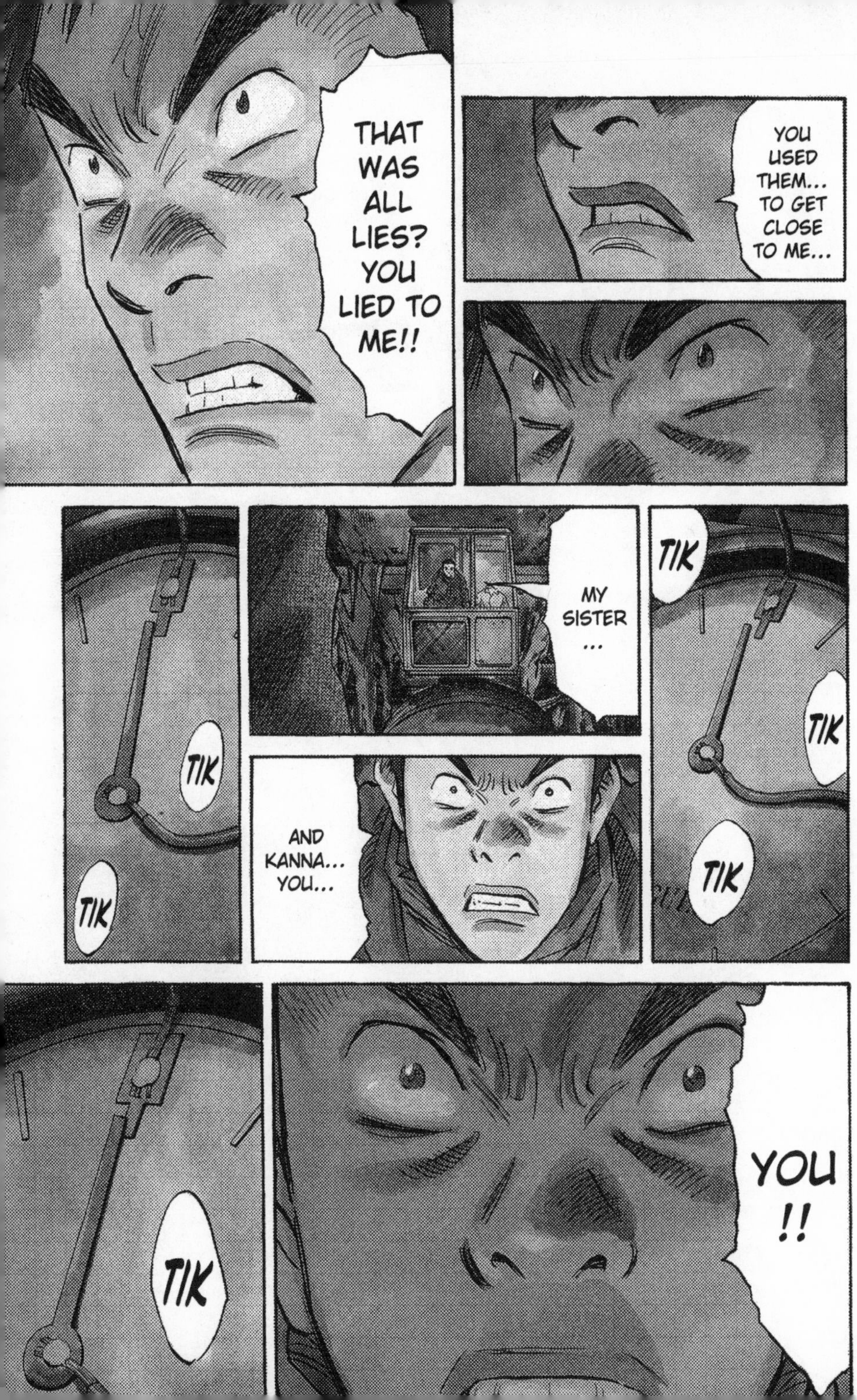
YOU USED THEM... TO GET CLOSE TO ME...
THAT WAS ALL LIES? YOU LIED TO ME!!
TIK
TIK
TIK
MY SISTER ...
AND KANNA... YOU...
TIK
TIK
YOU !!
TIK

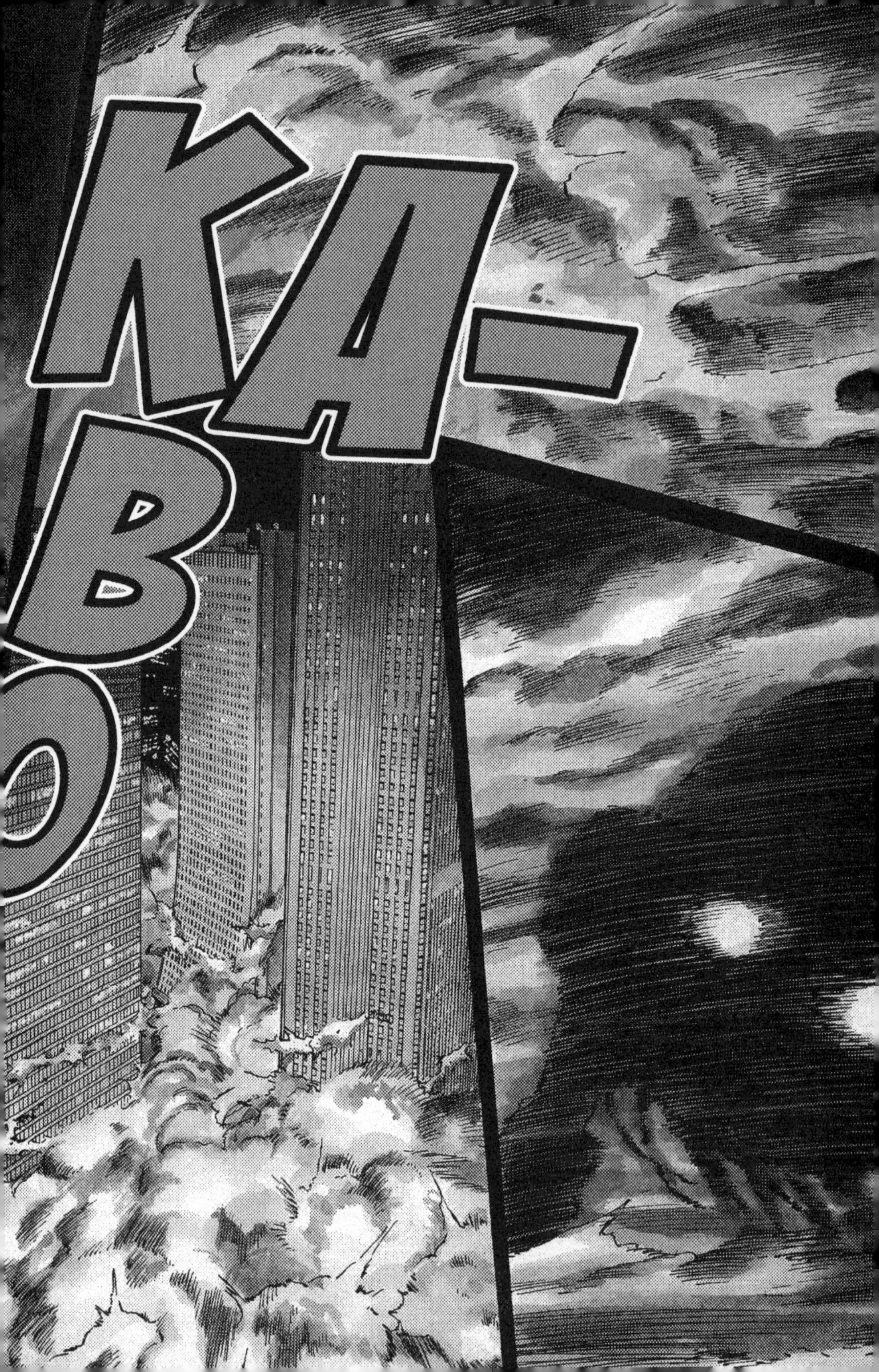
KA-BO

Chapter 12
Friend's Face

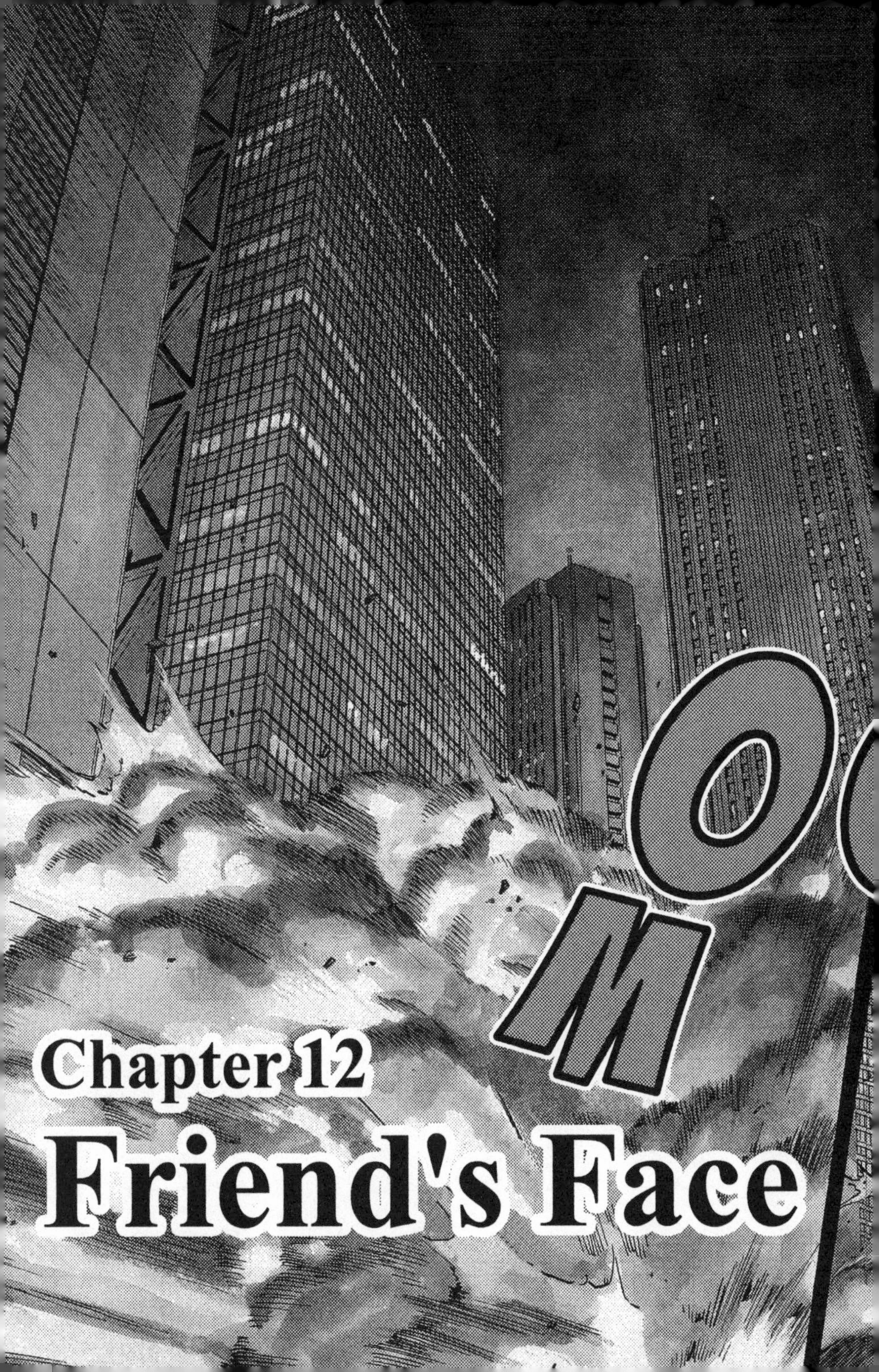
MO

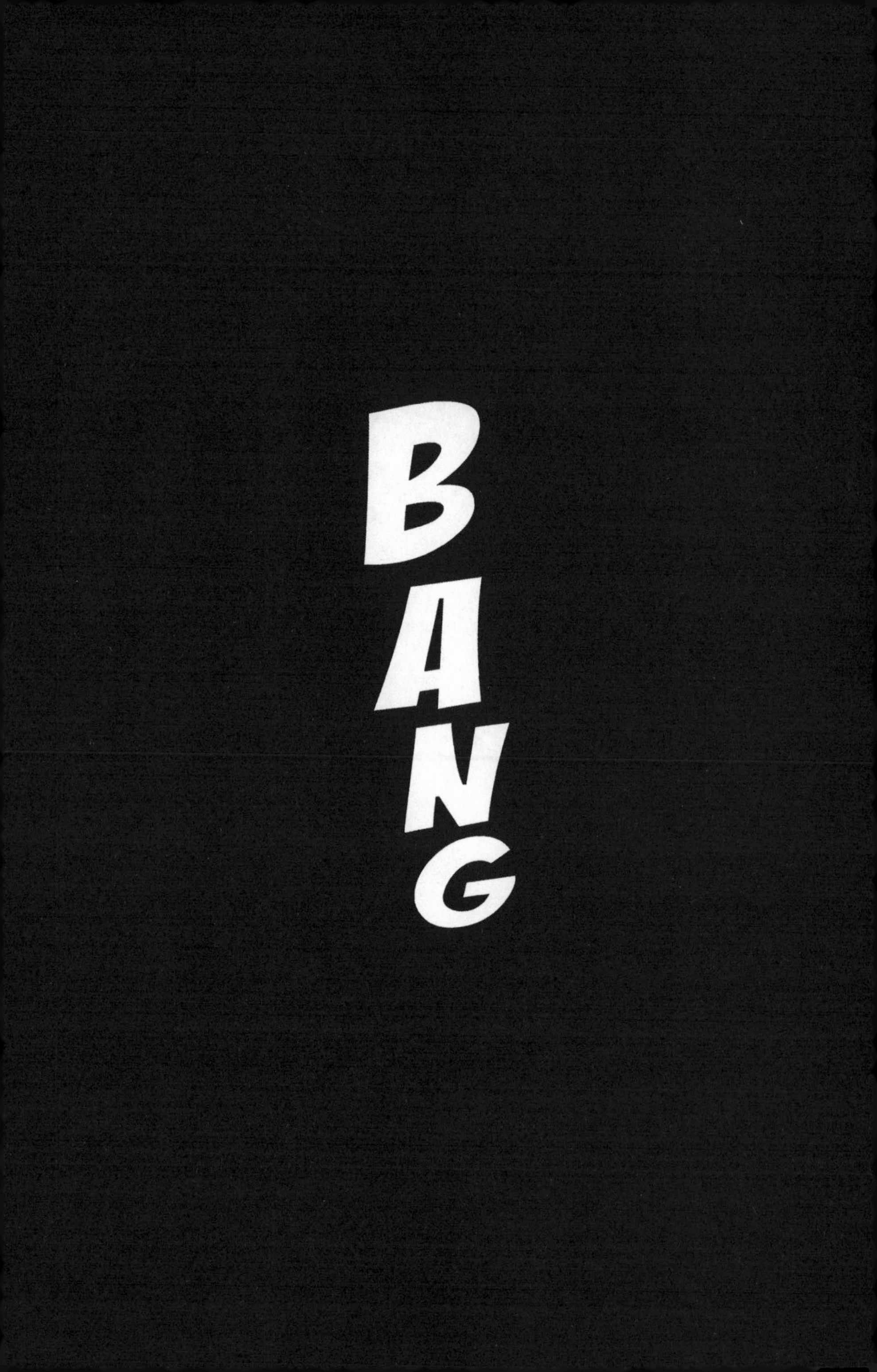
BANG

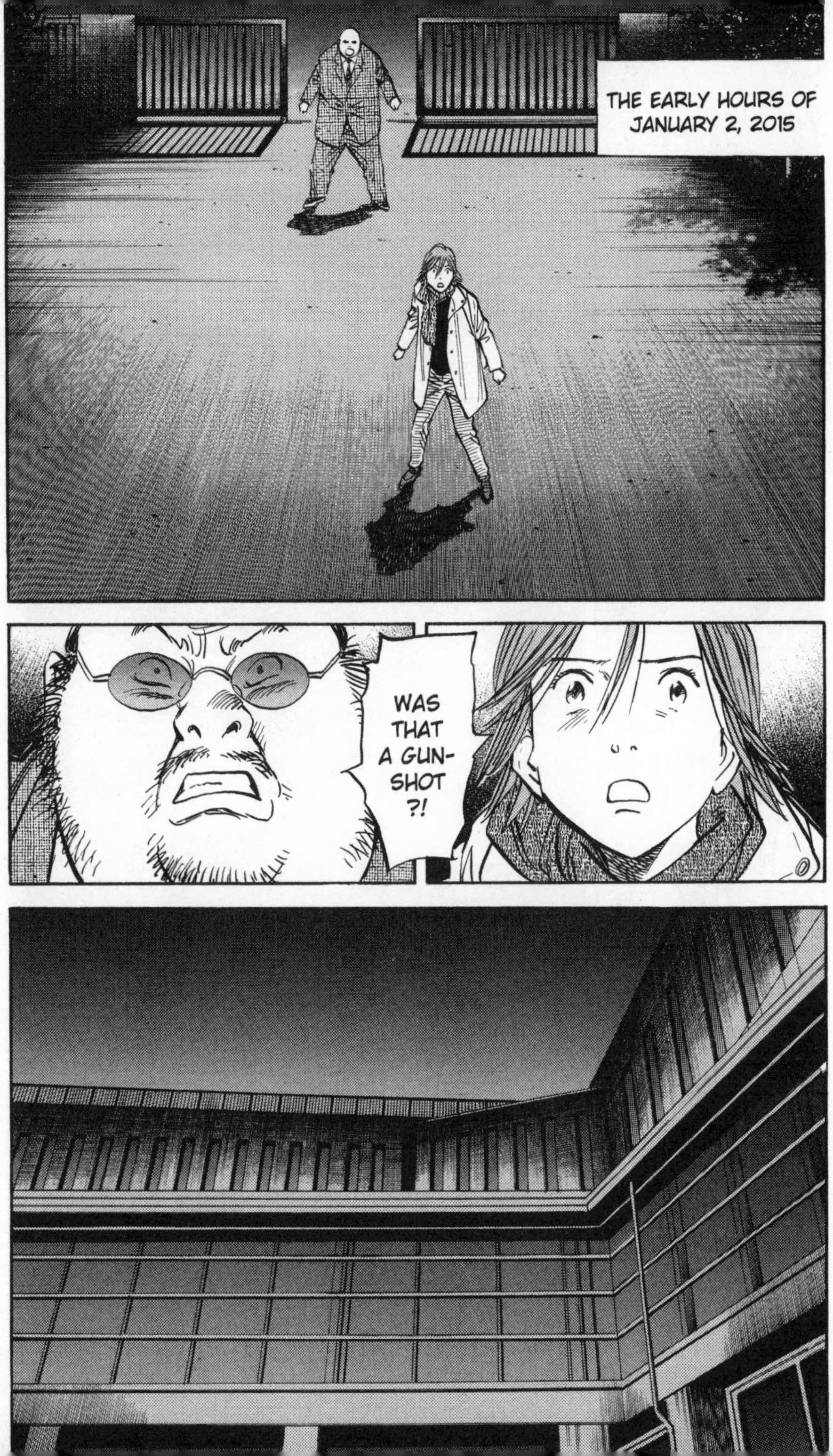
THE EARLY HOURS OF JANUARY 2, 2015
WAS THAT A GUN-SHOT ?!

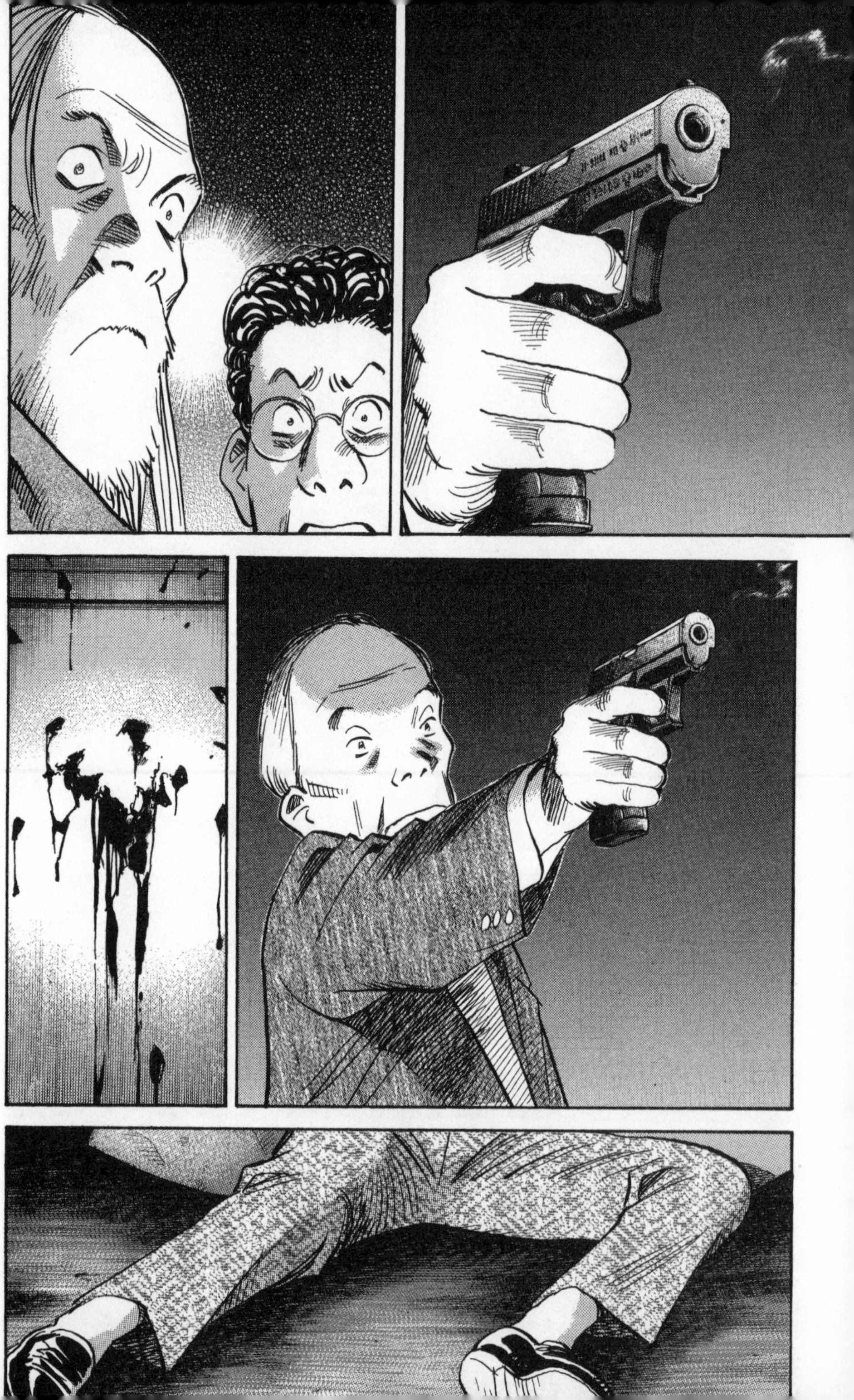

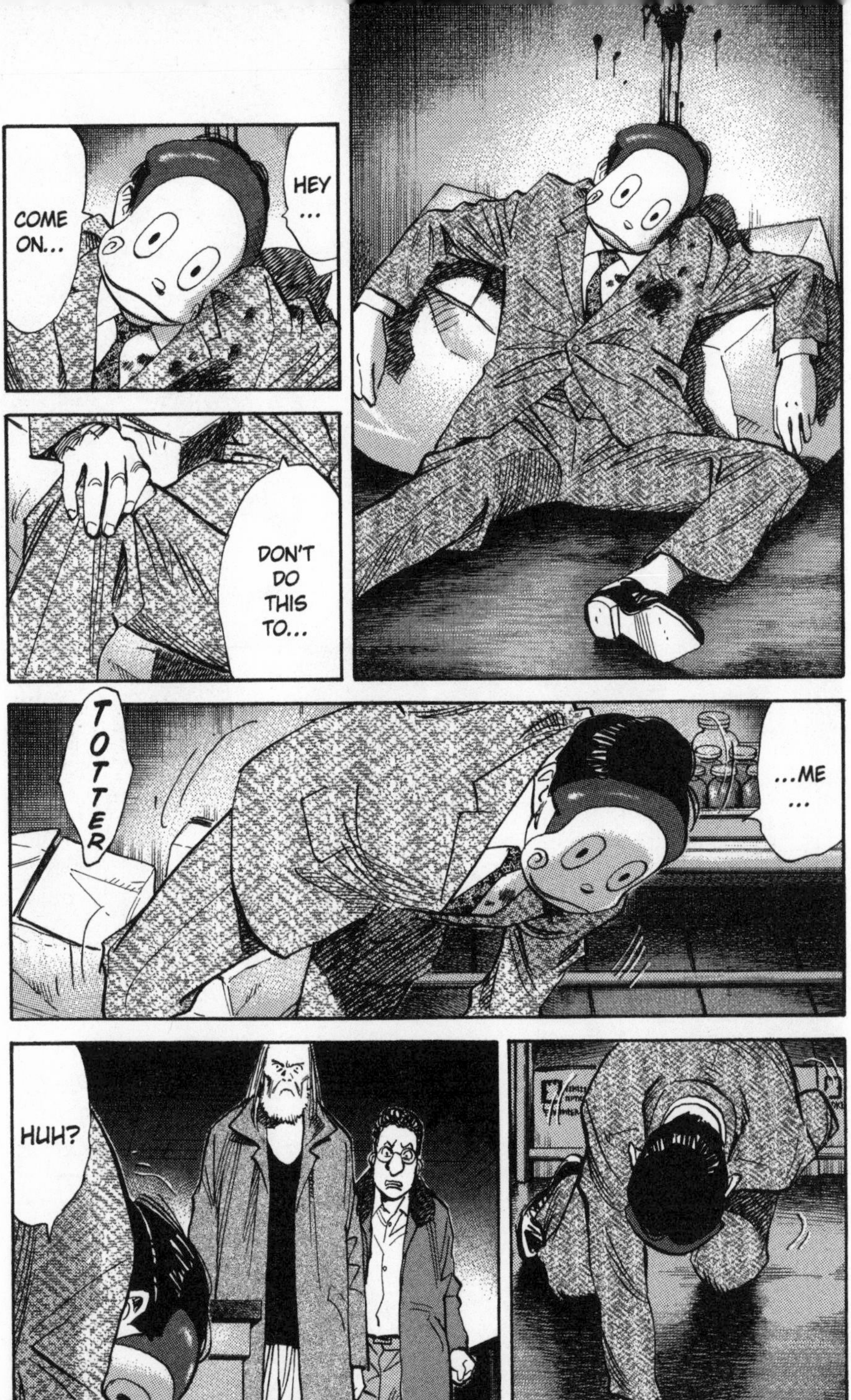
HEY ...
COME ON...
DON'T DO THIS TO...
...ME ...
TOTTER
HUH?

WAIT
...

WHAT?

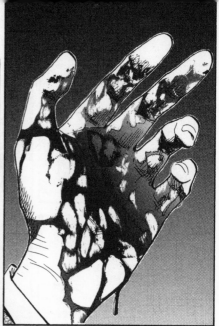

THIS IS A REPRISE ...

A REPRISE OF THAT NIGHT IN 1971.

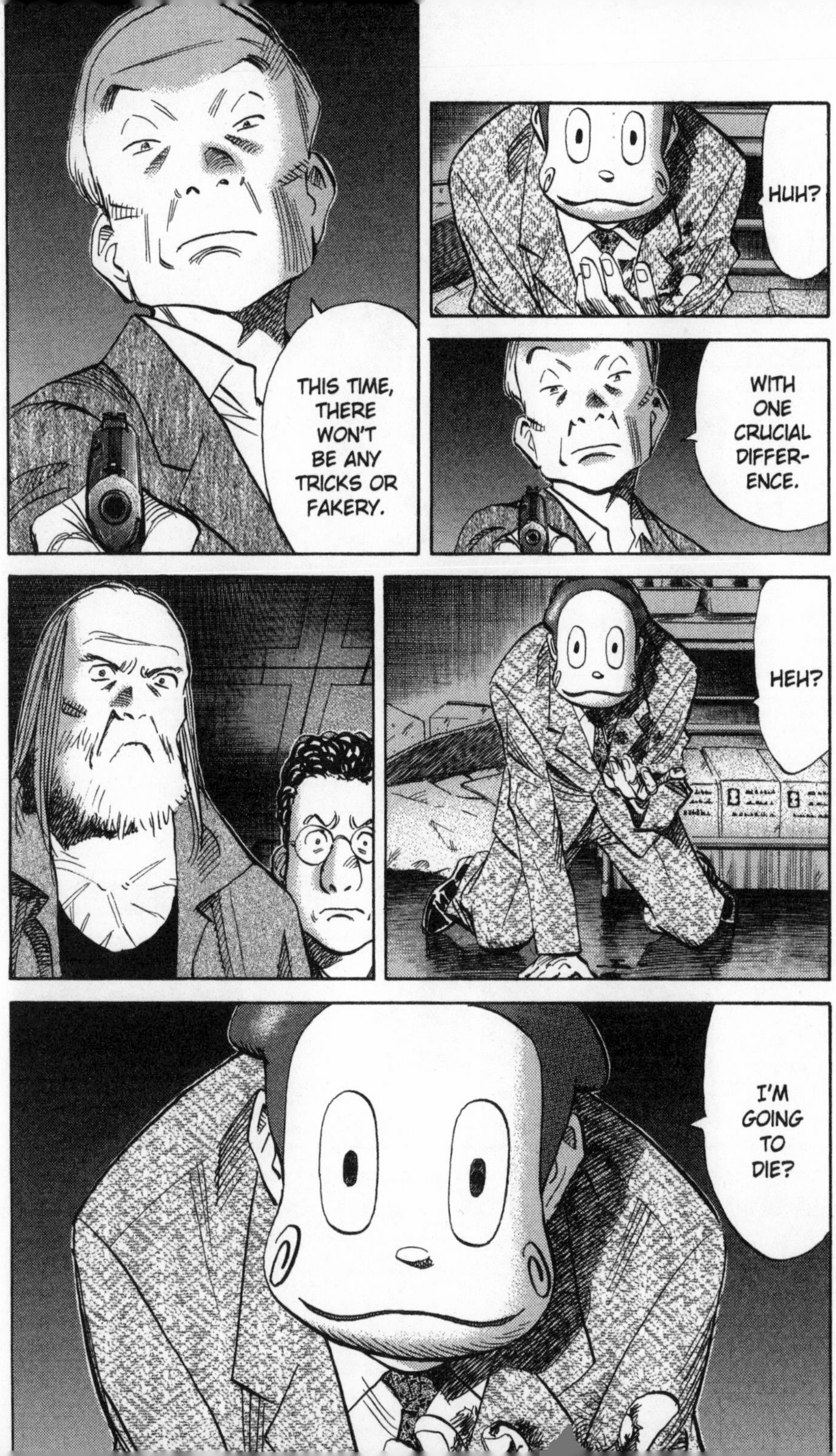
HUH?
WITH ONE CRUCIAL DIFFERENCE.
THIS TIME, THERE WON'T BE ANY TRICKS OR FAKERY.
HEH?
I'M GOING TO DIE?

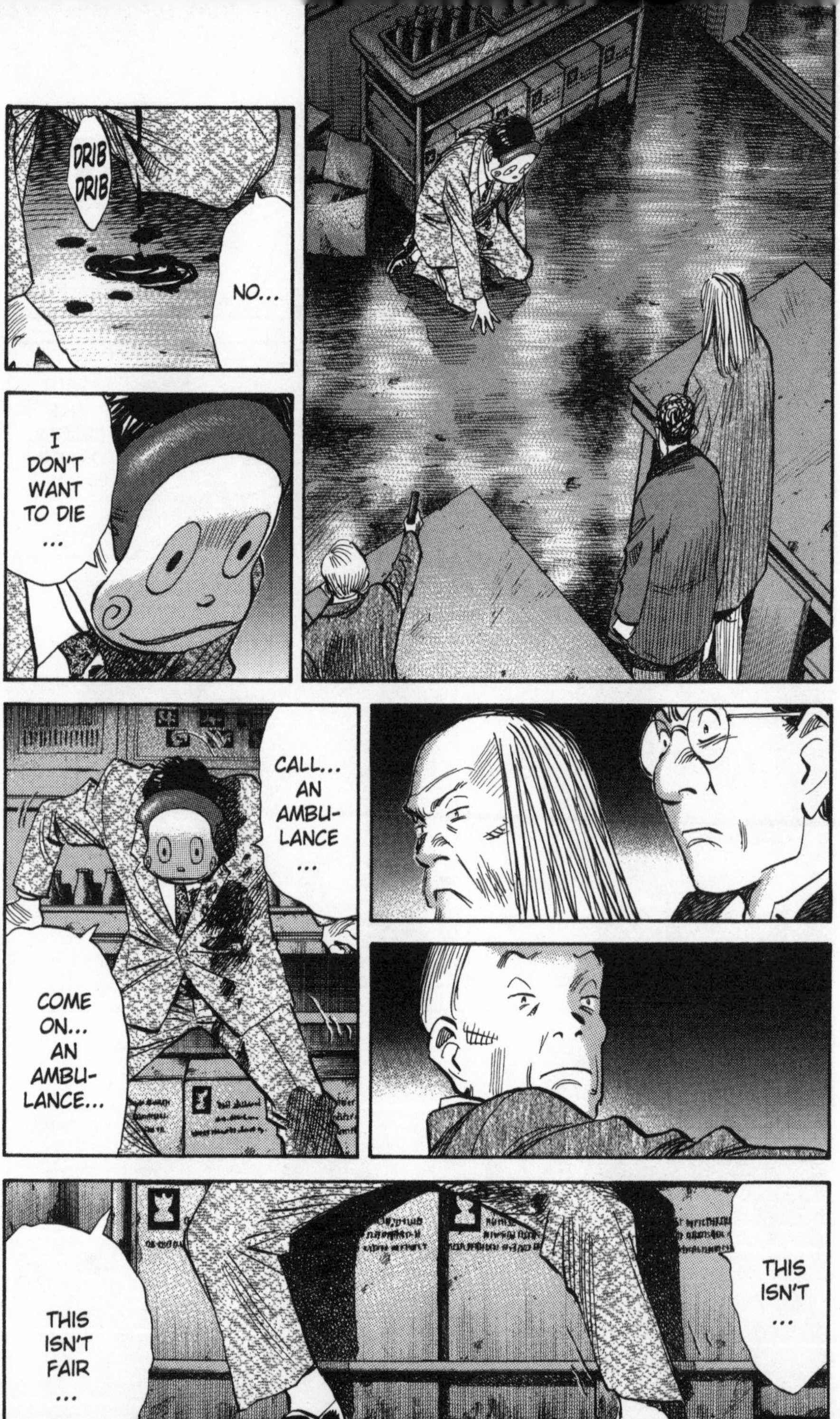
DRIB DRIB
NO...
I DON'T WANT TO DIE...
CALL... AN AMBU-LANCE...
COME ON... AN AMBU-LANCE...
THIS ISN'T...
THIS ISN'T FAIR...

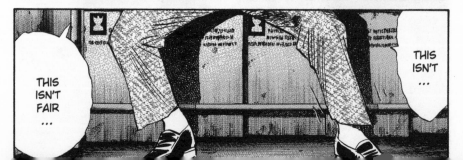

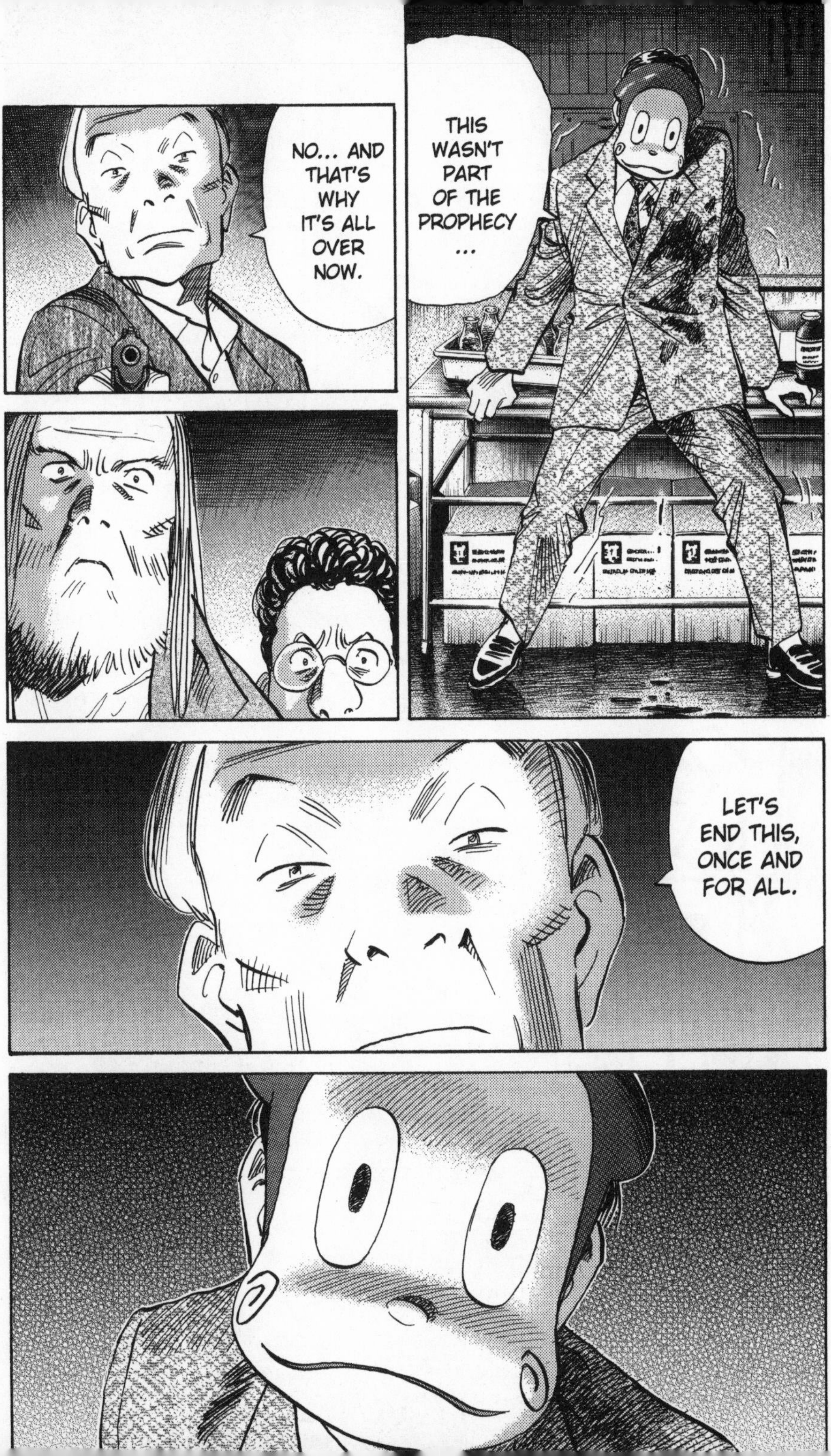
THIS WASN'T PART OF THE PROPHECY ...
NO... AND THAT'S WHY IT'S ALL OVER NOW.
LET'S END THIS, ONCE AND FOR ALL.

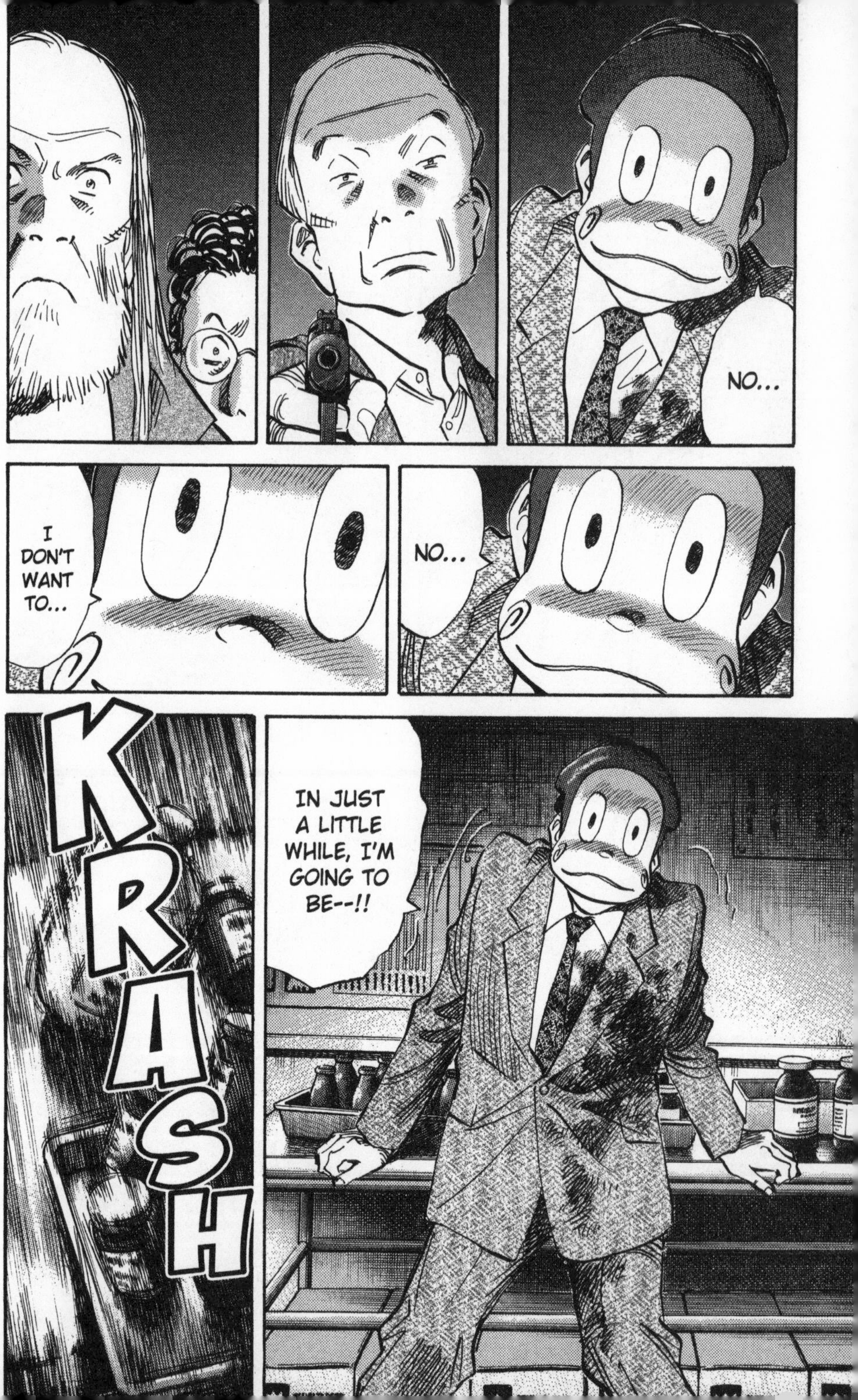
NO...
NO...
I DON'T WANT TO...
IN JUST A LITTLE WHILE, I'M GOING TO BE--!!
KRASH

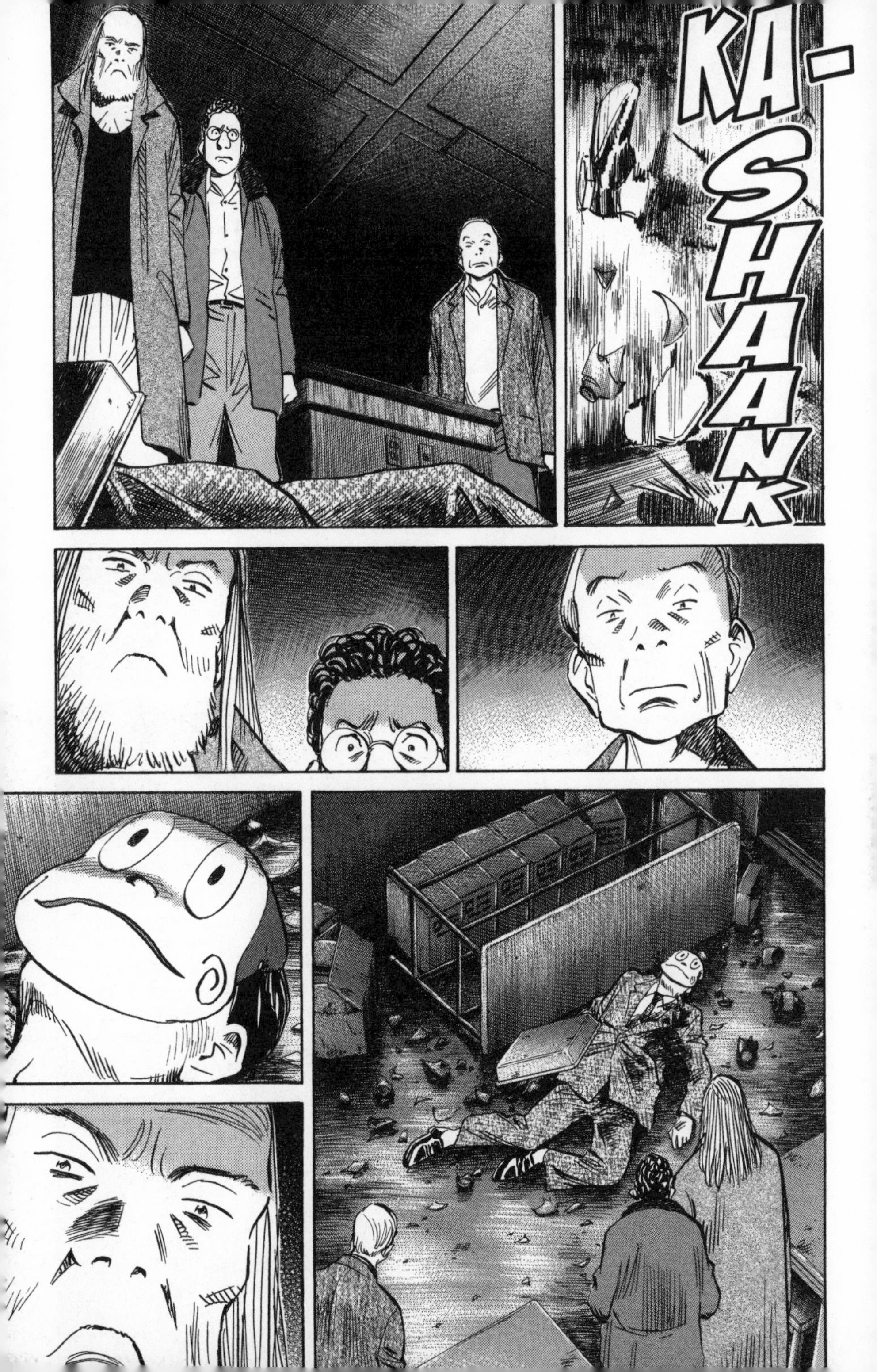
KA-SHAANK

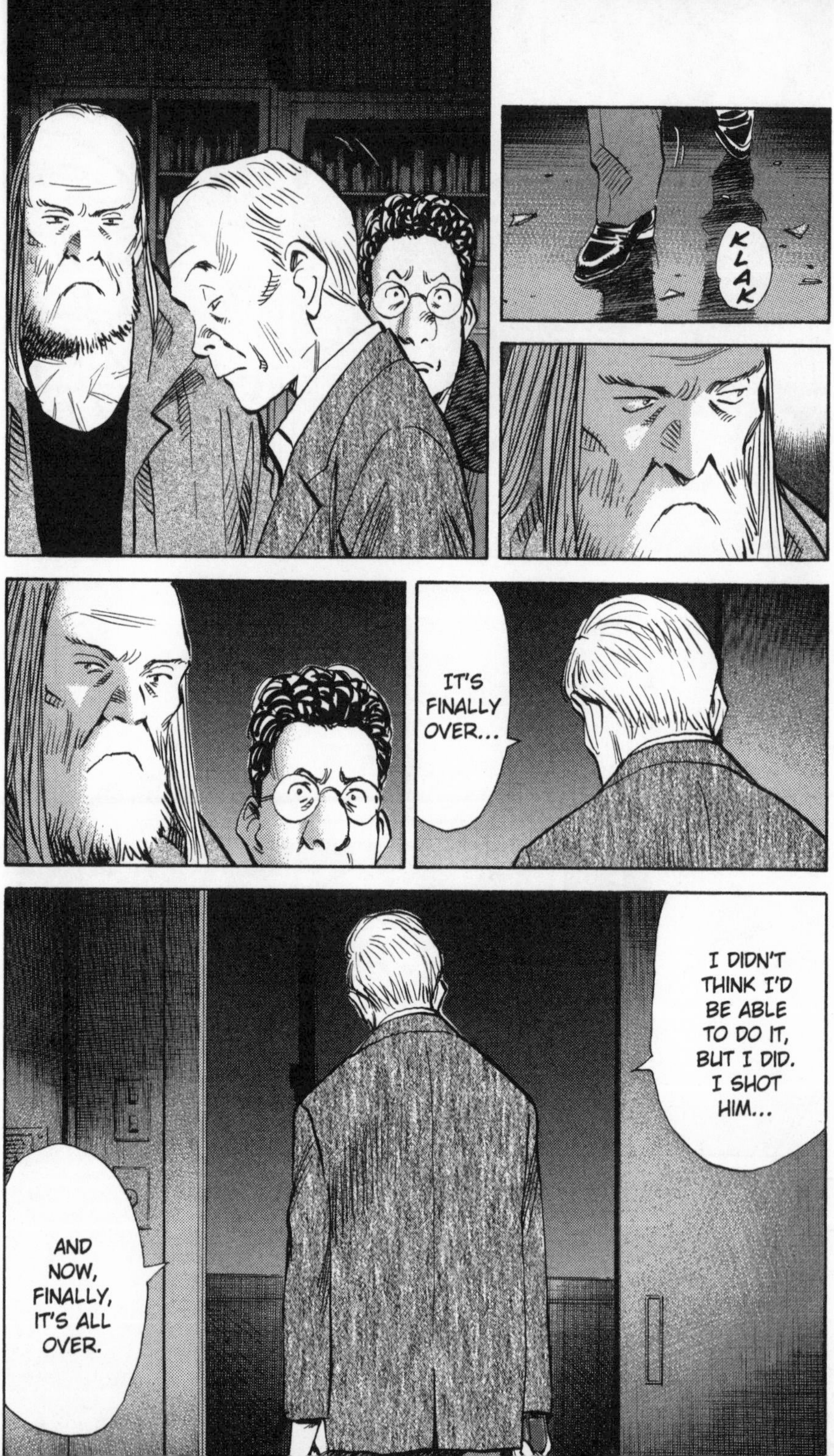
KLAK
IT'S FINALLY OVER...
I DIDN'T THINK I'D BE ABLE TO DO IT, BUT I DID. I SHOT HIM...
AND NOW, FINALLY, IT'S ALL OVER.

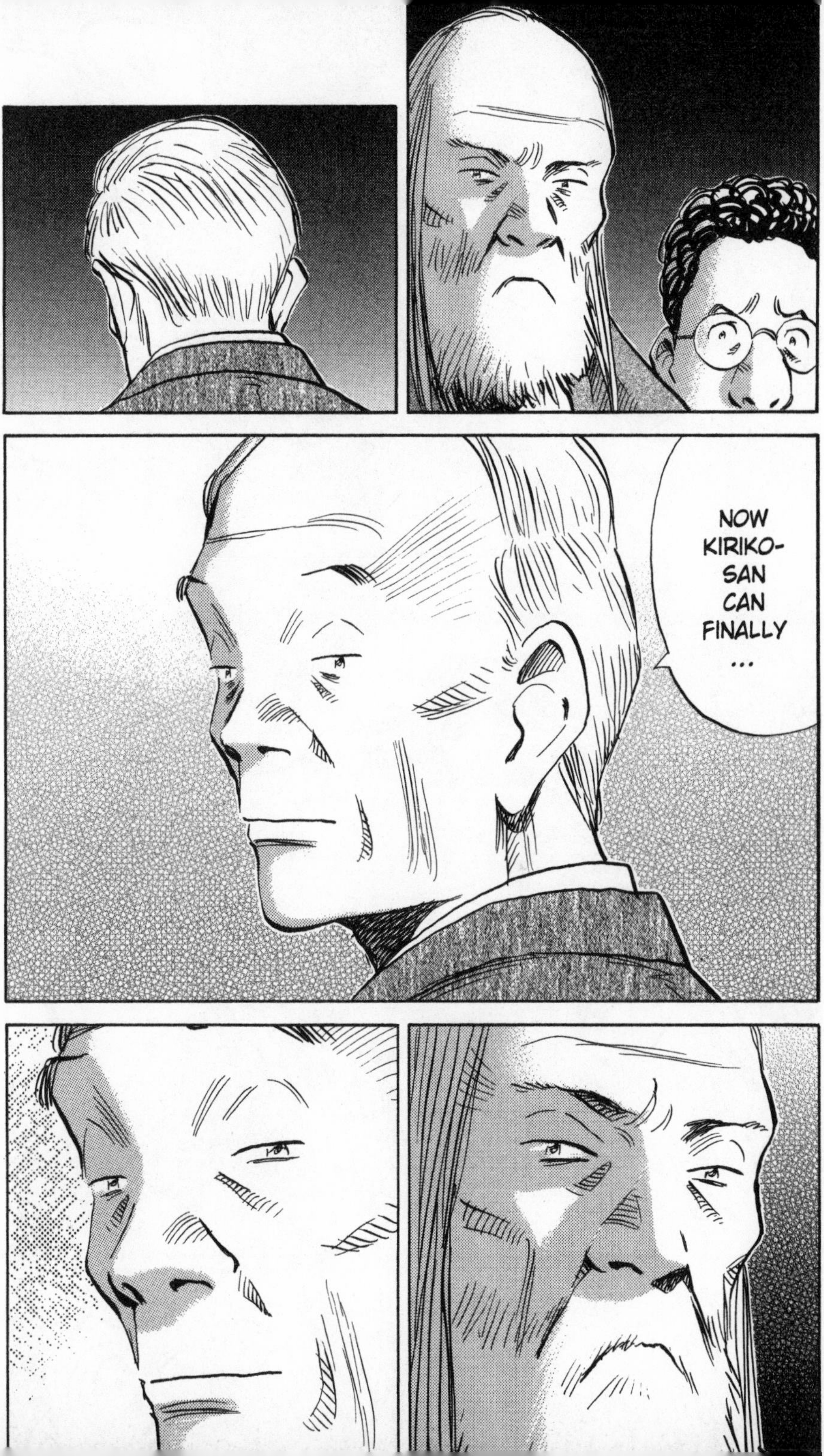
NOW KIRIKO-SAN CAN FINALLY ...

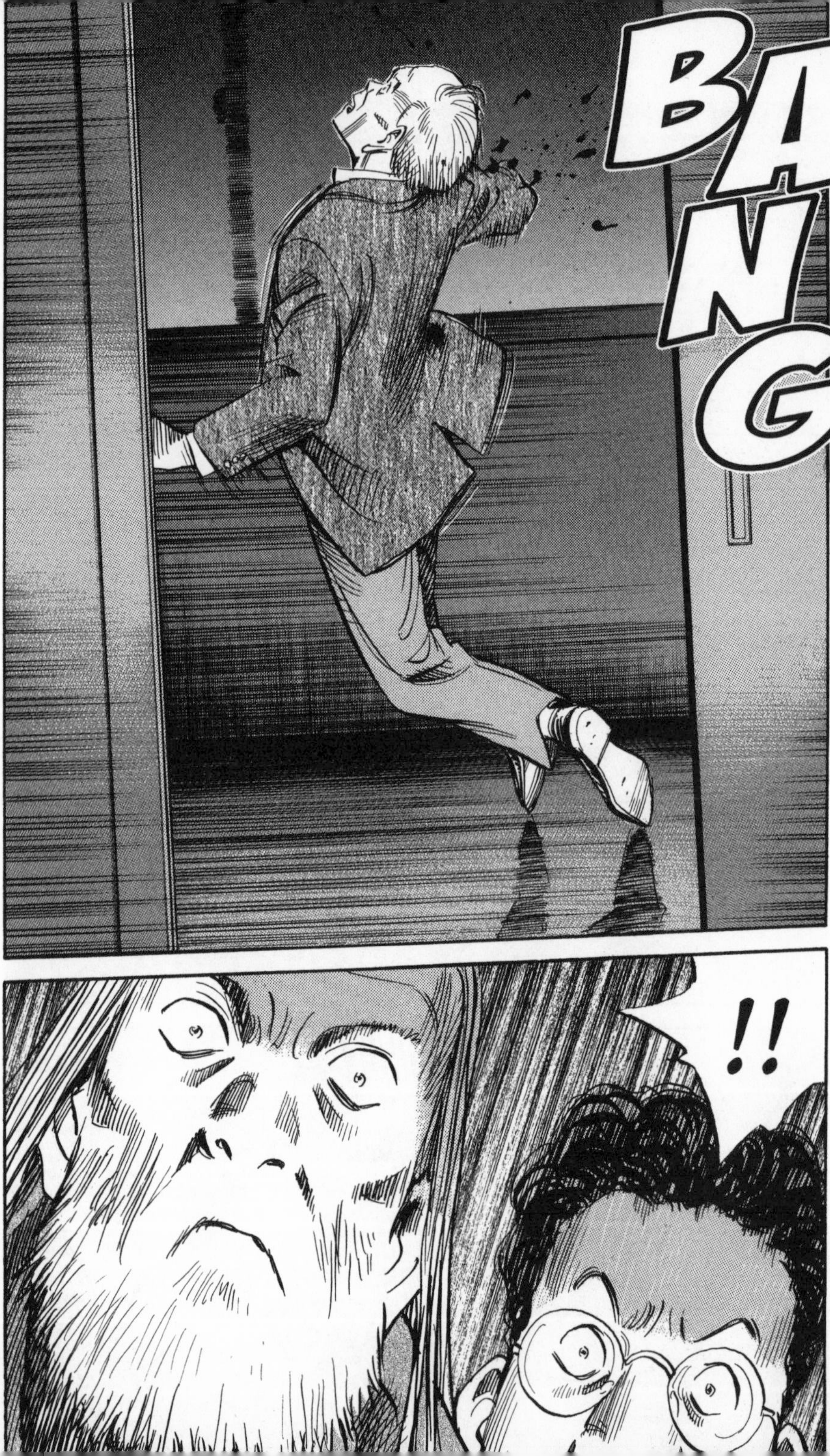
BANG
!!

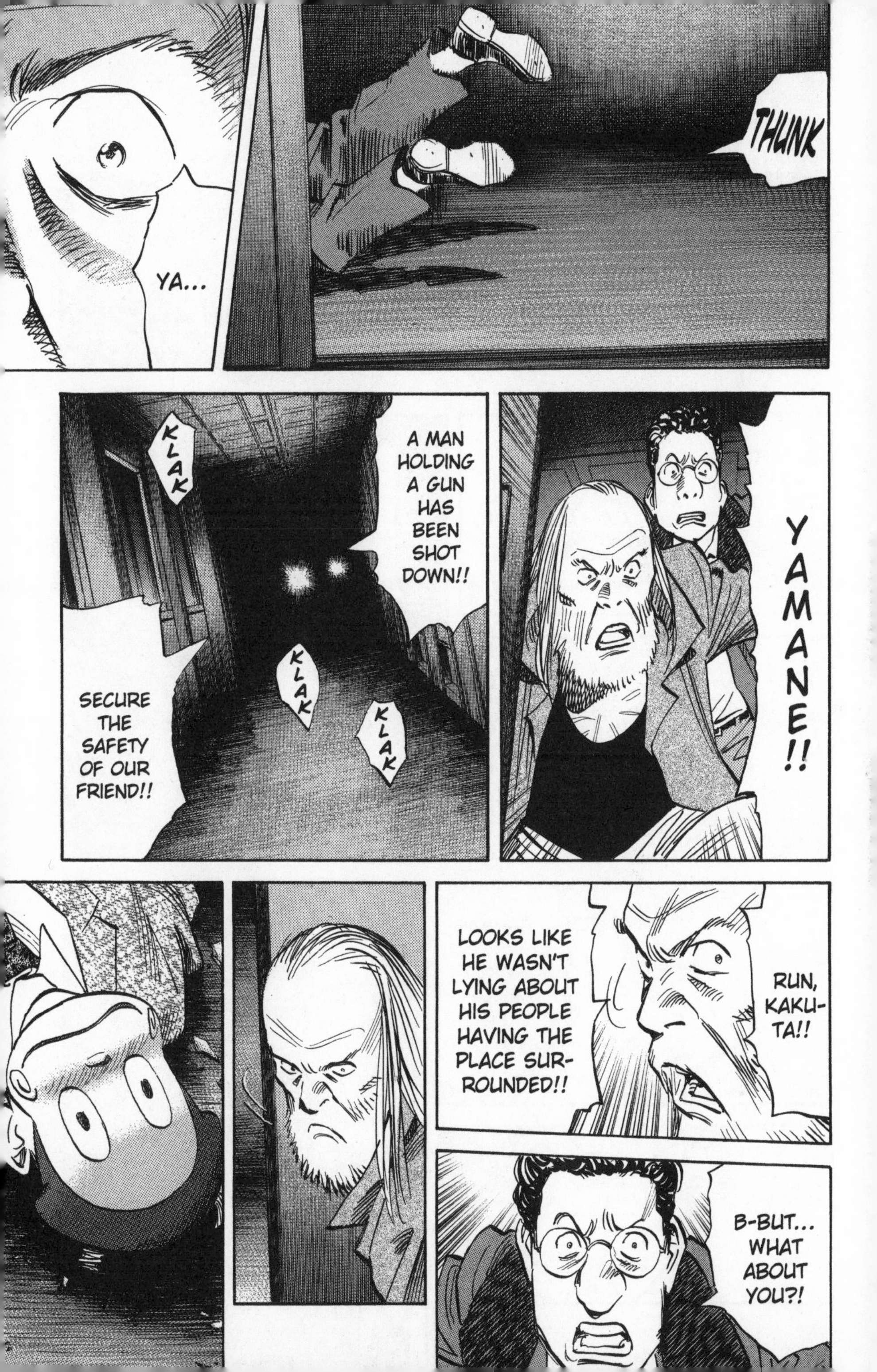
THUNK
YA...
YAMANE!!
A MAN HOLDING A GUN HAS BEEN SHOT DOWN!!
KLAK
KLAK
KLAK
SECURE THE SAFETY OF OUR FRIEND!!
RUN, KAKU-TA!!
LOOKS LIKE HE WASN'T LYING ABOUT HIS PEOPLE HAVING THE PLACE SUR-ROUNDED!!
B-BUT... WHAT ABOUT YOU?!

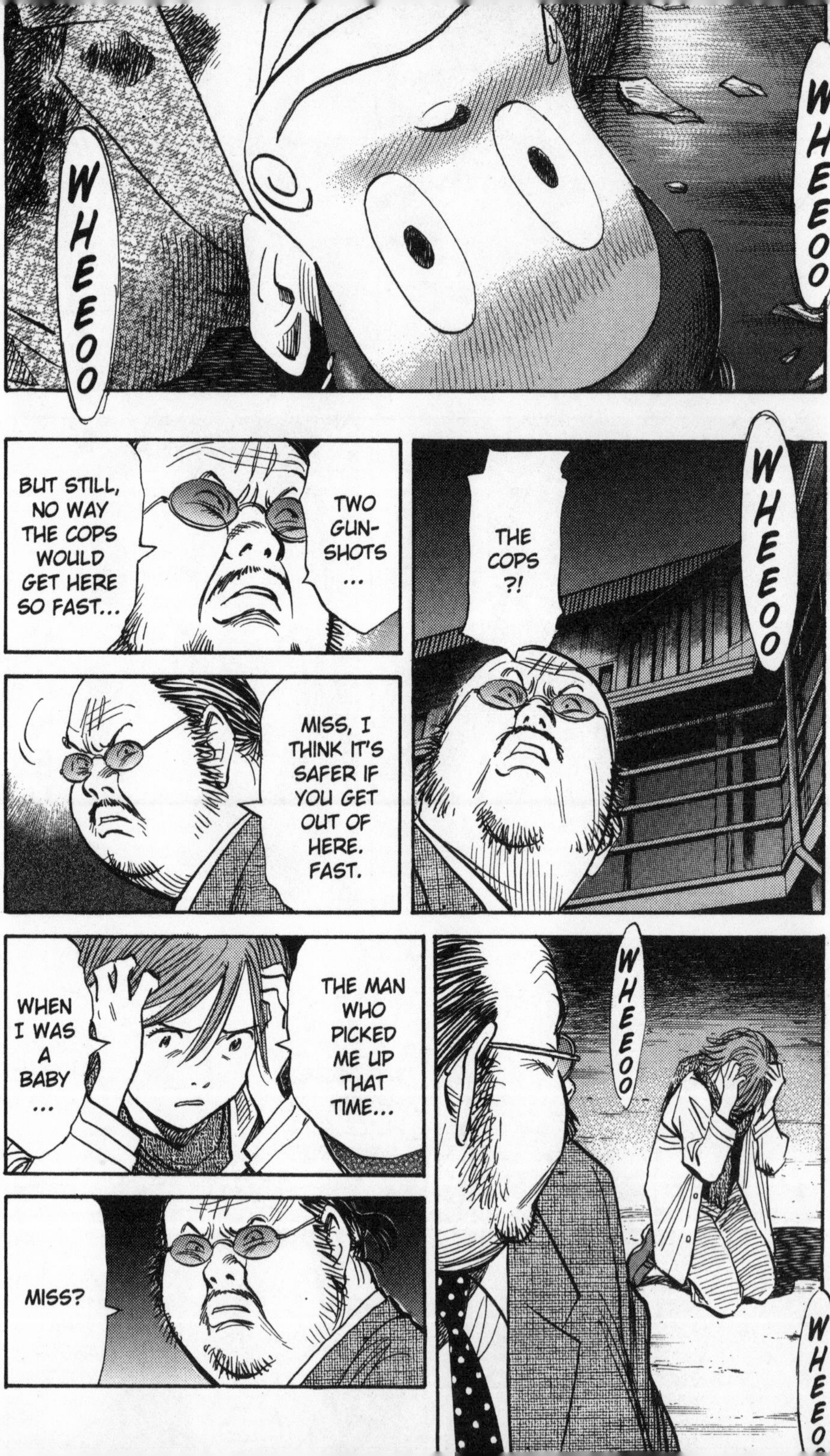
WHEEOO
WHEEOO
WHEEOO
THE COPS?!
TWO GUN-SHOTS...
BUT STILL, NO WAY THE COPS WOULD GET HERE SO FAST...
MISS, I THINK IT'S SAFER IF YOU GET OUT OF HERE. FAST.
WHEEOO
WHEEO
THE MAN WHO PICKED ME UP THAT TIME...
WHEN I WAS A BABY...
MISS?

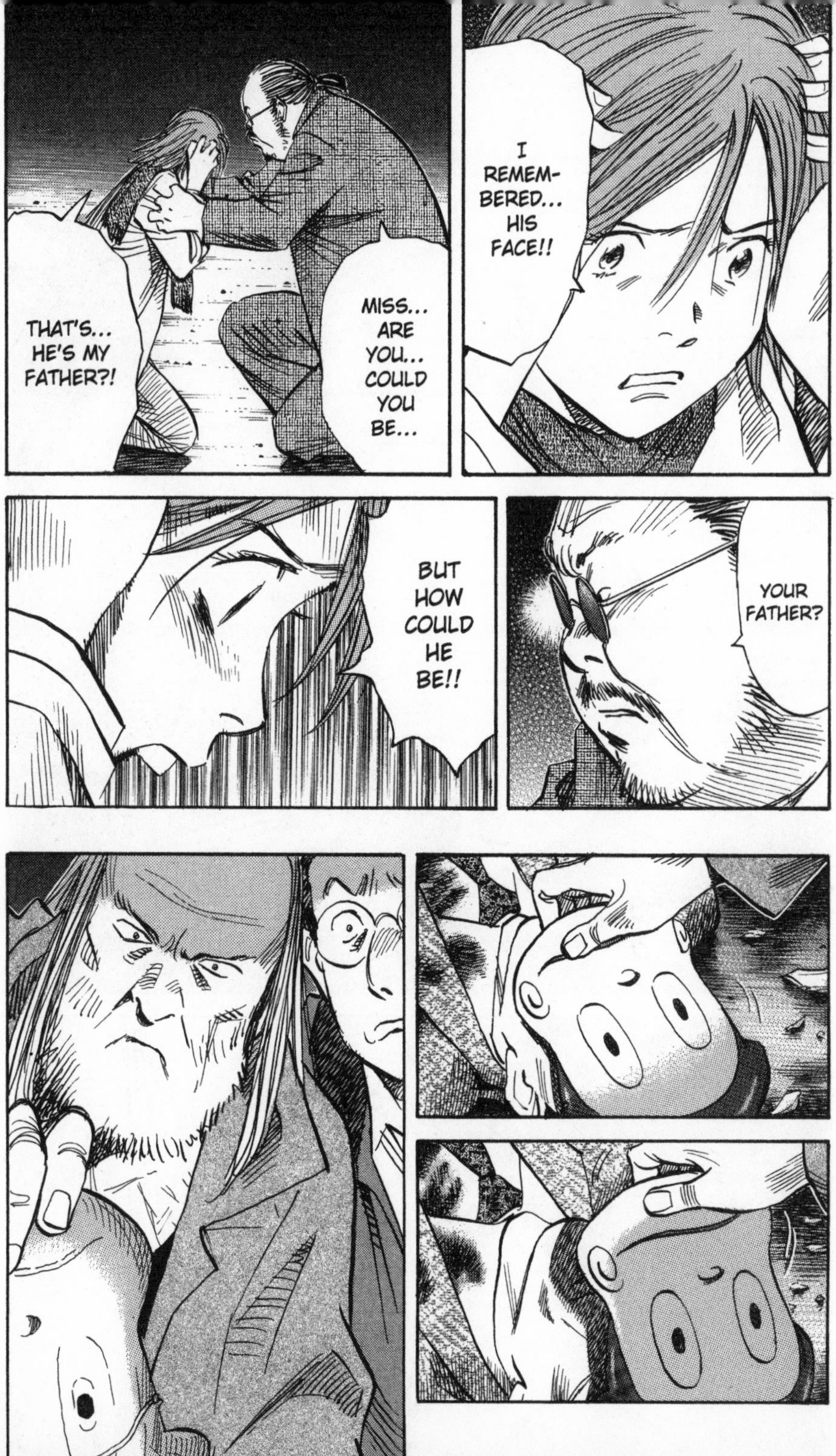
I REMEMBERED... HIS FACE!!
MISS... ARE YOU... COULD YOU BE...
THAT'S... HE'S MY FATHER?!
YOUR FATHER?
BUT HOW COULD HE BE!!

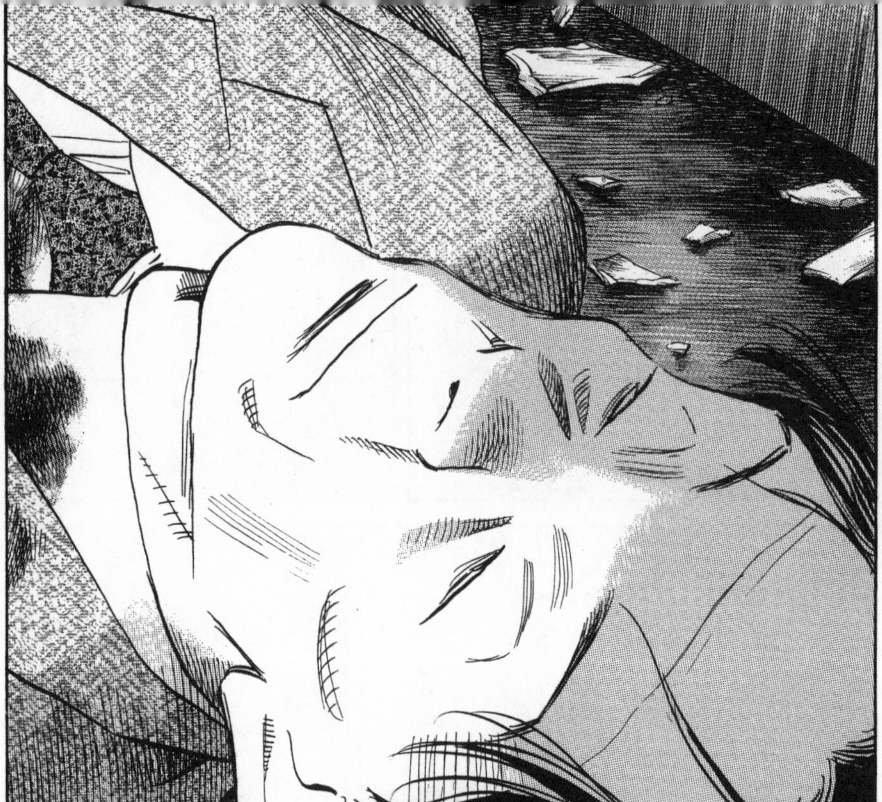

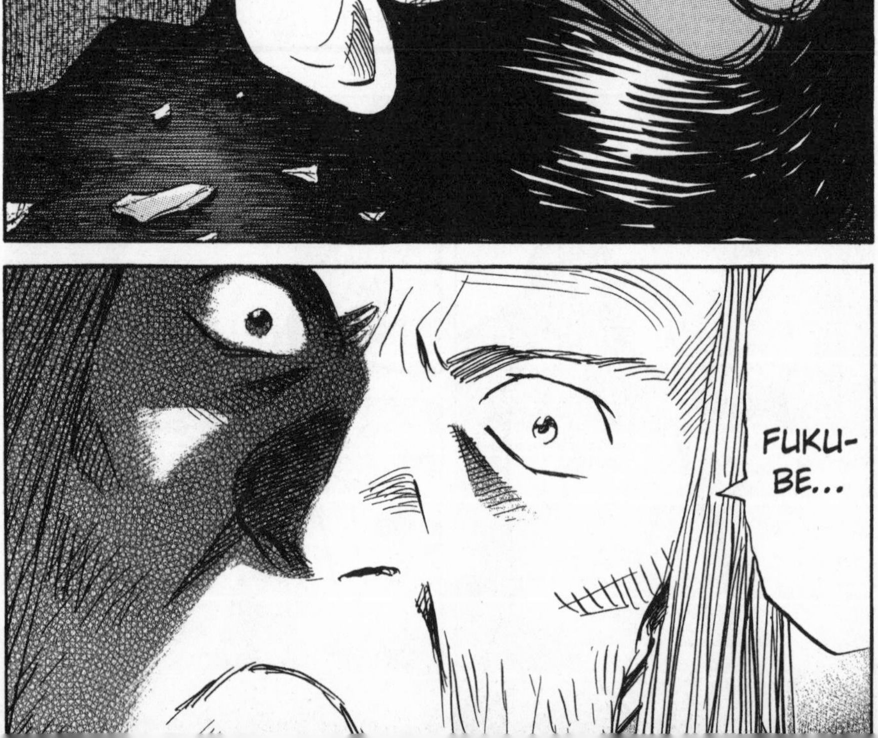
FUKU-BE...

TO BE CONTINUED

NOTES FROM THE TRANSLATOR

This series follows the Japanese naming convention, with a character's family name followed by their given name. Honorifics such as -san and -kun are also preserved.

Page 9: *Kouhaku*, short for *Kouhaku Uta Gassen*, is a yearly televised singing competition that airs on New Year's Eve in Japan. Broadcast on NHK, *Kouhaku* features musical performances from popular singers and groups.

Page 26: In Japan, when someone in the family dies the surviving members stay in mourning for one year, which precludes them from giving or receiving felicitations for the New Year.

Page 27: *Otoshidama* are gifts of money given to children by adults on New Year's Day in little envelopes of Japanese paper.

Page 34: It's common practice in Japan for successful entertainers to take on disciples and nurture them, much as in an apprenticeship system.

Page 46: Famous entertainers, especially those with disciples, are often called "Sensei," as are accomplished members of other professions, such as doctors, lawyers, and artists. The term is not solely reserved for teachers and professors.

Page 70: *Gakken no Kagaku* (Gakken Science) was a very popular science magazine for children. There was a different issue for each grade of elementary school.

Page 105: A *dagashi-ya* is a local neighborhood candy store.

Page 172: Notorious incident in 1972 in which The United Red Army, a leftist radical group, took a hostage at a mountain lodge near Karuizawa in Nagano Prefecture for ten days, eventually resulting in a shootout with the police.

Page 180: Minamoto no Yoshitsune is a legendary Japanese general who lived in the twelfth century.

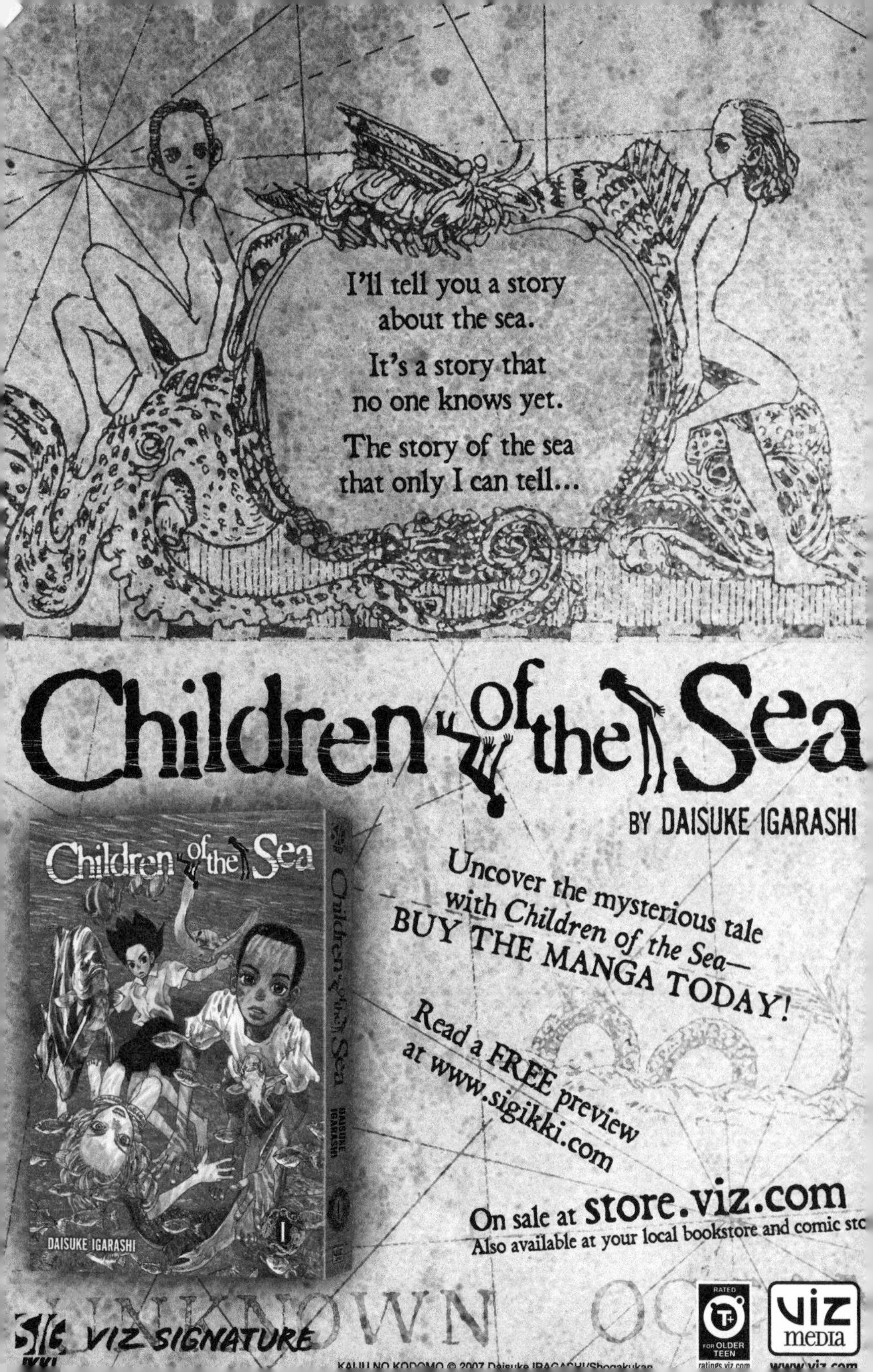

I'll tell you a story about the sea.
It's a story that no one knows yet.
The story of the sea that only I can tell...
Children of the Sea
BY DAISUKE IGARASHI
Children of the Sea
DAISUKE IGARASHI
Uncover the mysterious tale with Children of the Sea— BUY THE MANGA TODAY!
Read a FREE preview at www.sigikki.com
On sale at store.viz.com
Also available at your local bookstore and comic sto
VIZ SIGNATURE
RATED T+ FOR OLDER TEEN
VIZ MEDIA